Nordic Religions
in the Viking Age

The Middle Ages Series

Ruth Mazo Karras, General Editor
Edward Peters, Founding Editor

A complete list of books in the series
is available from the publisher.

Nordic Religions in the Viking Age

Thomas A. DuBois

PENN

University of Pennsylvania Press

Philadelphia

10 9 8 7 6 5 4 3 2 1

Published by
University of Pennsylvania Press
Philadelphia, Pennsylvania 19104-4011

Library of Congress Cataloging-in-Publication Data
DuBois, Thomas A. (Thomas Andrew), 1960–
    Nordic religions in the Viking Age / Thomas A. DuBois.
       p.   cm. (Middle Ages series)
    Includes bibliographical references and index.
    ISBN 0-8122-3511-8 (alk. paper). —
ISBN 0-8122-1714-4 (pbk. : alk. paper)
    1. Mythology, Norse.   2. Christianity and other religions—Norse.
I. Title.
BL860.D76   1999
293–dc21   99-22405
                                                                CIP

For Conor, Greer, and Brendan

Contents

Preface

This book, like the Nordic religions themselves, grew out of a combination of necessity and fascination. The necessity came when I was assigned to teach an introductory course on Scandinavian mythology at the University of Washington. Trained as a folklorist, with research specializations in Finnish and Sámi (Lapp) cultures in particular, I felt the need to examine all the pre-Christian religions of the Nordic region, not simply those of the Germanic-speaking peoples. I wanted to show how Nordic peoples interacted during the Viking Age, and how (or whether) their interactions left marks on the religions they practiced. In the materials written on the subject, I noticed a recurrent misperception that Scandinavians, Finns, and Sámi had lived in relative isolation from each other until the very recent past. My attempts at dismantling this assumption relied on the emerging consensus of contemporary archaeology regarding Nordic peoples in the Viking Age, and on lessons from the folkloristic and anthropological examination of mythology and religion. These areas of research became the foundation for the present work.

The fascination came from the materials themselves and the deeply human and transcendent concerns that I found reflected in the religious traditions of pagans and early Christian cults in the Nordic region. Students, too, saw immediate relevance in these concerns; even if the associated rituals appeared exotic and extreme, they saw the reasoning behind traditions like ancestor worship, the feud, spirit travel, personal devotion to a deity, and conversion. Many times their identification with the material was one of simple nostalgia—imagining a world more filled with wonder or wisdom than the one they knew. But often, students perceived a much deeper lesson in these materials: the very centrality of belief as a foundation upon which humans of all times construct their worlds. And—incredible though it may seem to the computer analysts quantifying evaluations of my course—students rated their introduction to Scandinavian mythology high in the category of "course relevance."

I wanted to write this book partly to fill the academic need and to gratify the fascination I had noted, but also simply to share with other researchers and students of Nordic religions the insights that my students and I had stumbled upon during the successive years of studying and teaching Nordic mythology. I was fortunate to receive a fellowship from the National Endowment for the Humanities for the project and supplemental funding from the Graduate School Fund of the University of Washington. Writing and reading diligently during the year of my fellowship, I came upon the hard words of John Lindow, who pointed out in his 1985 overview of Old Norse mythology and mythography what so many researchers in the field have tried to dismiss: the fact that the texts upon which we build many of our notions of religion in the pre-Christian Viking Age were written by thoroughly Christian intellectuals of the thirteenth century, men who wrote frequently in the vernacular but always with a clear and copious knowledge of contemporary continental thought and of Christian theology in particular. Thinking through this conundrum of sources led me at first into a deeper exploration of contemporary Nordic archaeology—evident in a number of the chapters included here—and subsequently into an exploration of the Catholic thirteenth century itself, a context reflected particularly in the readings of sagas included in the final chapter of this work.

I am grateful for the patience, encouragement, and suggestions of Patricia Conroy, Terje Leiren, James Massengale, Tracey Sands, Henning Sehmsdorf, Jan Sjåvik, and Guntis Smidchens. I am also deeply indebted to A. Gerald Anderson, Nordic Section Librarian for the University of Washington Libraries, for his assistance in finding books and sources, and to Linda Norkool of the Department of Scandinavian Studies, who facilitated my research and writing in many ways. The Finnish Literature Society (Suomalaisen Kirjallisuuden Seura) was crucial in supplying some of the works I needed, as was the Department of Sámi Studies at the University of Umeå, Sweden. I am also very grateful to the anonymous reviewers who read and commented on the text for University of Pennsylvania Press and who helped shape its final form. At the Press, Patricia Smith and Noreen O'Connor proved wonderfully helpful editors with whom I enjoyed working.

In bringing this study to its final form, I acknowledge with gratitude the assistance of the John Simon Guggenheim Memorial Foundation as well as the patience, keen criticism, and good humor of Wendy Vardaman.

Introduction

Communities of Belief

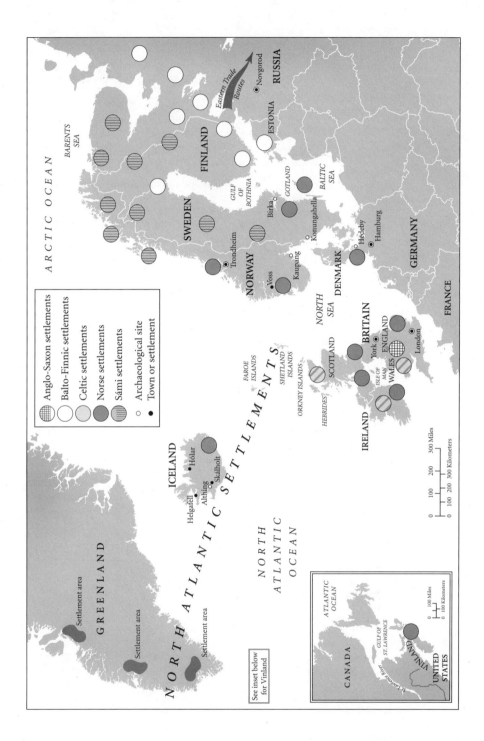

NORTH ATLANTIC SETTLEMENTS

Anglo-Saxon settlements
Balto-Finnic settlements
Celtic settlements
Norse settlements
Sámi settlements
Archaeological site
Town or settlement

ARCTIC OCEAN

BARENTS SEA

ARCTIC OCEAN

Eastern Trade Routes

Novgorod

RUSSIA

ESTONIA

FINLAND

GULF OF BOTHNIA

GOTLAND

BALTIC SEA

SWEDEN

Birka

Konungahella

Hedeby

Hamburg

GERMANY

Trondheim

NORWAY

Voss

Kaupang

DENMARK

NORTH SEA

FRANCE

BRITAIN

FAROE ISLANDS

SHETLAND ISLANDS

ORKNEY ISLANDS

SCOTLAND

York

ENGLAND

London

HEBRIDES

ISLE OF MAN

WALES

IRELAND

0   100   200   300 Miles
0 100 200 300 Kilometers

ICELAND

Hólar

Helgafell Althing Skálholt

NORTH ATLANTIC OCEAN

GREENLAND

Settlement area

Settlement area

Settlement area

See inset below for Vinland

CANADA

ATLANTIC OCEAN

GULF OF ST. LAWRENCE

St. Lawrence River

VINLAND

UNITED STATES

0   100 Miles
0 100 Kilometers

I.

Þórólfr kastaði þá fyrir borð öndvegissúlum sínum, þeim er staðit höfðu í hofinu; þar var Þórr skorinn á annarri. Hann mælti svá fyrir, at hann skyldi þar byggja á Íslandi, sem Þórr léti þær á land koma. En þegar þær hóf frá skipinu, sveif þeim til ins vestra fjarðarins, ok þótti þeim fara eigi vánum seinna. . . . Eptir þat könnuðu þeir landit ok fundu á nesi framanverðu, er var fyrir norðan váginn, at Þórr var á land kominn með súlurnar; þat var síðan kallat Þórsnes. Eptir þat fór Þórólfr eldi um landnám sitt, útan frá Stafá ok inn til þeirar ár, er hann kallaði Þórsá, ok byggði þar skipverjum sínum.[1]

Þórólfr threw overboard the posts which had been part of his temple; the image of Þórr (Thor) was carved on one of them. He said that he would settle in whatever part of Iceland Þórr came to shore. As soon as the temple posts had left the ship, they began to drift toward the west of the fjord, and it seemed to people that they drifted rather quickly. . . . After that, they came to land and found where Þórr had come to shore, at the end of a ness north of a brook; that place was called Þórr's Ness ever after. After that, Þórólfr brought fire around his land claim, out from Staf River and in to the river he called Þórr's River in the east and there he settled his crew.

II.

Var þá Eyvindr fluttr til tals við Óláf konung. Bauð konungr honum at taka skírn sem öðrum mönnum. Eyvindr kvað þar nei við. Konungr bað hann blíðum orðum at taka við kristni ok segir honum marga skynsemi ok svá byskup. Eyvindr skipaðisk ekki við þat. Þá bauð konungr honum gjafar ok veizlur stórar, en Eyvindr neitti öllu því. Þá hét konungr honum meizlum eða dauða. Ekki skipaðisk Eyvindr þat. Síðan lét konungr bera inn munnlaug fulla af glóðum ok setja á kvið Eyvindi, ok brast brátt kviðrinn sundr. Þá mælti Eyvindr: "Taki af mér munnlaugina. Ek vila mæla orð nökkur, áðr ek dey." Ok var svá gört. Þá spurði konungr: "Viltu nú, Eyvindr, trúa á Krist?" "Nei," segir hann, "ek má enga skírn fá. Ek em einn andi, kviknaðr í mann-slíkam með fjölkynngi Finna, en faðir minn ok móðir fengu áðr ekki barn átt. Síðan dó Eyvindr ok hafði verit inn fjölkunngasti maðr.[2]

Then Eyvindr was brought to see King Óláfr. The king commanded him to be baptized like other people. Eyvindr refused. The king commanded him to accept Christianity with fine words, and gave him many good reasons for it, as did the bishop. But Eyvindr would not consent. Then the king offered him gifts and great properties, but Eyvindr refused everything. So the king threatened him with torture, injury, or death. But Eyvindr would not consent. Then the king had a bowl full of hot embers brought in and set on Eyvindr's stomach and soon his stomach burst into pieces. Then Eyvindr said: "Take this bowl off me. I wish to say something before I die." And so it was done. Then the king asked him, "Eyvindr, will you now believe in

Christ?" "No," said he, "I cannot receive baptism. I am a spirit given life in human form by Sámi magic, for my father and mother were unable to have children otherwise." Then Eyvindr died and had been the most versed in magic of men.

III.

En er þeir kómu til Bjarmalands, þá lögðu þeir til kaupstaðar. Tóksk þar kaupstefna. Fengu þeir menn allir fullræði fjár, er fé höfðu til at verja. . . . Mælti Þórir: "Í garði þessum er haugr, hrœrt allt saman gull ok silfr ok mold. Skulu menn þar ril ráða. En í garðinum stendr goð Bjarma, er heitir Jómali. Verði engi svá djarfr, at hann ræni." . . . Þórir veik aptr til Jómala ok tók silfrbolla, er stóð í knjám honum. Hann var fullr af silfrpenningum. Steypði hann silfrinu í kilting sína, en dró á hönd sér höddu, er yfir var bollanum, gekk þá út til hliðsins. . . . Síðan rann Karli at Jómalanum. Hann sá, at digrt men var á hálsi honum. Karli reiddi til øxina ok hjó í sundr tygilinn aptan á hálsinum, er menit var fest við. Varð högg þat svá mikit, at höfuðit hraut af Jómala. Varð þá brestr svá mikill, at öllum þeim þótti undr at. . . . [K]ómu fram í rjóðrit varðmenninir ok blésu þegar í horn sín. . . . Þeir heyrðu, at herr Bjarma fór eptir þeim með kalli ok gaulun illiligri.[3]

When they arrived in Bjarmaland they came to a market town where a market was underway. They began to trade. Everyone who had money with them got a full load of goods. . . . Þórir said: "In this settlement there is a burial mound in which there is gold and silver and soil mixed together. . . . But in the settlement there stands the god of the Bjarmians who is called Jómali. No one should be so bold as to plunder him." . . . Þórir walked up to Jómali and took the silver bowl which lay on his knees. It was full of silver coins. He poured the silver into his cloak and hooked his hand around the handle of the bowl and then walked outside. . . . Then Karli ran toward Jómali. He saw that it had a great ring around its neck. Karli swung his axe and broke the cord which held the neck-ring on. He struck so hard that Jómali's head flew off. The din was so great that all thought it strange. . . . The watchmen came into the clearing and blew their horns at once. . . . They could hear the Bjarmian force coming after them with shouting and horrible cries.

The sagas of thirteenth-century Iceland teem with images of religious commitment and confrontation, depictions of pagan religiosity in an era three centuries earlier, when Christianity was new to the region and its eventual triumph uncertain. They depict the experiences of individuals, cults, and communities in a manner seemingly sympathetic to the views and devotions of the past. The three accounts above typify these descriptions; at the same time, they map the main topics and issues of this book. Through them, we see pagan religions as decentralized communities of belief, framing local relations with specific deities, interacting with the religious systems of neighboring peoples economically and geographically linked, and contributing to the social and political workings of the region as a whole. At the same time, we see in these texts signs of the thirteenth-century Christian outlook in which and through which they were written. An examination of each of these passages will clarify these points and introduce the subject of this book, the religious relations of the Viking Age (800–1300), defined broadly to encompass the era of Viking expansionism as well as the later era of consolidation and Christianity in which the sagas themselves were written.

The first passage above, taken from the classic *Eyrbyggja saga*, depicts the fervent devotion of a follower of Þórr (= Thor), a recurrent image in the sagas which deal with the ninth-century settlement and early history of Iceland. Hrólfr Mostrarskegg ("Mostur-Beard") starts out as a farmer of standing in Norway, where he also acts as a chieftain and proprietor of a local temple of Þórr, a role which we will examine in detail in Chapter 3. So great is his devotion to the god, in fact, that he has come to be called Þórólfr, his own name blending with that of the god he serves. The Þór- prefix was extremely common among Scandinavians settling Iceland, an indication of this god's particular popularity in the North Atlantic flank of the Viking world. When a series of events places Þórólfr in conflict with the acquisitive, irascible King Haraldr inn Hárfagri ("Fine-Hair")—a worshiper of Óðinn— Þórólfr consults with his god and then chooses to emigrate to Iceland. He brings most of the timbers of his former temple with him on the voyage, along with some of the soil upon which the temple had stood. Upon nearing Iceland, as the passage depicts, Þórólfr allows Þórr to determine his place of landing, using fire to claim the land and reserving part of the resulting property as a sacred site dedicated to Þórr. Þórr's Ness is dominated by a mountain that Þórólfr declares inviolable—Helgafell—a place protected by strict taboos, and the eventual resting place of Þórólfr and his kin. As we will see in Chapter 4, such sites could serve as localized otherworlds for families, a communal place of afterlife reserved for members of the clan and preserved by living descendants. Proper respect for this and other sacred sites in the area becomes a point of contention between Þórólfr's clan and other settlers, leading eventually to a protracted feud narrated at length in the saga.

Here, then, we see deep and personal relations between an individual and his god, ones which affect a man's political fate in Norway and help underscore or maintain his authority in Iceland. At the same time, we are confronted with the extratextual likelihood that *Eyrbyggja saga* itself was authored at the prominent Augustinian monastery at Helgafell, an institution founded in 1184 and important as an intellectual center in thirteenth-century Iceland. For the original audience of the saga, in other words, this depiction of pagan spirituality must have carried a double resonance: standing as a portrayal of pagan ways of the past but also as a reminder of Christian ways of the present. Perhaps, in fact, the Christian audience of the thirteenth century could appreciate commonalities in fidelity and devotion between the age of paganism and that of Christianity, commonalities which later audiences might fail to notice.

The second passage above is taken from Snorri Sturluson's *Óláfs saga Tryggvasonar*, a history of the first Norwegian king to undertake systematic Christianization of the realm during his brief but eventful reign (995–1000). This saga is discussed in detail in Chapter 8, and its author, Snorri Sturluson (c. 1178–1241), remains one of the prime sources of information about the religious life of the Viking Age. At this point in Snorri's narrative, Óláfr has prevailed in his efforts to Christianize the southern tracts of Norway, at least in name, and has turned attention at last to the vast northern district of Hálogaland, inhabited by Scandinavians and Sámi alike. Eyvindr figures as a steadfast adherent of the old religion, unwilling to accept Christ, even upon penalty of death. His reasons, however, do not lie in the kind of personal devotion to a single god depicted in the passage from *Eyrbyggja saga*. Rather, as Eyvindr explains to Óláfr before dying of torture, the circumstances of his birth make it impossible for him to reject the pagan faith: after a long period of infertility, his parents availed themselves of the services of a Sámi healer, who used some combination of magic and healing techniques to help them conceive a son. As we shall see in Chapter 5, procedures of this sort are common in extant accounts of healing among Scandinavians, Sámi, Finns, and Anglo-Saxons, and continued well into the Christian era, despite frequent Church disapproval. Further, the earliest Christian law tracts of this region of Norway explicitly forbid consultation with Sámi for magical assistance, indicating a frequency of intercultural exchange in this area, as we shall see in greater detail in Chapter 6. Snorri's text does not present Eyvindr as evil, however; instead, he appears imprisoned by the nature of the supernatural acts that have contributed to his birth. He dies unconverted, among the last of a disappearing generation of pagan holdouts. And his fidelity, though in Snorri's view misplaced, deserves the respect and memory which both Óláfr and Snorri accord it.

The third passage above derives from another of Snorri's works, *Óláfs saga helga*, the history of Norway's great King St. Óláfr (r. 1015–30), whose shrine at Trondheim had become a prime pilgrimage center for northern Europe by the thirteenth century. In an excursus regarding Viking raids to the east, Snorri includes the above account, in which the warrior-traders Þórir Hundr ("the Hound") and Karli í Langey ("of Langey," in Hálogaland) pay a visit to a Finnic settlement in the now indistinct region of Bjarmaland/Permia (between the White Sea and the Dvina River). As we shall see in the following chapter, Finnic peoples—speaking one or more of the variety of Balto-Finnic and Volga-Finnic languages then common in the region east of the Baltic Sea—had become major competitors of the Scandinavians in the northern fur trade, and attacks on such settlements are narrated repeatedly in the sagas. In the passage quoted above, however, this economic conflict becomes tied to religious desecration. The Vikings augment their profits made through trade by raiding a sacred grove, in which an image of a god, Jómali (Finnish *jumala*, "god") guards a hoard of gold and silver. The site is apparently a burial mound, with the treasure left as grave goods for a deceased kinsman (see Chapter 4). Þórir and Karli violate the site without fear, although the sin of greed eventually leads to their own downfall later in the saga. As if cursed through the act of desecration that led to its removal from the grove, the neckring will lead Þórir to murder Karli for its possession, and result in turn in Þórir's further estrangement from King Óláfr and their eventual open enmity. At the end of the saga (ch. 228), Þórir will deal the king one of his three deathblows in the Battle of Stiklastaðir, the final act in a series of worsening relations in which religion plays a muted but important role. After his death, however, the sainted King Óláfr's blood will miraculously cure Þórir's wounds, transforming Þórir into one of the first and most vocal proponents of the slain king's sainthood (ch. 230). Here, then, we see more clearly than in the previous two instances the interrelation of religious choice and politics, the use of belief as a symbol of loyalty or resistance to a king and as a device for strengthening or worsening relations between communities.

It is the contention of this study that in order to understand phenomena such as those depicted in these passages, we must look at the religious traditions of the Nordic region not as isolated, mutually exclusive language-bound entities, but as broad concepts shared across cultural and linguistic lines, conditioned by similar ecological factors and protracted economic and cultural ties. As I argue in Chapters 1 and 2, an areal focus on religious expressions—like its counterpart in areal linguistics—helps temper the isolating tendencies of past research, which has focused too exclusively on phenomena within single language families or cultures, for example, Germanic-Scandinavian, the broader Indo-European, or the distinct Finno-Ugric (Sámi and Finnish). A geographic perspective accounts for and makes relevant intercultural processes marginalized within studies that presuppose a strictly linear transmission of religious ideas from one generation of believers to the next, processes occluded in the history of research, not out of a lack of inherent interest or significance, but rather out of the limitations of research frameworks themselves. By looking at the interrelations between the various peoples who shared the Viking-Age North, we can perceive broad commonalities of worldview that served as conceptual bases for the comparison and exchange of more specific religious ideas: underlying views of death, for instance, which facilitated the shift from cremation to inhumation burial among Nordic pagans well before the actual adoption of Christianity, the ultimate source of the new custom itself. With this preexisting worldview in mind, we can understand the processes by which Nordic peoples perceived, interpreted, and eventually adopted Christianity in the course of several centuries. The arrival of Christianity becomes, in this light, not an end to the worldview of the Viking Age, but—as the saga writers themselves sometimes imply—its final chapter, toward which pagan and Christian adherent alike were progressing from the ninth through the thirteenth centuries.

The chapters of this study, then, examine some of the basic underpinnings of this Nordic worldview, focusing on tendencies and concerns central to all Nordic religions during the Viking Age. We will also explore the ways in which religious ideas diffused into the region from west, south, and east, that is, from the Christian British Isles, the European continent, Russia, and Byzantium. Textual evidence from the sagas, Eddaic poems, and other medieval texts are supplemented by insights from archaeology, the anthropology of religion, and the study of Nordic oral tradition. The final chapter of the study, for its part, examines the Christian agenda behind three important sagas of the thirteenth century, reminding us that although saga texts may contain fascinating glimpses of Nordic paganism, they do so for particular textual effects, often the advancement of integrally Christian themes. It is this dual nature of the sagas which makes them so interesting to the student of religion and so illustrative of the broad sweep of religious ideas from the early Viking Age to the era of saga composition. In the thirteenth century, as before, we can sense the workings of communities of belief, collectives of people whose juxtaposed religious ideals and practices contributed to the social and ethical realities of the day.

ONE

The Cultures
and History
of the
Viking-Age
North

This chapter establishes the premises for a detailed examination of religious interrelations during one of the most significant eras in Nordic history: the so-called Viking Age. The study elucidates the development and change of religious communities during a five-hundred-year period (c. A.D. 800–1300) that covers the era of Viking expansionism itself but also includes the conversion era that succeeded it. In the course of five centuries, Nordic peoples interacted closely through economic, marital, and religious exchange. Various groups of Sámi and Balto-Finns continued intercultural relations that had developed over millennia, although altered increasingly by the example and efforts of their Scandinavian neighbors. Speakers of the Scandinavian languages, for their part, spread settlements and political control throughout the region and beyond, driven by a combination of cultural ideals, economic necessity, and population growth. The Scandinavian Viking traders, particularly those of Sweden, Denmark, and Gotland, traveled eastward to Finland, the Baltics, and Russia. Raiders and displaced or disgruntled farmers from Norway and Denmark traveled westward to the British Isles and the insular North Atlantic (the Western Isles of Scotland, the Hebrides, Shetland, Orkneys, Faroes, Iceland, and Greenland, and apparently also coastal North America). They met and entered into long-term intercultural relations with a variety of other peoples, speaking languages sometimes reminiscent of their own (e.g., Old English), often, however, markedly different (e.g., Celtic and Slavic languages, Greenlandic Inuit). While economic and cultural choices differentiated the Scandinavians from their neighboring cultures, webs of interdependence soon developed through mutual need or as a result of direct conquest. And while cultural boundaries remained stable, individuals, goods, and cultural traits (including religious traditions) circulated regularly among the cultures.

By the end of the era under investigation, the North had become transformed from a complex mosaic of interdependent non-Christian communities to an increasingly consolidated and religiously unified region, diminished in range from its earlier expanse and merged into a few large royal realms. Christianity had become installed as the fruit and agent of this unity and had begun to make inroads, from its beachheads in Atlantic Scandinavia and the royal courts of the mainland, outward toward the marginalized farmsteads and forest settlements of the region. Iceland, now ruled by a well-established Christian aristocracy under the aegis of the Norwegian crown, looked nostalgically back at the era of local autonomy and allowed the religions of the pre-Christian North, still palpable in local legends and place-names, to symbolize individual conviction, familial tradition, and local identity. While the Christianity of the era may have represented, in fact, more a syncresis of pre-Christian practice and Christian dogma than an outright displacement of the old tradition, writers of the thirteenth century fixed their gaze wistfully on a period in which their ancestors had used religious adherence for consciously expressing personal identity and social outlook, a period in which religious diversity was considered a matter of course. At the same time, they wrote from a decidedly Christian viewpoint, commenting pointedly on the individual, institutional, and communal aspects of true Christianization.

In undertaking this exploration, we must first address some basic questions regarding the communities under examination and the religions to which they subscribed. Both have been subjected to extensive study over the course of at least a century and a half, and this research tradition presents a formidable and well-established interpretive apparatus.[1] Unfortunately, many nineteenth- and even twentieth-century scholars have tended to read into their observations of the Viking Age more recent Romantic notions of conquest, nationhood, and religion, in ways that have affected their conclusions significantly. In the area of religion, scholars have often regarded pre-Christian religions—as well as Christianity—as singular, unchanging entities, reconstructible through comparative analysis and reducible to a small set of myths or practices (see Chapter 2). This viewpoint offers little opportunity for a nuanced study of interreligious influence and change. The equation of religion and nation has also proved decidedly counterproductive for the study of intercult influences. In the area of cultural contacts, scholars have too often viewed the Viking Age through the distorting lens of eighteenth- and nineteenth-century imperial conquest and colonialism. Rather than looking toward ethnographic and historical data on the meetings and interrelations of "small-scale societies"—that is, moments at which economically differentiated but more or less equally viable and similarly sized communities come into extended contact—scholars have promoted notions of conquest possible only in later eras. Adopting a viewpoint that imagines the Viking "conquerors" as vastly more numerous, technologically superior, or somehow inherently more warlike loses the sense of exchange and cooperation which characterized much of the Viking Age. Finally, in the area of nationhood, scholars have often reduced locally variable communities of the North into monolithic ethnic units ("nations"), dramatically oversimplifying archaeological and textual evidence and often extending the national boundaries of the present day backward problematically into the realms of the medieval era. This line of scholarship in particular has received cogent critique in recent years.[2] In the following chapter, I offer some basic premises that attempt to avoid the biases of such past scholarship regarding Viking Age culture and economy. By rethinking scholarly assumptions, we may regard the Nordic peoples as engaged in a range of different relations, from positive cooperation to begrudging coexistence to occasional violent enmity. We may also see a context in which religious concepts passed between cultures and communities of belief, differing in language, economy, and location, but sharing a broadly similar worldview.

The Cultures of the Nordic Region

Sámi and Baltic Finns

Although Icelandic texts from the twelfth and thirteenth centuries show a passion for chronicling the details and history of the Scandinavian world, they offer relatively little firm commentary on the non-Scandinavian peoples of the North. Often, it is as if the presence of the Finns and the Sámi of mainland Scandinavia, as well as the Irish and Inuit of the Atlantic, is simply a given, taken notice of only when these peoples directly intrude into the events of a saga. Typically, they are portrayed as mysterious specters, lurking outside the saga's narrative focus and waiting to do mischief if allowed into the farmhouse or onto its roof. Scholars of later eras have been complicitous in this erasure: the Sámi, nineteenth-century archaeologists asserted, had lived only in the remote north during the Viking Age, regardless of what texts like Snorri's *Heimskringla* or occasional archaeological finds indicated.[3] The Finns, historians and archaeologists concurred, had hardly even arrived yet when the Viking Age began. Consider Will Durant's rendering of Finnish prehistory, a synopsis of the received historical and archaeological view of his day:

In the earlier Middle Ages the Finns, distant relatives of the Magyars and the Huns, dwelt along the upper Volga and Oka. By the eighth century they had migrated into the hardy, scenic land known to outsiders as Finland, and to the Finns as Suomi, the Land of Marsh. Their raids upon the Scandinavian coasts induced the Swedish King Eric IX to conquer them in 1157. At Uppsala Eric left a bishop with them as a germ of civilization; the Finns killed Bishop Henry, and then made him their patron saint. With quiet heroism they cleared the forests, drained the marshes, channeled their "10,000 lakes," gathered furs and fought the snow.[4]

Here, in a nutshell, we find the fundamental assumptions of much of earlier scholarship concerning the non-Germanic peoples of the North. They are viewed as unified ethnic entities, migrating en masse into the margins of Scandinavian civilization as pesky interlopers, where they are put in their place decisively by the superior military might and eventual Christian dominance of the medieval Scandinavian states. After subjugation, they recede again from the light, quietly going about their lives in the shadows of history.

Such a view, of course, promotes an array of logical conclusions that close off inquiry into processes such as productive intercultural relations or religious and cultural exchange. The very question of possible mutual interdependence of Nordic peoples in earlier eras becomes unlikely or even absurd. After all, one might ask, how could religious ideals—literally the heart and soul of culture—pass between mutually antagonistic populations, separated by a language barrier, a gulf in technology, and even anthropometric (i.e., racial) differences? Further, if religious traditions were to move at all, surely they must pass only from the superior (Scandinavian) society to its inferiors—an assumption critiqued forcefully by recent researchers in Sámi studies.[5] For the bulk of the nineteenth and twentieth centuries, the notion of permeable cultural boundaries—ones which permit the flow of material articles, personnel, and even abstract religious concepts in both directions—has remained outside of understandings of the Viking-Age North.

Our conceptions of Sámi and Balto-Finnic prehistory have changed considerably from that reflected in Durant's midcentury synopsis. Whereas consensus among archaeologists and historians from the turn of the century through the late 1960s favored a theory of late migration as the answer to the question of the origin of the Finns in particular, scholars in the latter half of the twentieth century have favored a theory of settlement continuity over a period of millennia for all the Finno-Ugric peoples of the North (the so-called *jatkuvuusteoria*—"theory of continuity"). Archaeological, palynological (pollen analysis), linguistic, and genetic data in recent decades confirm the revised hypothesis.[6] A clear notion of Finno-Ugric settlement and ethnogenesis in the region is crucial for an understanding of the relations of these peoples with each other and with Scandinavians.

Archaeological evidence today points to the arrival of Finno-Ugric-speaking populations in the Nordic region already c. 3300 B.C., when a population recognized by its distinctive pottery style (the "Combed Ceramic Ware culture") of the fourth millennium became regularized in terms of style and implement, implying, in the view of Siiriäinen and other archaeologists, "the unification of the ethnic and linguistic basis" of the region.[7] This hunter-gatherer population remained fairly uniform until around 2700–2600 B.C. At this point, new influences and a colony of Indo-European agropastoralists—now known as the Corded Ware or Battle-Ax culture (probably ancestors of the Baltic or Germanic populations of the region) became established in southwestern Finland. Over the course of a few centuries, this colony was assimilated into the preexisting population of southwestern Finland, bringing with it its technological advances and forming as a result the Bronze Age Kiukainen culture. This merging of Indo-European culture and population with the dominant Finno-Ugric culture of the region is regarded as the ethnogenesis of the Balto-Finns.

Meanwhile, inland populations of Finno-Ugric people did not undergo this cultural transformation toward agriculture and herding, but rather retained the older hunter-gatherer lifestyle. Other cultural influences, such as a new form of asbestos pottery, diffused into the inland area from further east as well, leading to the further differentiation of coastal and inland populations.[8] The decisive divergence of the shared Finno-Ugric language of the region into a coastal proto-Balto-Finnic and an inland proto-Sámi language, occurred at this time (c. 2000 B.C.), reflecting a cultural and economic division which is clearly observable in the archaeological evidence of the last millennium B.C. Continued close contact between the two cultures is reflected, however, in both archaeological and linguistic evidence.[9]

From the era of the Iron Age through to the early medieval period, this basic division of Finland into coastal agropastoral and inland hunter-gatherer cultures persisted. New influences from successive waves of Baltic and Scandinavian settlers to the coast further transformed Balto-Finnic culture and gradually led to its differentiation into the various Balto-Finnic languages and peoples of today (such as Finnish, Karelian, Estonian, Votic, Vepsian, Livonian).[10] By the Viking Age, a characteristic *eränkäynti* (seasonal wilderness sojourn) system had developed, whereby coastal agropastoralists migrated inland seasonally to hunt, practice slash-and-burn agriculture, and trade with the inland hunter-gatherers.[11] Forced taxation of the inland Sámi (mainly the taking of furs in tribute) appears to date from the first century A.D., and became regularized into a trading relation of such significance that Sámi in the area eventually abandoned the manufacture of both iron and ceramics, relying instead on imported trade-goods from agrarian populations to the south.[12] The Balto-Finns also became the source of prestige items for the Sámi, such as brooches and other ornaments, which in turn entered the coastal communities in part through trade with peoples to the south and east.[13] These relations extended to other Finno-Ugric peoples to the east, including the Balto-Finnic Vepsians, Votes, and Karelians, as well as the more distant Volga-Finnic, Permian, and Ob-Ugric peoples.[14] Linguistic and cultural affinities linked these populations, which began in some cases to develop urban cultures parallel to those of Germanic and Slavic neighbors.[15] The interplay between hunter-gatherer communities (the producers of the region's most valuable commodity, furs) and sedentary agriculturalists or traders became characteristic of the economy of the entire region. It was this set of relations that would eventually facilitate and attract Viking incursions into the area. Later increased migrations into the region by Slavic, Tatar, and Turkic peoples in more recent centuries, however, created gaps in the geographic continuity of this large and ancient Finno-Ugric complex.

It should also be noted that this eastern world received religious influences from a wide array of competing centers: far more, in fact, than impinged on the communities of western Scandinavia. Pre-Christian ethnic religions came to coexist with new religions brought by traders and settlers from the south. When the author of the twelfth-century Russian *Primary Chronicle* (*Povest' vremennikh let'*) describes the Christianization of King Vladimir the Great in 987, he depicts the king investigating a variety of options proposed to him by military and trade allies: Judaism, Islam, the Church of Rome, and Byzantine Orthodoxy. The chronicler's account must hold a kernel of truth, since each of these religions was well represented by significant communities of believers in Vladimir's realm. That Vladimir chose Orthodoxy in the end—moved, as the chronicler tells it, by reports of the beauty of its rituals—probably reflects in part his desire to form better relations with the most magnificent of his neighbors, the Byzantine Empire.[16] On the popular level, however, ideas from all of these religions appear to have circulated widely during his era and after. The eastern and specifically Orthodox influences on Nordic Christianization have received insufficient attention from both thirteenth-century saga writers and modern scholars, as we will see in Chapters 7 and 8.

A broader examination of the history of the North Eurasian region shows that economic relations between hunter-gatherers and agriculturalists of the sort described above occur frequently. In fact, so-called paired economies may develop as a result of long-term contacts and as a solution to environmental pressures facing each community.[17] In these cases, two small-scale societies develop in tandem, each arriving at an economy that relies upon the existence of the other to some extent. In North Eurasia, pastoralists, or agropastoralists (people living off a combination of farming and herding), relied upon neighboring hunter-gatherer communities for food, furs, and sustenance in times of famine. Hunter-gatherers, for their part, relied on their farming or herding neighbors for dietary supplements, hides or other animal products, and trade goods. Neither society was completely self-sufficient, nor was trade a foreign or extraneous concept. Such paired economies evolved over time, so that initial contact gradually developed into sustained interdependence, with a strong degree of economic specialization on each side. From an ethnological perspective, this pattern of intercultural commerce and interdependence calls into question earlier models of culture, in which a given people ("nation," "ethnos") was assumed to live or have lived in independence from all others.

In the Nordic region itself, the combination of linguistic affinities and paired economies ensured that Sámi and Balto-Finnic cultures exerted considerable influence on each other in the centuries leading up to the Viking Age. Archaeological evidence of sustained trade is augmented by observation of social transformations on both sides, including a normalization of annual regional meetings among the Sámi for the purposes of trade and taxation and a regularization of hereditary *eränkäynti* customs among the Balto-Finns.[18] Linguistic evidence points to the intimate exchange of cultural items as well as technology (such as skis) between the groups through the centuries and the existence of Balto-Finnic or Sámi cultures largely as choices in way of life rather than as impermeable ethnic entities.[19] Further, marked assimilation of southern Sámi populations into the expanding agropastoralist culture of Savo and eastern Finland during the medieval period reflects this permeability and may explain in part the tendency of early Scandinavian texts to refer to *Lapp* as a primarily economic category, as well as their failure to differentiate between Sámi and Finns in the use of the term *Finn*.[20]

The success of agriculture along the shores of the Gulf of Finland and Lake Ladoga led to a marked increase in Balto-Finnic population, a spread of the culture northward, and the birth of competitive relations between various Balto-Finnic communities.[21] Signs of fracture within the Balto-Finnic complex are evident in the differentiation of the common language of the Kiukainen culture into the various Balto-Finnic languages of today. Gradual differentiation in ritual and material culture is also evident in archaeological finds from west and east.[22] These competitive relations intensified during the Viking Age and era of conversions, as western and eastern Balto-Finns become absorbed into rival spheres of influence: the Swedish in the west and the Novgorodan in the east. Ottar's ninth-century account of the White Sea

Bjarmians (see below) is generally regarded as a reference to Karelian traders. *Egils saga* accounts of Balto-Finnic traders in the north refer to the Kven culture (see below), probably centered on the Tornio River Valley.[23]

Sámi communities, for their part, did not remain unchanged in economy or culture from the Stone Age to the era of Viking expansions. On the other hand, the changes appear more gradual and less cataclysmic than those experienced by the Balto-Finns during the same period. Linguistic, archaeological, and genetic evidence suggests that the initial Finno-Ugric (Sámi) population of the Nordic region was small in number, perhaps less than ten thousand people during the Bronze Age (c. 1300–500 B.C.).[24] As the coastal Balto-Finnic population "Indo-Europeanized," the inland Sámi maintained contact with their kindred people on the coast and arriving Germanic populations. Germanic loanwords entered proto-Sámi during this period both directly and (more frequently) through Balto-Finnic mediation.[25] Germanic loans include important technological terms (for example, northern Sámi *ruovdi*, Finnish *rauta* for "iron") as well as certain religious concepts (such as northern Sámi *vuor'bi*, Finnish *arpa*, "lot, fate"). Even though Sámi culture spread broadly across Finland and the Scandinavian and Kola peninsulas, it retained unity both in terms of material culture and language, implying a high degree of interrelations between the scattered inland communities.

Scandinavians in the North

Recent archaeology and other scholarship has also shed new light on the Germanic settlements of the North. By the beginning of the Viking Age, Scandinavians had become a ubiquitous and increasingly dominant part of the Nordic world, although localized primarily along the coasts and beside large bodies of water. The agropastoralist lifestyle brought by their ancestors to the region millennia before had become specialized in response to the variety of environments present in the area. In the dense forests of Sweden, Scandinavians combined farming with hunting, fishing, and lively trade with both Sámi and Balto-Finns. The islands of the Baltic became crucial trade centers, where ideas and artifacts from all sides of the sea exchanged hands.[26] In the fertile farmlands of Denmark, village life had taken root and prosperous trading cities like Hedeby had developed.[27] In the more rugged area of Norway, independent coastal settlements combined pastoralism with extensive fishing and trade and developed in the north a paired economy similar to that which had grown up between the Sámi and Balto-Finns. In the south, trading centers like Kaupang helped tie these communities to markets abroad and ample archaeological and artistic evidence points to very close links between southwestern Norway and the British Isles.[28] Increased population throughout the region had resulted in the taking of new lands between settlements, the expansion into higher or less fertile tracts, and the genesis of migrant populations seeking new settlement sites abroad. The need for additional land would lead particularly to the westward expansion of Scandinavians into the British Isles and eventually into the islands of the North Atlantic (see below).

Amid these economic and environmental specializations, however, the Germanic populations of the region appear to have viewed themselves as a more or less unified entity. They shared a single language—*Norrœna, norrœnt mál*, Old Norse—with relatively slight dialectal variation even over considerable distances. Further, saga texts frequently depict the inclusion of non-Scandinavians in these communities, provided the interlopers possess a mastery of the lingua franca. Such catholicity of outlook may not have been uniform among all Scandinavian communities, however; it is likely to have been more pronounced in the North Atlantic settlements, where migrants from different parts of the Viking world had converged to create a new society. In the less mobile local communities of mainland Scandinavia, in contrast, a greater degree of cultural exclusivity—even between communities sharing ostensibly the same language—is possible, or even likely. While the sagas narrate regular travel and commerce between the various communities of the mainland, they also depict frequent rivalries: conflicts hingeing on issues of trading rights, land ownership, or essential cultural differences.

Along with their language, these Germanic Scandinavians shared certain other cultural characteristics, ones which various scholars have tied to Indo-European cultures in general.[29] For instance, they possessed cattle and horses and a strongly patriarchal social system. Marked social stratification divided the populace into distinct classes, ranging from king or lord to slave. Class membership was hereditary but—to judge from the sagas—relatively fluid: the mighty could fall and the lowly could rise in the course of a generation or two. Men of wealth in tenth-century Iceland sometimes acknowledged slave forbears and even King Óláfr Tryggvason's mother could fall prey to piracy and enslavement (see Chapter 8).[30] Again, we must read these assertions of class permeability in the sagas with some reservation: what qualified as narratable (memorable) to saga authors may well have been the exceptional cases, not the norm. A fairly static situation from generation to generation may have been the overwhelming norm even at the outset of the Viking Age, as indeed it was by the thirteenth century. What fluidity existed during the height of Viking expansionism must have been greater in the migrant settlements like Iceland, where settlers of acumen and potential could escape the normative social pressures of the mainland.

Links of real as well as artificial kinship formed the basis of most social institutions among the Germanic Scandinavians. An individual's status and recourse to justice were determined by the strength and prominence of acknowledged kin, and the orphan enjoyed no status in society whatsoever. Families cemented friendships with distant trading partners through a form of temporary adoption of children (*fóstr*, fosterage). Fostering one's son or daughter ensured good relations in the parental generation and close friendships in the generation of the children. Marriage, too, was used as a strategic means of optimizing kinship alliances.[31] Gifts of various sorts helped maintain both real and artificial kinship ties and the systemic need for gifts helped drive the Viking raids.[32] One's responsibilities to kin survived even the grave: explicit duties toward the dead were well-established aspects of religious life (see Chapter 3), and the avenging of a kinsman's murder could become the basis of prolonged intergenerational feuds, the events of which were celebrated in Eddaic poems and sagas alike.[33]

In the manner of a true patriarchy, the imagery of fatherhood and attendant filial devotion extended beyond the family or clan (*ætt*) to other social institutions in general. The relations of a king (*konungr*) to his dependent farmers (*bönder*) and retainers (*liðmenn*) were often described in familial terms. Scandinavian kingship was an elected office, although in practice the ruler often possessed a hereditary claim to the throne. Snorri's *Heimskringla* is full of curious moments at which young men in their midteens are suddenly accepted as kings of Norway and take on a fatherly role in relation to retainers twice their age. The relation of a roving warlord (*dróttinn*) to his band of retainers was likewise conceptualized in terms of male kinship categories. While such imagery also appears in Sámi and Balto-Finnic societies, the greater degree of social stratification characteristic of Scandinavian communities accentuated this feature in Viking society. While Scandinavian women clearly played important roles in the workings of society and enjoyed legal rights of greater significance than in many other European societies of the era, these factors conflicted in some measure with the dominant ideology of the culture and receive a lessened or sometimes disapproving portrayal in the saga texts. Women appear to have played specific roles in religious life (see Chapter 3), for instance, which are mentioned only in passing in the sagas themselves.

The British Isles and North Atlantic

It is difficult to separate the process of *landnám*, or primary land-taking, from the activity of raiding in the British Isles and North Atlantic. Both activities were driven by the same cultural and demographic patterns facing Scandinavians of the mainland. In *landnám*, Scandinavians sought and settled tracts of land reminiscent of their home terrains, replicating Scandinavian life in coastal colonies. In many cases, these migrants found lands previously unsettled to any great degree, establishing new societies there with direct parallels to western Norway or Denmark. Such is the case in Orkney, Shetland, the Faroes, and Iceland.[34] Striking similarities of terrain and climate link northern Norway and the Skagafjörður/Skjálfandaflói district of northern Iceland, permitting the easy transferral of north Norwegian agrarian lifestyles to the region.[35] Settlers looked for landscapes which suited their farming and herding customs best, and some locales, such as the eastern coast of Scotland, received little or no settlement despite proximity to Norway and other positive features.[36] Often, raiding could supplement agricultural livelihoods in these tracts, as is reflected in the description of Sveinn Asleifarson's raiding customs in *Orkneyinga saga*.[37] Sveinn spends the winter with his eighty-odd men at his home on Gairsay, planting crops in the spring. Once the sowing is done, he leaves with his men for raids in the Hebrides or Ireland, returning at midsummer to reap and store grain. In the autumn, before winter has set in, he has a second opportunity for a raiding sojourn. Here, raiding helps the noble Viking maintain a lifestyle impossible on the basis of local agriculture alone. The Northern Isles settlements may have provided the bases and personnel for many of the raids into Ireland and other settlements to the south.[38] By the end of the ninth century, these archipelagos had become united under an earldom closely tied to the Norwegian king, possibly in an attempt to prevent their threatening Norway itself.[39]

In contrast to these uncontested settlements, however, Scandinavian *landnám* further south took place in regions already settled and inhabited by other peoples. Such was particularly the case in the Western Isles, the west coast of Scotland and England, the Isle of Man, and Ireland, all of which received strong (but ununified) migrant settlement from Scandinavia, chiefly from Norway.[40] England's Scandinavian settlements were dominated by Danish migrants, although finds like the Sutton Hoo ship burial prove evidence of early Swedish influence as well.[41] The Danelaw would eventually become a pivotal aspect of British history, leading to the culminating joint Danish-English realm of Cnut the Great (994–1035; r. 1016–35). The Isle of Man represented an area of clear and productive intermingling between Vikings and Celtic Manx, a union that had strong effects on local art and culture (see Chapter 7). The Vikings in Ireland were less successful in the long term, although their settlement-kingdoms in Dublin, Wexford, Limerick, and elsewhere played pivotal roles in the various wars and social transformations of the ninth and tenth centuries.[42] The lack of centralized kingship in Ireland at the time and the overwhelmingly rural character of the society hindered Viking attempts to dominate the island as a whole. When a unified kingship finally developed under King Brian Bóroime (Boru), it bent its powers toward removing the Viking threat, defeating the Norse warriors at the Battle of Clontarf (1014), and ending real Scandinavian rule on the island thereafter.[43] In these areas of prolonged intercultural contact, intermarriage and other forms of exchange could occur with greater productivity and the resultant hybrid Celtic-Scandinavian and Anglo-Scandinavian communities played important roles in the history of the British Isles.

Throughout subsequent migration, the Scandinavian communities of the British Isles proved significant in the settlement of Iceland, the Faroes, and other parts of the North Atlantic.[44] The Icelandic *Landnámabók* contains numerous references to British Isles migrants, and the Celtic portion of the Icelandic population is generally estimated at roughly 15–20 percent.[45] The earliest settlers from the British Isles were frequently Christian and introduced the religion on the island, although their descendants often converted to pagan cults in subsequent generations. The ongoing influence of British Isles culture in Iceland is reflected by the existence of early churches dedicated to St. Columba of Iona.[46] British Isle Scandinavians also seem to have returned to mainland Scandinavia in number as well. The wealth of Irish artifacts in Norwegian gravefinds signals not only frequent trade and raiding but also processes of return migration.[47] The most prominent such migrant was King Haraldr Gilli, son of King Magnús Bareleg, himself a Hibernized Norwegian. Haraldr returns to his ancestral Norway in young adulthood, claiming his royal title and proving his paternity through an ordeal of fire. Calling on St. Columba for help, he passes the ordeal without injury. Of Haraldr, Snorri writes:

Haraldr gilli var maðr hár ok grannvaxinn, hálslangr, heldr langleitr, svarteygr, døkkhárr, skjótligr ok fráligr, hafði mjök búnað írskan, stutt klæði ok létt klæddr. Stirt var honum norrœnt mál, kylfði mjök til orðanna, ok höfðu margir menn þat mjök at spotti.[48]

Haraldr Gilli was a tall man and slender, long of neck, rather long of face, dark-eyed, dark-haired, sharp and swift; he often wore an Irish costume: short clothes and light. It was difficult for him to speak Norse, and he searched much for the right words. And many men made much sport of that.

Haraldr's description matches well Norse stereotypes of the fleet-footed, dark Irish. Slaves, the product of trade as well as raids, could also bring intercultural and interreligious influences into the Scandinavian household, and British Isles slaves became common throughout the Viking world.[49] Through marriage or emancipation, British Isles slaves and their descendants could become important members of Scandinavian society. Possibly because of close connections between his foster father Jón Loftsson (d. 1197)—a natural grandson of King Magnús Bareleg—and the British Isles settlements, Snorri devotes considerable attention to these influences in his history of the Norwegian kings.

Raiding constituted a central part of the Viking experience.[50] The Eddaic poem *Hávamál* exhorts listeners to be free with gifts to friends and retainers:

Vápnom oc váðom   scolo vinir gleðiaz,
    þat er á siálfom sýnst;
viðrgefendr oc endrgefendr   erost lengst vinir,
    ef þat bíðr at verða vel.[51]

Raiment and weapons   cheer your friends
    as much as they do you;
through receiving and giving back   friends last the longest
    if it is destined to be so.

Young leaders appear to have made their fortunes, names, or marriages through raiding sojourns, returning to their home tracts later with acquired booty, slaves, and prestige. Sagas such as *Egils saga* and Snorri's *Heimskringla* portray raiding as a nearly obligatory rite of passage, one far surpassing the merchant trade in bravery, honor, and literary significance. Surplus males made up the bulk of such expeditions, and young men could also travel abroad to serve in a king's army, sometimes venturing as far afield as England or Byzantium. This menacing aspect of Viking life was transformed by the ennobling lenses of honor and heroism, and even Christian saga writers of the thirteenth century could relate Viking raids of the past with some nostalgia.

Scandinavian, Sámi, and Balto-Finnic Interrelations

The expansion of Scandinavian settlements on the Scandinavian peninsula itself between the fourth and ninth centuries A.D. brought about great changes in Sámi culture. While Sámi living in closest contact with expanding Balto-Finnic populations were gradually assimilated, Scandinavian and Sámi populations in the west remained distinct.[52] Sámi cultural changes attributable to this era appear of two sorts: a gradual specialization from overall hunter-gatherer lifestyles toward more particular hunting and fishing economies (fishing communities along the Arctic coast, hunting communities in the inland forests), along with further adjustment to long-term contact and trade with agropastoralist communities. As the earlier unity of Sámi lifestyle disappeared, the proto-Sámi language developed into the variety of Sámi languages in evidence today (North, Central, Eastern, and South Sámi, along with more localized dialects, such as Inari, Lule, Skolt), reflecting a fragmentation of the once more uniform pan-Sámi culture.[53]

Inger Zachrisson has demonstrated the extensiveness of Scandinavian influence in eleventh- and twelfth-century Sámi graves from the district of Härjedalen along the present Norwegian-Swedish border.[54] Here, in proximity to Scandinavian settlements, Zachrisson finds a community using land in the traditional collective manner of the Sámi institution known as the *siida*.[55] At the same time, the community's close trading ties to Scandinavians and pronounced degree of cultural exchange are evident in findings of wool and linen clothing, brooches and rings from both western and eastern Scandinavia, and caches of Norwegian coins. Burial evidence also points to the strong maintenance of non-Christian religion in the community at this time, however, despite the introduction of Christianity into neighboring Scandinavian settlements. In this sense, the continuities of society and tradition afforded by the *siida* system appear to have acted as an effective cultural sieve, allowing in adaptive technological and cultural innovations while retaining Sámi links to the ancient life modes and belief systems of northern Eurasia.[56]

As the above evidence indicates, Sámi and Scandinavians appear to

have entered into paired economic relations similar to those observed between Sámi and Balto-Finnic populations. The classic proof of this fact is
Ohtere's (Ottar's) ninth-century account of his lifestyle for the English King
Alfred, which survives in manuscripts from the tenth and eleventh centuries.
Ottar, a native of Hálogaland, provides details on the yearly tribute he col-
lects from local Sámi (*Finnas*), including hides, feathers, walrus tusk, and
ship rope made from either walrus or seal. Although he owns livestock
(oxen, sheep, swine, horses, and reindeer) and does some farming, he counts
this tribute as his principal source of wealth: "His greatest income is that
which the Finnas yield him."[57] The specificity of the terms of this tax indicates that it was well established by this point and that, in order to meet it,
Sámi were compelled to produce surplus goods of the types required.

Ottar also describes Ter Sámi (*Terfinnas*), Bjarmians (*Beormas*), and
Kvens (*Cwenas*) in the north and White Sea areas, the latter two groups
representing Balto-Finnic populations.[58] Trade/taxation between the Bjarmians and their Sámi neighbors seems to be facilitated by the fact that, in
Ottar's view, they speak practically the same language.[59] The Kvens, Ottar
relates, reside in and around the Tornio River Valley and are engaged in
occasional hostilities against the Norwegians (*Norðmen*). Eventually, as *Egils
saga* indicates, Kvens and Norwegians are able to cooperate in the competition against Bjarmian and Russian traders for Sámi goods.[60] Such cooperation, however, remained sporadic and temporary.

Ottar's ninth-century account of Scandinavian taxation of the Sámi is
matched by details in *Egils saga*, where the Sámi tribute and trade system is
represented as a well-established part of the Norwegian royal income. Björ-
gólfr, his son Brynjólfr, and Brynjólfr's son Bárðr—residents of the island of
Torgar, in Hálogaland—hold the hereditary right to collect the king's taxes in
Finnmörk, a right which is later reconfirmed by King Harald Finehair when
he visits the province.[61] Upon dying, Bárðr passes this trading privilege, his
wife, and the rest of his inheritance on to his friend and kinsman, Þórólfr
Kveld-Úlfsson. Þórólfr is the paternal uncle of Egill Skalla-Grímsson, the
hero of the saga. Chapter 10 presents Þórólfr's first expedition into Sámi
territory:

Þórólfr gerði um vetrinn ferð sína á fjall upp ok hafði með sér lið mikit, eigi minna
en níu tigu manna; en áðr hafði vandi á verit, at sýslumenn höfðu haft þrjá tigu
manna, en stundum færa; hann hafði með sér kaupskap mikinn. Hann gerði brátt
stefnulag við Finna ok tók af þeim skatt ok átti við þá kaupstefnu; fór með þeim allt í
makendum ok í vinskap, en sumt með hrælugœði.[62]

That winter, Þórólfr made his foray into the mountains with a large troop of retainers, no less than ninety men. Previously, agents had usually brought thirty men
with them, sometimes fewer. He took along a large number of goods. He called a
meeting with the Sámi quickly, collected their tribute, and started a market. Everything proceeded properly and in friendship although with some trepidation.

Here, we see a number of important details on the workings and significance
of the Sámi tribute. First, the collecting takes place in the winter, corresponding to the period of winter group encampments within the Sámi *siida*
tradition.[63] The collecting of the tribute appears completely normalized by
this period, although the Sámi vary the quality and size of their payment
according to the degree of impressiveness or intimidation displayed by the
collector. Further, we may note that the tribute payment appears to be only
the first part of the interaction between the Scandinavians and Sámi. Þórólfr
brings with him trade goods, further increasing the quantity of riches he is
able to carry away in exchange. Presumably, the Sámi are free to trade or
not at this point, depending on their interest in the goods being offered.
In this sense, the initial tribute payment represents a ritualized economic
acknowledgment of the difference in advantage between the two groups,
after which normal trading may ensue. It is, in this way, very much a tax,
although one which implies no guarantee of benefits or security for the
payers. Negative Sámi views of this system, which transformed their communities from subsistence economies to paired economic relations with
outside groups, are well reflected in Sámi oral tradition concerning evil
marauder troops of *čuðit*.[64] In *Egils saga*, the booty from such trade eventually makes its way to England, where it is traded again for a cargo of wheat,
honey, and cloth.[65]

Textual evidence indicates that Scandinavian and Balto-Finnic agropastoralists competed with each other for access to the furs and products of
the north. *Egils saga* furnishes details of Þórólfr's efforts to maintain the
royal monopoly in the vast stretches of Finnmörk, as he patrols its forests in
search of tribute seekers from other kings, whom he murders and loots.[66]
Such accounts indicate a highly decentralized trading system, in which various groups, Scandinavian as well as Balto-Finnic and possibly Slavic, circu-
late among the Sámi *siidas*, extorting or enticing riches from the indigenous
population. Later in the same saga, Þórólfr allies himself to a King Faraviðr of
Kvenland, helping the Kven king force his neighboring trade competitors the
Karelians (ON *Kirjálar*; F *Karjalaiset*) out of the district. Relations between
Kvens and Norse were not always so productive, however. It is with certain

envy that Ottar describes the Kvens' lightweight boats that they are able to portage from lake to lake in their raids on Norwegian settlements:

Ðonne is tōemnes þǣm lande sūðeweardum, on ōðre healfe þæs mōres, Swēoland, oþ þæt land norðeweard; and tōemnes þǣm lande norðeweardum, Cwēna land. Þā Cwēnas hergiað hwīlum on ðā Norðmen ofer ðone mōr, hwīlum þā Norðmen on hȳ. And þǣr sint swīðe micle meras fersce geond þā mōras; berað þā Cwēnas hyra scypu ofer land on ðā meras, and þanon hergiað on þā Norðmen; hȳ habbað swȳðe lȳtle scypa and swȳðe lēohte.[67]

Bordering that land [Norway] from south to north, on the other side of the mountains, lies Sweden, and further to the north, Kvenland. The Kvens sometimes make raids on the Norwegians over the mountains; sometimes the Norwegians make raids on them. There are many freshwater lakes throughout these mountains and the Kvens portage their boats overland onto the lakes and in that way raid the Norwegians; their boats are very small, very light.

The Vikings' dominance in the region came only gradually, thanks in large measure to superior weapons and a larger population.

While conflicts between Scandinavians and Balto-Finns were frequent in the north, archaeological evidence also indicates more amicable trade relations between the groups, particularly in the south. The Merovingian and Viking Age graves of Eura, in southwestern Finland, demonstrate the extensive commerce between western Finns and Swedish centers such as Vendel, Birka, and Gotland.[68] Until the tenth century, Scandinavian ties with the Balto-Finns of the southwest appear dominated by Ålanders, who carried on extensive trading/raiding along the eastern Silver Road.[69] At the turn of the millennium, however, more westerly Vikings came to dominate the trade, reflected by a shift in Finnish coin hoards from Arabic coins to Anglo-Saxon and German, and a decline in hoards in Åland itself. This turn of events correlates with shifts in power related in the sagas and reflects the gradual triumph of western European and western Christian influences on the region. Germanic swords and spearheads, common in Finnish graves from the sixth century onward, proliferate in this latter era, and prestigious swords of central European and Frisian origin give evidence of strong trading relations between Balto-Finns and Scandinavians.[70] At the same time, Balto-Finnic hilltop fortifications and signs of temporary habitation there reflect the activities of Viking raiders in the region. In *Óláfs saga helga*, Torgny the Jarl boasts of a Swedish king, Eric Emundson, of some generations before, who had reportedly subjugated much of the eastern Baltic, including the regions of the Sámi, Karelians, and Estonians, as well as Kurland.[71]

The importance of the long-term development and coevolution of these various intercultural relations becomes clear in accounts of Viking activities to the far west, where settlers in the Greenland and Vinland colonies attempted unsuccessfully to replicate a paired economic relation.[72] Here, in dealing with Inuit and other indigenous hunter-gatherers, and equipped with farming tools and cattle, the Scandinavians failed utterly in their attempts to establish long-term trading relations. Although the beginnings of trade between the groups is described in *Eiríks saga rauða*, the relation soon sours, perhaps in part because the hunting population was unable or unwilling to accept the dairy products offered by their pastoralist neighbors. The lucrative exchange Scandinavians enjoyed in their dealings with Sámi could not be duplicated overnight with a new society of hunters, particularly when the indigenous population maintained the advantage over the invading agropastoralists in warfare and sheer numbers. The productive trade and intermarriage evidenced in parts of the British Isles and Balto-Finnic tracts finds no counterpart in this short-lived experiment in the west.

Whatever else we may say about the various peoples of the North during the Viking Age, then, we cannot claim that they were isolated from or ignorant of their neighbors. Sámi and Balto-Finns were bound by age-old systems of exchange and intercultural influence, ones which linked their communities to each other and to similar societies farther afield. Scandinavians appear to have adopted some aspects of this earlier tradition, seizing upon the Sámi fur trade as a key source of revenue. Raiding and *landnám* east and west extended the Scandinavian settlement area from its mainland hearth eastward across the Baltic and Russia and westward toward the British Isles and North Atlantic.

From the above discussion, it also becomes clear that any examination of religion in this era and region should take into account the integral nature of these intercultural contacts and their effects on religious practices. Evidence of intercultural borrowing or syncretism should not be regarded as mere addendas or as instances of late devolution of some earlier isolated belief system. Rather, such evidence should be seen as the logical product of ongoing cultural adaptation. As religion expresses the concerns and experiences of its human adherents, so it changes continually in response to cultural, economic, and environmental factors. Ideas and ideals passed between communities with frequency and regularity, leading to an interdependent, intercultural region with broad commonalities of religion and worldview. At the same time, myriad distinctions between and within the various linguistic communities of the North ensured constant variety and change. These commonalities as well as distinctions will be explored in the following chapters.

TWO

Religions in the
Viking Age

Contexts and Concepts for Analysis

Northern Europe from the ninth through thirteenth centuries was a world of gradual and sometimes violent change. As outlined in the last chapter, Scandinavian settlements spread widely during the era, entering into long-term relations—productive or antagonistic—with their neighbors at every turn. They had become a cultural force to reckon with throughout the region and it is for this reason that the common title of their most infamous subset—the Viking raiders—has become a synecdoche for the entire era. We write and think of the "Viking Age."

But the same era can be seen from other perspectives. From the point of view of religion, the Viking Age was a time of consolidation: an era in which the variety of pre-Christian belief systems diminished in number and in variation as an increasingly more unified and dominant western Christianity prevailed. Both of these related processes derived from intercultural contacts and the developing economic relations that tied the various peoples of the North to each other and to the world of central and Mediterranean Europe. Such contacts and changes brought with them particular views of religious diversity and strategies for managing the interactions of peoples of different faiths.

This chapter surveys what we know about Nordic intercult relations, particularly examining Christian attitudes toward non-Christian populations. Since the bulk of data regarding all religion in the Viking Age was preserved by Christian writers and communities, it is important to understand the ways in which Christian culture viewed religious variation. A clear understanding of the cultural norms of this community will in turn provide a basis for comparison with what is known about pagan religions in the region and their attitudes toward rival or neighboring faiths.

Defining Religion

Before proceeding to such an examination, however, it is necessary to specify what we mean by *religion*. Although researchers in the anthropology of religion have advanced a vast array of definitions for this central and complex term, two definitions in particular inform the current study. The first of these appears in Karl W. Luckert's 1984 introduction to volumes 8 and 9 of the series *American Tribal Religions*.[1] The second, an older one, appears in Clifford Geertz's 1965 classic essay "Religion as a Cultural System" and was developed further in his seminal work *The Interpretation of Cultures*.[2] Luckert defines religion as "man's response to so-conceived greater-than-human configurations of reality."[3] All people, Luckert contends, and all cultures, divide their experiences of the world into several categories. Elements or experiences that the culture or individual regards as less than human are "handled": controlled, analyzed, conquered, dismissed. Elements or experiences viewed as equal to human are treated as such: shared and communicated with, or competed against. Finally, elements or experiences recognized as greater than human evoke some sort of religious experience, be it mild (fascination), heightened (terror, awe), or extreme (mystic or physical surrender). Cultures vary as to how they perceive any given entity and where on this scale they place it. They also vary in the quantity and types of entities they place in each of the three categories. It is a truism, as Luckert points out, that Westerners today define more things as less than human and fewer things as greater than human than did their ancestors a millennium ago. Religious experience (the confrontation of the self with a perceived greater-than-human entity), for both Christians and non-Christians, was once much more a given in life than it is for many today. In addition, whether we study the tribal religions of North America or the Viking-Age religions of northern Europe, the equal-to-human category of experiences (those entities recognized as partners or competitors) can also be much larger than it is for many Westerners today. Nordic peoples of the Viking Age had a vast array of equals—human, near-human, and nonhuman, mobile and immobile, visible and invisible—with which they shared and competed on a daily basis. These included other people (alive and dead), elements of the landscape and nature, items of flora and fauna, and unseen spirits, all of which (as we will see in Chapter 3) required or expected communication and negotiation from the human community. Religious experience—recourse to the greater-than-human—figured as an important means of gaining advantage over these equals in this comparatively crowded middle world.

Geertz, for his part, attempts to encompass within his definition the processes by which a given religion substantiates itself and shapes the behavior of its adherents. He sees religion as a meaning-making enterprise, the social construction and maintenance of a system of understandings and symbols that imposes order on the chaos that (Geertz asserts) is the true reality of the universe. Through the system of meaning offered by the religion, one is able to view the world with a sense of coherence. And this sense—embodied in what Geertz terms "deeply felt moral and aesthetic preferences," or in that which Luckert later terms the experience of the greater-than-human—becomes, in turn, a means of asserting the validity of the system of symbols that gave rise to it. While many of the details of

Geertz's definition have been questioned by later anthropologists, the usefulness of recognizing religion as not simply an experience but also a social institution is generally recognized.[4] The particular strength of Geertz's formulation is that it maintains the cogency of the personal experience while recognizing and exploring its social construction, maintenance, and use.

In discussing these definitions, I make no claim about their applicability to all the world's religions (as do their authors), nor do I intend to test their validity using Nordic materials as a body of evidence. Rather, I hope to arrive at a conceptual basis that helps make sense of features and issues in the material at hand. Finding a definitional basis that promotes an understanding of both the transcendent religious experience and its attendant social role(s) is important in the present study for a number of reasons. First, it allows us to focus on the crucial issues of life and human relations that underlie many of the religious traditions of the Viking Age. Second, it shifts our attention toward the dynamics of religious experience and away from questions of the pedigrees of particular religious traditions—a line of investigation too prevalent in the philological inquiry into Scandinavian and Finno-Ugric mythologies.[5] Finally, it matches in large measure the emphases of the writers of the sagas themselves. Time and again in these works of thirteenth-century Iceland, authors depict non-Christian religious experiences—rituals, prophecies, acts of piety—as intense, highly personal, and valid, even though the characters in question subscribe to religions that could not be condoned. The writers seem to recognize, I argue, some unifying, underlying verities within all such religious experience, just as they recognize and depict the various social uses—both aboveboard and underhanded—to which religion was put by their characters. Religion in the sagas is both a human institution and something greater.

With these definitions in mind, it becomes evident that religion exerts a shaping effect on an individual's and a community's outlook on life. This deep perceptual shaping, encapsulated in the term *worldview*, pervades all aspects of human experience, regardless of whether or not an individual notices these effects or views them as related to the religion in any way.[6] Thus, by looking at key issues of human experience—for instance death and health—it often becomes possible to discern aspects of the religion only hinted at in more explicitly religious discourse like myth or the discussion of deities, rituals, or conversion. On this deep, partly unconscious level of worldview, similarities may emerge between religious polities that appear at first mutually exclusive or even openly antagonistic toward one another.

Christianity in the Viking Age

Given the above definitions, what can we say about the religions and under-lying worldviews of the Viking world from the ninth through thirteenth centuries? It is clear that we know more about Christian populations than about their pagan counterparts. But the same distortions of perception which, as we saw in the last chapter, have clouded research into Viking-Age economies and intercultural relations, have likewise obscured scholarly un-derstandings of Christianity. Scholars have too often relied on later notions or configurations of Christianity as a basis for understanding the religion as it existed in the Middle Ages, depicting in their studies a Christianity some-how static and well defined, ignoring both historical and local variations. Such a view has little to do with the processual, locally variable religious complex known as Christianity in the ninth through thirteenth centuries.[7] So, too, scholars have tended to focus on formal theological concepts of Christianity, taking these as representative of the culture of the religion's adherents as a whole. While such a tendency may be warranted to a degree in the Mediterranean region of late antiquity, in the Viking-Age North, a marked distinction between formal Christianity and its popular expression among laity must be acknowledged.[8] It is this lived Christianity of the Viking Age that I sketch below, examining its relations—sometimes tentative, some-times close—with the formal theology and learning of the faith.

By even the beginning of the Viking Age, Christianity was well on the way to becoming the dominant religion in northern Europe. The Viking marauders who appear first in the famed account of the sacking of Lindis-farne in 793 outraged their monastic victims not only because of their vio-lence but also because they remained obstinately and anomalously pagan. The British Isles of the eighth century were well Christianized, and mission-ization began in earnest in Scandinavia and Iceland at least by the middle of the following century.[9] During the tenth century, Christianization was pro-moted by Nordic kings in Denmark, Norway, and Sweden, and by the end of the century, Christians were numerous enough even in the once indepen-dent Iceland to push successfully for universal conversion.[10]

This broadly accepted Christianity was by no means a uniform or static religion, however, even in its most formal details. On a theological level, variation of rite and tradition continued in the Church of the West through the thirteenth century. Differences in the form of the mass and other liturgi-cal issues reflected the varying roles and histories of the Church in Rome,

France, Ireland, and Britain and helped map a pattern of missionization and resultant loyalty that persisted in areas of secondary missionization like Scandinavia.[11] In monastic and clerical life, this variability produced differing networks of houses and dioceses, and even nearby sees could be split by longstanding rivalries.

On the popular level, devotions to particular local or national saints often recapitulated these clerical differences and helped separate one Christian community from the next. Local saints frequently became the subject of fierce pride and attendant regional rivalries. Gurevich's account of the struggle between Poitiers and Tours for the relics of St. Martin (316–97) finds ample counterparts in northern Europe in the history of various local saints and the translation of their relics.[12] One need only consider the account of King Cnut's secretive translation of the relics of St. Ælfheah in 1023, as recounted by Osbern: the canny Danish monarch sought to win favor with his British subjects by translating holy relics but did so under the cloak of night lest the residents of London discover the fact before the relics arrived in Canterbury.[13] A similar tale can be gleaned from the hymn to the tenth-century Irish anchorite St. Sunniva (Synnøve), who was murdered by her neighbors on the island of Selja in coastal Norway.[14] While the *Breviarum Nidrosiense* of Trondheim specifies celebration of the saint's feast on the day of the translation of her remains to Bergen (July 8, 1170), the hymn specified for performance on that day still refers to the church on Selja, commissioned by King Óláfr Tryggvason in 995. For the islanders of Selja and their local Benedictine house, the translation of St. Sunniva's relics had been a cause for great sorrow. Such issues of pride took on national significance when the saint in question was a glorious king-saint of old, such as Óláfr (r. 995–1030) or the twelfth-century King Eric of Sweden (r. 1150–60).

Also consequential for Christians of the North was the split between the Roman church and the Orthodox tradition of the East. Differences between the eastern and western churches had grown gradually over time, culminating in the Great Schism of the mid-eleventh century. From the 1220s through the 1240s, papal legates urged crusades from the Latin realms of Denmark and the Baltic against the Orthodox Novgorod Empire, and some warfare did occur along the border between the two spheres of interest (chiefly in Ingria and Karelia).[15] At the Second Council of Lyons in 1274, Pope Gregory X believed he had reunited the severed halves of the Church with Orthodox promises of fidelity to the Latin church and a universal recognition of the supremacy of the pope. But the reconciliation did not take. Although thirteenth-century authors like Snorri Sturluson downplay the significance of the Eastern Orthodox religion in the history of Nordic Christianization, archaeological evidence and the historical facts of Scandinavian contacts with the Byzantine and Novgorod empires indicate a closer relation than might at first be assumed.[16] Its significance in eastern Nordic regions like Karelia and Gotland is clear from archaeological evidence, and *Hungrvaka* mentions eleventh-century Armenian missionaries in Iceland, who are said to have preached a less demanding (and thus more appealing) form of the faith.[17] While such contacts could occur between rank-and-file Nordic populations and Orthodox faithful, royal marriage between Scandinavian and eastern European dynasties occasionally brought the Orthodox religion into the very heart of Nordic court life.

The intellectual life of western Christianity relied on Latin language and learning. For northern Europeans—none of whom spoke a Romance language natively—this Latin dominance represented both a barrier and a bridge to the rest of Europe. For those clerics of the region fortunate enough to gain facility in the language, Latin offered the prime medium through which they became acquainted with the major ideas of the Classical and Christian world. It also allowed them to contribute to that body of knowledge in their own ways. The Northumbrian Venerable St. Bede's eighth-century *Historia ecclesiastica gentis Anglorum*; the English Alcuin's late eighth-century *De virtutibus et vitiis liber*; the English nun Huneberc's eighth-century *Hodoeporicon of Saint Willibald*; the eleventh-century Adam of Bremen's *Gesta Hammaburgensis ecclesiae pontificum*; and the Danish Saxo Grammaticus's early thirteenth-century *Gesta Danorum* all brought the thoughts of northern European authors into the intellectual discussions of the Christian world. Their voices were joined to many others of the region who became proficient in Latin in monastic schools either within Scandinavia or in central Europe.[18] Even in remote northern Iceland, the twelfth-century maiden Ingunn was reported to have learned Latin well enough at the clerical center of Hólar to school her fellow pupils, listening to them read aloud while she played draughts or embroidered scenes from saints' lives.[19] Through this shared Latin learning, in fact, the twelfth-century English cleric Nicholas Breakspear rose to unprecedented heights in the Church of Rome, serving as a cardinal, as papal legate to Norway, and eventually as Pope Adrian IV (1154–59).

For the vast majority—pagan, Christian laity, and even some Christian religious—however, the written texts of the South remained inaccessible but for their oral translation and interpretation in homilies and visual iconography. Early religious texts in Irish, Anglo-Saxon, and Scandinavian languages give us a glimpse of the ways in which Christian learning was presented to the masses, and it is unwise to discount the degree or effectiveness of oral channels in the spread of such continental learning. As the English missionary Winfrid (St. Boniface, 680–754) pointed out in his work in Saxony, the ideal cleric could not only read and comprehend Latin texts, but also translate them meaningfully into the vernacular for the benefit of those around him.[20] In the *Biskupa sögur* account of the Swedish Gísli Finsson's preaching at Hólar in Iceland, the learned monastic is said to have read (apparently in the vernacular) from a book of homilies. His listeners, Gísli felt, were more likely to treat his words with respect if they saw that they came from a book.[21] Translation of Latin works into Scandinavian languages began early, and the twelfth-century Norwegian homily book and Stockholm homily book—compilations of vernacular sermons organized according to the church calendar—draw on a variety of sources, including the scriptures, apocrypha, and the Latin essays of Gregory the Great, Honorius Augustodunensis, Hrabanus Maurus, and the Venerable St. Bede.[22]

In the thirteenth century, the crucial work of extending Latin religious knowledge to the masses became the focus of the new mendicant orders, the Franciscans (founded in 1209) and the Order of Preachers (the Dominicans, founded in 1216). Following the example of their founders St. Francis of Assisi (c. 1181–1226) and St. Dominic (1170–1221), friars in these new orders devoted themselves to preaching among the peasantry and townsfolk of Europe, bringing the learning of the monastery and court to the broad public. Their rapid spread throughout Europe extended into the Nordic realms, where they added their voices to the religious activities of the Benedictines, Cistercians, and the secular clergy.

Scholars have debated the extent to which the Icelandic texts of the thirteenth century, our most valuable sources regarding the pre-Christian religions of the North, are influenced by this extensive ecclesiastical literature. Scholars such as Sigurður Nordal and Einar Ól. Sveinsson have argued vehemently for the existence of a largely independent and secular literary tradition in Iceland during the thirteenth century; other authors have stressed the interrelations between Latin and vernacular writing during the era.[23] Most scholars today would agree that works such as Snorri's *Prose Edda*—which begins by asserting a historical origin for the god Þórr in the family of a Trojan King Agamemnon—blend native concepts and lore with the concerns, learning, and even narrative plots of continental Christian literature. Even such a blending, however, could be seen as an aspect of Christian theology, as von See has shown in his examination of Christian euhemerism (reading myths as history) in relation to pre-Christian deities.[24]

Pagans, Heretics, and Infidels

In this light, then, it becomes crucial to understand the ways in which Christian literature and thought of the era portrayed non-Christian faiths. It was within and perhaps partly against this tradition that the writers of the sagas and histories of the thirteenth century presented their accounts of Nordic paganism. Non-Christians in general were depicted as enemies, prone to violence, deviousness, ignorance, and sometimes utter stupidity. Several different varieties of non-Christians can be discerned in continental Christian literature, including Jews, Moslems, heretics, and members of pre-Christian cults; in Scandinavia, however, these different categories tend to run together into the vague overarching category of "pagan."

A text in the Norwegian and Stockholm homily books details the symbolism of the church building. The two long walls of the nave are said to symbolize the Jews on the one hand (*gyðingum*) and the pagans (*heiðnum þjóðum*) on the other, separate nations joined by the short wall that symbolizes Christ.[25] The symbolism derives from standard Christian works of the Continent, including the ninth-century *De universo* of Hrabanus Maurus, reflecting the special respect accorded to the (converted) Jews in official Church theology and the dual Jew-Gentile categories prominent in New Testament scripture.

In the saints' legends and other pious literature of the medieval period, however, the image of the Jew is seldom positive: Jewish characters are presented as mean-spirited and recalcitrant. Typical is a Latin legend that takes place near the end of the Virgin's life in Jerusalem. When Christians in the town of Lydda convert a synagogue into a church, the Jewish leaders make a protest to the Christian leader. In response, the Christian orders the building shut for forty days in anticipation of a sign from God. When the building is reopened, the Jews discover a miraculous portrait of the Virgin on one of its walls. They are too afraid to touch or remove the image and thus forfeit possession of the building. But as is typical in such accounts, they remain stubbornly resistant to the new faith nonetheless, rejecting the acknowledged miracle.[26] In the Icelandic *Jóns saga*, we find a reference to the *Flagellatio Crucis* legend, in which a group of Jews are depicted railing against the image of a crucifix. When they chance to pierce it with a spear, however, they discover that it is filled with healing blood and water. Terrified, the Jews repent their action but still refuse to convert.[27] The negative spirit of these legends was paralleled by periodic pogroms in central and eastern Europe, as well as the development of saints' cults explicitly based on anti-Semitic lore (e.g., the cults of the twelfth-century William of Norwich and Richard of Pontoise, as well as the thirteenth-century Hugh of Lincoln).[28] In a strange expression of Nordic curiosity, however, the Icelander Brandr Jónsson (d. 1264) used a version of Josephus's *Antiquities* to author a history of the Jews at the time of Jesus (*Gyðinga saga*), a work which resembles the *Sturlunga saga* in many respects.[29]

Even more important as an image of the Infidel was Islam. After the death of Mohammed in 632, the Islamic world had begun to develop with striking speed and zeal. Winning over nearly the entire Middle East in a matter of a few generations, Islamic civilization had spread across northern Africa all the way to the Strait of Gibraltar by the beginning of the eighth century.[30] Arabs came to dominate commerce throughout the Mediterranean and plied their trade northward all the way to Novgorod and Hedeby in Denmark.[31]

In medieval popular culture, the incursions of Muslims on Spain, eastern Europe, and above all the Holy Land were regarded as direct affronts to Christ.[32] By the thirteenth century, the Holy Crusades had turned the professional soldier into a sacral hero, and legends of his exploits abounded. The connivance of the infidel versus the honor of the Christian knight had already become established as a favorite narrative theme, and legends of Christian-Muslim conflicts from both the Holy Lands and the Iberian Peninsula soon diffused into Scandinavia. Typical is the thirteenth-century *Elis saga ok Rósamundu*, an adaptation of a French chanson de geste. Here, however, the saga writer shows little knowledge of Islam itself, as the characters are presented as pagan idolators, worshipping statues and falling victim at last to the righteous hand of God.[33]

If Islam was perceived as the ultimate threat from without, heresy remained an endemic threat from within. Heresies—fundamental ideological breaks with accepted theology—plagued the faith, and church authorities East and West were faced with constant challenges to doctrinal and ritual unity.[34] Often, these challenges grew out of the persuasive teachings of charismatic individuals who offered their views from the pulpit or fireside. The preaching of the British monk Pelagius (c. 360–420) engendered a serious heresy that spread to various parts of Europe and northern Africa in the fifth century. A plenary synod of all bishops in the Frankish kingdom was called in 745 to combat two wildly popular heresies of the day: one led by a charismatic Adalbert (who dedicated churches to himself and distributed pieces of his hair and nails as holy relics) and the other led by the Irish bishop Clement (who rejected aspects of the Church fathers' writings and refused the rule of celibacy).[35] Ralph of Coggeshall, a British Cistercian monk and abbot of the thirteenth century, wrote stirringly of the heresy of a townswoman in Rheims who knew the Scriptures well enough to quote and (mis)interpret them freely, leading many of her fellow villagers astray.[36] The Protestant Reformation of the sixteenth century had ample predecessors, from the earliest era of the Church onward.

Arianism—based on the teachings of the charismatic fourth-century Greek theologian Arius—had beset the era of Constantine and remained important among south Germanic peoples for centuries. Its longevity helped engender a body of legends dealing with its threat. St. Martin of Tours's account of God's judgment against an Arian priest enjoyed considerable popularity for centuries after the threat of Arianism itself had subsided. As the story is presented in his *Liber de gloria martyrum*, the wedding feast of a Catholic bride and an Arian groom is blessed by priests from each religion. While the Arian priest dies suddenly from ingesting the food, his Catholic counterpart eats undisturbed.[37] As with accounts of Jews and Muslims, legends regarding heretics depict the villains receiving their punishment directly from the hand of God, to the consternation of their supporters and the joy of the Christians they had assailed.

Meanwhile, in remote northern Europe, the threat against Christianity was even nearer at hand. Along the shores of the eastern Baltic, pagandom persisted, leading to Danish and especially German crusades modeled after those of the Holy Land. The Fratres Militiae Christi (Swordbrothers) and the Teutonic Knights brought the methods and imagery of Middle Eastern wars to the frontiers of northern Europe, and Scandinavian kings such as King St. Eric IX of Sweden (d. 1160) and Valdemar II of Denmark (1170–1241) mounted their own expeditions into neighboring, ostensibly pagan realms (modern-day Finland and Estonia).[38] Orthodox schismatics of Novgorod were also targeted in attempted holy wars of the mid-thirteenth century.[39] Farther to the north, Sámi remained still largely non-Christian and rural Finns and Scandinavians alike often remained quietly faithful to traditions seemingly inimical to Christian doctrine. Where later medieval writers would see secret pacts with the devil as the silent threat from within Christian society, Scandinavians of the thirteenth century recognized stubborn pagan recalcitrance as their perennial adversary. The pagan god or spirit— like the devil—was a real threat, even if it remained inferior to the might of the Christian God.

Continental learning provided its own tales of pagan conversion. Pope St. Gregory the Great's sixth-century account of the conversion of Totila the

Goth by St. Benedict served as the narrative basis for a similar story in Snorri's *Óláfs saga Tryggvasonar*.[40] In both accounts, the pagan chieftain attempts to deceive a pious hermit by disguising one of his men as himself. The hermit sees through the disguise, however, and his prescience convinces the leader to convert. Even more memorable as an image of pious courage in the face of pagan resistance was St. Boniface's eighth-century destruction of the sacred tree at Geismar. The missionary steadfastly felled the tree, convincing his German audience to convert, and used the tree's wood to build a church on the spot.[41] Bishop Daniel of Winchester summed up the strategy behind such acts in his letter of advice to his countryman St. Boniface: "[Y]ou will have to contrast the truths of our Christian faith with their superstitions, in such a way that you stir their feelings at the same time; the pagans, confounded rather than embittered, will then blush over their superstitions; and moreover, they will see that we are really aware of their shameful practices and myths."[42] The missionary must show superior knowledge of the cosmos, calling on the might of the almighty God over the more limited powers of the demonic false gods of the pagans. Daniel recommends increasing the resulting embarrassment by linking it to an observation of the greater natural endowments of Christian lands over those still given over to paganism. He writes: "And why do the Christians possess fertile countries, rich in oil and wine and teeming in other treasures, while the pagans who still worship false rulers, the gods banished everywhere else, are left the countries always benumbed with cold?"[43] Such a strategy appears ideal for dealing with the acute code of honor, status, and shame that governed Scandinavian life and finds such memorable depiction in the sagas.

In dealing with their own pagan past, Icelanders often evinced a certain sympathy, however, as we shall see in Chapter 8 in our examination of specific sagas. At times, their representations could even take on the form of a kind of "noble pagan" construct, in which the pagan characters act in a laudable manner despite their religious affiliations.[44] Such is the thrust of the account of the steadfast Eyvindr in *Óláfs saga Tryggvasonar*, presented in the Introduction.[45] This Icelandic tendency becomes more evident when we compare it with the pitiless depictions of contemporaneous Baltic pagans included in works such as the German *Livonian Rhymed Chronicle*.[46]

Pagan Views of Religious Diversity

It is possible to imagine the pagan religions of the Nordic region as somehow inherently more pluralistic and respectful of neighboring faiths than was

Christianity. Such a view involves privileging certain pieces of evidence over others. One can look, for instance, at the pagan reasoning depicted in the celebrated accounts of the Icelandic conversion in the year 1000 as a kind of censure of Christian exclusivity.[47] Since the petulant Christians—missionized by the unmanageable foreigner Þangbrandr—would not tolerate religious diversity, we are told, the reasonable and mature pagan response was to accept universal baptism. But such a view mistakes the nature of Nordic ethnic religions and the dynamics at work within and between them. The bulk of our evidence points to the notion that these smaller religious communities, like the localized Christian enclaves around them, were markedly exclusive and apparently highly ethnocentric as well. The Finno-Ugric tendency to adopt the name of a neighboring people's chief deity as the title of their own religion's principal demon illustrates cogently the kind of inherent rivalry and discourse of ethnocentrism that characterized religious life in the region.[48] John Lindow has pointed to similar long-lived tendencies among Scandinavians and these attitudes certainly do not appear to date only from Christianization.[49] But given the small size of individual cults and the economic and cultural ties of populations during the Viking Age, it was inevitable that such groups would engage in intimate contact with peoples of other faiths. The very exclusivity of native religions could spawn interest in comparing (and deprecating) neighboring cults. That such awareness of other religions eventually led to a convergence of religious outlook is one of the principal findings of the present study.

It is probably foolish to view the existence of a statue of the Buddha in an eighth-century grave on Helgö in Sweden as evidence for a true Scandinavian interest in Asian religions during the Viking Age.[50] Likewise, many of the Scandinavian cult objects that appear in eastern Baltic and Sámi graves over the course of the same era may represent—at least at the outset of their appearance—little more than indications of productive trade relations.[51] The thorny question of how to interpret such votive objects in gravefinds will be examined in depth in Chapter 7 in connection with images of the Cross.

Yet even if we entirely discount such evidence in our examination of intercult relations, it remains a fact that by their very nature the ethnic religions of the Nordic pagans were brought into contact with each other in substantive and prolonged fashion. Ancestral cults (discussed in the following chapter) necessarily entailed intercult contact, as marriage partners were recruited or acquired across clan lines. Long-distance trading partnerships, fosterage, and migration all led to further contacts between peoples of different religious identity. In areas like Iceland, where settlers had arrived from an array of different locales, real religious exclusivity was only possible on an abstract philosophical level. Intercult contact was an inevitable aspect of life, finding manifestation both between and even within clans or communities.

Awareness of neighboring religious diversity was undoubtedly intensified by the lack of unity in the beliefs of even purportedly related local cults. The non-Christian belief systems of the Nordic region seldom if ever underwent the processes of open codification that characterized Christianity from its earliest stages onward. We have only a few instances in which pagan religious leaders appear to call for the open inculcation of succeeding generations in specific cult verities. The early tenth-century Rök Stone calls for the reader to instruct the youth (*ungmenni*) in the history of various heroes of the past, detailing a list of at least thirteen pieces of sacred history that should be passed on.[52] The knowledge itself—barely sketched in the inscription—remains murky, however. Even the Eddaic poems, standardly viewed as our most direct textual sources for pre-Christian Scandinavian religion, tend to refrain from direct enunciation of key beliefs, preferring instead to hint at these nuggets of wisdom in cryptic, truncated allusions. The inherent secrecy of pagan religious knowledge appears to have rendered problematic any open sharing of efficacious information. Where we do have multiple versions of specific myths—such as the varying accounts of the Baldr story,[53] or the multiple textual and pictorial versions of the myth of Þórr's fishing for the world serpent[54]—the evidence points to widely divergent accounts of ostensibly the same lore. Adding to that the conflicting, sometimes parodic representations of principal gods like Óðinn and Þórr (as we shall see in the following chapter), it becomes clear that Nordic paganism was subject to extensive local variation and a fair degree of intercult rivalry.

The use of pagan cults as a means of promulgating collective unity—a hallmark of Roman as well as Christian practice—did find counterparts in Nordic pagan practices, however. In at least some cases, pagan temples and sacred sites appear to have been publically recognized and their maintenance as well as defense viewed as a point of public duty. The account of the Bjarmian temple in *Óláfs saga Helga* (quoted in the Introduction) indicates that Balto-Finnic temples could be situated near settlements with their location known to both native and stranger alike.[55] A similar situation is implied by Tacitus's accounts of continental Germanic sacred groves and islands during the first century.[56] Sámi *seidit* (altars) appear to have remained hidden, but this practice seems related to a desire to prevent desecration of the site by women or other unworthy beings. The fact that, at least in some cases, women were not even allowed to look in the direction of such sites implies that their location, although covert, must have been at least vaguely known to all and that proper maintenance of their sacrality was viewed as a communal responsibility.[57]

A few accounts depict an even more organized approach to public expressions of cult affiliation. *Landnámabók* details the number and distribution of pagan temples formerly maintained by law and public temple dues (*hoftollar*) in each of the quarters of Iceland, a system much like the tithes that arrived with Christianity.[58] The Icelandic law tract *Úlfljótslög* decrees that all persons wishing to conduct legal business at court must swear to three gods on a sacred arm ring, conserved at a particular temple.[59] Adam of Bremen records similar public requirements in his eleventh-century account of the temple at Uppsala.[60] The temple, containing golden ornamentation, carved images of three gods, a sacred grove, spring, and tree, shows all the signs of a consolidation of cult and a public insistence on submission to the religion of the realm.

Pagans do not appear to have shown great tolerance of Christian refusals to submit to these public displays of religious unity. Adam reports that Christians unwilling to attend periodic sacrifices at the temple at Uppsala were compelled to pay for their absence by a fine. Snorri's account of the pagan demands that the Christian King Hákon partake in the annual feast in honor of the gods and deceased ancestors at Þrándheimr (Trondheim) appears rooted in the same insistence on Christian submission to the pagan public cult.[61] Jónas Gíslason points out the political disenfranchisement that Icelandic Christians faced because of their religious convictions prior to the conversion: their agitation for universal baptism, it would seem, arose in part from their exclusion from the political life of the island otherwise.[62]

The inevitable drawback of maintaining publicly acknowledged sacred sites lay in the opportunity for desecration that they afforded one's rivals or enemies. Here, the ethnocentrism of pagan cults appears as virulent as that displayed by Christians, as warriors raided and desecrated the sacred sites and objects of all rivals. Holy reliquaries, looted from Christian churches, were emptied of their sacred contents and made into personal treasure boxes.[63] It may be that Sámi concealment of their *seite* sites arose in part as a defense against such practices of sacrilegious theft. In addition to defilement through looting, pagans were known to desecrate each other's sacred sites as a form of insult, as when, in *Eyrbyggja saga*, the hallowed meeting grounds at Þórsnes are intentionally defiled by excrement.[64] Similarly, when a farmhand in *Hrafnkels saga* carelessly defiles a stallion dedicated to the god Freyr, its owner Hrafnkell feels honor-bound to slay the perpetrator.[65] The maintenance of public sacrality required an investment of time and manpower, and desecration called for immediate and decisive retribution.

As with sacred grounds and objects, the holy men of other religions seem to have received little mercy when the intent was to shame or injure another's cult. St. Ansgar's fellow priest Gautbert was robbed and martyred by tenth-century Swedish pagans,[66] and the English priest Ríkarðr (Richard) was savagely mutilated in twelfth-century Norway, ostensibly for becoming too friendly with a woman of high standing.[67] More tempered is Hákon the Jarl's actions when rejecting the faith that his ally King Haraldr has imposed upon him: he simply strands the priests whom he has agreed to bring to Norway, leaving them to fend for themselves while he renews his allegiance to Óðinn (see Chapter 8 for further discussion).[68] It is not surprising in this context of honor and shame that Christians built their churches at times upon the remains of former pagan worship sites: such an act demonstrated the superiority of one religion over another in terms comprehensible to the pagan world.

Given the conflicts which appear common between the various religious groups of the Viking-Age North, it is hard to imagine any degree of productive religious exchange or rapprochement. Yet, as we shall see in the coming chapters, such developments did indeed occur. Ideas and personnel from different religions crossed cultural lines and became incorporated into new and changing belief systems; these processes then affected the cultural history and achievements of the entire Viking Age.

THREE

Gods, Guides, and Guardians

Spiritual Aids

Amid the vagaries of life in the Viking Age, people sought and found guidance in a variety of spiritual allies, conscious beings of greater-than-human power who had chosen to manifest themselves to humans on earth.[1] Human adherents, for their part, expressed their knowledge of and relation to these beings through myth and ritual: narratives and symbolic actions which served as communications both with particular spirits and with other human adherents of the religion.[2] This chapter surveys the variety of supernatural allies known to Nordic peoples during the Viking Age, with particular reference to commonalities that obtain across cultural lines. The comparison of Nordic gods and myths presents difficult challenges, since the evidence left to us is scant and usually cryptic. Yet it is important to attempt a comparison, not only to understand the centrality of these beings in the spiritual lives of pagans as well as Christians, but also to appreciate the comparative issues facing Nordic peoples themselves during the centuries of the Viking Age.

It has become a practice in the study of Nordic religions to approach gods from the point of view of environment, ecology, and economy.[3] One can speak of the gods of hunter-gatherer communities, for instance, or the agrarian cults of farmers. The following overview follows these tendencies but without positing any historical evolution from one type to the next. In fact, given the variety of livelihoods practiced in the Viking Age and the intimate interconnections between peoples occupying different economic niches (as discussed in Chapter 1), we may view all of these religious expressions as more or less contemporaneous during the Viking Age. I argue further that nearly all of these different traditions regarding deities were familiar to most Nordic peoples, regardless of their own particular ways of life. Historical continuities as well as intercultural contacts ensured a wide range of common knowledge and worldviews regarding the supernatural world and its helpful (as well as harmful) denizens.

Worship of Ancestors

Ancestors constituted one of the most ancient and widespread types of deity worshipped in the Nordic region. Archaeological evidence from eighth-century graves at Vainionmäki, Finland, suggest the practice of making food offerings and gifts of other objects to dead ancestors.[4] Such devotion to deceased relatives appears to have been common among Finno-Ugric peoples in general, and the significance of ancestors in the spiritual lives of even Christianized Finns and Sámi remained strong throughout the medieval period.[5] Scholarly fascination with the more fantastic gods and myths of the Vikings has drawn attention away from such customs among Scandinavians during the same era, but some sort of ancestor worship was probably an element of the private religious practices of the farmstead and village.[6] Certainly similar food offerings occur in Swedish graves of the era.[7] In demanding that King Hákon participate in their annual feast at Þrándheimr (Trondheim), the tenth-century Norwegian pagans insisted that the king drink toasts to the gods Óðinn, Þórr, Njörðr, Freyr, Bragi, and "their kinsmen who lay in barrows."[8] As we shall see in Chapter 4, sacred mountain and other ancestor worship customs among Sámi, Finns, and Scandinavians remained of great importance throughout the Nordic region during the era.[9]

Gods of the Hunt

Scholars have examined the evidence for the characterization of the earliest period of Nordic religions, an era millennia before the beginning of the Viking Age.[10] From archaeological evidence, we can tell that bands of hunter-gatherers, closely dependent on seasonal patterns of abundance in fish, mammals, and birds, replicated their concerns for survival in art and ritual. In the most ancient rock paintings of the Nordic region, practical information on the bodies or movements of likely food sources merges with representations often interpreted as hunting magic or even as depictions of deities. Mikkelsen argues that the frequent depiction of the bull moose in petroglyphs attributed to the Nøstvet culture of the Oslo fjord region reflects the moose's possible status as a totemic figure (a mythical ancestor for the clan or community).[11] At the same time, the relative paucity of depictions of the bear—held as supernaturally powerful throughout ancient North Eurasia—may also indicate totemic status, this time through taboos against representation. In the eastern Baltic, in areas of the Combed Ceramic Ware culture of the fourth millennium B.C., depictions of waterfowl as well as moose and bear are found on objects of stone, bone, antler, and wood.[12] Waterfowl in particular figure as sacred animals throughout the Finno-Ugric world, and their pictorial distribution, corresponding to the region stretching from the eastern Baltic to the Ural Mountains, closely maps the habitation areas of Finno-Ugric peoples during this early period.[13] Finds from the same area frequently also contain figurines of human form, characterized by a large face and prominent nose and occasional tattoos or facial painting.[14] It is possible that some or all of these objects represent deities, including gods of the forest or hunt documented among Finno-Ugric peoples in postmedieval ethnographic literature.[15]

Interpretation of mute archaeological evidence left by hunter-gatherer peoples of ages past depends on insights gained from observing recurrent patterns in the rituals and concepts of such populations in the world today. Through picture and word magic, hunting cultures often attempt to gain advantage over other entities in nature, maintaining or monopolizing the limited quantity of luck residing in the cosmos. Man's interactants in daily life—animals and plants, the landscape, diseases—must be compelled to act with goodwill toward humans, goodwill that is achieved only by a careful combination of respectful behavior and magical control. When an animal appears capable of signaling or even causing important events (e.g., seasonal shifts in the case of migratory waterfowl), the sacral relevance of the species rises. Finnish epic songs preserve instances of the world-egg and earth-diver myths (widespread throughout Eurasia), in which the origin of the cosmos results from the actions of a nesting or diving waterbird.[16] These traditions certainly remained active in the Viking Age, even when they were combined with other notions of deities and ritual. The luck-based worldview of hunting peoples remained an enduring stratum of religious belief observable in hunting customs among all the Nordic peoples for centuries after the close of the Viking Age.

A variety of evidence points to the bear as a key object of veneration among Nordic peoples during this period as well. The Finno-Ugric ceremonial bear hunt sought to remove a fierce competitor from the local environment, while winning its power for the hunter and community and assuring its eventual reincarnation or return to the sky.[17] Among Sámi and Balto-Finns, such hunts included selection of the hunter by divination or lots, a welcoming of the slain bear's carcass as an honored guest or even wedding partner, ceremonial consumption of the bear's meat, recounting of its mythic origins in the sky, and placement of its bones or skull in a place of honor (such as a sacred grove or fir tree, or, in tundra areas, a stone cairn). Aspects of this tradition survived among Sámi and Finns into the eighteenth and nineteenth centuries and find close parallels among the Finno-Ugric Khanty and Mansi peoples of Russia as well.[18] Although we possess fewer indications of such traditions among the Germanic Scandinavians, the myth of an astral origin for the bear is widespread throughout Europe, and taboos surrounding utterance of the animal's name occur in many cultures of the region, including the Germanic, where word roots referring to the color brown have replaced the earlier name of the beast.

Closely related to the concept of luck are ritual implements for testing chance. Terms for thrown lots (ON *fella blótspánn*, F *arpa*, SáN *vuor'be*) appear to have spread from Germanic to Finno-Ugric languages at an era before the separation of proto-Finnic and proto-Sámi (second or first millennium B.C.) and thus represent extremely ancient examples of Nordic religious contact.[19] In *Njáls saga*, the kinsmen Gizurr and Geirr draw lots to decide which of them will assume the onerous task of prosecuting the case of their second cousin Otkell's killing.[20] Allowing seemingly random processes such as lots to determine important acts could be seen as resigning human destiny to the inevitability of fate (a concept of great importance), or (if magic were involved) allowing one's store of luck to be heightened or stolen through supernatural means. On the other hand, if the community looked to the guidance of some powerful deity (e.g., Óðinn, God), the same act could be viewed as an appeal to divine judgment. In this way, the ancient concept of chance could take on a new meaning in rituals such as the ordeal, common to late pagans and Christians alike.[21] The ordeal settled issues that could not be determined otherwise in the community: for instance, the guilt or innocence of a woman accused of adultery (as in the case of Guðrún in the Eddaic poem *Guðrúnarqviða in þríðia*), or the veracity of a pretender's claim of royal paternity (as in the case of King Haraldr Gilli in *Magnússona saga*).[22] As the latter example illustrates, such tests were fully accepted within the Christian worldview as well: in Snorri's account, the rightful prince calls on St. Columba for assistance while undergoing his trial by fire.

Gods of Menace

While nearly any god could prove deleterious if angered, certain Nordic deities—particularly gods of disease or death—were regarded as especially menacing. These gods seldom appear the recipients of warm affection: ritual acts directed toward them were calculated to prevent the deity's potential wrath or to purchase their begrudging restraint. Such gods' anger could erupt in failed luck, injury, illness, or death. Offerings to the Sámi god Ruto— related to other Finno-Ugric gods of disease and misfortune across North Eurasia (see Chapter 4)—were intended to secure the god's absence rather than any particular assistance.[23] By sacrificing a piece of livestock to the god (e.g., a black horse), the community could ensure that Ruto would remain in his own underworld, thereby avoiding the onset of dangerous disease or famine. Alternatively, Nordic communities could call on the assistance of a more powerful god to limit or counteract the aggression of such demonic spirits. This approach became particularly pronounced in Christianity, distinguishing the Christian devil from the more ambiguous demons of pagan tradition, the trickster/demon Loki, for example, or the ill-willed but occasionally marriageable giant (*jötunn*) folk. Scholars have debated the extent to which figures like Loki reflect Christianizing worldviews in late paganism and the exact nature of such pre-Christian spirits as the giants before Christian influence.[24] During the Viking Age, however, the concept of "demon" certainly incorporated both pre-Christian and Christian conceptualizations and encompassed a range of beings including fiends from beneath the world, ogres from the edge of the world, personified diseases, and deceptive false gods.

Localized Deities

All Nordic peoples recognized a range of spirits dwelling in particular objects or places, such as stones, trees, groves, waterfalls, houses, and small idols. Such deities were common throughout northern Europe: Anglo-Saxon terms for sacred groves, rocks, or trees (e.g., *hearg, bearu, friðgeard*) correspond closely to Scandinavian terms like *stafgarðr* (a Gotlandic designation for a sacred enclosure), *lundr* (a sacred grove), and *vé* (a sacred field or sacrificial site), as well as the Finnish term *hiisi* (sacred grove, demon).[25] In Tacitus's description of religious comportment within the sacred grove of the Semnones, adherents are said to exercise supreme care so as not to anger their divine host, viewed as the source and ruler of the community.[26] If one fell within the grove, he had to roll out rather than return to his feet in an act which could be interpreted as resistance to the god's will. Sámi *seidi* altars occurred in forests or mountainsides and were maintained as inviolable sanctuaries for specific deities.[27] Cult leaders could be assured of a deity's receptiveness to offerings made at these altars, whose sacrality was guarded through the careful observance of taboos, particularly regarding sacrifices and women. The Sámi tradition resembles the account of a male spirit residing in a rock on a tenth-century Icelandic farm in *Kristnisaga*.[28] Here, the *goði* Koðrán brings sacrifice to the deity, *ármaðr*, on behalf of his family and community. Attempts to root out these localized cults accompanied Christianization throughout northern Europe and often involved the deliberate destruction of such sacred sites, as in the case of St. Boniface's felling of the sacred tree at Geismar (discussed in Chapter 2) or the decisive pouring of holy water on the rock discussed in *Kristnisaga*.

Archaeological finds throughout Scandinavia indicate a widespread custom of making various offerings in bogs and swamps as well.[29] Swords, tools, votive objects, and even human remains have been recovered from peat bogs in particular. It is unclear, however, whether pagans intended these items as offerings to spirits actually dwelling in the bog or whether they viewed these sites as the appropriate place to sacrifice to gods who resided elsewhere. Tacitus's account of crimes punishable through submersion in a swamp probably reflects such areas' negative symbolism for ancient Scandinavians.[30]

While some deities dwelled in field and forest, others lived beneath the floorboards of human dwellings. Fall or midwinter sacrifices (*blót*) to female household spirits (*dísir*) or the god Freyr figure frequently in saga accounts and appear particularly associated with women's religious expression.[31] In the poem *Austrfaravísur* (c. 1020), the Christian skald Sigvátr complains of being locked out of all the local farms in the area of Sweden he visits due to the celebration of a sacrifice in honor of elves (*elfblót*).[32] In the description of the Winter's Nights ceremony included in *Njáls saga*, Þiðrandi dies as a result of improper behavior on the night of the ritual, falling victim to the *dísir* when he breaks a taboo against opening the door.[33] *Blót* ceremonies appear to have involved sacrifices of blood made inside the house and general feasting among the human participants. Travelers' accounts of the Viking city of Hedeby indicate the display of slaughtered animal carcasses outside of houses as testimonies to household rituals within.[34]

The Sámi deities Máttaráhkká, Sáráhkká, Juksáhkká, and Uksáhkká evince many of the characteristics typical of such household spirits and may serve as indications of the cosmological significance and roles of these beings among Nordic peoples in general. Each of the spirits dwelled within her own portion of the house: Máttaráhkká (the mother of the other deities and creator of human bodies) resided under the floor, while her daughter Sáráhkká (the subsequent guardian of female fetuses and helper of women in childbirth and menstruation) lived beneath the hearth. Juksáhkká (guardian of male fetuses), and Uksáhkká (guardian of small children and the doorway) both resided near the entrance of the house. Their roles apparently varied in detail from one Sámi community to another but were characterized in general by clear delimitations of duty and normalized reciprocity-based sacrifices.

Scholars have suggested that these spirit *ahkkas* (women, wives)—as well as possibly the Scandinavian spirits of the household and fate, the *dísir* and *nornor*—derive ultimately from ancestor worship: a bride brought her clan's ancestral spirits with her when moving to her husband's home, and these deities settled in the women's sections of the house, remaining distinct from the spirits of the man's clan.[35] With time, the deities became associated with their place of residence rather than their originating clan. Traditional wedding ceremonies among various Finno-Ugric and other northern European peoples involve the bride's ritual leave-taking of such natal household spirits and formal introduction to the household spirits of the husband's home, implying the stasis of the spirits themselves.[36] Máttaráhkká has also been compared with Mother Earth cults across North Eurasia, however, while Sáráhkká bears affinities to the widespread North Eurasian cult of Mother Fire, protectress of families and helper in childbirth and healing.[37] This latter interpretation helps explain the continued significance of Sáráhkká, in particular, among Christianizing Sámi of the seventeenth and eighteenth centuries. The early eighteenth-century missionary Thomas von Westen reports that before receiving Holy Communion, for instance, Sámi drank a toast to Sáráhkká as well as to their astral god (see below), asking forgiveness for their act of disloyalty.[38] Olaus Rudbeck noted in 1695 that Sámi regularly addressed their calls for help to Mary and a St. Sara, the latter of whom must represent a Christianization of the pre-Christian deity.[39] The relation indicated here between the deity and the people under her protection is warm and loyal, similar to the personalized friendships characteristic of devotions to saints and to Jesus in Christianity (see below).

More intimate and more mobile were the relations between individuals and their guardian spirits, supernatural beings who hovered beside or near a person during life. All the Nordic cultures appear to have possessed concepts of such beings, and this idea became augmented in both shamanism and Óðinn worship. In Christianity, the concepts of guardian angels as well as saints eventually filled a similar role. In Scandinavian paganism the presence of the guardian spirit often went unnoticed until the time of one's death: in the Eddaic poem *Helgaqviða Hjörvarðzsonar*, for instance, the hero Helgi's female guardian spirit (*fylgior*) appears in the form of a woman riding a wolf with snakes for reins.[40] When Helgi hears of the vision, he knows that his death is near. In *Víga-Glúms saga*, the Icelandic chieftain Glúmr dreams of his Norwegian grandfather's guardian spirit (*hamingja*), who appears to Glúmr at the time of the elder's death to offer her services to him.[41] In shamanism, these spirits—often taking animal form—assumed particular roles, especially during ecstatic trance (see below). In Óðinn worship, for its part, they merged with Óðinn's own *valkyrjor* (corpse-choosers): attendant spirits of the battlefield.[42] In the Eddaic poems *Helgaqviða Hundingsbana in fyrri, Helgaqviða Hundingsbana önnor,* and *Sigrdrífomál,* these valkyries appear as warrior-princesses, taking human form but also assisting their chosen warrior-lovers on a supernatural plane during battle.[43] Improper behavior toward one such valkyrie forms the basis of the prolonged conflict in the Eddaic poems of Sigurðr and their prose rendering in *Völsungasaga.*[44] While pagan guardian spirits appear transferrable, particularly between men in the same family, the Christian guardian angel was not. Nor are saints as clearly bound in service to one person at a time as the guardian spirits of paganism.

Shamanism

The roles and significance of shamanism in North Eurasia has received considerable scholarly attention.[45] In shamanic traditions, when crises of health or need drove a community toward the limits of its capacity to negotiate with guardian spirits, the spirits of animals, the dead, or deities of other kinds, it could turn to the greater expertise of a religious specialist, whose relations with such spirits had become regularized and frequent. Acting as an advocate for human clients and a medium for interested non-human spirits, the shaman could restore or assure productive relations between the human community as a whole and its surrounding spirit milieu, generally through undergoing ecstatic trance during which one or more of the shaman's souls would travel forth on supernatural quests.

In the cross-cultural morphology of shamanism as put forward by Eliade and echoed convincingly by later ethnographic cases, the shamanic role is seen not so much as one of leadership but as one of discipleship: human practitioners describe themselves as attendants or followers of spirit guides, who demand submission to their communicative urges.[46] In Sámi shamanism, about which we know the most of any shamanic tradition found in the Nordic cultures, the *noaide*'s (shaman's) helping spirits took three theriomorphic forms: the bird (*sájva-lâddie*), the fish (*sájva-guölie*), and the reindeer bull (*sájva-sârvá*).[47] The *noaide*'s negotiations involved ecstatic trance usually accompanied by animal sacrifices at sacred sites (*seidi* altars or special lakes), thus purchasing or ensuring the assistance of helpful spirits. In Balto-Finnic shamanism, spirit guides appear to have taken the form of squirrels as well as waterfowl, and sacred groves or trees often figured in associated rituals.[48]

This idea of marginalized ritual specialists consulted at times of communal need appears common to all Nordic peoples during the Viking Age.

The shaman, the Germanic warrior class associated with battle fury and bear or wolf skins (the *berserkr* tradition), the *seiðr* practitioner (see Chapter 6), and the holy hermit of Christianity all represented liminal figures in Nordic societies, beings whose sacral powers arose in part from their choice to assume a marginal, even pariah-like existence. The Christian hermit tradition had deep roots in both Judaic prophecy and Eastern eremitism, but it also resembled in key respects the special status of marginal ritualists in Nordic pagan life. That deities chose such figures as channels of communication reflects certain deep-seated assumptions about divine prerogatives and the attitudes of spirits toward human society. It is the physical—sometimes also the cultural—outsider who may be selected to relay the god's message to the community.

Agrarian Deities and Rituals

The arrival of agriculture in the Nordic region brought with it distinct and revolutionary religious concepts.[49] Celestial bodies—stars, the moon, the sun—rose as favored motifs in rock paintings dating from the second millennium B.C. and after, coincident with the spread of agricultural practices in the region.[50] As the coital act emerged as a prime metaphor for the mystery of agricultural fecundity, the gods responsible for the seasonal cycle, sunshine, rain, and plants took on the characteristics of human sexuality: gender, reproductive organs, and appetites. Although anthropomorphic in many respects, these gods are often marked by sexual ambiguities, theriomorphic elements of physique (such as the antlers of the Celtic god Cernunnos), and appetites akin to animals in rut. The sagas contain stray images of worship of farm animals, as well, possibly as representatives of these gods: individual boars, bulls, cows, and horses all appear as the occasional objects of ritual veneration.[51] This stratum of Nordic religious life appears to have held great significance for people dependent on the seasons and the vagaries of agricultural production.

 The deities of the earth—the Vanir of Scandinavian texts—were on the whole a passionate, lascivious lot. Within the worldview of early agriculturalists, the magic of natural regeneration—the very basis of agriculture—leads naturally to magic of other types. The Eddaic poem *Völuspá* depicts Vanir magic as a redolent, intoxicating force, wielded with might and success against the weapons of the Æsir.[52] In his discussion of Vanir gods Freyja, Freyr, and Njörðr in the Prose *Edda*, Snorri portrays the deities as exotics, possessed of their own strange customs, such as incest, and given to fits of rage and desire. In the Eddaic poem *För Scírnis*, the god Freyr pines for a giant maiden, sending his emissary to coerce her into marriage.[53] By lending Skírnir his sword for the journey, Snorri notes chidingly, Freyr deprives himself of the weapon he needed in his battle against Beli.[54] In describing the Vanir magic in *Ynglingasaga*, Snorri notes its cooption by Óðinn but also its compromising or embarrassing qualities for men.[55]

At every turn within his texts, in fact, Snorri depicts the Vanir as ambiguous figures: powerful and even essential to the proper functioning of the cosmos, but dubious as emulative role models. That Snorri's views reflect Christian moral appraisals of pagan deities is certain: the same view can be seen in the jibes against gods' foibles in the Eddaic poem *Locasenna*[56] (generally regarded as a late poem conditioned by Christianity), as well as in the Christian Hjalti Skeggjason's immortalized blasphemy against the Vanir at the Icelandic Althing in 999:

Vilk ek eigi goþ geyja
grey þykke mér Freyja.[57]

I will not blaspheme the gods
but Freyja seems a bitch to me.

While this Christian disapproval of Vanir customs is clear, it remains difficult to appraise pagan views of these gods' behavior. Although the deities are clearly important to Viking Age pagans, their status does not mean that their behaviors were intended for daily emulation by human beings: they may have represented instead transgressive behaviors designed to invert the natural order of the cosmos for the duration of a ritual. The assumption that gods are meant to be imitated is itself a Christian view, based on a Hellenistic notion of discipleship, and one that can cloud our views of pre-Christian religious systems.[58]

Recurrently throughout Nordic agrarian religions, we see such mysterious deities of the earth and fertility engaged in procreative sexual relations, a concept known by its Greek title *hieros gamos*, "divine marriage." From the union of male god and female earth comes the harvest or the fertility of the cosmos. The Eddaic poem *För Scirnis* depicts the Vanir god Freyr's courtship of the giantess Gerðr, a bride who lives among the frost giants. Freyr's eventual success signals the triumph of fertility over the frigidity of the giants, beings associated with winter, the mountains, and lifelessness.[59] A similar marriage occurs between the Vanir god Njörðr and the mountain-dwelling giantess Skaði, as recounted in Snorri's *Gylfaginning*.[60] Tacitus's description of the Germanic Nerthus cult of the first century A.D. depicts a ritual possibly related to the *hieros gamos* tradition: the goddess Nerthus is paraded through the vicinity in a wagon accompanied by her priest.[61] Peace and celebration occur wherever the wagon travels. Skaldic poets of the Viking Age also describe Óðinn as the bridegroom of Jorð (Earth), a fact which would tie him to the *hieros gamos* complex as well. And Mikael Agricola's sixteenth-century description of Finnish planting customs mentions a thunder god, Ukko, and his wife, Rauni, who also seem connected to the tradition there.[62]

Gods Above

In Scandinavian mythology, as evidenced in Snorri's *Skáldskaparmál* and the Eddaic poem *Völuspá*, the agrarian gods of the earth are depicted as a distinct clan—the Vanir—once living entirely apart from the gods of the sky (Æsir) but now sharing hostages after the conclusion of an earlier feud.[63] The myth of the war between the Æsir and Vanir may represent an ancient aspect of Indo-European agrarian mythology, and it appears that gods of the sky and weather arrived at the same time and within the same religious system as deities of earth fertility.[64]

The dominant astral gods of all Nordic pre-Christian religions evince similar, widespread characteristics and fall into several recurrent categories.[65] They reside in an upper world much parallel to the world of humans and connected to it by a route represented as a rainbow, a pole, a tree, or the Milky Way.[66] This bridge is traversed by gods, ritual specialists, and the souls of the dead. The male gods are often depicted as powerful chieftains or rulers such as the Scandinavian Óðinn, Týr, or Freyr, the Finnish Ukko, or the Sámi Radien/Vearalden-olmmái. Through association with thunder, they may alternatively be envisioned as powerful warriors or smiths, such as the Scandinavian Þórr, Finnish Ilmarinen, Sámi Dierpmis/Bajánolmmái/Hovrengaellies or rulers of the wind and weather, such as Þórr, Ilmarinen, or the Sámi Biegga-olmmái/Ilmaris. Gods of similar characteristics are found throughout North Eurasia, among Indo-European peoples and Finno-Ugric peoples alike.[67] They are engaged in the shaping of the world, the fighting of cosmic battles, the ordering of human society, the control of weather, and the impregnation of the earth, but they are distinct from the sun, which was viewed as a separate deity, generally female in gender. They are often married to queenly goddesses such as the Scandinavian Frigg, Þórr's wife, Síf, or the Finnish Rauni, but they often show little marital fidelity.[68]

While male astral gods are frequently identified as prime recipients of worship among Nordic populations, individual gods of this type often vary in distribution and name. Among Sámi, for instance—whose mythology we know of through stray, localized reports rather than through a creative synthesis such as Snorri's writings—the father/chieftain god went by the name *Raedie* in south Sámi regions, *Vearalden-olmmái* in Pite, Lule, and southern Tornio River regions, and *Dierpmis/Tiermis* in the far north and east. Many of these names are epithets ("ruler," "world-man"); only the last of these appears to represent a distinct proper name connectible to divine names among other Finno-Ugric peoples. Variation in nomenclature corresponded to variations in characteristics, functions, or modes of sacrifice as well, however. The Sámi thunder god, on the other hand, went by the names *Hovrenåarja* and *Hovrenskodje* in the south, *Hovrengaellies* somewhat farther north, *Áddjá* ("Father," "Old Man") epithets in the Ume, Lule, and Pite regions, and *Bajánolmmái* in the north. In the east and along the northern coast, on the other hand, the father god and thunder god merged (or remained unseparated), going by the single name *Dierpmis/Tiermis*.[69]

In a similar fashion, Scandinavian gods show inconsistencies of their own. Textual and place-name evidence indicates that Þórr may have enjoyed a favored status among Germanic peoples before the rise of Óðinn: a situation reflected, for example, by his equation with the Roman Jupiter in the third-century development of Germanic names for the days of the week.[70] Óðinn, associated by Roman sources with Mercury,[71] may have started out as a god of exchange, rising to the status of Scandinavian "All-Father" only in late paganism, particularly in the royal courts of Denmark and Norway.[72] Both gods go by a variety of other names, appellations that Snorri dutifully notes in his prose *Gylfaginning*, and which may reflect confusions, amalgamations, or localizations over time.[73] After listing some fifty-two such names for Óðinn, Snorri notes:

[F]lest heiti hafa verit gefin af þeim atburð at svá margar sem eru greinir tungnanna í veröldunni, þá þykkjask allar þjóðir þurfa at breyta nafni hans til sinnar tungu til ákalls ok bœna fyrir sjálfum sér.[74]

[M]ost of these names have been given him because the many different nations in the world, all speaking different tongues, felt the need of translating his name into their several languages in order to worship and pray to him.[75]

The Eddaic poem *Hárbarðzlióð* reflects an era in which Óðinn and Þórr appear to vie directly for adherents, with Óðinn appealing to aristocratic tastes and Þórr attracting the devotion of farmers and fishermen.[76] The little evidence left to us regarding the paganism of Sweden, on the other hand, indicates the worship of Freyr or a Freyr-like deity as a leading god there. As Snorri notes in his *Skáldskaparmál*, Freyr had become part of the astral community of Ásgarðr after the famous battle between the Vanir and Æsir, leaving his old ways partly behind as he settled into life as a hostage.[77] The sagas furnish ample evidence of these and possibly other gods, all different in certain respects but sharing overall similarities.

If we can point to evidence of Þórr or Freyr worship in some Nordic communities of the Viking Age, the case for Óðinn is far more emphatic, at least among the aristocrats and poets who were responsible for the formal poetry that has come down to us from the pagan era. In the retrospective view offered by Snorri in his thirteenth-century *Prose Edda*, Óðinn stands as the uncontested ruler of all, the All-Father, who counts Þórr as a son and leads the other gods in counsel at Ásgarðr. His missing eye (ransomed for wisdom), attendant ravens, and eight-legged horse make him easily recognizable in iconographic as well as narrative depictions.[78] Although presiding as the leader of the Æsir as well as dead warriors, he also seems to have subsumed older aspects of both Vanir magic and shamanic tradition into himself, figuring as an ever-present and resourceful deity, one always behind the corner, waiting to enlist the dying hero in the afterlife wonders of Valhalla (see Chapter 4) or plotting to gain a new type of magic or wisdom. Tellingly, Óðinn's apparent rise to power in the Scandinavian pantheon finds reflection in recurrent images of him as a crafty, usurping, duplicitous deity, lacking in many accounts the unambiguously admirable qualities of Þórr. Again, we are led to wonder whether worshippers of the Viking Age could have regarded Óðinn's exploits as completely worthy of emulation, or whether instead, they represented the extreme acts of a divine being or the marginalized behaviors of a practitioner of magic.

Vying for Adherents

The tenth-century English cleric Ælfric addresses the issue of Scandinavian gods in his sermon *De falsis diis*, which was translated into Old Norse in the collection of homilies known as *Hauksbók*.[79] The homilist relies largely on Latin sources for his characterizations of pagan gods, railing against the

Classical pantheon at length and drawing some parallels with Danish counterparts. Ælfric notes the "erroneous" Danish view of Óðinn as Þórr's father and appears secure in the superiority of the Christian God over these pagan demons. As Pope puts it: "What he has written is much more a reassuring celebration of God's triumph over a series of foolish pretenders than a frontal assault on contemporary evils."[80] If the English homilist could view the struggle between pagan and Christian deities as settled in the tenth century, however, his Scandinavian counterparts certainly could not.

Intercult rivalry between Óðinn, Þórr, Freyr, Njörðr, and God appears strong during the Viking Age, and it appears that different individuals or communities found different gods of appeal over time, depending on cultural, regional, economic, familial, or occupational factors. So direct and parallel are the linkages between human and divine endeavors in Scandinavian mythology, in fact, that they have led some theorists to posit a unified, class-based mythological system, in which worshippers directed their devotion toward the god who most closely matched their own way of life.[81] Such choices must have varied, however, as livelihoods and the imagery of the gods themselves underwent change during the era.

The sagas offer a number of images of conversion from the worship of one astral god to another.[82] In *Egils saga*, the crafty skald Egill SkallaGrímsson finds an ideal personal leader in Óðinn, apparently abandoning the Þórr worship of his Icelandic childhood.[83] That Egill meets with the Óðinnic cult chiefly during his visits to continental courts reflects the geographic and social localization of Óðinn worship; place-name and personal naming practices in Iceland as well as the other Atlantic settlements clearly indicate the dominance of Þórr worship in the region.[84] Similarly, the Icelandic chieftain Víga-Glúmr seems to abandon his childhood worship of Freyr for a reliance on Óðinn after traveling to visit prominent relatives in Norway (see Chapter 8).[85] At the end of his life, he switches yet again to Christianity. In recounting the ninth-century settlement of Iceland, *Landnámabók* recounts how the descendants of the Christian Auðr in Djúpúðga ("the Deep-minded") reverted to paganism after her death.[86] At the end of the tenth century, the pagan chieftain Snorri of *Eyrbyggja saga* can switch his allegiance to the Christian God without losing his local ritual or political authority.[87] That such intercult rivalry may have deep roots in Scandinavian paganism is indicated by the existence of additional male astral gods (e.g., Týr, Ullr), attested in placenames and some myths but largely forgotten by the Viking Age.[88]

Rivalry between the cults of Þórr and Christ figures prominently in both Swedish archaeological finds and the saga accounts of Iceland and the Atlantic settlements.[89] *Landnámabók* includes a description of the settler Helgi the Lean, who worships both deities, depending on whether he is on land or sea. On migrating to Iceland from Ireland, Helgi is said to have called upon Þórr to guide his landing and advise him in selecting a place to settle. Once settled, however, he names his district *Kristnes* (Christ's Headland), and is said to have remained Christian until his dying day.[90] In the tenth-century Greenland of *Eiríks saga rauða*, Þórr worship is pitted against Christianity through the secret backsliding of nominally Christianized converts.[91] Christian and pagan vie with each other by comparing the ways in which each deity provides for them during their sojourn in Vinland (see Chapter 8). In *Njáls saga*, the pagan Steinunn even claims that Þórr had challenged Christ to a duel.[92] The latter, she asserts, had proved too cowardly to fight. Her description pits the ideal warrior behavior of Þórr against the ideal pacifism of Christ, distilling key elements of each religion's code of ethics.

While individual gods could thus be brought into direct contrast with the Christian deity, pagans of the tenth and eleventh centuries also appear to have consolidated various gods into more unified cults, opposing these in turn to the highly institutionalized cult of Christianity. Such appears to be the case at the eleventh-century temple at Uppsala which, according to Adam of Bremen, contained statues in the likeness of Óðinn, Þórr, and Freyr, as well as a sacred grove, tree, and spring.[93] The tenth-century King Óláfr Tryggvason is said to have attacked and desecrated a temple in Rogaland containing images of multiple gods, with Þórr at their center.[94] One of Óláfr's tenth-century predecessors, the Christian King Hákon, faces a similarly united cult at Lade: there, his pagan subjects try to force him to participate in a ritual combining elements of Óðinn, Þórr, and Freyr worship. Writes Snorri:

En er it fyrsta full var skenkt, þá mælti Sigurðr jarl fyrir ok signaði Óðni ok drakk af horninu til konungs. Konungr tók við ok gerði krossmark yfir. Þá mælti Kárr af Grýtingi: "Hví ferr konungrinn nú svá? Vill hann enn eigi blóta?" Sigurðr jarl svarar: "Konungr gerir svá sem þeir allir, er trúa á mátt sinn ok megin ok signa full sitt Þór. Hann gerði hamarsmark yfir, áðr hann drakk."[95]

When the first cup was poured, Sigurðr the Jarl spoke before it and blessed it in honor of Óðinn and drank to the king from the horn. The king took it and made the sign of the Cross over it. Then Kárr of Grýting said: "Why does the king do that? Will he still not sacrifice?" Sigurðr the Jarl answered: "The king does as all do who trust in their might and main; he blesses the cup in honor of Þórr. He made the sign of Þórr's hammer over it before he drank."

The beleaguered king is also bullied into breathing in the odors of a soup made of horseflesh (implying a sacrifice to Freyr), an act that relieves him of the demand that he actually consume some of its meat or fat. At the end of his life, despondent at having to die in a still un-Christianized land, Hákon permits his followers to bury him as they choose, accompanied by his weapons and bound for Valhalla (see Chapter 4). His skald Eyvindr skáldaspillar composes a lament that commends his spirit to Óðinn.

What is crucial about accounts such as that of King Hákon the Good is not the triumph of paganism but rather, the comparability of pagan and Christian cults. Both Hákon and his pagan men share a set of assumptions regarding the relations of deities and humans and the acts of loyalty and ritual demanded of true adherents. Hákon is depicted trying to nullify a pagan blessing by substituting a Christian one, an act which his supporter Sigurðr can gloss as an invocation of a different pagan god. The shared assumptions reflect a tradition of comparison, in which the Christian Lord appears at first as just one more deity of the sky, vying with others for the best of adherents. In his *Óláfs saga Tryggvasonar*, Snorri presents Óðinn as a powerful visible entity, capable of beguiling the Christian King Óláfr with tales of the glorious past.[96] His efforts to win the monarch over are foiled, however, by the king's vigilant bishop and Óláfr's own suspicions regarding his garrulous, one-eyed guest. Such accounts must be seen in the light of Christian imaginings of an earlier age, but they also reflect the historical fact of intercult comparison during the centuries of conversion in the Nordic region.

The Distinctiveness of God

While Nordic pagans and Christians engaged in such comparisons of their gods, Christian theology itself offered a new image of omnipotence for its deity, a quality entirely novel to the Nordic region. In the writings of Pope St. Gregory the Great (c. 540–604), for instance, crucial to Christian theology of the twelfth and thirteenth centuries—God is envisioned as an all-powerful, all-scrutinizing entity, who knows the every action and most inward secret of each person.[97] Gregory's is the God of Job and Genesis, an all-knowing and majestic deity who remains intensely interested in the behaviors of mankind. Attitudes hold as great an importance for this God as actions, and nothing short of complete fidelity can please the Lord.

Christian theology of the period possessed its own particular views of Jesus as well. In prayer, legend, and iconography, the North European in general favored an image of Christ in Judgment, drawing on the imagery of the Gospel of Matthew.[98] Here, Christ sits at throne, escorted by angels and engaged in the orderly separation of the righteous from the damned, just as a shepherd separates sheep from goats. Those who have proven themselves worthy through acts of Christian kindness on earth are welcomed with words of praise and cheer; those who failed in their Christian duties are cursed and banished to eternal damnation. The imminence of the Last Judgment, combined with the total, ineluctable justice of the Lord led to the further conception of Jesus as a warrior, grimly prepared to carry out the work of his Father, in heaven, hell, or earth. This martial Christ becomes evident in the crucifixes of North European craftsmen, which remain stolid and heroic throughout the Viking Age (see Chapter 7).

Christian Intercessors: The Cult of the Saints

In Gregory's writings, God—be it the Father or the Son—is a solicitous and merciful deity, constantly offering living individuals opportunities to approach him through obedience and forgiving them readily when pride causes them to choose disobedience instead.[99] At the same time, mankind is always distanced from God, unable to regain the original closeness of understanding or communication enjoyed before the Fall. Into this breach stepped first Jesus and then Mary, the martyrs, and the saints, providing both exemplary models and modes of communication for humans struggling toward a perfect relation with God.[100] In the cults of Mary and the saints in particular, Viking-Age Christians found that their confidants and advocates, as sainted humans already enjoying the paradise of the hereafter, used their status to intercede with God in heaven and to cause miracles on earth. While images of God and Christ remained fairly static, Mary and the saints were allowed to shine forth in all the particularity of character and preference that typify humans. Having aided their living charges well, the saints received generous gifts at their shrines and churches, often bestowed in conjunction with a pilgrimage and/or a recounting of the saint's miraculous offices.

In the world of Christianizing Scandinavia, saints of central and southern European origin were soon joined or rivaled by the cults of local missionary-saints. Charlemagne's missionary to Denmark and Sweden, St. Ansgar (c. 801–65), was celebrated in Rimbert's *Vita Anskarii*, authored soon after the saint's death.[101] Its inclusion of detailed descriptions of the saint's visions in life reflects the personal testimony of the dying monk and of monastic interests in documenting sacral experiences in preparation for canonization. English missionary-saints included St. Eskil of Södermanland (who died c. 1080), St. David of Västmanland (early eleventh century), and St. Henrik of Uppsala and Finland (died c. 1156). The Swedish St. Botvid (d. 1120), on the other hand, was said to have gained the faith when trading in England. In Iceland, Bishop Jón Ögmundsson (1052–1121) of Hólar and Bishop Þorlákr Þórhallsson (1133–93) of Skálholt became important local saints and a cult of Guðmundr the Good (1161–1237) became popular as well.[102] Humble and ascetic at least in memory, these saints displayed their wondrous faith in God through lives of self-mortification and a powerful ability to lead others to Christ. Their shrines became favorite but often highly localized sites of devotion, included in the calendars of a single diocese or region.

By the thirteenth century, monastic saints had also been joined by the figures of sainted national kings, modeled on traditions of royal sanctity derived from continental Europe and England. Monarchs credited with the Christianization of their realms became natural objects of eventual devotion, often through the efforts of royal descendants. The tenth-century Swedish King Olof Skӧttkonung was credited retrospectively with the Christianization of his realm.[103] King St. Erik of Sweden (d. 1160) was said to have led a holy Crusade to Finland, bringing St. Henrik with him to accomplish the task. The Norwegian King St. Óláfr (995–1030) became the most popular of all such saints, his shrine at Trondheim attracting pilgrims from throughout the Viking world. A stalwart military leader, he combined the esteem of the monarch-saint with the fire and conviction of the warrior-saint of the Crusades, epitomized throughout Europe by the archangel St. Michael.

Throughout Europe, some of the traditions or devotions formerly associated with pagan deities became reattached to "legendary saints," sometimes with little alteration. Whereas historical saints and their miracles were verifiable through reference to other records and evidence, legendary saints often emerged out of the mists of a nebulous past, their lives ascribed to an era of hardship, war, or conversion a century or two earlier. In northern Europe, the legendary saint was often tied to the arrival of Christianity in the region and was credited with acts of wonder and bravery. Given the vast number of saints' legends common in the period, it would have been difficult for the laity to distinguish between the cults of historical saints and those which represented Christianizations of earlier belief systems, even if they had understood such distinctions. The unofficial assimilation of native cults into the communion of saints may have eased the process of Christianization for many converting populations, in the Nordic region as elsewhere in Europe.

While Christians yearned to approach God for the goal of final salva-

tion, the saints were often entreated for more immediate ends. Many of the
prayers addressed to Mary and the other saints asked for miracles, supernatural manifestations of God's interest and reminders of the miraculous
power of the sacraments and faith. In Gregory's view—and those of the
Church as a whole—God permitted miracles to help win over human adherents; they demonstrated God's control of the universe and his interest in
attracting human followers.[104] As miracles were essential to the enterprise of
conversion, God had allowed more of them to occur in the days of the
Apostles, lessening their frequency with the triumph of Christianity in Europe but still allowing some for the benefit of the living faithful. Gregory
himself noted with joy the frequency of occurrence of miracles in the newly
Christianized land of England, where Augustine and his assistants had begun to win over the Angles.[105] Gregory's views suggest a possible reason for
the frequent reference to miracles and other wonders in sagas recounting the
era of Nordic conversions. Writing in the predictable Christian world of
thirteenth-century Iceland—an era bedeviled by political intrigue and social
unrest but largely stable in terms of religious outlook—the writers of the
sagas imagined an era of abrupt clashes between the old religion and the
new, when pagan gods still lingered in the shadows and the Christian God
allowed all sorts of wonders in his quest for souls.

Characteristic of the cult of saints in general was the strong supernatural
properties of relics, fragments of the saint's body or possessions. Brown sees
this aspect of the cult of saints as a unique innovation of late antiquity, one
which separated Christian practice in the Mediterranean markedly from its
pagan counterparts, which generally shunned contact with the dead (see
Chapter 4).[106] By the Viking Age, the *translatio* (translation) of saints' relics
(*reliquiae*) or former possessions (*benedictiones*) had become a highpoint of
liturgical life, a means of sanctifying or exalting a place of worship. The dates
of translations were celebrated in liturgical calendars, along with the dates of
saints' "birthdays" (dates of death), and ecclesiastical leaders could enhance
the sacrality of specific churches or dioceses by conferring valued relics.
Sturlunga saga describes the effectiveness of St. Sunniva's relics once they had
been transferred to Bergen, where they aid in extinguishing a city fire:

Þá brann Björgyn um vetrinn. Þá var in heilaga Sunnifa fœrð ór Selju áðr sumarit, ok
störðvaði þat eldsganginn, er skrín hennar var í móti borit.

Bergen caught on fire that winter. St. Sunniva had been translated there from Selja
the summer before [1170], and the fire's progress was stopped when her reliquary was
brought forth against it.[107]

Kings such as Charlemagne and Cnut enhanced their own reputations by assisting in key translations, winning favor among the clergy and laity alike and hopefully gaining spiritual pardon for sins committed in a life of rulership (see Chapter 7). Aristocrats, merchants, and even humble peasants in turn could mark their devotion to saints by offerings deposited at saints' shrines. If the Viking Age gave western Europe one of its final flourishings of pagan spirituality, in other words, it also produced one of the most fervent embraces of the sacrality of saints.

The Role of Priest

While both paganism and Christianity included ritual roles for marginalized spiritual guides—such as the shaman, *seiðr* practitioner, or hermit—a more central priesthood was also characteristic of many Nordic faiths. In closing this overview of Nordic concepts of deities, it makes sense to examine this priestly role more closely, as it represented one of the prime movers in the change of religions during the Viking Age.

The office of pagan priest, *goðorð*, appears in both runic and saga evidence. Runic inscriptions present the Scandinavian *goði* as an empowered and revered figure, one who inherited his office from a father or other kinsman and who performed rituals for the benefit of the entire vicinity. The Danish Glavenstrup Stone, carved c. 900–925, commemorates a *goði* named Alli, who is described as "respected thane of the temple."[108] The inscription also calls on Þórr to hallow the runes, emphasizing the linkage between the *goði* and his god.[109] An even more authoritative image of the *goði* can be seen in the roughly contemporaneous Swedish Rök Stone. Here, on a stone raised in memory of a chieftain named Wæmoþ, the priest and rune-carver Biari exhorts men of knowledge to pass on myths of the heroic past to the rising youth.[110] Biari's catalog of thirteen important pieces of knowledge—truncated references to myths that have tantalized scholars ever since—suggests the array of history and myth possessed by the wise *goði* and used as a means of shaping the behaviors and ideals of each new generation. Biari seems to hold the same rights to exhortation and reverence that later Christian priests would enjoy among Christians, rights tied to personal discipleship with a god and the willingness in turn to mentor disciples of one's own.

The sagas depict Icelandic *goðar* as canny and empowered figures in Icelandic society. *Eyrbyggja saga* includes a portrayal of the loving relationship between the Norwegian Hrolf and his "beloved friend" (*ástvinr*) Þórr.[111]

Hrolf changes his name to include his god's, becoming Þórólfr, and relocates his temple to the god when migrating to Iceland, bringing with him some of its timbers and soil. Throwing the pillars of the temple overboard upon approaching the island, Þórólfr allows the god to guide him to shore and establishes a sacred site near his point of landing. He confers his god's name upon his son Þorsteinn as well, and establishes the authority of his temple through demanding tributes from neighboring farms. Similar characteristics can be noted in the figure of Hrafnkell, priest of Freyr in *Hrafnkels saga*, as well as Þórólfr's descendant Snorri the priest in *Eyrbyggja saga*. While Hrafnkell appears deeply affectionate to his horse Freyfaxi (an animal dedicated to Freyr), he is characterized as crafty and hard-edged in his dealings with men:

Hann þrøngði undir sik Jökulsdalsmönnum til þingmanna hans, var linr ok blíðr við sína menn, en stríðr ok stirðlyndr við Jökulsdalsmenn, ok fengu af honum øngvan jafnað.[112]

He forced the men of Jökulsdal to become his supporters ("thingmen") and was kind and pleasant to his own men but harsh and stubborn with the Jökulsdal men, and they received no fair treatment from him.

While it appears that the *goði*'s sacral significance may have lessened over time in Iceland, he remains a key figure in the sagas, serving as chieftain in his district, maintaining order among his following of *þingmenn*, and negotiating the settlement of legal disputes through tact, diplomacy, and force.[113] His world exactly mirrored that of the divine Ásgarðr, where the gods lived in their own society and held divine counsels and feasts.[114]

While women appear central to ritual practices occurring within the household, they seldom emerge as leaders of such public cults. The *Landnámabók*, however, includes references to two women who hold the title of *gyðja* (priestess); in both cases, the priestesses appear to belong to chiefly families of their districts.[115] *Kristnisaga* depicts the tenth-century Þorvaldr Koðránsson assisting in the preaching of Christianity at the Icelandic Althing while his wife Friðgerðr remains at home offering a sacrifice at a temple.[116] In the *Njáls saga* account of Icelandic missionization, the pagan woman Steinunn forcefully defends the pagan faith, even attempting to convert King Óláfr Tryggvason's bad-tempered emissary, the Christian priest Þangbrandr.[117] Such exceptional status may have been more common among worshippers of the Vanir, in which the concept of divine marriage and the siblings Freyr and Freyja played a central role.[118] More usually, however, women's public roles in religious matters appear to have been limited to outward shows of religious allegiance, as when Swedish women commissioned memorial rune stones for their deceased Christian husbands or used their wealth and status to advance their families' faith within local and familial circles.[119]

In the struggle between paganism and Christianity during the final stages of Nordic conversion, pagan chieftain-priests appear to have played an expectably central role. In *Óláfs saga Tryggvasonar*, King Óláfr challenges his pagan opponents to a debate.[120] When the normally eloquent chieftains on the side of paganism are miraculously stricken with speech impediments, the victory goes naturally to the king and his God. When dealing with a continued, and apparently more centralized, *seiðr* cult in Tunsberg, the king lures the practitioners to a feast and has them burned to death once they have fallen drunk.[121] Those who escape Óláfr's ruse are later captured and left on a tidal skerry to drown. Similar persecution met Christian priests at the hands of resentful pagans, as we saw in the previous chapter. In a world in which persuasive priests and oratory were essential for success in conversions, it is not surprising to find the eighth-century St. Willibrord as well as the ninth-century St. Ansgar purchasing Danish slave boys to raise as future priests.[122]

We have seen, then, a variety of relations between deities and humans in Nordic religious life. In the luck-based worldview of hunters and gatherers, deities of nature and the hunt demanded both respect and tactful manipulation, accomplished through a combination of sacrifices, rituals, and taboos. From the earliest era onward, ancestors and spirits nearer at hand offered humans more intimate relations, requiring their own specific sacrifices and observances. Individuals could manage these relations personally, especially when deities occupied localized, static sites. Familial or communal leaders, male as well as female, could also represent the collective. In times of crisis, communities could consult with human specialists who possessed close relations with certain spirits and access to culturally esteemed altered states of consciousness. These specialists included the shaman, skilled in ecstatic trance and useful in discovering information or cures through spirit travel and consultation with the world of deities. A similar role developed for the hermit of Christianity, at least as reflected in saints' legends and other narratives.

Agrarian life brought its own deities to the fore, ones connected to the earth, fertility, and the sky and associated with particular rituals and mythic imagery of lasciviousness and fecundity. Astral gods in this system demanded high regard from their human adherents, developing toward a regularized system of discipleship or priesthood. Of the various gods known to us from Scandinavian tradition, Njörðr, Freyr, Freyja, Óðinn, and Þórr appear to have competed first with each other and then with the Christian God for followers, eventually losing out to the supremely omnipotent Christian deity, whose conceptual dimensions and earthly promoters towered above them.

The Christian God exceeded all others in his ability to see into the minds and motives of humans, judging not solely actions but also attitudes. At the same time, the exalted, all-powerful nature of the medieval Christian God made the intimate relations of humans and saints important: in these, the close and loving relations of human individuals and greater-than-human entities could thrive, affording adherents the comfort of a close friendship within the broader framework of a universe whose order and significance remained firmly in the hands of a single Almighty. It was perhaps from this standpoint in particular that saga writers of the thirteenth century imagined the pre-Christian religiosity of their forebears, seeing in those earlier relations between deities and their followers the same affection and loyalty that they enjoyed with saints.

FOUR

Visitors from Beyond

Death, Afterlife, and the Problem of Ghosts

You take the people you most love and honor and throw them in the ground and the earth and creeping creatures and growing things destroy them. We, on the other hand, burn them in an instant, so that they go to Paradise in that very hour.
—Rus man to Ibn Fadhlan, c. 922[1]

The great mystery of death found interpretation in all of the religions of the Nordic world, not least in Christianity. Issues of the care and disposal of the body were tied integrally to concepts of afterlife and a recurrent, if not ever-present, fear of subsequent haunting. Tradition or dogma specified the otherworlds that might receive the dead, the rulers of each, and the concourse between the beings of that world and this. By the Viking Age—as the exchange quoted above between the tenth-century Arab traveler Ibn Fadhlan and a Rus Viking illustrates—Nordic peoples had become very aware of differences in burial or cremation customs, differences which became symbolic of larger religious divergences. By the thirteenth century, a thoroughly Christianized Icelandic populace could still recall pagan burial traditions and use the contrast between pagan and Christian customs as a device for characterizing figures from the settlement era. A strong and pervasive interest in ghosts, paralleled throughout Europe, had acquired a particular ethnographic bent, as the burial customs of non-Christians became the source and sometimes the cure of malevolent returns from the dead. At the same time, a warm and positive relation obtained between some dead—those who had attained sainthood—and the prayerful living of the Christian world.

In this chapter, then, we will examine the variety of practices and ideas related to death in the Nordic region during the Viking Age. Views of death and its ritual commemoration show clear processes of transformation, as pagan cults become aware of each other's customs and react particularly to Christian concepts of inhumation and its theological import. Variation in burial form, grave goods, and placement or decoration of the grave all evolve in a manner independent of the stipulations of any one religious system. Finally, I discuss three thirteenth-century saga texts—*Laxdœla saga*, *Eiríks saga rauða*, and *Eyrbyggja saga*—to illustrate the ways in which Icelandic Christians of that era used burial customs as symbols of character and morality, remembering in this literary guise the variability and interest that must have fascinated their ancestors in previous centuries.

While care for the dead is generally regarded as a particularly stable and telling aspect of religious life, the cremation and burial practices of the Viking Age showed anything but stability. Even long-lived customs such as

the ship burial (see below) underwent modification, depending, for example, on whether the deceased and/or ship was cremated, cremated and
buried, or simply buried. Literary texts make reference to even a further
variation: the launching of the boat unmanned to drift upon the sea, sometimes aflame. Variation occurs over both space and time, with a decided
evolution toward inhumation that can only be due to the influence or example of Christianity but that begins well before the real Christianization of the
region. Grave goods, too, show an exchange of materials and ideas that
contrasts with the nineteenth-century view of the different Nordic groups as
isolated entities. On the whole, the funereal customs of the Nordic region
show both a lively intercultural concourse as well as a lack of strict dogma
regarding the disposal of the dead, an expectable state of affairs in religions
which varied locally and were presided over by local or familial priests. This
variability even affected early Christian graves, which show varying degrees
of adherence to the Christian burial rite.

Both Viking-Age archaeological findings and later ethnographic reports from the seventeenth and eighteenth centuries indicate a similar, recognizable burial tradition among Sámi.[2] The body was wrapped in birch
bark, sometimes in pelts, and laid in the ground or a stone cist, generally
away from the village or encampment. The body was sometimes buried in a
sled or hollowed-out log as further protection. In any case, the grave was
shallow; in eastern parts of the Sámi region, it could even be above ground,
encased in a wooden chest such as that built by Sámi for the storage of meat,
fish, and milk. Bodies were buried with gifts or personal items (axes, knives,
flints, bows and arrows, sewing equipment, scissors, and so on), occasionally
with food provisions as well. In southern regions, grave goods show extensive trading with Scandinavian and Finnish communities.[3] The practice of
burying the dead in graveyards was known in some Sámi communities,
although individual graves in disparate sites were more usual.

Finnish chamber graves, lovingly provided with grave goods and long
the site of Finno-Ugric forms of ancestor worship (see below), showed many
features common to Scandinavian graves as well.[4] By the era of the Viking
Age, the body was first cremated and then buried with an array of items
necessary for a comfortable life in the otherworld: for example, weapons, a
dog, jewelry, or treasure. Snorri describes the raiding of a Finnic grave in his
Óláfs saga Helga, in which the deceased's treasure is mixed with soil and
placed in a mound under the protection of an idol.[5] With time, however, the
custom shifted from cremation to inhumation of the body, which remained
fully dressed and ready for the next life. This shift occurred already in the

sixth century in those parts of western Finland most exposed to foreign contacts and trade. By the eleventh century, as Christianity began to spread across the region, inhumation became the norm elsewhere as well. Some of the men buried in this period are scarcely distinguishable from their Scandinavian counterparts.[6] Their weapons, brooches, and burial form show lively intercultural exchange.

Among Scandinavians, similar trends occurred. The body, first cremated and buried, later buried fully clothed, was accompanied by extensive grave goods, animals, possibly even sacrificed women or slaves. Snorri credits Óðinn with the institution of such pagan burial customs. According to Snorri, men were to be burned on a pyre with their possessions. Objects and treasure buried by the man himself would be available to him after death.[7] The deceased's ashes could be borne out to sea or buried in the earth. While some graves were left unmarked, others—those of men of note—had stone cairns or mounds raised over them. Deliberate damage to grave goods, especially swords and knives, may have prevented their theft by impious grave robbers. The greatest difference between these Scandinavian graves and their Sámi or Finnish counterparts is the degree of social stratification evident in them: graves vary according to the status and wealth of the deceased, with both men and women receiving elaborate burials if their stations in life warranted it.[8] This stratification is particularly evident in market towns such as Hedeby and Kaupang, in which rich grave mounds filled with valuables lie beside the humble graves of peasants and slaves. Rich or poor, however, the graves of these areas were respected for only so long: in Hedeby, burial grounds were repeatedly leveled and built over with houses and shops.[9]

In Scandinavian settlements in the British Isles, both pagan graves and Christian cist graves coexist in the same sites.[10] Graves could be rectangular (with the body outstretched) or oval shaped (with the body crouched); occasionally they were surrounded by stones arranged in the shape of a boat. Although many Christian as well as pagan graves contained grave goods, a certain number showed the Christian custom of burial without such objects, reflecting a strong embrace of the new religion (see below). Grave goods only gradually disappeared from Christian burials in mainland Scandinavia, making identification of the deceased's religion difficult in cases in which a pagan graveyard gradually became Christianized. An east-west orientation of the grave, indicating careful observance of the Christian burial rite, occurs increasingly in both the British Isle sites and Scandinavia. On the whole, the burial customs of migrant Scandinavians show a remarkable degree of variation that, when coupled with the gravity of the occasion, must have proved of intense interest to the settlers.

Christianity attached great importance to the proper burial of the dead, as we will see in greater detail below. Burial in sanctified ground—either in a churchyard, Christian graveyard, or in the walls or floor of a church—prepared the body for its eventual reuniting with the soul on the Day of Judgment. On that day, body and soul together would receive eternal reward or punishment. Because burial with grave goods signaled continuity of pre-Christian concepts of the afterlife, the custom was strongly resisted by medieval clergy, who advocated the burial of the body in a simple shroud, oriented eastward, toward the Holy Land. Such simple burial remained only a distant goal in many Christianizing communities, however. The expectation that the body would remain in place until the final day of judgment led to difficulties when churches or graveyards moved. Reinterment of bodies could occur with the reconstruction or enlargement of churches. Sometimes such renovations created new places of honor for revered figures, special chapels or crypts. In the case of saints, reinterment took on even greater significance (see below).

While Christian attention to proper burial spread among the general populace of Scandinavia, pagans of status and wealth availed themselves of elaborate boat burials, a tradition with its roots in eastern Sweden, but best known today for the remarkable royal ship burials of Oseberg and Gokstad in southern Norway.[11] As the Sutton Hoo burial of East Anglia, England, demonstrates, this form of burial could appeal to even the non-Scandinavian noble.[12] The same kind of noble burial was practiced for multiple generations at Vendel and Valsgärde, Sweden, from the seventh through twelfth centuries.[13] Ibn Fadhlan's remarkable description of a tenth-century Rus funeral on the Volga also follows this form, although body, accompaniment, and ship are all burned rather than buried in this depiction.

While the ship burial spread as a favored form of pagan aristocratic funeral, the tradition democratized in western Norway and insular North Atlantic settlements. Boats buried reduced in size according to the means and status of the deceased: over a thousand such burials have been discovered in coastal Norway and the Atlantic colonies. Two similar boat burials from the Orkneys show small crafts, probably used previously for fishing or transport among the many islands of the vicinity.[14] In large trading settlements such as Kaupang, boat burials crowded into cramped burial grounds. The orientation of boats here appears wholly a matter of convenience, and a new boat could be placed over an old. Further, a single boat could be used as the resting place for several persons. The eventual decline of the boat burial in favor of rectangular cist graves may owe as much to overcrowding in such urban areas as to a change in worldview.[15]

To see the boat as a symbol of a journey to the otherworld is tempting, even though the textual evidence discussed below tends to speak of land journeys between this world and the next. While the ferry to the otherworld is a widespread motif in world mythology, its appearance in Scandinavia may also reflect adoption of Mediterranean funereal imagery, as we will see in our discussion of the Gotlandic picture stones in Chapter 7. It may also reflect the rise in importance of boat travel in the scattered and diversified settlements of western Norway and the North Atlantic. In addition, however, it is difficult to miss the impression that the boat burial rose in prominence during the Viking Age in part as a response to Christian ideals of proper burial, much as Þórr's hammer amulets appear to gain popularity in response to the wearing of the Christian cross (see Chapter 7). The testimony of the Rus Viking quoted at the outset of this chapter, at least, attests to pagans' strong awareness of the burial traditions of their neighbors and trading partners and interest in comparing them with their own.

The pre-Christian burial customs of the Nordic peoples vary in some respects but share an overall common belief in the idea of preparing the dead materially for an afterlife. In contrast, Christianity preached spiritual preparation of the dying for the afterlife, although strong rules governed the disposal and care of the body nonetheless. All the Nordic peoples, pagan and Christian alike, possessed concepts of multiple otherworlds awaiting them after life, generally located beneath or above the earth and ruled by particular beings. Passage to the otherworld did not prevent continued contact between the deceased and the living, who remained anxious about the status of their dead and watchful of their possible return.

While burial customs provide us with a very concrete indication of religious outlook, concepts of afterlife are too complex to reconstruct solely on the basis of archaeological evidence. Fortunately, textual accounts and oral tradition can fill out the picture. As we turn to these sources of information regarding Nordic views of the afterlife and otherworlds, we find the same kinds of variation and trends as in burial form. Although internally variable, the views of each Nordic group regarding the hereafter nonetheless present a similar overall profile, allowing us to speak of a general Nordic view of the afterlife, which comes into contact and partially fuses with the new view presented by Christianity. This complex evolution can be discerned in its broadest lines.

The closest and conceptually perhaps the oldest otherworld for Nordic dead merged with the grave itself. Forms of familiar ancestor worship occurred among all the Nordic groups to varying degrees and often took place on or near the grave. Balto-Finnic peoples practiced varieties of ancestor worship which had their roots deep in the Finno-Ugric past.[16] Dead relatives remained valued members of the family or clan and were venerated at sacred sites, often burial grounds or shrines near the home. Memorial feasts and other rituals ensured the contentedness of the deceased and secured the dead person's aid for the living community. The dead were seen as essential guardians, watching that the family's members upheld the rights and responsibilities incumbent upon the clan. They wielded great power—nearing or equaling that of even the sky god—but focused singlemindedly on the fortunes of one family or set of descendants. Sámi traditions concerning the dead were apparently less elaborate than the ancestor worship posited for Finns, although offerings were made to the dead during times of sickness.[17] A form of reincarnation also occurred in Sámi tradition, by which a pregnant woman or shaman might see a vision of a dead relative in a dream and determine to name a new child after the deceased. This act was seen as allowing the dead to return to the family as a living member and has extensive parallels in other Arctic cultures.

On the other hand, persons who had disgraced themselves in death became outcast ancestors and were left to roam the world as ghosts.[18] Writes Honko: "The exclusion of the 'restless dead' from ancestor worship was comparable to the outlawing or banishment of the living."[19] This notion of an unsettled afterlife for some of the dead became so seamlessly merged with later Christian concepts of purgatory and hell that it is difficult to see it in its pre-Christian light. But "disgracing oneself in death" appears to have been defined by Finns as any act which brought *shame* on the family or ancestors (e.g., suicide). Thus, the concept of the restless dead can be seen as part and parcel of the tradition of ancestor worship with which it might at first appear to contrast. Honored ancestors expected honorable deaths of their descendants and dishonorable deaths deserved no honor in the afterlife. Dead and living were united in adherence to a single code of honor against which none, living or dead, dared transgress.

A holy-mountain tradition placed the spirits of the dead in specified underground locations on particular mountains. These were known in south Sámi as *Sájva-ájmuo* or simply *Sájva*; in northern Sámi communities the term was *Passe-vare*.[20] Both *sájva-* and *passe-* denote a state of holiness marked by strong taboos regarding who could be present at the site and what they were allowed to do there. Women in particular were barred from contact with such sacred sites, a tendency paralleled by the concept of *pyhä* ("taboo," later "holy") in Finnish tradition.[21] Spirits from these holy mountains could prove useful as helpers or guides for shamans and they could be won over by living humans through the sacrifice of reindeer.[22] *Sájva-ájmuo* was regarded as a pleasant place to spend the afterlife, one which contrasted markedly with the miserable *Jabme-ájmuo* or the demonic *Rut-ájmuo* (see below).

These traditions find close parallel in the holy-mountain cults of Norway and Iceland.[23] In *Landnámabók* as well as *Eyrbyggja saga*, Þórr worshippers Þórólfr Mostrar-skegg ("Moster-beard") and his son Þorsteinn Þorskabítr ("Cod-biter") are both said to retire after death to a particular familial mountain, where they dwell and feast in the company of their ancestors. Þórólfr brought the tradition with him from Norway, where he served as a priest of Þórr. Helgafell, the familial mountain, is guarded from defilement by either bloodshed or excrement. No one is allowed to look at it without having washed. In *Eyrbyggja saga*, Þorsteinn's departure into the next life is described as follows:

[S]auðamaðr Þorsteins fór at fé fyrir norðan Helgafell; hann sá, at fjallit lauksk upp norðan; hann sá inn í fjallit elda stóra ok heyrði þanat mikinn glaum ok hornaskvöl; ok er hann hlýddi, ef hann næmi nökkur orðaskil, heyrði hann, at þar var heilsat Þorsteini þorskabít ok förunautum hans ok mælt, at hann skal sitja í öndvegi gegnt feðr sínum.[24]

[A]s Þorsteinn's shepherd was tending sheep north of Helgafell, he saw the whole north side of the mountain opened up, with great fires burning inside it and the noise of feasting and clamor over the ale-horns. As he strained to catch particular words, he was able to make out that Þorsteinn Cod-biter and his crew were being welcomed into the mountain, and that Þorsteinn was being invited to sit in the place of honor opposite his father.[25]

Nordland posits that this tradition came to Iceland from the districts of western Norway where similar beliefs persist. *Landnámabók* notes that the descendants of Icelandic settler Auðr Djúpúðga ("the Deep-minded"), a Christian, reverted to holy-mountain worship after her death: "Þar höfðu frændr hennar síðan átrúnað mikinn á hólana. Var þar þá gör hörg, er blót tóku til; trúðu þeir því, at þeir dœi í hólana" (Later her kinsmen worshipped these hills, then when sacrifices began, a pagan temple was built there. They believed they would go into the hills when they died).[26] Ellis sees the tradition as bound to Þórr worship, since the Óðinnic cult would place the dead in Óðinn's Valhalla.[27] In any case, such localization of cult to a particular mountain would pose problems in the case of emigration, and thus may have become less prominent in Iceland. Helgafell itself, by the thirteenth century a thriving monastic center and scriptorium, appears to have held particular familiarity or interest for the saga writer.

A number of sagas, as well as the Eddaic poem *Helgaqviða Hundingsbana önnor*, contribute to this localized otherworld tradition by describing the dead as conscious postmortem inhabitants of their graves.[28] In *Hervarar saga ok Heiðreks konungs*, the dutiful Hervör visits the grave of her slain father and brothers to obtain a sword with which to avenge them.[29] She awakens them and threatens a curse that will bring uneasy rest if they do not surrender the sword to her:

> Svá sé yðr öllum   innan rifja,
> sem þér í maura   mornið haugi,
> nema sverð selið   þat sló Dvalinn;
> samira draugum   dýrt vápn fela.[30]

> May you writhe within your ribs,
> your barrow an anthill where you rot,
> if you deny me Dvalinn's sword—
> ghosts should not wield costly weapons.[31]

In the Eddaic poem, on the other hand, the hero Helgi, a warrior of the Óðinnic Völsung clan, does indeed reach Valhalla in his afterlife (see below) but is drawn back to his barrow at Sefafell once to comfort his grieving widow, Sigrun. There, he tells her:

> Ein veldr þú, Sigrún   frá Sefafiöllom,
> er Helgi er   harmdögg sleginn;
> grætr þú, gullvarið,   grimmon tárom,
> sólbiört, suðrœn,   áðr þú sofa gangir;
> hvert fellr blóðuct   á brióst grami,
> úrsvalt, innfiálgt,   ecca þrungit.[32]

> You alone,   Sigrun of Sefafells,
> steep Helgi's shroud   in the dew of sorrow.
> My sun-bright lady,   the bitter tears
> you shed each night   before you go to sleep
> are drops of blood   falling on my breast,
> cold as rain, heavy   with your heart's grief.[33]

Sigrun's sorrows, although welcomed by Helgi as noble mourning of his death, seem to attract him back to the land of the living, accessed primarily through his own barrow.[34]

As this example from *Helgaqviða Hundingsbana önnor* illustrates, the proximity of dead ancestors in familial otherworlds near at hand was partly contradicted by belief in other destinations beyond the world of the living. All Nordic peoples possessed beliefs in further otherworlds, usually situated in a vertical array underground and open as destinations for the dead. In general, each was presided over by a deity or spirit. In Finno-Ugric cultures, the dead needed to be escorted to the appropriate underworld, a task often carried out by the shaman.[35] The family also played a role in the transference, however, with women's laments in particular acting as soothing entreaties and encouragement from the living to the dead.[36] The same kind of lament role for Scandinavian women can be glimpsed in the Eddaic poems *Guðrúnarqviða in fyrsta* and *Helgaqviða Hundingsbana önnor.*

In Sámi tradition, a more or less generic land of the dead *Jabme-ájmuo* (Jabmeaimo) was ruled by the goddess *Jabme-áhkká*, while a deeper and darker *Rut-ájmuo* was reserved for the wicked and was presided over by the evil god of death, disease, and calamity, Ruto.[37] Both otherworlds have extensive counterparts in other North Eurasian Finno-Ugric cultures and certainly belong to an ancient stratum of Finno-Ugric religion. The specific characteristics of Ruto were influenced however, by the widespread Finno-Ugric tendency to model demon figures after the high gods of neighboring peoples: thus, the evil god in Finnish religion becomes known as *perkele* (from the Baltic thunder god, Perkunas) while the south Sámi renderings of Ruto acquire Óðinnic traits (a phenomenon misinterpreted as borrowing in a number of early studies).[38] Some regions or sources of the eighteenth century indicate a further Sámi otherworld for the good as well—Radienaimo, ruled by the sun god, possibly a newer concept influenced by Christian eschatology.[39]

Drawings on the surface of drums used in rituals provided Sámi shamans with a cognitive map of these contending otherworlds.[40] Symbols for the buildings, landmarks, and denizens of holy mountains, Jabmeaimo, and Rutaimo gave *noaidit* (shamans) knowledge of how to pass between these realms in search of wisdom or magic objects. Strong continuities of form exist between the extant drums of the eighteenth century and Viking Age finds, and some scholars posit that some of the earliest skaldic mythological poems—the so-called "shield poems"—were performed with reference to Sámi drums.[41] *Noaidit* enlisted the dead in their service either as guides or as guardians for reindeer herds, and thus travel between these lands held special importance. In general, the need to know the location of such realms was linked to shamanic goals in all Nordic religions.

Finnish epic songs preserve glimpses of lands of the dead—Tuonela, Manala—their rulers, and the elaborate trek necessary for the shaman or the dead to reach them.[42] In Ingrian songs, the road to death's domain is paved with nails and knife blades, a detail which may derive from a medieval Christian image of purgatory. The traveler needs sturdy shoes (possibly built of righteous deeds in life) and a worthy horse for the journey.[43] In the classic epic poem *Tuonelanmatka*, the shamanic hero Väinämöinen makes a journey to a Finnic land of the dead in pursuit of magic items. He is greeted at the river border of the land by Death's daughter (*Tuonen tytär*), who recognizes him as a living man and attempts to imprison him there. Väinämöinen escapes, however, in the shape of a serpent.[44] The image of a female guardian at death's door finds parallels in Scandinavian myths of Hel (see below).

Snorri's *Prose Edda* mentions a great number of places outside the world of men, at least four of which receive the dead. Hel, the daughter of Loki, is said to rule a multilevel general land of the dead, open to men and women alike. Writes Snorri:

Hel kastaði hann [= Óðinn] í Niflheim ok gaf henni vald yfir níu heimum at hon skipti öllum vistum með þeim er til hennar váru sendir, en þat eru sóttdauðir menn ok ellidauðir.[45]

[Óðinn] threw Hel into Niflheim and gave her authority over nine worlds, on the condition that she shared all her provisions with those who were sent to her, namely men who die from disease or old age.[46]

In the Eddaic poem *Helreið Brynhildar*, the valkyrie-queen Brynhildr is depicted en route to this land of the dead, riding there in a chariot.[47] Even the god Baldr ends up in Hel's realm after his untimely death.[48] The god Hermóðr journeys there in an Orphean attempt to rescue his brother, entering into a conversation with the maiden Móðguðr, who guards the bridge across the River Gjöll at the land's border. This generalized afterlife destination, depicted as cold, damp, and dark, appears typical in Scandinavian visions of the beyond.

On the other hand, Snorri reports that half of the slain in battle join the goddess Freyja at her home in Fólkvangar following their deaths.[49] Her hall, Sessrúmnir, is described as large and beautiful. Further, in accounting for the goddesses, Snorri mentions Gefjun, noting that women who die unmarried end up in her service.[50] And finally, of course, skaldic poetry as well as Snorri's *Prose Edda* provide ample details of Valhalla (*valhöll*—hall of corpses), the shining hall of eternal battle and feasting for the slain who have followed Óðinn.[51] In Snorri's euhemeristic account of Óðinn in *Ynglinga-saga* the god-cum-chieftain is credited with mandating cremation for his followers, stating that men would arrive in Valhalla with the goods that had gone with them on the pyre:

Svá setti hann, at alla dauða menn skyldi brenna ok bera á bál með þeim eign þeira. Sagði hann svá, at með þvílíkum auðœfum skyldi hverr kom til Valhallar, sem hann hafði á bál; þess skyldi hann ok njóta, er hann sjálfr hafði í jörð grafit.[52]

He commanded that all the dead should be burned on a pyre along with their possessions. He said that each man would come to Valhalla with those things he had had on the pyre with him; he could also use those things which he himself had buried in the ground.

Skaldic poets elaborated endlessly on the form and furnishings of this hall for the slain, its customs and purpose. The men of Valhalla, attended by Óðinn's valkyries, were to feast on boar and mead, engaging in battle every day and healing miraculously afterward. The Valhalla host, the *einherjar*, were to fight on the side of the Æsir at Ragnarök. Like the other afterlife destinations of Scandinavian belief, Valhalla is apparently open to only some of the dead: men who show prowess at war and offer themselves up to Óðinn in their lives and dying acts.

Significantly, although Ellis sees connections between the holy-mountain tradition (above) and the cult of Þórr, neither Þórr's great hall Bilskirnir, in Þrúðvangar, nor Njörðr's seaside Nóatún is depicted by Snorri as the destination of humans after death.[53] Not all Scandinavian gods appear interested in hosting the dead, even if their halls are known to men and wondrous to behold.

In his further discussion of Ragnarök, Snorri mentions still further afterlife destinations.[54] The otherworld region Gimlé has a hall called Brimir, which serves good drink to the dead lucky enough to arrive there. In the hall Sindri, in the Niðafjöll Mountains, good and righteous men will find quarter. The vile Nástrandir, a hall of woven serpents, will house perjurers and murderers, while Hvergelmir, the well at the vortex of the underworld, reappears in Snorri's text as the closest correspondent to the Christian hell: a place of torment for the wicked. Quoting a poetic account of the land, Snorri writes:

Þar kvelr Níðhöggr
nái framgengna.[55]

There [the serpent] Níðhöggr
torments the bodies of the departed.

Christian influence in this description is clear but the general idea of multiple otherworlds for the dead appears to predate contact with the new religion.

In the Christianity arriving in the region, visions of afterlife realms were frequent and important. Biblical accounts of heaven and hell were juxtaposed to numerous visions of heaven, hell, and purgatory.[56] Gregory's sixth-century *Dialogues* contains numerous references to afterlife visions, as when the saintly hermit at Lipari sees a vision of King Theodoric being thrown into a volcano as retribution for a life of sin.[57] The monk Reparatus sees a vision of purgatory at the end of his own life: an immense pyre has been prepared for the priest Tiburtius as punishment for lifetime carnal pleasures, and a similar pyre reaching the sky awaits Reparatus himself.[58] St. Ansgar sees a vision of purgatory early in life, according to the ninth-century *Vita* authored by Rimbert soon after the saint's death.[59] Images of near-death visions of otherworlds also occur frequently in accounts of the miraculous intercession of Mary or the saints.[60] Since these accounts often found their ways into homilies—especially in the hands of Dominican and Franciscan friars—they were translated frequently into the languages of Scandinavia.[61] Gregory's *Dialogues*, in fact, forms the basis of one of the supernatural episodes in *Njáls saga*, as Einar Ól. Sveinsson has shown, and at least one Icelandic translation of the *Dialogues* survives.[62] Hultgård argues for the influence of such Christian homiletic literature on late pagan eschatological constructs such as Snorri's depiction of Ragnarök.[63]

Even more important than Christian imagery of the otherworlds, however, was the concept of ritual purity at the moment of dying, a state referred to in medieval Christianity as the "Good Death." This set of beliefs held extreme importance for Christians of the thirteenth century and influenced dramatically the way they viewed pagan death.[64] Dying a good death necessitated a clear conscience, coupled with absolution of all sin, recent receipt of pertinent sacraments (e.g., the *viacum*, the Eucharist) and guarantee of burial in sanctified ground. The realities of early Christianity in Scandinavia made the attainment of this ideal impossible for all but a lucky few. Even into the nineteenth century, as Storå shows, for instance, Sámi Christians were obliged to bury their dead in shallow temporary graves without Christian rites, reinterring the bodies later with a proper ceremony once the district minister had arrived. In some cases, the body was even hung and dried in the wind—like meat or fish provisions—to be more easily transported to the churchyard when the opportunity arose.[65]

These realities of death in a world with too few clerics and limited sanctified ground must have plagued thirteenth-century Scandinavians, who expected an immanent end of the world and attached great importance to the eschatological significance of the Resurrection. While the rich could retire to monasteries in their final years, the ordinary peasant or merchant, especially in youth, risked untimely death with even the shortest of journeys. Life in the un-Christianized settlements presented a constant dilemma as well. In *Óláfs saga Helga*, Snorri informs us that prior to his final battle, King Óláfr considered a pilgrimage to Jerusalem or life as a monk, deciding to return to Norway to regain his kingdom only after a sacred vision.[66] In *Grœnlendiga saga*, the able and saintly Guðríðr (see Chapter 8) travels "south" upon her son's marriage, returning to his estate as a "nun and anchorite" to live beside the church in her old age.[67] Archaeological evidence and local oral tradition indicate the existence of a convent of Scandinavian nuns even in the remote Orkney setting of Murkle, where, it is said, both a queen of Norway and an earl of Caithness were buried in the tenth century.[68] Although such claims must be seen in light of later Christian customs and imaginings, they do indicate the ideals of the Good Death among thirteenth-century Icelandic saga writers. The continental custom of late-life monasticism appears familiar and laudable to these Christians of Snorri's generation.[69]

Likewise, the Good Death figures as an unattainable goal in saga writers' portrayals of early Christian Scandinavia. When Þorvaldr Eiríksson died in Vinland, as *Grœnlendiga saga* points out, he asked to be buried on a hill with crosses set at his feet and head as a makeshift substitute for proper burial.[70] In *Landnámabók*, the Christian settler Auðr the Deepminded is said to have been buried below the high tide mark upon her death in the as-yet-unChristianized Iceland: better to be buried technically at sea than interred in unsanctified dry land (see below).

A further illustration of the Christian concern for proper burial can be found in the tendency to reinter pagan ancestors in sanctified ground after the conversion of a descendant. In the late tenth century, King Haraldr Bluetooth not only raised a memorial stone in honor of his father and mother at Jelling (see Chapter 7); he also appears to have reinterred his father in the large church he had built there. The transferral of Gorm from his pagan burial mound to the sanctity of the east nave may have been undertaken to ensure him everlasting peace; theologically, it held no such significance, since righteous pagans were not bound by the laws of the church. Such fine points of theology were usually missed in the early era of conversions, however. The reinterment may have also represented an attempt to create "retrospective continuity," a favorite interest of Scandinavian monarchs even when they wished to claim—as Haraldr does in the Jelling Stone's runic inscription—the notoriety of having Christianized the kingdom.[71] Illustrative of the same tendency among nobles of lesser birth (but with substantial financial means) is the reinterment of the intractable pagan Egill Skalla-Grímsson in the church at Borg.[72] Here, the irascible worshiper of Óðinn is removed from his burial mound, where he had lain with grave goods and clothing, to be placed beneath the altar of the new church at Hrisbru. Apparently, the skald's Christian niece Þórdís has him reinterred out of concern for his soul. When the church is later demolished, the priest Skapti Þórarinsson has Egill's remains reburied in the churchyard at Mosfell, although not in the same place of honor as before. Situated on the periphery of the church's sanctified ground, Egill's grave now expresses spatially the skald's spiritual position in life: standing at the threshold of the faith that his descendants will later embrace. The edges of cemeteries became the standard grounds for the burial of the unshriven, unrepentant, excommunicated, or unbaptized in medieval Christianity.[73]

This generalized attention to proper burial in Christianity found further elaboration in the cult of the saint. Christians' loving attention to the graves, bodies, and possessions of the deceased built on earlier pre-Christian concepts but took these to a level unparalleled by pagan cults.[74] The Roman *refrigium* (a ceremonial feast for the dead) and its Scandinavian and Finno-Ugric counterparts, and the Nordic holy-mountain tradition supply a partial but incomplete basis for this important conceptual innovation. In Christian sainthood, the deceased became an invisible friend, capable of interceding with God on behalf of the living. Sanctity could be recognized by the miracles occurring at a saint's grave and by the miraculous resistance of the saint's lifeless body to processes of natural decay. The saint's power to heal also resided in personal possessions that became treasured items of families and churches alike. Once a person had become known as a saint (in most cases, long before any attempt at official canonization), his very flesh and bones became treasured relics, buried in altars, at monasteries, and presented to foreign bishops and kings. Disinterment and redistribution of such sacred human remains (*translatio*) became a high point in liturgical life and the foundation for the establishment of pilgrimage centers and other aspects of devotion to a particular saint.

Medieval and postmedieval traditions concerning burial reflect this concept of the Good Death. Throughout Scandinavia, an attempt was made to ensure that no ties would bind the person to this world—that the person's tasks were completed, that old disputes were settled, and that the person's goods were disposed of in the desired manner (see discussion of *Eyrbyggja saga*, below).[75] Failure to take these precautions could lead to haunting, and thus such actions were taken both out of compassion for the dying and as a precaution against the person's possible return. The practice of bearing the body out of a hole in the wall (so that the ghost would not be able to find its way back, should it choose to return)—a detail common in thirteenth-century sagas and persistent in Iceland during the centuries which followed—appears wholly motivated by fear. An example of such preparations occurs in *Eyrbyggja saga* in connection with the death of the cantankerous Þórólfr Bægifótr ("Twist-Foot"):

Gekk Arnkell nú inn í eldakálann ok svá inn eptir setinu á bak Þórólfi; hann bað hvern at varask at ganga framan at honum, meðan honum váru eigi nábargir veittar; tók Arnkell þá í herðar Þórólfi, ok varð hann at kenna aflsmunar, áðr hann kœmi honum undir; síðan sveipaði hann klæðum at höfði Þórólfi ok bjó um hann eptir siðvenju. Eptir þat lét hann brjóta vegginn á bak honum ok draga hann þar út. Síðan váru yxn fyrir sleða beittir; var Þórólfr þar í lagiðr, ok óku honum upp í Þórsádal, ok var þat eigi þrautarlaust, áðr hann kom í þann stað, sem hann skyldi vera; dysjuðu þeir Þórólf þar rammliga.[76]

When Arnkell went into the living-room, he crossed the hall to get behind Þórólfr, warning people to take care not to pass in front of the corpse until the eyes had been closed. He took Þórólfr by the shoulders but had to use all his strength before he could force him down. After that he wrapped some clothes around Þórólfr's head and got him ready for burial according to the custom of the time. He had a hole broken through the wall behind Þórólfr, and the corpse was dragged outside. After a yoke of oxen had been hitched to a sled, Arnkell laid Þórólfr on it, and they began driving it up through Þórsárdal. It was hard work hauling Þórólfr to his burial-place. When they got him there, they built a solid cairn over him.[77]

Although much of the ghostlore common in postmedieval agrarian Scandinavia has international sources and distribution, a few traditions seem to represent distinctive Nordic beliefs. Icelandic legends of wrestling with ghosts persisted well into the nineteenth century.[78] Similarly, Sámi traditions about a being called Stallo may reflect the early contact era: the evil Stallo, equipped with iron teeth and the desire to devour the flesh of the living, is associated with scattered mounds in the region, possibly remnants of non-Sámi burial or settlement places.[79] So, too, Finnish and north Estonian traditions about Hiisi appear associated with particular pre-Christian burial grounds or places of sacrifice.[80] In Finnish legendary, Hiisi figures as an evil guardian of particular forest tracts and mountains and as an ill-willed denizen of the subterranean realm of the dead. Hiisi sites were guarded through extensive taboos and a generalized fear. During the thirteenth century, papal bulls granted the Church the right to confiscate and control these sites in an attempt to suppress ongoing pagan rites there.[81] As in other Nordic folklore related to the dead, pre-Christian practice, continental traditions, and Christian theology meld into a strikingly complex syncretic understanding.

Death, Burial, and Haunting in the Sagas

Given the variety of burial customs prevalent in the Nordic world of the Viking Age and the significance attached to the dead in both pre-Christian and Christian religions, it is not surprising that pagans and Christians alike took active interest in the details of their neighbors' final resting places. In thirteenth-century sagas, however, this interest often becomes developed into an elaborate symbolic system in which type of burial is described as a key device for characterizing men and women of the conversion era. Christian and pagan burials are juxtaposed in ways which illustrate the morals, quality, and sanctity of the persons buried. Haunting—the unwanted return of the dead—is juxtaposed to the instrumental return of helpful dead within the framework of Christian miracles. It is one of the marvels of these texts that their authors can accommodate and distinguish between different meanings of supernatural reanimation and that their original audiences, attuned to the issues of burial and ghosts, would have comprehended the nuances of these distinctions. Burial and reanimation became prime items in the symbolic economies of saga texts.

Three texts figure as classic distillations of this thirteenth-century use of ghost lore. In these, we see the ghost as a menacing physical presence, intent on injuring the living and infecting them with the same curse of haunting. In the first, *Laxdœla saga*, the haunting characterizes a particularly acquisitive and selfish pagan, Hrapp, as opposed to the dignified, generous and unhaunted passing of the noble pagan, Unnr. In the second, *Eiríks saga*, the pagan hauntings of Garðar are juxtaposed to the positive resuscitation of the Christian Þorsteinn, who returns to ensure proper conduct among the living and observance of God's laws. In the third, *Eyrbyggja saga*, the saga writer employs both pagan-pagan and pagan-Christian contrasts in his use of burial type, haunting, and the reanimation of Christian dead. His text combines the rhetorical strategies of both *Laxdœla saga* and *Eiríks saga*. In all three examples, portrayal of pagan death plays a thematic role in the saga narrative.

Laxdœla saga illustrates this symbolic economy in its depiction of the burials of Unnr the Deep-minded and Killer Hrapp.[82] *Landnámabók's* description of Auðr Djúpaúðga's scrupulously Christian interment is replaced by the image of Unnr Djúpúðga's pagan ship burial, in which the wealthy leader departs from the world of the living with extensive feasting, abundant grave goods and a picturesque ship-grave.[83] This imagistic replacement allows the saga writer to reserve the prestige of introducing Christianity for the later character Kjartan. It also permits the writer to juxtapose the noble and generous pagan passing with the vindictive and miserly death and burial of the brutal pagan Killer Hrapp. Hrapp, buried upright beneath the threshold of his home that he may better guard its possessions, becomes a dangerous ghost. His hauntings chase wife and descendants from the farm and remain unchecked until he is later disintered, cremated, and scattered to the winds of the sea.[84] His discovery in his grave—undecayed after many years—betrays further the influence of Christian legend, although here the miraculous preservation of the body highlights the deceased's demonic nature.

Similarly, in *Eiríks saga*, the saga writer constructs a tale of ghost haunting that revolves around issues of burial. Just as *Laxdœla saga* borrows and refigures details of a death recounted in *Landnámabók*, so *Eiríks saga* transforms the account of deaths at Lysafjörðr in *Grœnlendiga saga*. The *Grœnlendiga saga* account describes epidemic deaths at the Lysafjörðr farmstead and preparations made for the burial of the corpses. They are carefully stored aboard ship in coffins for later interment in the church at Eiríksfjörðr.[85] In *Eiríks saga*, this base is expanded into a full exploration of the causes and effects of haunting and its relation to burial customs. The Lysafjörðr settlement—now portrayed as recently Christianized—harbors pagan backsliders like the foreman Garðar, who dies first in the recounted epidemic. As more of the farmstead die, they appear to the dying farmwife Sigríðr in the form of a frightening vision, in which she sees herself and Þorsteinn Eiríksson among the host of the dead. Garðar figures as a demon, tormenting the other dead with his whip:

"[H]ér er nú liðit þat allt it dauða fyrir durunum ok Þorsteinn, bóndi þinn, ok þar kenni ek mik, ok er slíkt hörmung at sjá!" Ok er þetta leið af, mælti hon: "Föru vit nú, Guðríðr, nú sé ek ekki liðit." Var þá ok verkstjórinn horfinn, er henni þótti áðr hafa svipu í hendi ok vilja berja liðit.[86]

"Here is now the entire host of the dead before the door, and Þorsteinn your husband with them, and I recognize myself there too. How dreadful it is to see such a thing!" And when this passed off, "Let us go now, Guðriðr," she begged. "I do not see the host any longer." The foreman too had disappeared, who she thought earlier had had a whip in his hand and sought to scourge the company.[87]

What is crucial about this expanded account of the Lysafjörðr epidemic is the fact that burial customs become the primary explanation and solution of the problems. Þorsteinn Eiríksson revives from the dead for a brief time—with God's permission and endorsement—to criticize the settlement's handling of the deceased. In his words to his widow and the assembled farmstead he makes their failings in this area clear; rather than carefully laying their dead to rest in sanctified ground, they have chosen an expedient but improper alternative:

Skyldi setja staur upp af brjósti hinum dauða, en síðan er kennimenn kómu til, þá skyldi upp kippa staurinum ok hella þar í vígðu vatni ok veita þar yfirsöngva, þótt þat væri miklu síðar.[88]

A stake would be set up from the breast of the dead, and in due course, when clerks came that way, the stakes would be pulled up and holy water poured into the place, and a service sung over them, even though this might be a good while later.[89]

The revenant Þorsteinn states that while the good Christian dead are to be reintered in a church, the body of Garðar is to receive cremation, the pagan burial form. Since he is responsible for the hauntings, he must be disposed of in a manner in keeping with his demonic, pagan tendencies. In this way, burial becomes a key device for determining the postmortem rest of the dead, and reanimation takes on different meanings according to the religious adherence of the revenant. Cremation, the once-standard pagan method of disposing of the body, symbolizes hell fire, juxtaposed to the peaceful repose of Christian inhumation, slaked by the cool blessings of holy water and sanctified ground.

The connection between pagan burials and subsequent hauntings, employed to effect in Laxdœla saga, figures prominently in Eyrbyggja saga as

well.[90] Here, as in *Laxdœla saga*, pagans of differing character undergo
contrasting burial rituals. Þorsteinn Þorskabítr ("Cod-biter")—generous to
the end and a vigorous defender of his clan's sacred site—is depicted as being
welcomed into Helgafell, his family's holy mountain. His death leads to no
hauntings. On the other hand, the embittered Þórólfr Twist-foot—manipulative and unkind to his son Arnkell—dies an unsettled death, rising soon
from his cairn to plague the countryside with his haunting.[91] Only late in the
saga (ch. 63) are attempts made to stop Þórólfr's haunting, characteristically
by exposing his corpse to pagan cremation:

[F]ara þeir út til Bægifótshöfða ok til dysjar Þórólfs; síðan brutu þeir upp dysina ok
fundu þar Þórólf; var hann þá enn ófúinn ok inn trollsligsti at sjá; hann var blár sem
hel ok digr sem naut; ok er þeir hrœra hann, þá fengu þeir hvergi rigat honum; lét
Þóroddr þá fœra undir hann brot, ok við þetta kómu þeir honum upp ór dysinni;
síðan veltu þeir honum á fjöru ofan ok kvistuðu þar bál mikit, slógu síðan eldi í ok
veltu þar í Þórólfi ok brenndu upp allt saman at köldum kolum, ok var þat þó lengi,
at eigi orkaði eldr á Þórólf. Vindr var á hvass, ok fauk askan víða, þegar brenna tók,
en þeiri ösku, er þeir máttu, sköruðu þeir á sjó út.[92]

Off they went to Twist-Foot's Knoll, where Þórólfr was buried, broke open the grave,
and saw Þórólfr still lying there, uncorrupted with an ugly look about him. He was as
black as death and swollen to the size of an ox. They tried to move the dead man, but
were unable to shift him an inch. Then Þóroddr put a lever under him, and that was
how they managed to lift him out of the grave. After that they rolled him down to the
foreshore, built a great pyre there, set fire to it, pushed Þórólfr in and burnt him to
ashes. Even so, it took the fire a long time to have any effect on Þórólfr. A fierce gale
had blown up, so as soon as the corpse began to burn the ashes were scattered
everywhere, but all that they could get hold of they threw into the sea.[93]

Due to the wind, not all of the ashes are disposed of at sea, however, and the
ghost enjoys a short reprieve from final banishment in the form of a mon-
strous bull.[94] Here, then, the intricacies of pagan burial customs—be it the
holy-mountain tradition of Helgafell or the cremation burial instituted by
Óðinn—find textual representation and reuse as symbolic devices for characterization. In a Christian text, their outlandish details serve a broader
rhetorical strategy in delineating characters and clans of the past. At the
same time, it is clear that pagan burial remains a useful means of disposing
of pagan ghosts: the traditions of the pre-Christian era thus live on in
attenuated form as a special treatment for the restless dead.

If *Eyrbyggja saga* were to contain only these references to pagan deaths
and ghosts it would play a valuable role in the study of Nordic religion, but

the text goes further in recounting yet more details of hauntings, providing one of saga literature's most memorable accounts of tenth-century ghost lore in its Fróðá Marvels.[95] In this case of haunting—which appears to have become well known in oral tradition—the death of the Christian Þórgunna and envy of the farmwife Þuríðr combine to create evil supernatural events.[96] Christian and pagan reanimation are juxtaposed in the manner of the *Eiríks saga* account, to which it is closely linked by the character Þórgunna and the testimony of the *Eiríks saga* text. This pagan-Christian juxtaposition falls midway between the first appearances of Þórólfr Twist-Foot as a ghost and his final laying, and is tied narratively to the Christianization of Iceland.

The account of the Fróðá Marvels occurs in the saga directly after the mass Christianization of Iceland, in which Snorri Goði ("the Priest") and other notables of the narrative's locale build churches on their estates.[97] The saga stipulates, however, that the lack of Christian priests hinders the performance of the religion's rituals in the area. Thus, when the mysterious Christian visitor from the Hebrides, Þórgunna, dies, she asks that her body be brought to Skálholt, where priests can sing Mass for her. Along the way, she reanimates to ensure that her pallbearers receive proper hospitality. Denied food and dry clothes by the farmhouse at Nes it nerða, the pallbearers choose to sleep in the farm's living room without welcome:

[E]n heimamenn fóru í dagsljósi í rekkju. Ok er menn kómu í rekkjur, heyrðu þeir hark mikit í búrit; var þá farit at forvitnask, hvárt eigi væri þjófar inn komnir; ok er menn kómu til búrsins, var þar sén kona mikil; hon var nökvið, svá at hon hafði engan hlut á sér; hon starfaði at matseld; en þeir menn, er hana sá, urðu svá hræddir, at þeir þorðu hvergi nær at koma. En er líkmenn vissu þetta, fóru þeir til ok sá, hversu háttat var; þar var Þórgunna komin, ok sýndisk þat ráð öllum, at fara eigi til með henni. Ok er hon hafði þar unnit slíkt er hon vildi, þá bar hon mat í stofu. Eptir þat setti hon borð ok bar þar á mat. Þá mæltu líkmenn við bónda: "Vera má, at svá lúki við, áðr vér skilim, at þér þykki alkeypt, at þú vildir engan greiða gera oss." Þá mæltu bæði bóndi ok húsfreyja: "Vit viljum víst gefa yðr mat ok gera yðr annan greiða, þann er þér þurfuð." Ok þegar er bóndi hafði boðit þeim greiða, gekk Þórgunna fram ór stofunni ok út eptir þat, ok sýndisk hon eigi síðan.[98]

The household went to bed before it grew dark. They hadn't been long in their beds when they heard loud noises coming from the larder, and some of them went to see if thieves had broken into the house. When they came to the larder, there was a tall woman, stark naked, not a stitch of clothing on her, getting a meal ready. The people of the household were too scared when they saw her to come anywhere near. As soon as the corpse-bearers heard about it, they went to see for themselves what was going on. The woman was Þórgunna, and everyone thought it best to leave her in peace.

When she had finished doing what she wanted in the larder, she carried the food into the living-room, laid the table, and served the meal.

"Before we part, you may end up very sorry that you didn't treat us more hospitably," said the corpse-bearers to the farmer.

"We'll gladly give you food and anything else you need," said the farmer and his wife.

And as soon as the farmer had made them welcome, Þórgunna walked out of the room and didn't reappear.[99]

In contrast, the dead who reanimate at Fróðá do so for no positive purpose. Local ghosts who have died on land and at sea return to the hall in the evenings, driving away the living even from the warmth of the yuletide fire. Their appearance is first said to be viewed as a sign of approval from the goddess Ran, who allows the sea dead to attend their own funerals if she is pleased to welcome them to her realm.[100] This detail finds no counterpart in any other account of pre-Christian Scandinavian belief and seems created to underscore the conflict of old and new understandings of death during the era of conversions. As the saga writer confides: "At that time a good many pagan beliefs still prevailed, though people were baptized and supposed to be Christians."[101] The return of the dead is accompanied by ill omens (bloody rain, a mysterious half-moon appearing on the wall) and seal-like tormenters who rise from the floor and devour the farmstead's stores. Such hauntings continue until Þórgunna's possessions are burned—in accordance with her dying wishes—and the ghosts are banished through legal action. The exposure of the ghosts to lawsuit, a colorful and again unparalleled detail of the text, underscores the physicality of the Icelandic ghosts. They must be handled as one would deal with the living, while guarding against their return through the liturgical arsenal of Christianity:

Síðan gengu þeir Kjartan inn; bar prestr þá vígt vatn ok helga dóma um öll hús. Eptir um daginn syngr prestr tíðir allar ok messu hátíðliga, ok eptir þat tókusk af allar aptrgöngur at Fróðá.[102]

Then Kjartan and the others went back inside, and the priest carried holy water and sacred relics to every corner of the house. Next day he sang all the prayers and celebrated Mass with great solemnity, and there were no more dead men haunting Fróðá after that.[103]

Here, then, as in *Eiríks saga*, pagan and Christian reanimation find direct juxtaposition, a contrast that contributes to broader thematic attention to the Christianization of Iceland.[104] Ethnographic details of pagan burial are sometimes accurate, sometimes fanciful, but always deployed in the service of a Christian theme.

Death, burial, and the return of the dead thus represent a key nexus for the interaction of differing cults during the Viking Age. Surface differences between Sámi, Finnish, and Scandinavian customs and beliefs regarding burial and afterlife mask an underlying unity in worldview that emphasized the importance of material preparation for the next life and the existence of multiple otherworld destinations. Christian notions of burial—strikingly divergent in a number of ways—began to make inroads into the practices of Nordic pagans long before Christianization per se, altering age-old but variable traditions of the disposal of the dead. Concepts of afterlife underwent transformations as well, with pagan communities adjusting their beliefs in line with Christian doctrines prior to the real conversion to the new faith. It is likely that Christian rites and beliefs affected traditions like the ship burial and Ragnarök, which rise in prominence during the late pagan era. Later, Christians of the thirteenth century still retained cultural memories of pre-Christian burial rites and beliefs, casting these in the light of continental demonology and saints' legends. This complex set of transformations underscores the interrelation of pagan and Christian ideas during the Viking Age and the immense complexity of the process of conversion in Nordic cultures.

FIVE

Concepts of Health and Healing

The definition, achievement, and maintenance of health represents one of the central and most widespread functions of religion worldwide. During the Viking Age, Scandinavians, Finns, and Sámi practiced a variety of healing acts derived from both pagan and Christian worldviews. Health and disease were conceptualized through continental theories first developed by Greek and Roman physicians and spread through a set of extremely popular medical tracts copied, translated, and annotated throughout medieval Christian Europe. The British Isles served as a major conduit for the passage of this knowledge northward to the Nordic peoples. At the same time, especially in the Nordic region itself, older native ideas of spirit loss and possession, characteristic of shamanism, underlay many approaches to disease. Health entailed not only the lack of disease but also the presence of luck, and it could be stolen by the ill will or machinations of supernatural beings. In these moments of need, the reestablishment of personal health sometimes required consultation with a healer who could both diagnose and treat the problem at the root of the symptoms. In this chapter, we examine the Nordic healer and view of health and disease common during the Viking Age. While many present-day Westerners may draw unproblematic distinctions between the realms of religion and that of medicine, no such boundaries existed in the world of the Vikings, pagan and Christian alike.

Gift of the Ancients: Classical Medical Lore

Classical learning of Greece and Rome supplied Christian Europe with its principal medical treatises, among which the *Herbarium* of Apuleius enjoyed particular prominence.[1] Copied and circulated throughout monastic Europe, its herbal remedies were diligently translated into north European languages. An examination of the contents of the Old English translation of Apuleius provides a notion of the kinds of medical learning offered by the Christian intelligentsia of the Viking Age.

At the first, most basic level, Apuleius gives us a glimpse of medical understandings of health and illness. The kinds of ailments identified are as indicative of medieval life as the cures offered. The work of Apuleius is devoted particularly to chronic aches and pains, be they sore teeth, aching bones, or headaches. Urinary and gastrointestinal irregularities receive dozens of remedies, as do dropsy, bladder ailments, and eye problems. The same remedies often cure several such ailments. Rue (*Ruta gravolens*), for instance, could be used to treat bloatedness when taken internally, soothe sore eyes when applied as a salve, amend lethargy when mixed with vinegar and applied to the forehead, improve eyesight if given with wine to a fasting patient, or cure headaches when taken with wine.[2]

Acute illness takes a secondary place in Apuleius, although it remains prominent in some particulars. Above all, snake bites occupy the attention of the ancients: scarcely a page goes by without the characterization of some plant or animal as useful in treating snake bites. These include betony (*Betonica officinalis*), catmint (*Nepeta cattaria*), gorse (*Ulex europæus*), field larkspur (*Delphinium consolida*), and parsley (*Apium petroselinon*).[3] Poultices applied to the sore spot are roughly as common as remedies taken internally (usually mixed with wine). The same holds true for the treatment of wounds and burns, which are covered to some degree in Apuleius. A poultice of halswort (*Campanula trachelium*), flour, and oil is recommended for wounds, as is dittany (*Diptamnus alba*), either taken internally or applied directly to the sore.[4] Celandine (*Chelidonium maius*) mixed with goat's cheese could be applied to severe burns, as could members of the herbaceous borage genus *Anchusa* (*Boraginaceae*) mixed with oil and wax.[5] Wounds caused by iron are treated differently from those caused by other agents: a poultice of groundsel (*Senecio vulgaris*) and lard prepared in the morning or at midday or one of grease and yarrow (*Achillea millefolium*) are two of a number of specialized remedies for this type of wound.[6] Fever that goes beyond the second or third day warrants medicinal treatment as well: among other remedies, lettuce (*Prenanthes muralis*) laid secretly under the patient's pillow is recommended.[7]

Despite the inevitable male bias of this learning—reflected not least in the plethora of remedies for varieties of prostate trouble—women's ailments also receive some attention. The starting and stopping of menstrual flow can be controlled by plant elixirs: for example, comfrey (*Symphytum officinale*) or bramble (*Rubus fruticosus*), and infertility could be treated with a bath of wild parsnip (*Pastinaca sativa*).[8] Successful labor and delivery could be brought about by placing coriander seeds (*Coriandrum sativum*) in a linen pouch by the left thigh during parturition.[9] Equally or even more common, however, are prescriptions for expelling stillborns, including pennyroyal (*Mentha puligium*) and dittany.[10] That some of these remedies may have been used as abortives is reflected by the explicit identification of a few substances as useful in stimulating abortive parturition, among them cucumbers (*Cucumis* sp.), a hare's heart, and wolf's milk.[11] In a culture of long-term lactation, however, sore breasts receive far more extensive attention. This ailment can be treated by application or ingestion of henbane (*Hyo-

scyamus niger), iris (*Iris pseudocorus*), rue, licorice (*Glykyrrhiza glanduli-fera*) or hemp (*Cannabis sativa*).[12]

While plants supplied the bulk of the healer's medicinal arsenal, animal parts were plied as cures as well, as the widely translated *Medicina de quadru-pedibus* of Sextus Placitus illustrates.[13] In Anglo-Saxon translation, Classical learning recommended an elixir made of dried hare's belly for the man and woman wanting to conceive a son, and a combination of goat turd and honey could be rubbed on cancerous sores.[14] Goat urine could be ingested as a cure for dropsy or the affected area could be rubbed with hound's vomit.[15] Placing a wolf's head under one's pillow at night brought sound sleep, and the sight of frightening apparitions could be countered by consumption of a drink made from a white hound's feces.[16] Dried bull's testicles made an effective aphrodisiac when steeped in wine, and consumption of a newborn puppy—its eyes yet unopened—was recommended as a cure for almost any sore, if eaten in the early summer.[17] A hare's foot possessed curative proper-ties if worn on one's upper garment and carrying a hound's heart prevented attacks by dogs.[18] Further remedies entailed elephant ivory (good for remov-ing blemishes) and lion's flesh (good for various pains).[19] The paucity of remedies using fauna unique to northern Europe reflects the Classical roots of this learning and the derivativeness of the medical thought of the era.

A similar overall approach to medicine is found in the tenth-century *Bald's Leechbook*, a carefully compiled and meticulously organized work which provides many insights into Anglo-Saxon concepts of health and disease.[20] General aches and pains of the anatomy comprise about a third of the text, with a second third devoted to major and acute ailments, such as skin eruptions, shingles, urinary disorders, jaundice, and cancer. The re-maining third covers ailments that intrude upon the patient through outside agents, be they "worms" (worms, maggots, insects), supernatural beings, animals, or circumstances of life. The ailments of this last category could nearly all be sent by the devil or persons engaged in witchcraft. The author includes detailed instructions on amputation and some twenty different treatments for Anglo-Saxon *átor* (poisons), a term which covers snake bites, gashes, and even swellings. These receive magical treatment as well as physi-cal: incantations in English, Latin, and even Irish are combined with holy water, prayers, appeals to St. John, and an array of plant extracts.

Many of the remedies noted in Anglo-Saxon materials find counter-parts in Scandinavia. As in Anglo-Saxon England, violets (*Viola odorata*) could be used to treat burns, and the peony (*Paeonia* sp.) could cure lunacy or epilepsy.[21] Hemp (*Cannabis sativa*) was administered as a salve as well as ingested for the treatment of sores, poisons, and cough in Scandinavia as in the British Isles.[22] The association of remedies and Christian intercessors is reflected by such cures as an elixir made from wine and *Hypericum perfora-tum*—in Danish, *Sankt Johannesurt*, English St. John's wort—used for treating depression and other ailments both natural and supernatural.[23] Some remedies, however, clearly antedate continental sources, as in the case of the various medicinal uses made of species of the broad-leafed dock (*Rumex* sp.).[24] Widely reflected in place-names, remains of the plant have been found in the stomach of the Tollund Man and pollen analysis confirms its early and widespread cultivation. *Hávamál* includes recommendations for the use of various substances for the maintenance of health in daily life, advice which appears widespread, if not necessarily native to the region:

> Ráðomc þér, Loddfáfnir,   enn þú ráð nemir,
> nióta mundo,   ef þú nemr,
> þér muno góð,   ef þú getr:
> hvars þú öl dreccir,   kiós þú þér iarðar megin!
> þvíat iörð tecr við ölðri,   enn eldr við sóttom,
> eic við abbindi,   ax við fiölkyngi,
> höll við hýrógi   —heiptom scal mána qveðia—
> beiti við bitsóttom,   enn við bölvi rúnar;
> fold scal við flóði taca.[25]

> I recommend, Loddfáfnir,   take these counsels;
> you'll do well to follow them,
> they will serve you well if you learn them:
> if you are drinking ale,   avail yourself of the power of earth.
> For earth prevails against ale,   fire against disease;
> the oak against constipation,   the ear of grain against witchcraft,
> elder against strife at home   —the moon soothes ill will—
> alum [or "the worm"] against cattle disease,   runes
>   against misfortune,
> earth will prevail against the flood.[26]

This section of *Hávamál* is open and matter-of-fact, and it seems likely that these words of wisdom represent the kind of herbal lore common among well-informed Scandinavians of the Viking Age. When the monasteries and convents of the region began to produce their own compendia in the fifteenth century, their texts included details specific to the flora of northern

Europe: the fifteenth-century *Nadhentals closters bok*, for instance, produced
at the Benedictine convent at Naantali, Finland, includes information on the
healing potential of such native plants as juniper (*kataja*; *Juniperus* sp.) and
stinging nettle (*nokkonen*; *Urtica* sp.), both popular in folk remedies down
to the present day.[27]

Some Scandinavian texts indicate the development of an identifiable
medical profession. When King Magnús selects men to become healers for
his army at the Battle of Hlýrskogsheiðr, it is implied that the chosen men receive subsequent further instruction, which may have entailed travel abroad
and study of the great medical tracts like Apuleius. Writes Snorri:

En af liði Magnúss konungs fell ekki mart, en fjölði varð sárt. Eptir orrostu lét
Magnús konungr binda sár sinna manna, en læknar váru ekki svá margir í herinum
sem þá þurfti. Þá gekk konungr til þeira manna, er honum sýndisk, ok þreifaði um
hendr þeim, en er hann tók í lófana ok strauk um, þá nefndi hann til tólf menn, þá er
honum sýndisk sem mjúkhenztir mundu vera, ok segir, at þeir skyldu binda sár
manna, en engi þeira hafði fyrr sár bundit. En allir þessir urðu inir mestu læknar. Þar
váru tveir íslenzkir menn, var annarr Þorkell Geirason af Lyngum, annarr Atli, faðir
Bárðar svarta í Selárdal, ok kómu frá þeim margir læknar síðan.[28]

Although few of King Magnús's men fell, many were wounded. After the battle, King
Magnús ordered his men's wounds bandaged, but there were not as many healers in
the army as needed. Then the king went up to those men who seemed suitable and
examined their hands and once he had taken their hands and felt them he chose the
twelve men who seemed to have the softest of hands and said that they should
bandage the men's wounds although none of them had ever bandaged before. But all
of these men proved the best of healers. There were two Icelandic men—Þorkel
Geirason from Lyngar and Atli, the father of Bárðr the Black of Selárdal—and from
them have come many healers since.

We know of at least one Icelandic healer—Hrafn Sveinbjarnarson (d. 1218), a
descendant of Atli—who left his native land to gain more extensive medical
training on the Continent.[29] The likelihood of enslaved British healers, acting either as practitioners or as trainers, is certain, as all classes and occupa-
tions were fair game for capture even among Christians, and healing skills
only increased their value.[30] By the end of the thirteenth century, the law of
Uppland, Sweden, could require a person who injures another to produce
three "lawful" healers (*lagha lækir*) from which the victim may choose.[31]
Such healers were defined as those capable of treating major wounds as well
as broken limbs, although no mention is made of their ability to treat

disease. Clearly, by this time, continental medicine had become well established in the region, as reflected by the establishment of Sweden's first hospital in 1269.[32]

While the ethnic origin of the healing woman depicted in Snorri's *Óláfs saga Helga* is unspecified, her methods and medicinal arsenal match those of the Anglo-Saxon or broader continental healer. So, too, her patient Þormóðr appears wryly aware of the various medicinal uses of plants and clinical in his approach to his own fatal wound. Snorri includes a long description of the healer's consultation as an illustration of the grim courage of King Óláfr's faithful soldier in the face of certain death:

Þá mælti læknirinn: "Láttu mik sjá sár þín, ok mun ek veita umbönd. Síðan settisk hann niðr ok kastaði klæðum af sér. En er læknir sá sár hans, þá leitaði hon um þat sár, er hann hafði á síðunni, kenndi þess, at þar stóð járn í, en þat vissi hon eigi til víss, hvert járnit hafði snúit. Hon hafði þar gört í steinkatli, stappat lauk ok önnur grös ok vellt þat saman ok gaf at eta inum sárum mönnum ok reyndi svá, hvárt þeir hefði holsár, því at kenndi af laukinum út ór sári því, er á hol var. Hon bar þat at Þormóði, bað hann eta. Hann svarar: "Ber brot. Ekki hefi ek grautsótt." Síðan tók hon spennitöng ok vildi draga út járnit, et þat var fast ok gekk hvergi, stóð ok lítit út, því at sárit var sollit. Þá mælti Þormóðr: "Sker þú til járnsins, svá at vel megi ná með tönginni, fá mér síðan ok lát mik kippa." Hon gerði sem hann mælti.[33]

The healer said: "Let me take a look at your wounds and I will treat them." He [Þormóðr] sat down and took off his clothes. And when the healer saw his wounds, she examined the one in his side and noted that there was a piece of iron in it, although she couldn't say for sure where the iron had traveled. She had put some leeks and other herbs in a stone cauldron and brewed it together, and this she gave to the wounded man to eat, trying in this way to discover whether he had serious wounds, because it would smell like leeks around any wound that was deep. She brought the mixture to Þormóðr and told him to eat it. He answered: "Take it away. I do not have a porridge illness." Then she took a pair of tongs and wanted to extract the piece of iron, but it was stuck and would not budge; it stuck out just a little because the wound was swollen. Then Þormóðr said: "Cut away down to the iron so that it can be grasped firmly with the tongs; then give them to me and let me wrench it." She did as he instructed.

Þormóðr disputes the use of leek for treating iron-caused wounds and recommends an incision deep enough for the removal of the arrowhead. *Bald's Leechbook* recommends placing leek leaves and salt as an anesthetic on wounds which must be cauterized and makes similar stipulations regarding the depth of incisions for successful amputation.[34] The notion of a female healer is supported by references in *Njáls saga* to Hildigunnr Starkaðardóttir, who is depicted treating her kinsmen's battle wounds.[35]

Sauna and Ritualized Health Maintenance

The awareness of medical practices reflected (but almost certainly exaggerated) by Snorri's depiction of Þormóðr was matched by routinized health rituals in daily life. Among the Finno-Ugric peoples of the Nordic region, the sauna dates from at least the era of early agriculture; the custom was also common among western and eastern Slavs as well as Balts. During the Viking Age, it seems to have spread to Scandinavians as well. While the Finnic word for the sauna stove (*kiuas*) is probably an early loan, other terms associated with the tradition possess deeper Finno-Ugric roots. For instance, *löyly*—the term for sauna steam, personified in Finnish charms as a healing spirit— finds a counterpart in the Hungarian term for soul or life-force, *lélek*.[36]

The Russian *Primary Chronicle* (*Povest' vremennikh let'*, c. 1040–1118) describes saunas (*bani dreveni*, wooden bathhouses) in the city of Novgorod. Flagellation with twig switches is mentioned along with anointing the body with tallow.[37] Nestor records the testimony of two Russian witches in 1071 who assert that man was created from sweat shed by God in his heavenly sauna.[38]

Tacitus mentions a hot-bath tradition among continental Germanic peoples: "Statim e somno, quem plerumque in diem extrahunt, lavantur, saepius calida, ut apud quos plurimum hiems occupat"[39] (Right after sleeping, which usually extends into the day, they bathe: often in hot water, for it is usually winter where they live). Although the tenth-century Arab traveler Ibn Fadhlan makes no mention of the sauna or other hot baths in particular in his description of Viking hygiene on the Volga, the twelfth-century *Sverris saga* describes bathhouses in Norway. Here, the men of King Sverri are able to surprise the warriors of Niðaróss by marching upon the town while the men are in an apparently large bathhouse. *Arons saga* includes a description of a royally commissioned bathhouse which has two rooms: one for undressing and one for bathing. Each room is said to have accommodated fifty men.[40]

Eyrbyggja saga (ch. 28) describes the form and use of an Icelandic sauna (*baðstofa*) at Hraun: it is partly dug into the ground and has a hole in the top for pouring water on the stove from the outside. The landowner Styrr uses it as a means of murdering a pair of troublesome *berserkr* (see Glossary) warriors, who have demanded his daughter in marriage.[41] In *Sturlunga saga*, the Icelanders Svarthöfði and Þórðr Bjarnarson hide in a small sauna at the farmstead of Skógar, and deacon Móðólfr retires to a sauna to warm himself after swimming across an icy river in a flight from enemies.[42]

While the steam bath thus appears to have gained popularity both in continental as well as insular Scandinavia, Icelanders soon took advantage of the hot volcanic springs of their island to create baths of a different kind. The hot springs at Laugardal are described as a key meeting place for allies in *Sturlungasaga*, and Snorri Sturluson's own outdoor bath at Reykjaholt figures as a similar meeting place for the chieftain and his supporters.[43] The Christian priest Dálkr's attempted healing treatment at Borg apparently uses a hot spring rather than a steam bath and demonstrates the importance of this resource in Icelandic medical practice:

Guðmundr biskup fór ok vestr af þingi. Með honum var prestr sá, er Dálkr hét; hann kallaðisk vera læknir góðr ok atgerðamaðr at meinum mann. En er Guðmundr biskup gisti at Borg, þá var talat um, hvárt Dálkr mundi nökkut kunna at gera at sjúknaði Hallberu; hon var þá mjök sjúknuð. Dálkr kveðsk kunna at gera henni laug, þá er henni mundi batna við, ef hon fengi staðizk. En hon var fús til heilsunnar, ok vildi hon hætta á laugina. Eptir þat réð prestr til at gera laugina, en hon fór í. Síðan vóru borin at henni klæði; sló þá verkjum fyrir brjóstit ok andaðisk hon litlu síðarr.[44]

Bishop Guðmundr also traveled west after the assembly. With him was a priest named Dálkr, who was said to be a good doctor [*læknir*] and the healer of many men's ailments. And when Bishop Guðmundr was staying at Borg, talk arose about whether Dálkr might be able to do something about Hallbera's sickness; she was then suffering from a great sickness [*sjúknuð*]. Dálkr said that he could prepare a bath [*laugr*] for her, and she would be cured, if she could stand it. But she was eager for a cure, and wanted to try the bath. After that, the priest ordered the bath prepared, and she stepped into it. Then her clothes were brought to her, but pains struck within her breast and she died soon after.

Even with occasional fatalities, sauna and hot bath alike provided a salubrious activity in a world full of aches and disease. It became a prime context for important rites of passage, including birth and death.

Epidemic Disease and Hospitals

While the sauna custom—and frequent recourse to massage and bloodletting (phlebotomy)—represented a strong tradition of health maintenance and preventive medicine among Viking-Age Nordic peoples, the onset and treatment of epidemic disease was met with little else but resignation. Infectious disease was often viewed as the result of arrows shot by supernatural beings (a belief with ancient Greek roots).[45] In Anglo-Saxon as well as Nordic healing traditions, terms like *elfshot* or *stitch* referred to ailments arising from this kind of agent.[46] Classical sources also attributed epidemic disease to corruptions of the air, however, and this theory, too, gained proponents in north European medicine.[47] Imbalance of the four humors—blood, phlegm, yellow bile, and black bile—accounted for many diseases.[48] Biblical sources and exegesis viewed at least some plagues as divine punishment, and the merits of a king could be judged on the frequency of epidemics or famines during his reign.

Whatever its theorized etiology, epidemic disease figures as a constant scourge in the chronicles of England and Ireland from the sixth century onward. The most common pandemics were typhus and relapsing fever, often accompanied by jaundicelike effects.[49] Smallpox and dysentery were also common, the latter sometimes accompanied by bloody discharge. Murrain of cattle and other livestock epidemics were prevalent as well, and human epidemics were often worsened by the combined effects of crop failure and livestock death. Bonser provides a detailed tabulation of major bouts of pestilence in the British Isles from the sixth century through the relatively salubrious reign of King Cnut and into the disastrous era of Edward the Confessor (eleventh century).[50] Some of these epidemics afflicted the Scandinavian colonies in particular, as in the case of a fierce epidemic of leprosy and bloody discharge among the Vikings of Dublin in 949, recurring among the same population in 951. William of Malmesbury reports a major outbreak of *dolor viscerum* (pain of the internal organs—probably dysentery) among the Danish soldiers in Kent in 1010. The *Chronicon Scotorum* records a disease of the legs and plague of rodents among the Scandinavians of Ireland in 1015.[51] The rodents, arriving on the island from Scandinavian boats, soon overran British and Irish ports.

Hospitals provided the urban sick with a measure of comfort and sacraments during their dying days. At times of epidemic, they became cramped with the ill, huddled together with several patients to a single bed with clerics providing what care they could. England had a comparatively well-developed hospital system, with some 21 known hospitals at the time of the Norman invasion (1066) and fully 113 such institutions by end of King Stephen's reign (1154).[52] Figures like St. Sebastian (d. c. 288)—reported in legend to have been both a great healer and the recipient of great healing—became popular throughout Europe, as monarchs, monasteries, and wealthy merchants provided for the founding of hospitals. Henry I's Scottish queen, Edith, became famed for the hospitals, leprosaria, and lavatories she founded. She was also attended by Italian physicians during her first confinement (1101).[53] Medical practitioners from England occasionally traveled to the Continent for further training, especially after the Norman Conquest; there they were able to meet with a growing body of medical knowledge coming from Classical as well as Arabic sources.[54]

In comparison with the British Isles, Scandinavia had little in the way of centralized health care. Epidemics were treated where they occurred, with farms or settlements becoming the dying places of all who fell ill. Both *Eiríks saga rauða* and *Eyrbyggja saga* contain descriptions of farmsteads stricken by protracted epidemic disease. In *Eiríks saga*, Guðríðr and her husband Þorsteinn Eiríksson battle a winter epidemic at their estate in Lysafjörðr, Greenland.[55] The sick lie abed in the main room, while those still in health sit by dutifully, helping them walk out to the outhouse or to prepare for death. In *Eyrbyggja saga*, the sense of dread at the outset of an epidemic is artfully depicted, as members of the household at Fróðá witness an eerie half-moon that appears on the wall by the hearth during the evening hours. Its significance is interpreted by Þórir Viðleggr ("Wooden Leg"), one of the first residents to die:

Þóroddr spurði Þóri viðlegg, hvat þetta myndi boða. Þórir kvað þat vera urðarmána; "mun hér eptir koma manndauðr," segir hann. Þessi tíðendi bar þar við viku alla, at urðarmáni kom inn hvert kveld sem annat.[56]

Þóroddr asked Þórir Wooden-Leg what it boded. Þórir said it was a moon of fate. "People will die here now," he said. This sign continued for the entire week: the moon of fate appeared every evening as before.

Despite this indication, however, neither Þórir nor other farm residents flee the site. By midwinter, the predicted epidemic has taken its toll: of the thirty servants formerly in residence at the farm, eighteen have succumbed to the disease, and five have deserted. The pestilence is portrayed as due to the failure of the farmwife Þuríðr to burn the bedclothes of Þórgunna, an interloper from the Hebrides who is the first to die on the farm.[57] Burning of the deceased's bedstraw was customary throughout Scandinavia, and the direction of the smoke flume could predict the severity of the epidemic among the remaining residents.[58] The circulation of migrants throughout the Viking world and the sustained close contact inherent on farmsteads during the winter made infectious disease an inevitable problem.

Among Sámi, victims of disease were isolated from their communities, their ailments viewed as possible possession by evil spirits (see below). In contrast, Scandinavians, at least with Christianization, appear to have viewed disease in less personified forms, although the onset of an epidemic in particular could reflect the ire of God toward the general populace or its ruler.

Magic Medicine

While the Classical and native pharmacopeia represented one set of treatment options for the ailments of life, magic represented another. Magical medicine—be it the following of meticulous ritual procedures, consultation with a religious specialist, or recitation of charms—appears from all accounts the more common means of treating diseases and maintaining health in body, livestock, and household. Sometimes these methods could be employed singly; often, however, they were accompanied by healing methods which did not appeal to magic powers—for example, medicinal herbs or physical binding or cleaning of a wound. It is difficult at times to draw a distinction between magical acts and those healing treatments that, correctly or incorrectly, appeal to nonsupernatural scientific verities of the day.[59]

Among Finno-Ugric peoples, the shaman (Sámi *noaide*, Finnish *noita*, later *tietäjä*) played a pivotal role in the diagnosis and magical control of disease. Hultkrantz points to healing as the most common shamanic activity cross-culturally, and it appears that Finno-Ugric shamanism was no exception in this respect.[60] Among Viking-Age Finns and Sámi, the healer's role was clearly important, as shamans battled against instances of either soul loss (when the patient's soul became stranded in some otherworld) or soul intrusion (in which a foreign soul invaded the patient's body). Ecstatic trance and the accompanying spirit journeys narrated by the shaman upon his return allowed the shaman to rescue souls, discover the etiology of a disease, or find out details useful in controlling an entity's activities (e.g., its secret name or origin). At least some of the charms collected from later generations (see below) may owe their composition to these important early healers. The twelfth-century *Historia Norwegiae* contains the first written account of a Finno-Ugric shamanic healing session, in which two shamans attempt to revive a woman who lies catatonic, apparently from soul loss.[61]

Siikala sees continuities between oral epic representations and Finnish folk healers of the seventeenth, eighteenth, and nineteenth centuries, who used a combination of charms, sauna, massage, and ecstatic trance to treat various ailments.[62] Court records from a Finnish witchcraft trial of 1678 depict the healer subjecting his patient to frequent sauna baths (seven or eight times a day), recitation of Christian prayers, and performance of non-Christian charms. The healer diagnosed the disease by casting lots and eventually transferred the spirit of the disease into a wooden object which he later bound to a tree and abandoned in the forest.[63] We can note strong continuities between this early description of the healer's magical art and later observations made during the nineteenth and early twentieth centuries throughout Scandinavia.[64]

The vulnerability of humans in relation to harmful spirits, typical of Finno-Ugric religion in general, is illustrated in many of the materials collected from Finns and Sámi in recent centuries.[65] Finno-Ugric gods of disease like the Sámi Ruto or Finnish Loviatar required sacrifices, appeasement, or forceful banishment through charms in order to be controlled. Spirit intrusion served as the prime metaphor for infection by disease. Eighteenth-century records of Sámi views of smallpox show that Sámi refrained from speaking around people with the disease, lest the dangerous male spirit of the disease (known as *sueje*) take an interest and plague them as well.[66] Even at the turn of the twentieth century, such views persisted among traditional Sámi.[67] According to the Sámi writers Johan and Per Turi, breathing in the odor of a dead body, too, could bring on fatal illness within two years of the mishap. Men could even be infected by pregnancy cravings (*vuosmes*) if they ate from the same bowl as a pregnant woman without first knowing of her condition.[68] The Finnish custom of confining the ill to the sauna reflects a view toward disease similar to that of the Sámi.

A further important element in Finno-Ugric conceptions of disease and healing was the notion of inherent power, known as *väki* in Finnish.[69] *Väki* resided in objects or entities in relation to their cosmic significance: thus, for instance, bears, fire, or iron contained heavy charges of *väki*, reflecting their mythological importance and physical ability to wound or do harm. *Väki* was not stored in the core of a being: in fact, even a small piece of the being (such as a bear's claw or a bit of wolf's fur) possessed a share of the power inherent in the animal from which it derived. This property of physical matter made it useful for the curing of diseases and the magical manipulation of objects otherwise too powerful for human control. Principles similar to *väki* appear to underlie at least some of the magic uses of objects described in Scandinavian and Anglo-Saxon magic as well.

Also crucial to northern European magic healing with the concept of transference, by which disease could be transferred from a patient to some disposable or distant object.[70] Trees were common recipients of transference throughout Europe; their use in medieval England is deplored in the *Canones Edgari*, where several forms of disease transference are singled out for castigation: "tree worship and stone worship and that devil's art in which children are drawn through the earth."[71] The closely related custom of *smörjning*—drawing a sick child through an opening in a known "healing tree"—persisted as a practice of folk medicine in many parts of Scandinavia into the turn of the twentieth century, and trees were used extensively in the magical healing of Finland.[72]

Charms

Word magic—the use of powerful incantations—played a central role in Nordic magical healing. The oldest extant text of a Finnish charm, written in Cyrillic characters on a piece of birch bark in Novgorod, dates from the mid-thirteenth century. It appears addressed to lightning, although it incorporates the Russian word for the Christian God (*Bog*):

> Jumolanuoli 10 nimiźi
> noulisëhanoliomobou
> ioumola soud'niiohovi.

> Arrow of God—ten are your names.
> The arrow—it verily belonged to God.
> God will guide my fate.[73]

Here, the importance of naming the deity is coupled with assertions of his assured good will toward the human user of the charm. The formula appears crafted to convince the powerful supernatural listener of the close and faithful relation which obtains between the deity and his follower on earth. Using this same divine friendship as a base, the second oldest recorded charm in Finnish—a formula jotted in the account register for the royal estate at Korsholm, Sweden, in 1564—aggressively banishes the offending ailment:

> Benedicite Dominus
> Tyydy sille kuin sinä ottanut olet
> anna jäädä jotka sinä jättänyt olet
> pyhän hengen väki olkohon minun kanssa.
> Kaikki tuskat, kaikki vaivat
> mene Ruskian kallion rakoon
> kuin sinäkin tullut olet.[74]

God bless
be content as you have taken
let things stay as you have left them
may the force of the Holy Spirit be with me.
All pains, all troubles
go into a hole in Ruskia rock
from which you also emerged.

The overall form and content of these charms finds close parallels throughout northern Europe. Grendon's early characterization of the recurrent elements in Anglo-Saxon charms may describe the whole. He identifies ten frequent elements, the first five of which pertain to the form of the charm itself: it may contain an epic portion, an appeal to a superior spirit, the enunciation or writing of potent names or letters, the listing of ways to bind or dispose of the offending ailment, and the performer's boast of power over the enemy.[75]

The ninth-century second Old High German Merseburg charm illustrates the ways in which the epic portion could function in pagan Germanic practice:

Phoelnde uuodan   uuorun zi holza
du uuart demo balderes uolon   sin uuoz birenkit
thu beguolen sinthgut   sunna era suister
thu biguolen friia   uolla era suister
thu biguoleb uuodan   so he uuola conda
sose benrenki   sose bluotrenki
sose lidirenki
ben zi bena   bluot zi bluoda
lid zi geliden   sose gelimida sin.[76]

Phol and Wotan   rode through the forest.
There the steed of Baldr   sprained his leg.
That was charmed by Sinthgut,   [and] her sister Sunna;
that was charmed by Freyja,   [and] her sister Volla;
That was charmed by Wotan,   as he well could:
So bone ailments   as blood ailments
as limb ailments:
bone to bone,   blood to blood,
limb to limb   fuse as by glue.

The first five lines of the text recount the story of how Wotan (the continental Germanic counterpart of Óðinn) healed a sprained leg on Baldr's horse. After goddesses fail to cure the ailment, Wotan accomplishes the task handily. By reminding the god of his past benevolence and success, the performer or owner of the charm seeks to spur him toward a similar action in the present.[77] The subsequent lines in the charm may represent a quotation of the god's own healing words or a summary of their effects. In any case, the implication is that the deity may be more likely to act if he knows that his services in past have been acknowledged. Similar strategies are followed in Christian charms addressed to Christ and Mary. While some charms cajole higher allies, others chide, threaten, or bully porported subservients, particularly personified diseases.

The power of words could become extended easily to orthography. In the Eddaic poem *Sigrdrífomál*, the valkyrie Sigrdrífa explains the use of runes as healing implements. Three examples from her catalog of useful charms illustrate the uses of writing in Viking magic:

> Sigrúnar þú scalt kunna,   ef þú vilt sigr hafa,
>   oc rísta á hialti hiörs,
> sumar á véttrimom,   sumar á valböstom,
>   oc nefna tysvar Tý.

> Ölrúnar scaltu kunna,   ef þú vill, annars qvæn
>   vélit þic í trygð, ef þú trúir;
> á horni scal þær rísta   oc á handar baki
>   oc merkia á nagli Nauð.

> Limrúnar scaltu kunna,   ef þú vilt læcnir vera
>   oc kunna sár at siá;
> á berki scal þær rísta   oc á baðmi viðar,
>   þeim er lúta austr limar.[78]

> I shall teach you   the runes of triumph
> to have on the hilt of your sword—
> some on the blade,   some on the guard;
> then call twice on Týr.

> Ale-runes you will want   if another man's wife
> tries to betray your trust;

scratch them on your drinking horn,   the back of your hand,
and the need-rune on your nail.

Here are the limb-wounds   that heal the sick
and close the worst of wounds;
write them on the bark of a forest tree
with eastward-bending branches.[79]

The very letters for sounds had acquired names, so that, for instance, the sound *t* was expressed by an arrow-shaped letter that was named for the god of war, Týr. So, too, the sound *n* was expressed through the rune called *nauð* (need), which related to a crucial state of being in the economy of magic. With great conciseness, then, each rune could represent not only its sound but also the entity for which it was named, rendering the runes both phonemic markers and idiographs. Later in the same poem, the valkyrie enumerates the many places where runes could be written, including the bodies of mythological beings and animals. Scraped off into mead, they became potent healing elixirs:

Á scildi qvað ristnar,   þeim er stendr fyr scínanda goði,
á eyra Árvacrs   oc á Alsvinnz hófi,
á því hvéli, er snýz   undir reið Rungnis,
á Sleipnis tönnom   oc á sleða fiötrom,
á biarnar hrammi   oc á Braga tungo,
á úlfs klóm   oc á arnar nefi,
á blóðgom vængiom   oc á brúar sporði,
á lausnar lófa   oc á lícnar spori,
á gleri oc á gulli   oc á gumna heillom,
í víni oc virtri   oc vilisessi,
á Gungnis oddi   oc á Grana briósti,
á nornar nagli   oc á nefi uglo.[80]

On the shield that stands before the shining god,
on Árvakr's ear   and Alsvinn's hoof,
on a wheel revolving   under Hrungnir's chariot,
on Sleipnir's teeth,   on scraps of a sled,
on a bear's paw,   on Bragi's tongue,
on the claws of a wolf   and an eagle's beak,
on bloody wings   and a bridge's head,

on a midwife's hand,   on the footprints of help,
on glass, on gold,   on good-luck charms,
in wine, in beer,   on the wished-for chair,
on Gungnir's point   and Grani's breast,
the nail of a Norn,   a night-owl's beak.[81]

In *Egils saga*, Egill Skalla-Grímsson cures a woman of a wasting sickness that has plagued her for some time. In an earlier attempt to cure her, a local farmer's son has carved runes on a piece of whale bone and laid it under her as she slept. Egill inspects the runes and recognizes them as crudely and improperly executed. He scrapes them off into the fire (presumably erasing their potency) and reinscribes them artfully, placing the new inscription beneath the woman's pillow. In the morning, her recovery has begun and Egill receives the grateful thanks of the household.[82]

This same extension of word magic to writing finds parallels in Anglo-Saxon charms, in which prestigious ecclesiastical language often figures as the script of power. In a remedy for an anemic condition reminiscent of that suffered by Egill's patient, *Bald's Leechbook* recommends the writing of a long prayerlike formula in Latin.[83] The prayer is then steeped in a medicinal drink made of herbs and holy water. A remedy for bleeding recounted in the *Leechbook* prescribes another written charm:

Sume þis writað: + ægryn • thon • struth • fola arȝrenn • tart • struth • on • tria • enn • piath • hathu • morfana • on hæl + ara • carn • leou • ȝroth • weorn ℍ • ffil • crondi • w • [X] • mro • cron • ærcrio • ermio • aeR • leNo • ȝe horse ȝe men blod seten.

Some write this: . . . to stanch the blood of either horse or man.[84]

Although we do not know where the Anglo-Saxon healer wrote this, or what he understood these words to mean, the same principle underlies this cure as those of the Eddaic poems: it is the act of writing itself, of linguistically encapsulating an entity in a web of efficacious, divinely inspired words, which accomplishes the healer's task. In the Anglo-Saxon charms, the tendency to reproduce magic words in their original language—be it Latin, Greek, Irish, or a mixture of dubious syllables (labeled "Hesperic" by later scholars) reflects notions of exactness common in magical thought.[85] At the same time, the linguistic fidelity of the charms affords us an interesting look at the intercultural diffusion of magic formulas in medieval northern Europe. The concept of an ailment as a separable spiritual entity underlies all such methods.

Within the corpus of charms presented in various sources, it is difficult to distinguish between procedures intended to cure specific physical ailments (what westerners today might define as medicine) and broader attempts to maintain or regain luck. Good fortune in life figures as an overarching category, in the context of which the maintenance or loss of health is merely a symptom of the broader state of affairs. If one loses luck, one's cattle or kidneys may fail; if one maintains luck, all aspects of one's life will proceed smoothly. Thus *Bald's Leechbook* can present not only cures for sore eyes, but also procedures for assuring success in a long journey: one must collect a sprig of mugwort (*Artemisia vulgaris*) before sunrise, sign it with the cross, and address it with a Latin charm. The sprig is then placed inside one's shoe for magical effect.[86] The same text recommends a drink made of baby swallows or sand martins (*Hirundines vipariae*) steeped in wine for the man wishing success in battle.[87] That these cures are included in a compendium of medicinal remedies reflects an undifferentiated, flowing concept of illness and its control: illness is largely an instance of ill luck.

Although actual charm texts dating from the Viking Age are few, several Old Norse poems from the period present striking portrayals of charm use. One such work is *Oddrúnargrátr*, which depicts a midwife chanting incantations in her assistance of a woman in labor.[88] *Grogaldr*, a narrative poem depicting a young man's consultation with his dead mother to obtain her store of charms, offers a catalog of some nine incantations, although none of the charms themselves are included in the text.[89] Similar catalogs occur in both *Hávamál* and *Sigrdrífomál* as well.[90] These allow us to examine the conceptualizations of overall health as reflected in the choice and use of magic charms.

The latter three Eddaic poems mentioned above each presents a list of charms offered by a supernatural entity to an adherent. In *Grogaldr*, a deceased woman passes on her knowledge to her son; in *Hávamál*, the source of wisdom appears to be Óðinn; and in *Sigrdrífomál*, an Óðinnic valkyrie proffers her wisdom to the hero Sigurðr. Although the actual charms are not revealed, the poems make explicit reference to their use and effectiveness.

Of the thirty-five charms listed in the three poems, only four refer specifically to healing in the narrow sense. These address healing in general, treatment of aches and pains (frostbite), midwifery, and limb healing (treatment of fractures and breaks).[91] *Hávamál's* first charm—a general formula for people in sorrow or need—may also refer in part to healing illness.[92] Of the remaining charms, ten confer success in battle[93] and fully nine aid the user in social interactions, amorous and otherwise.[94] One such charm—

that for guarding against the effects of poisoned ale served by an ill-willed hostess—combines notions of medieval healing (e.g., counteracting poison through use of a leek) with the maintenance of favorable social relations.[95] Of the remaining charms, five refer to dealings with supernatural beings (giants, witches, the dead, elves, Æsir, dwarfs),[96] four are useful for calming waters,[97] and one is useful in putting out fires.[98] This survey shows that the healing of ailments represented only one of the tasks for which magic was used in Viking-Age Scandinavia, figuring in only about 14 percent of the cataloged charms. Luck in battle represents a more pressing goal (roughly 28 percent), and manipulation of social relations also takes a greater share (26 percent). Supernatural beings figure in some way in 14 percent of the charms, while the remaining 14 percent provide assistance with the practical needs of everyday life.

Childbirth

In Nordic midwifery practices, we see the merger of magic and physical treatments, as well as the uniting of Classical and native lore that we might expect on the basis of the above discussion. It is thus useful to examine this healing context in detail as an illustrative aside. Although a number of studies examine aspects of Scandinavian childbirth in detail, a more generalized Nordic overview is useful.[99]

Sámi culture is distinctive in the North for its preservation of a distinct deity of childbirth, the household goddess Sáráhkká, who also functioned as the spiritual guardian of female fetuses and of menstruation (see Chapter 3). The closest parallel in Scandinavian mythology is the goddess Eir, whom Snorri describes in passing as a healer of great accomplishment.[100] The Eddaic poems *Oddrúnagrátr* and *Sigrdrífomál* also make reference to appeals to Freyja, Frigg, and dísir in connection with childbirth.[101] Finnish charms mention some spirits related to birth, but tend to rely on the Virgin Mary. Sáráhkká's important roles in women's experiences led to her retention well into the Christian period, during which she became associated closely with both Mary and with a St. Sara, who seems to represent a Christianization of the deity. Sáráhkká's longevity as a recipient of entreaties reflects both the importance of her duties in the eyes of Sámi women and the lack of competing figures or customs in the Christianity that the Sámi adopted. In fact, since Christianity retained few if any of the Judaic rituals associated with women's physical experiences (e.g., the postmenstrual purification ceremony known as *mikva'ot*), the new religion offered little competition in the areas of childbirth and women's health.[102]

Some aspects of more generalized Nordic childbirth traditions reflect Classical origins, however, and must have diffused into the region along with Christianity. The injunction against crossing or knotting in the presence of a woman in labor—a piece of sympathetic magic seeking to create an environment of looseness and ease for the emerging infant—finds a Classical source in Ovid's account of the birth of Hercules. The tradition of loosening ties of all kinds—uncrossing arms, unbraiding hair, and so on—remained a standard part of folk midwifery in the Nordic region into the twentieth century.

This assimilation of continental and Christian elements is sometimes difficult to recognize, as in the Eddaic poem *Oddrúnargrátr*. Here, the noblewoman Oddrún is depicted using charms in her attempts to ease the difficult labor of Borgný:

> ríct gól Oddrún,   ramt gól Oddrún,
> bitra galdra,   at Borgnýio.[103]

> mightily chanted Oddrún,   magically chanted Oddrún,
> powerful charms   for Borgný.

Borgný, in turn, invokes a blessing from spirits, the goddesses Frigg and Freyja and other gods as well, upon Oddrún once she has been delivered of her twins:

> Svá hjálpi þér   hollar vættir,
> Frigg oc Freija   oc fleiri goð,
> sem þú feldir mér   fár af höndum.[104]

> So may the holy spirits help you,
> Frigg and Freyja   and other gods,
> as you delivered me   from near death.

On the other hand, Borgný's difficulty in bearing her twins is attributed to their illegitimacy, a concept with strong Christian overtones. So, too, Oddrún's vow of indiscriminant service to all in need recalls Alcuin's words on love for one's neighbor in *De virtutibus et vitiis liber*, a text contained in an early Norwegian homily book as well as in other Christian texts of the conversion era.[105] Such altruism, indeed, contrasts with the clan-based system of loyalty and duty associated with pagan practice and so strongly reflected in the sagas.

Whatever the case regarding these possibly Christian details of the poem, however, the use of charms in childbirth is substantiated further by references in *Sigdrífomál* (see above) as well as by later Sámi, Finnish, and Scandinavian charms. While many of these later formulas appeal to the Virgin Mary for assistance, they may also address pagan spirits such as the Finnish goddess of death and disease, Loviatar. Still others contain an epic account of a small man who rose from the sea to open the closed doors of the mother's cervix. Even in the most seemingly non-Christian of these charms, Mary may be invoked at the end. Finnish charms collected at the outset of the nineteenth century combine direct appeal to Mary with vivid descriptions of the saint bursting through the door of the mother's cervix, freeing the infant to slip easily into sight.[106]

Johan and Per Turi (1918–19) provide a detailed description of childbirth practices among traditional Sámi women of the turn of the twentieth century. The Turis' account reminds us of the fact that no aspects of culture are completely universal. While most Nordic women gave birth *à la vache* (on all fours), or with the ubiquitous birthing stool of Nordic farmsteads, Sámi women were kept on their feet or at least in an upright kneeling position.[107] The Turis write that when the woman's strength failed, she was urged to hold onto a rope strung between tent poles. Failing that, the attending women endeavored to maintain her in a standing position, maximizing gravitational pull as the infant proceeded down the birth canal. If the infant's progress was impeded in the uterus, the mother was placed on a blanket and inverted to allow the child to turn. These remarks remind us of the wealth of specific practical knowledge that healers possessed, little of which remains available to us in written records.

Witchcraft

The same powers which made the healer a valued adversary against disease could lead to acts of supernatural aggression. Demonization of magical practices after Christianization affects our ability to discern pagan views of negative magic, especially following the publication of the seminal *Malleus maleficarum* (1486) and the violent witchcraft trials it spurred or reflected throughout Europe.[108] Although sixteenth- and seventeenth-century opponents of witchcraft saw its rise as a recent and pressing threat to Christianity, the phenomenon had become recognized and discussed in both official and unofficial arenas of the Church already in the twelfth century.[109] Outright condemnation of all magic, including that intended to cure, had been declared already in St. Augustine's *De doctrina christiana* (c. 396–427).[110] From the evidence available to us from textual and oral sources, it appears likely that pagans, like Christians, recognized and feared the human use of supernatural forces for the accomplishment of evil.

In his *Historia de gentibus septentrionalibus* (1555), bishop Olaus Magnus describes the magic activities of Sámi and Finns. After a close description of divinatory trance, the learned bishop gives an account of malevolent sending of disease among the denizens of Bothnia:

Nec minoris efficaciæ perhibentur in hominibus diversa ægritudine prosternendis. Faciunt nanque de plumbo iacula magica brevia ad modum digiti: ea emittunt per quæuis dissita loca in eos, de quibus vindictam expetunt. Hi oborto carcinomate à crure, vel brachio intra triduum vehementia doloris exanimantur.[111]

They are also said to be no less potent in destroying men with various sicknesses; for they make short magic darts of lead, about the length of a finger, and launch them over any distance they like against folk they seek vengeance on. These, infected by a cancerous growth in the leg or arm, die within three days in agonizing pain.[112]

This description of mortifying darts finds parallels in Anglo-Saxon as well as Nordic witchlore and medicine.[113] An Anglo-Saxon charm for curing a sudden onset of pain cites human witches as one of several possible sources of such arrows.[114]

The use of *seiðr* to cause psychological restlessness will be discussed in Chapter 6. This distinctive dis-ease of mind appears characteristic of malevolent magic in general, leading otherwise safe heroes into dangerous situations against their conscious wills. In *Eyrbyggja saga*, however, we find a further account of a witch using her powers to harm an enemy.[115] At the farmsteads of Mávahlíð and Holt, mature farmwives figure as practitioners of magic arts. At Fróðá, on the other hand, the young Gunnlaugr Þorbjarnarson—object of the desires of both purported witches—turns up badly scratched and maddened one morning after having visited both women's farmsteads. His wounds reach to the bone and are universally recognized as the work of witchcraft. Such accusations of witchcraft are far more common in the family sagas of the early thirteenth century than in the Sturlunga sagas of the late thirteenth century, a shift which may reflect either the decline of magic in the face of overall Christianization or structural changes in the relations between chieftains and their followers over the course of the century.[116] Legends of shamanlike witches persisted in Iceland into recent times, however.[117]

From the sources left to us, it appears clear that magic had both a positive and a negative potential in Nordic society. Because it gave people access over an otherwise unpredictable and precious commodity—personal good fortune, both in terms of events and in bodily health—magic was seen as a powerful tool. In a world of limited resources and unequal justice, its power could balance the scales in the favor of the weak or disfavored. Nonetheless, its divisive and manipulative nature, coupled with its strong demonization in the Christian era, made it a problematic tradition by the time of the sagas. The extent of its importance, however, was such that even persons consciously opposed to magic of all kinds appear to have accepted certain magic procedures in daily life, as the Anglo-Saxon charms indicate.

Christianity and Magic Healing

One way that magic continued to play a part in the management of health and disease was through Christianization of the charm tradition itself. Many of the charms included in the Anglo-Saxon medical texts derive from Latin or Greek prayers, and Nordic peoples added or substituted the Christian God, saints, and narratives into the charm texts they performed. The examples provided in the preceding sections illustrate this process amply, but it may be useful to mention a further example to underscore the point. In his introduction to Cockayne's anthology of Anglo-Saxon charms, Singer points out the liturgical basis of one of the more inscrutable "Hesperic" charms for nosebleeds. After smearing some of the blood on the patient's forehead (in the sign of the cross), the healer writes the following words: "Stomen calcos. Stomen meta fofu." Although these words make no sense in Old English or in Latin, they represent a rendering of a line from the Greek Mass of St. John Chrysostom, a figure closely linked to the cult of the Holy Cross (see Chapter 7). In Singer's reading, the *co* of *calcos* actually represents the Greek letter ω, while *fofu* represents the Greek *phobou*. The corresponding phrase in Greek would thus read "Let us stand properly; let us stand in awe," and occurs in the Greek liturgy immediately before the solemn elevation of the Host. It is, then, a perfect call to attention and stasis for the running blood. Tellingly, the same line serves as a blood-stanching charm in Greece today.[118] Yet it is difficult to say whether this liturgical allusion was anything more than a mysterious formula for the Anglo-Saxon cleric who recorded it at the beginning of the twelfth century in distant England. In any case, if the same charm reached the hands of a less educated healer, its ecclesiastical flavor would soon have been lost. Yet the Christian root of the charm text itself remains intact, to be rediscovered by scholars examining the texts centuries later.

The remedy for anemic conditions contained in *Bald's Leechbook* illustrates the variety of Christian liturgical elements which could be brought to bear upon a disease.[119] The Latin charm is written in the form of a prayer with invocations to God the Father, Jesus, and holy scripture. The written text is steeped in water from a baptismal font, mixed with healing herbs. Signs of the Cross are made on the patient's limbs with the chrism used in the last rites and in baptism, and the ritual calls for a liturgical refrain, *Pax tibi*, reminiscent of the Mass. Other central prayers are called for as well, particularly the Credo and Pater Noster. The treatment, although presented in the *Leechbook* as a remedy for a specific ailment, is recommended in closing in broader terms: "[T]his craft works against every temptation of the demon."[120] It is hard in this case to imagine a healer who did not recognize his procedure as absolutely dependent on Christian symbolism and the healing powers of the Christian faith.

Notwithstanding this powerful Christianization, however, Church authorities often took a dim view of healing through charms and other magic. St. Bede describes the efforts of the seventh-century St. Cuthbert to prevent the newly Christianized Northumbrians from reverting to magical medicine during times of epidemic. Bede writes: "[A]t the time of the pestilence, forgetting the sacred mystery of the faith into which they had been initiated, they took to the delusive cures of idolatry, as though by incantations or amulets or any other mysteries of devilish art they could ward off a blow sent by God the Creator."[121] Thus it is not surprising that the early Christian law tracts of Scandinavia explicitly forbid recourse to the old healing traditions. In the elder *Gulaþingslög*, traditionally credited to King Hákon the Good's era (933–59) and in force until revised in 1267, prophecy (*spá*), charms (*galdra*), and sacrifice (*blót*) are explicitly grouped together and roundly forbidden.[122] Church law at times even forbade all practice of medicine by its clerics: a synod at Ratisbon in 877 prohibited priests from studying medicine, and this prohibition was repeated at the Council of Rheims in 1131 and at the Lateran Council of 1139.[123]

While Christianization brought with it strong pressures to abandon older magical practices, Sámi practitioners, and other Nordic communities further away from the eye of bishop or monarch, appear to have maintained these practices unabated. At times, in fact, Christian community members appear to have availed themselves of this alternative source of healing, consulting with pagan magic practitioners when in need. Such is the case with *seiðr*, as discussed in Chapter 6. This practice is also evident in the account of Eyvindr in *Óláfs saga Tryggvasonar*, quoted at the outset of this study.[124] Here, the pagan Scandinavian Eyvindr refuses to undergo baptism because he was conceived only after his parents resorted to the magic assistance of a Sámi or Finnish healer. Apparently, with his very conception a product of pagan magic, Eyvindr is unwilling or unable to accept the Christian faith.

In the Christian view, magic charms offered healing at the cost of damage to one's soul. But healing could also be accomplished through positive supernatural forces in consonance with the Christian faith, as when contact with a saint's relics or prayer to God or an intercessor resulted in miraculous cures. Indeed, as discussed in Chapter 4, the cult of the saints had become an importance source of healing by the Viking Age, extolled already by Augustine and Gregory and transformed into a lively system of pilgrimage sites and relics by the thirteenth century. The cult of the saints developed quickly in the North and Scandinavians soon came in contact with myriad accounts of miraculous healings at springs, cathedrals, or graves. The existence of demonic magic as well as divine assistance made discernment of true miracles problematic, however, and led to the development of a complex system for authenticating true miracles and the intercessors responsible. Pilgrimage to the sites of verified miracles became an ubiquitous part of medieval life and a central means of healing: an afflicted person might go to numerous domestic or foreign shrines before obtaining the hoped-for cure.

As the cult of the saints grew and diversified, particular saints became known for their healing capabilities or sympathies toward persons with particular diseases. St. Cuthbert himself, while fighting against Northumbrian backsliding into magical healing, performed several miraculous cures during his life with consecrated oil, blessings, and prayer. His relics became important in later healing and were carefully guarded from pagan invasions.[125] The bones of the Anglo-Saxon St. Milburga (d. 715), rediscovered in 1101, were said to cure leprosy.[126] King St. Óláfr's first miracle, recounted in *Óláfs saga Helga*, appears to his contemporaries at first a simple instance of Christianized magic healing: the king combines massage with pieces of bread laid out in the shape of the Cross and then fed singly to the patient (see Chapter 7).[127] After the king's death, however, this instance of healing became recognized as a divine manifestation of Óláfr's sanctity. The same saga recounts the miraculous healing of a hand wound touched by Óláfr's blood, the curing of a man long blind through similar contact with the holy blood, and the curing of many ills through contact with water from a spring beside Óláfr's resting place.[128] The miracles attributed to Bishop Jón Ögmundarson (bishop of Hólar, 1106–21) after his death recall the typical categorization of health and disease noted in Anglo-Saxon and magic medicine: the saint is credited with cures of bodily aches and pains (e.g., toothache, insomnia, hacking cough), acute ailments (fractures and hand injuries), and congenital disorders (crippled legs).[129] Only the last of these categories—reminiscent of Christ's healing of paralytics and others with congenital defects—stands out as distinct from the usual healing repertoire of the *medicus*. In fact, as Koppenberg points out, such corporeal cures far outnumber the explicitly spiritual miracles credited the saint.[130] Such tendencies are typical of medieval saint's legends in general and illustrate the congruity of this kind of healing with the concepts of overall good fortune and health discussed above. In summarizing the miracles attributed to the new saint, Óláfr, Snorri provides a characterization that might as easily describe the healing repertoire of the medical physician:

Vetr þann hófsk umrœða sú af mörgum mönnum þar í Þrándheimi, at Óláfr konungr væri maðr sannheilagr ok jartegnir margar yrði at helgi hans. Hófu þá margir áheit til Óláfs konungs um þá hluti, er mönnum þótti máli skipta. Fengu margir menn af þeim áheitum bót, sumir heilsubœtr, en sumir fararbeina eða aðra þá hluti, er nauðsyn þótti til bera.[131]

That winter, many men in Trondheim began saying that King Óláfr had been a saintly man and many signs of his sanctity appeared. Many raised their prayers to King Óláfr about those things which seemed most important to them. Many people's prayers were answered: prayers for health, or successful journeys, or other things which seemed necessary.

Clearly, Christian healing continued in part the conceptualizations of good fortune and its maintenance central to Nordic magical thought.

If we take seriously Luckert's definition of religion, presented at the outset of this study as "man's response to so-conceived greater-than-human configurations of reality," then the phenomena described in this chapter fit perfectly into the framework of religion.[132] Among the Nordic peoples of the Viking Age, neither health nor disease were seen as less-than-human entities, to be managed, controlled, or forgotten. Rather, people sought the aid of greater-than-human allies—deities, intercessors—and made use of specialized procedures—therapy, rituals, magic, prayer—to try to secure for themselves and their communities some measure of good fortune, a commodity sensible in large measure by the concomitant or resultant lack of illness. Human ailments—aches, diseases, fractures, psychological trauma— were indications of misalignments on the supernatural plane, problems which could be healed by a combination of physical and spiritual treat- ments. While the Church grappled with the difficult philosophical issues of the meaning of misfortune, its significance in the eyes of ordinary people, pagan and Christian alike, appeared clear. And the healer, whether lay, cleric, monarch, foreign, or canonized, offered means for addressing the vexing supernatural problems that found somatic expression in illness. In a world of staggering epidemics, hand-to-hand combat, and hard manual labor, the healing traditions of the Nordic Viking Age provided a link between the needs of the human community and the powers that lay beyond.

SIX

The Intercultural Dimensions of the Seiðr Ritual

The previous chapter demonstrates how a focus on a given human issue—health, for example—allows for the comparison of religious traditions. In the Viking Age, certain commonalities of worldview among Nordic cults found expression in similar approaches to healing. This common worldview in turn encouraged the borrowing evident in Nordic healing traditions over time, borrowing that occurred even when religious leaders consciously opposed all such potentially heretical acts.

The current chapter focuses not on an issue of universal human significance but on a distinctive religious ritual known in the sagas by the ambiguous title *seiðr* (see Glossary).[1] By examining the circulation of this ritual tradition among the various pagan communities of the pre-Christian North, we can observe more closely dynamic processes of syncresis in a context in which borrowing was not only tolerated but seemingly embraced. An examination of seiðr shows us both the extent of intercultural exchange in the pre-Christian North and the complexities of religious fusion involved in the assimilation of a new religious tradition. As we shall see in Chapter 7, the syncretic tendencies of Nordic religions offered a substantive challenge to the Christianizers of the era.

Defining Ritual

Before proceeding to our examination of seiðr, however, it is important to specify what we mean by *ritual*. Along with *myth* and the very definition of religion itself, this term has attracted considerable theoretical debate. Its notoriety arises partly because of the variety of actions it denotes and partly because of the crucial nature of ritual in the workings of religion. In the following discussion, I follow Zuesse's now largely accepted definition of ritual as "those conscious and voluntary, repetitious and stylized, symbolic bodily actions that are centered on cosmic structures and/or sacred purposes. (Verbal behavior such as chant, song, and prayer are of course included in the category of bodily actions.)"[2] Ritual is an enacted communication that may be intercepted or shared by other humans but that is directed primarily toward an efficacious god or intermediary. It can record, reenact, even reactivate an earlier act of communication in the here and now, drawing on a symbolic idiom established during a seminal communication in the past. It can persuade its supernatural audience to act favorably toward the human community.

Seiðr is only one of a variety of rituals depicted in the sagas, standing alongside such efficacious acts as baptism (both a Christian and a pagan variety are mentioned), funerals, sanctifications of land or temples, oath taking, the Christian mass, and the mysterious midwinter sacrifices (*blót*) associated with the pagan household and its spirits. Some of these are accomplished by religious specialists—chieftains or priests, for example. Others are enacted by heads of households (male or female) or even ordinary individuals. They may be undertaken in response to moments of the lifecycle (birth, death), the passage of the seasonal cycle, or situations of crisis. Occasionally, pagan rituals are described in detail, as in Ibn Fadhlan's famed account of a Viking funeral on the Volga (see Chapter 4) or the explicit portrayals of seiðr discussed below. Often, however, they are merely sketched in the sagas: tantalizing hints at a system of religious thought and symbolism that can only be guessed at today. In many cases, the rituals were probably mysterious to the writers of the sagas themselves, who may have learned of them from textual accounts or hearsay reports.

Within this array of pagan rituals, seiðr appears to respond primarily to situations of crisis and is undertaken by a religious specialist (usually a woman) at the request of a client and within the context of a communal gathering. The ritual appeals to some sort of spirit helpers, either for divinatory information or help in controlling the minds and wills of others. Typical is the detailed account included in the thirteenth-century *Eiríks saga rauða*, in which an itinerant seiðr practitioner named Þorbiörg is invited to a Greenland farmstead to help the community discover whether its current run of ill luck will continue. As the saga writer recounts:

Þat var háttr Þorbjargar um vetrum, at hon fór at veizlum, ok buðu þeir menn henni mest heim, er forvitni var á at vita forlög sín eða árferð; ok með því at Þorkell var þar mestr bóndi, þá þótti til hans koma at vita nær létta mundi óárnai þessu, sem yfir stóð. Býðr Þorkell spákonunni heim, ok er henni þar vel fagnat sem siðr var til, þá er við þess háttar konum skyldi taka.[3]

It was Þorbiörg's practice of a winter to attend feasts, and those men in particular invited her to their homes who were curious to know their fate or the season's prospects. Because Þorkell was the leading householder there it was thought to be his responsibility to find out when these hard times which now troubled them would cease, so he invited her to his home, and a good reception was prepared for her, as was the custom when a woman of this kind should be received.[4]

Clear norms of decorum operate in this exchange between community, leading householder, and seiðr practitioner. Þorbiörg is fed a meal including a ceremonial food made from different animals' hearts and she is treated in a dignified, if not exceedingly warm manner. Her elaborate garb is described in near-touristic detail:

þá var hon svá búin, at hon hafði yfir sér tuglamöttul blán, ok var settr steinum allt í skaut ofan. Hon hafði á hálsi sér glertölur ok lambskinnskofra svartan á höfði ok við innan kattskinn hvít; ok hon hafði staf í hendi, ok var á knappr; hann var búinn með mersingu ok settr steinum ofan um knappinn. Hon hafði um sik hnjóskulinda ok var þar á skjóðupungr mikill, ok varðveiti hon þar í töfr sín, þau er hon þurfti til fróðleiks at hafa. Hon hafði á fótum kálfskinnsskúa loðna ok í vengi langa ok á tinknappar miklir á endunum. Hon hafði á höndum sér kattskinnsglófa, ok váru hvítir innan ok loðnir.[5]

[T]his is how she was attired: she was wearing a blue cloak with straps which was set with stones right down to the hem; she had glass beads about her neck, and on her head a black lambskin hood lined inside with white catskin. She had a staff in her hand, with a knob on it; it was ornamented with brass and set around with stones just below the knob. Round her middle she wore a belt of touchwood, and on it was a big skin pouch in which she kept those charms of hers which she needed for her magic. On her feet she had hairy calf-skin shoes with long thongs, and on the thong-ends big knobs of lateen. She had on her hands catskin gloves which were white inside and hairy.[6]

The saga's details here link the portrayal to Sámi and Balto-Finn shamanic traditions, as we shall see below. We may also note, however, the simple exoticism of everything associated with Þorbiörg: she is clearly distinguished from the other women present at the farmstead, and the details of her dress underscore her alterity.

After a customary exchange of hospitality (a stay of one day and night), Þorbiörg consents to perform her service for her host. Crucially, however, the seiðr practitioner alone is insufficient for the ritual: Þorbiörg needs a chorus of women and at least one assistant familiar with a magic song or incantation called *varðlokkur*, requisites which her host must supply. In the *Eiríks saga* account, this song is supplied—somewhat unwillingly—by Guð-ríðr, a Christian woman who learned the mysterious *varðlokkur* from her pagan foster mother in Iceland. The account culminates with a description of the ritual itself, performed while Þorbiörg lies on a raised platform in the middle of the hall:

Slógu þá konur hring um hjallinn, en Þorbiörg sat á uppi. Kvað Guðríðr þá kvæðið svá fagrt ok vel, at engi þóttisk heyrt hafa með fegri rödd kvæði, sá er þar var hjá.

Spákonan þakkar henni kvæðit ok kvað margar þær náttúrur nú til hafa sótt ok þykkja fagrt at heyra, er kvæðið var svá vel flutt, er áðr vildu við oss skiljask ok enga hlýðni oss veita. En mér eru nú margir þeir hlutir auðsýnir, er áðr var ek dulit, ok margir aðrir. . . ." Síðan gengu menn at vísindakonunni ok frétti þá hverr þess, er mest forvitni var á at vita. Hon var ok góð af frásögnum, gekk þat ok lítt í tauma er hon sagði.[7]

The women now formed a circle round the platform on which Þorbiörg was seated. Guðríðr recited the chant so beautifully and well that no one who was present could say he had heard a chant recited by a lovelier voice. The seeress thanked her for the chant, adding that many spirits had been drawn there now who thought it lovely to lend ear, the chant had been so admirably delivered—spirits "who before wished to keep their distance from us and give us not hearing. And now many things are apparent to me which earlier were hidden from me as from many others. . . ." After this men approached the prophetess and inquired, each of them, about what they were most concerned to know. She was free with her information and little indeed of what she said failed to come about.[8]

Here, then, we see the use of a platform, a chant, and special roles not simply for the practitioner herself but also for other women and especially female singers present in the community. It is a collective and communal ritual, performed within the home, but its central figure, Þorbiörg, comes from the outside, leaving the farm on the following day when another potential host sends her an escort. The ritual thus unites stranger and local community, specialist and competent audience in a set of symbolic actions directed toward a listening spirit world.

The image of Þorbiörg as an itinerant practitioner parallels the account of a seiðr ritual in *Vatnsdæla saga*.[9] On the Norwegian island of Hefniey, Farmer Ingialdr invites a Finnish or Sámi woman skilled in magic (*finna ein fiölkunnig*) to attend a feast and predict the future and fates of the assembled guests. As in the above account, the practitioner takes her place on a high seat and prophesies about each person who approaches her. When Ingialdr's foster son Ingimundr Þorsteinsson refuses to consult her (preferring, he maintains, to learn about his future as it comes, not before), the practitioner offers her prediction of his future settlement in Iceland unsolicited. Later in the saga, when Ingimundr is considering emigrating to Iceland, he consults several other Sámi. The same idea of a host engaging a seiðr specialist as part of a feast is repeated in other texts as well—for example, *Örvar-Odds saga* and *Þáttr af Norna-Gesti*.[10]

If the above accounts characterize seiðr as a useful divinatory ritual, they also hint at its negative potential. The seiðr practitioner's access to otherwise unknowable information could lead to unfair advantages in the struggle for survival, and the fact that specialists in the art performed their services for pay could pull them into interpersonal conflicts between clients. Both saga accounts contain characters who explicitly refuse to consult with the seiðr woman during her visit, even though she has access to information about their fates. Their refusals do not deprive the specialist of her ability to see into their futures, however. The negative potential of the seiðr ritual is highlighted in accounts of the Danish King Fróði in *Hrólfs saga kraka* and Saxo's *Gesta Danorum*.[11] Both accounts detail Fróði's attempts to locate and murder his royal nephews, who have gone into hiding at the death of their father, the rightful king, by hiring an itinerant seiðr woman. The seiðr practitioner's prying mind appears fully able to locate the boys but a bribe convinces her to remain silent on their whereabouts. Both accounts include details that link the scene to other descriptions of seiðr, albeit with some variation. In *Hrólfs saga*, the woman mounts her raised platform and appears to hyperventilate as a means of inducing divinatory trance, a behavior closely paralleled in Sámi and Finnish shamanism, as we shall see.[12] In Saxo's more divergent account, the woman falls into a deathlike trance, but only after receiving the bribe, feigning a collapse under the stronger magic powers of the princes' protectors. The texts clearly refer to the same ritual tradition as that depicted in *Eiríks saga* and *Vatnsdœla saga*, though now with its abusive possibilities underscored.

While Fróði's attempt illustrates the way in which the seiðr practitioner and ritual might be coopted for evil purposes, other accounts provide more explicit details of the intentional use of seiðr with harmful intent. The vengeful Queen Gunnhildr of *Egils saga Skalla-Grímssonar* uses her own seiðr skills to disquiet and ultimately to manipulate the skald Egill's mind.[13] Through her spell, Egill can find no rest in Iceland and eventually wanders to Scotland, where he falls into the hands of his enemy, Gunnhildr's husband, King Eiríkr Blood-ax. Similarly, the Icelandic Þorgrímr uses seiðr to curse his enemy Gísli in *Gísla saga Súrssonar*. Plagued by nightmares and premonitions of horrid events, the beset Gísli can find no peace of mind anywhere in Iceland, apart from the overlooked island of Hergilsey. Snorri illustrates this aspect of seiðr in his *Ynglingasaga*, when the Finnish or Sámi Queen Drífa hires a seiðr practitioner to disquiet the mind of her errant husband, King Vanlandi of Sweden.[14] Immediately upon the working of the seiðr practitioner's spell, the king is seized by the desire to return to "Finnland." When the king's men prevent his return, Drífa has her seiðr practitioner send an incubus (*mara*) to beset and finally to murder the king.

Even more emphatic in its portrayal of seiðr as a tool of evil, however, is the striking account of the Hebridean seiðr practitioners in *Laxdœla saga*.[15] Here, a family of specialists arrives in Iceland from the mixed Celtic-Scandinavian settlement of the Hebrides. Led by a man named Kotkell (a Celtic name), they are welcomed by the local chieftain Hallsteinn. Soon, however, their magic wiles become known to the neighborhood through occasions of magical theft and malicious plotting. When the householder Þórðr Ingunnarson summons them to answer charges at the Althing, the family retaliates with a seiðr spell. Erecting a platform and singing incantations (*galdrar*), the family effects a storm which causes Þórðr's boat to capsize on his way home; he drowns as a result.

Kotkell and his family also disquiet minds, as subsequent events in the saga reveal. The family is hired by Þorleikr Höskuldsson to humiliate Þorleikr's uncle Hrútr Herjólfsson after a quarrel. In response, the family climbs on top of Hrútr's house at night to sing an enchanting but malevolent song:

En lítlu síðar gera þau heimanferð sína, Kotkell ok Gríma ok synir þeira; þat var um nótt. Þau fóru á bœ Hrúts ok gerðu þar seið mikinn. En er seiðlætin kómu upp, þá þóttusk þeir eigi skilja, er inni váru, hverju gegna myndi; en fögr var sú kveðandi at heyra. Hrútr einn kendi þessi læti ok bað engan mann út sjá á þeiri nótt—"ok haldi hverr vöku sinni, er má, ok mun oss þá ekki til saka, ef svá er með farit." En þó sofnuðu allir menn. Hrútr vakði lengst, en sofnaði þó. Kári hét son Hrúts, er þá var tólf vetra gamall, ok var hann efniligastr sona Hrúts. Hann unni honum mikit. Kári sofnaði nær ekki; því at til hans var leikr gørr; honum gerðisk ekki mjök vært. Kári spratt upp ok sá út. Hann gekk á seiðinn ok fell þegar dauðr niðr.[16]

A little while later, Kotkell, Gríma, and their sons started off for home during the night. They mounted Hrútr's roof and began a great seiðr ritual there. When the seiðr sounds started, no one inside knew what to make of it but the singing they heard sounded pleasant to listen to. Only Hrútr realized what the sounds were and he bade everyone not to look outside during the night, "and everyone who can should keep watch," he said, "and nothing will happen to us if we follow my advice." But nonetheless, everyone fell asleep. Hrútr stayed awake the longest, but then he fell asleep as well. Hrútr had a son named Kári whom he loved very much. He was twelve years old and the worthiest of Hrútr's sons. Kári could hardly sleep at all, for the spell was aimed at him; he could find no rest. Finally, he got up and looked outside. He stepped into the seiðr magic and fell down dead.

Here, we find the imagery of sweet music, so prominent in the *Eiríks saga* account of divinatory seiðr, combined with the notion of magic that unsettles and eventually compels a victim's mind. As in *Eiríks saga*, the ritual is performed on a raised surface (this time a roof), in the presence of a community. It is commissioned by a man who pays for the ritual to be performed.

The various accounts of seiðr in these narratives thus combine to create a fairly consistent, if nebulous, overall picture of the tradition. The phenomenon appears to be composed on the one hand of concrete ritual practices, performed in a specified manner by recognized specialists and on the other hand of complex interactions of spirits operating on an unseen, supernatural plane. While the former characteristics are fully observable even to those opposed to the tradition, the latter are shrouded in mystery. On the material plane, the accounts depict the predominant (but not total) association of the tradition with female practitioners, the use of induced trance, the frequent communal nature of the ritual performance, and the recurrent image of itinerant, employable practitioners, who sell their skills, for good or evil, to wealthy clients. On the supernatural plane, the tradition involves the specialist's own spirit, those of the people whom she scrutinizes or controls, and those of unseen, hovering spirits attracted by the ritual itself, its music or symbolic acts. Raised above the human community on a platform, the seiðr practitioner appears positioned to interact with both human and spirit worlds at the same time, acting as a point of convergence between natural and supernatural realms.

Even while depicting seiðr as an important ritual in Scandinavian religious life, however, the same sagas frequently portray the tradition as unfamiliar, even exotic, to many in the community. In the still pagan Greenland colony of *Eiríks saga*, for instance, no one besides Guðríðr knows the song needed for the ritual, and the community appears surprised and engaged by its beauty when they eventually hear the *varðlokkur* performed. Seiðr practitioners are frequently depicted as foreigners, people with Sámi or Finnish connections or (more rarely) links to the British Isles. In these ways, seiðr gives the impression of relative novelty, of representing an instance of late intercultural borrowing. As we shall see below, this interpretation is well supported by the textual evidence as well as comparative ethnographic data from the Finno-Ugric shamanic traditions of the Nordic region.

It is worthwhile noting the prevalence of Sámi and Balto-Finnic characters in these various accounts of seiðr. In addition to those in which the practitioners are explicitly labeled as "Finns" (as, for example in *Vatnsdøla saga* and *Ynglingasaga*, above), many sagas note the Finno-Ugric origins of the practitioner's skills themselves. As Snorri relates in *Haralds saga ins Hárfagra*, for instance, Gunnhildr has learned her skills from Sámi practitioners in Finnmark, where Eiríkr Blood-ax first meets her. There, she lives in a Sámi hut, apprenticed by her Hálogaland father to a pair of Sámi magicians "to learn the knowledge of these two Finns who are the wisest in the forest."[17] Likewise, *Landnámabók* reports that Þuríðr Sundafyllir ("Sound filler"), a settler from Hálogaland, had learned how to use seiðr to fill her home sound with fish, a skill she brought with her to Iceland.[18] Finno-Ugric parentage may account for the interest in seiðr evinced by Rögnvaldr Réttilbeini, King Haraldr's son by his Sámi wife Snæfríðr in Snorri's *Haralds saga ins Hárfagra*.[19] The Sámi connection lives on in Rögnvaldr's grandson Eyvindr Kelda, who is executed as a seiðr man by King Óláfr Tryggvason.[20] Although the art spreads to the Icelandic and Greenland colonies, it appears most frequently associated with areas of Scandinavian Finno-Ugric contact, such as Hálogaland, Finnmark, and the nebulous "Finnland."

If we hypothesize that the seiðr ritual practiced by Finno-Ugric and Scandinavian specialists in these saga accounts represents a borrowing from Sámi or Balto-Finnic religious traditions into Scandinavian ritual life (a conclusion reached by Dag Strömbäck in his authoritative study of the phenomenon),[21] then we must assume first Scandinavian familiarity with the rituals of the other Nordic peoples. Such is evidenced by explicit legal bans against consultation with "Finn" (Sámi or Balto-Finnic) seers in both the eleventh- and twelfth-century Christian *Borgarthings Kristenrett* of coastal Norway and in the Christian law code of the Norwegian interior from this same era, *Eidsivathinglag*. Penalties imposed included outlawry and forfeiture of property for anyone convicted of consulting with such specialists or obtaining cures from them. Such clear regulations imply that pagan and Christianizing Norwegians had previously made significant use of the divinatory and healing skills of their neighbors. In *Borgarthings Kristenrett*, the act of consulting is referred to as *trúa á finna* ("to believe/trust in a Finn"), *fara til finna* (or *Finnmerkr*) *at spyria spá* ("travel to the Finns or Finnmark to have one's fortune read"), or "gera finnfarar" ("pay a visit to Finns").[22]

Further evidence of Scandinavian awareness of Finno-Ugric shamanism is furnished by the account of a Sámi shamanic ritual in the *Historia Norwegiae*, a Norwegian text dated to between 1178 and 1220.[23] In the Latin account—based purportedly on the testimony of a Christian eyewitness—two Sámi shamans attempt to retrieve the missing life-soul of a woman struck unconscious by an unknown adversary. Spreading a cloth as a stage for the ritual, each shaman in turn combines drumming, dance, and incantations to effect a spirit ecstasy, during which they are able to pursue the woman's missing soul and its malevolent thief. One of the two practitioners dies while in trance, mortally wounded by a trap laid in a lake by his spirit adversary during the chase. The other shaman, however, succeeds, returning not only to revive the woman but also to explain the sudden death of his colleague. This account resembles reports of Sámi shamanic procedures by later Lutheran missionaries of the seventeenth and eighteenth centuries.[24] Other saga and law references confirm the notion that Scandinavians who lived in areas of close contact with Sámi or Finns were aware of their neighbors' religious traditions and sometimes consulted them for assistance.

While the *Historia Norwegiae* report of a Sámi ritual strongly resembles saga accounts of seiðr, it also differs in certain key respects, both in terms of the outward physical ritual and of its unseen spiritual component. Both practitioners are male and employ a combination of drumming and dance to enter the spirit realm. They undertake the ritual with the intent to heal, not to divine the future or to manipulate others' minds, as in saga accounts of seiðr. Their spirit quest for the woman's soul differs from anything detailed in the saga texts. All of these characteristics are paralleled in later accounts of Sámi shamanism, although divination and malevolence also figure at times in the Sámi tradition. If we hypothesize an origin for seiðr within Sámi *noaidevuohtta* (shamanism), then, we must also recognize its significant alteration within the Scandinavian religious system. An examination of the drum explicates these changes.

The Sámi shamanic drum survives in both textual and archaeological evidence.[25] It played a central role in the Sámi ritual and was targeted for destruction by missionaries of later eras. The *Historia Norwegiae* account describes the form and meaning of symbols inscribed on the drum face:

Cetinis atque cervinis formulis cum loris et ondriolis navicula etiam cum remis occupatum, quibus vehiculis per alta nivium et devexa montium vel profunda stagnorum ille diabolicus gandus uteretur.[26]

It was carved with figures of sea creatures and (rein)deer, skis and a boat with oars, all of which could conduct the diabolical spirit across high snowcaps, steep mountains, or deep slopes.

Ernst Manker has examined recurrent symbols on surviving drums, finding images closely related to the mythological explication of the shaman's spirit journeys. Symbols include deities of both high and low orders (e.g., the sun, sky gods, áhkkás (household goddesses), Ruto, guardian spirits) as well as key seasons or economic activities (hunting, fishing, reindeer husbandry, planting, burial, etc.). Reports by Lutheran ministers frequently note that by watching the movements of a metal ring placed on the vibrating drum skin, shamans could use such symbols as tools in divination. The images have been interpreted as encapsulations of Sámi mythology, local wisdom regarding hunting and prey, cosmic maps of the spirit world, and even celestial maps of major star constellations.[27] The drum face appears to have acted as a nexus at which the shamanic ritual—broadly similar cross-culturally—united with the distinctive ethnic religion of the Sámi people and perhaps also the personal religious experiences of a single practitioner.[28]

Despite its importance in Sámi shamanism, the drum does not appear to have transferred to any great extent into the neighboring cultures of the Nordic region. The Finnish *tietäjä* (shaman) Antti Tokoi, convicted and punished for witchcraft in 1663 and 1681, admitted to using a drum that he had acquired from a Sámi *noaidi*.[29] Both a Sámi term for the *noaidi*'s drum, *kannus*, and the Finnish word for the five-stringed harp, *kannel, kantele*, may derive from the same proto-Finnic root **komta* ("lid"), indicating an earlier unity between the instruments. Epic songs indicate the importance of the *kantele* in the ancient *tietäjä*'s art and Siikala suggests that the *kantele* may thus represent a musical descendant of an earlier Balto-Finnish drum tradition.[30] It has also been suggested that the decorated "shields" described in some skaldic poems (e.g., *Haustlöng, Ragnarsdrápa, Húsdrápa*) may also represent Sámi drums borrowed into Scandinavian usage.[31] In any case, however, we find no evidence of seiðr practitioners in the sagas either owning or using shamanic drums.

If our evidence were limited to these accounts of Scandinavian seiðr on the one hand, and Sámi *noaidevuohtta* on the other, our examination of the linkage between them could proceed no farther. Fortunately, however, it is also possible to examine the shamanic traditions of the Balto-Finnic peoples. These traditions demonstrate an overall continuum between the various ecstatic rituals discussed above. Such evidence must be used cautiously in any appraisal of Viking Age religion. Nonetheless, Balto-Finnic peoples probably possessed shamanic traditions akin to those explicitly documented among medieval Scandinavians and Sámi, and the rituals and oral tradition collected at a later remove among Balto-Finnic peoples may bear some relation to these pre-Christian phenomena. At least some of this material may represent later borrowings of traditions from either Sámi or Scandinavians, a notion suggested by the report of the seventeenth-century Finnish healer Antti Tokoi with a Sámi drum, as mentioned above. Both Haavio and Pentikäinen note aspects of Finnish and Karelian epic song that clearly reflect borrowing from Sámi as well as Scandinavian oral tradition.[32] But it would also be surprising if Balto-Finnic peoples of the Viking Age failed to possess any shamanic traditions of their own, given the commonness of the tradition among Finno-Ugric peoples, the native terminology for aspects of the ritual, and its widespread use in later eras.[33] It is with this likelihood of medieval shamanism in mind that we survey the following later accounts of Finnish and Karelian shamanic traditions.

In many aspects of the outward ritual, the Finnish *tietäjä*'s art resembled saga accounts of seiðr. The *Eiríks saga* account of Þorbiörg's distinctive ritual dress (quoted above), for instance, strongly resembles garb used by Finnish and Karelian *tietäjät* during their healing rituals. Paraphernalia included a distinctive headdress, mittens, belt, and pouches, items which remained a part of the tradition into the late nineteenth century.[34] Court records of the witchcraft trial of the soldier and healer Heikki Heikinpoika Räisänen in 1742 report that he wore snakeskin belt from which hung pouches of ashes, hair, and other magic items.[35] Both belts and other garb were often lined with the pelts of animals helpful in Finnish shamanic spirit travel: waterfowl (especially loons), squirrels, and snakes—creatures notable for their abilities to scramble or soar upward into higher realms or to slither or dive down into the underworld. In 1896, a practitioner from Lonkka explained the significance of his own paraphernalia in detail, collecting similar accounts from other healers of his vicinity. From these testimonies, we know that items such as the healer's hat required sanctification through rituals performed over a number of nights and with a variety of different materials, including the brains of ravens, sauna soot, and alder bark.[36] The substitution of cat fur in the *Eiríks saga* account of seiðr garb may reflect details of European witchlore later grafted onto the tradition, as we shall discuss below.

Trance induction also bears a strong resemblance to the saga accounts: here we find both the performance of enchanting song (without drumming), hyperventilation (as in the *Hrólfs saga* account) and a merging of musical performance with incantations, the *galdrar* (Finnish *loitsut*) of the healing tradition (see Chapter 5). In his 1789 study *Mythologia Fennica*, Christfrid Ganander details a Finnish *tietäjä*'s hyperactive rage, a display which combined incantations with intense physical activity, sauna, spitting, scowls, convulsions, rolling of eyes, and clenching of teeth.[37] Epic songs of the shamanic hero Väinämöinen, for their part, stress the shaman's wondrous singing, which has the power to captivate all who listen: human, animal, and deity alike. He can also use it to punish his enemies and manipulate their wills.[38] Elias Lönnrot describes the Finnish *tietäjä*'s trance induction and experience as follows:

Kivillä istuen sanottiin tietäjien kulkeneen yli jokien ja järvien ja heidän henkensä ruumiista erillään matkustaneen muilla kaukaisillakin paikoilla tietoja saamassa ja sitten jonkun tiiman perästä jälleen yhdistyneen ruumiiseen. Semmoiseen henki- matkaan olivat jonkun taikarunon hiljaisella hyrinällä valmistautuneet, siitä tain- noksiin joutuneet eli "loveen langenneet," ja sillä aikaa, kun henki itsepäällänsä kulki, ruumiin, kuin hengetön ruumis ainaki, kuoleena maanneen, sitten hengen matkoiltaan palattua jälleen vironneen.[39]

Sitting on stones, *tietäjät* were said to pass over rivers and lakes and their spirits, separate from their bodies, were said to travel to other remote places obtaining knowledge and after some time reuniting with their bodies. They prepared for such spiritual journeys by quietly humming a magic poem, from which they fell into a trance ("slipped into the crack") and while the spirit was traveling by itself, the body, like a lifeless body at least, lay as if dead, to recover again after the spirit's return from its journeys.

These varying accounts of the Finnish practitioner's music may suggest something about the musical component of the shamanic ritual in both Balto-Finnic and Scandinavian cases alike: performed songs were probably not "beautiful" in the sense of later musical aesthetics, but compelling in a powerful emotive as well as supernatural sense.[40]

   Accounts of Balto-Finnic shamanism also resemble Scandinavian seiðr in the range of functions associated with the ritual. Although healing is the most common function in the Finnish cases (as in Sámi shamanism and shamanic traditions in general cross-culturally),[41] divination and the ma- nipulation of spirits or luck also figure as prime activities. The Finnish *tietäjä* could be hired to divine future events, to secure greater luck for clients, or to steal the luck of others. In both of the latter tasks, manipulation of spirits—be they of animals, objects, or people—was necessary for obtain- ing the desired flow of luck from one entity to another. The lack of a healing function in the seiðr tradition as we see it in the sagas appears the single greatest difference between the Balto-Finnic forms of shamanism and their Scandinavian counterparts or adaptations. The prominence of continental healing traditions among Scandinavians, as we have seen in the last chapter, may account in part for the absence of this important shamanic function.

   The second largest point of divergence between Sámi and Balto-Finnic rituals on the one hand, and Scandinavian seiðr on the other, is the gender ascription associated with each. In contrast to the female-dominated seiðr tradition, male predominance of Finno-Ugric shamanism appears clear in all evidence, from the early *Historia Norwegiae* account through reports from later eras and Finnish epic poems. Male dominance squares well with what we know of women as sources of desecration in both Sámi and Balto-Finnic religious thought.[42] Later instances of female practitioners in both culture areas have been interpreted as products of a late breakdown of the religious system, although subservient female assistants are noted in shamanic rituals of earlier eras.[43] Our examination of seiðr must thus account for this seeming inversion of the Finno-Ugric taboo in its apparently derivative Scandinavian variant. For an explanation of this transformation, we must turn to the practice of divination and women's broader spiritual roles within Scandinavian paganism itself. Our examination helps reveal the logic of assimilation and syncresis that underlies the intercultural borrowing of rituals in the Viking Age.

If we remove healing from the range of shamanic activities identified in depictions of Sámi and Balto-Finnic shamanism, we are presented with a repertoire of ritual functions closely associated with women in Germanic religious practice. Tacitus writes that the Germanic peoples of the first century A.D. view woman as powerful diviners: "[I]nesse quin etiam sanctum aliquid et providum putant, nec aut consilia earum aspernantur aut responsa neglegunt"[44] [(T)hey are believed to have something holy and provident about them, nor do their counsels meet with disdain or inaction]. Tacitus illustrates his point with reference to the Vespasian oracle Veleda, who was treated as nearly a goddess among her people. In Scandinavian mythology, this divinatory role becomes embodied in Freyja, who, Snorri notes, was the first among the gods to practice seiðr, an art associated with the Vanir.[45]

The notion of women being particularly prone to malevolent spiritual manipulation—witchcraft in its most deleterious sense—is also clear in the sagas, even when the pre-Christian society is depicted. In *Eyrbyggja saga* (ch. 15–20), for instance, the male protagonist, Gunnlaugr Þorbjarnarson, is beset by witchcraft arising from his female neighbors.[46] The idea of dangerous female witches is present in a number of the most important mythological poems of the *Edda*, including *Völuspá* and *Hávamál* (str. 155), and it is noteworthy that some of the saga accounts of seiðr (*Hrólfs saga, Ynglingasaga*) describe the practitioner as a witch. Even the *Eiríks saga* account of Þorbiörg includes details (an association with cats, for example) reminiscent more of European witchlore than Finno-Ugric shamanism. It is probable that saga writers saw little difference between seiðr of the past and thirteenth-century notions of witches; it is more difficult to ascertain the degree of overlap between these two concepts among pagans of the ninth or tenth centuries. Whatever the case, it appears that seiðr itself became assimilated into a preexisting set of gender norms regarding supernatural entities: as the ritual's divinatory and manipulative functions became central, its gender ascription shifted from male to female.

The Eddaic poem *Völuspá* incorporates this gendered portrayal of magic into its narrative frame and explicit mythological details. The poem depicts a meeting between a female seer (*völva*) and the god Óðinn, who compels her to speak to him of times past and future. She relates the beginning of the cosmos as well as its end, providing details about the ancient war between the Vanir and Æsir that resulted in the arrival of Njörðr, Freyr, and Freyja in the celestial fortress of Ásgarðr. Principal in this battle was a powerful female figure named Gullveig, whose magic protected her even from fire. The *völva* declares:

> Heiði hana héto,   hvars til húsa kom,
> völo velspá,   vitti hon ganda;
> seið hon, hvars hon kunni,   seið hon hug leikinn,
> æ var hon angan   illrar brúðar.

> She was called witch,   as she came toward a house,
> a seer [*völva*] skilled in prophecy,   she knew how to work spells;
> she practiced seiðr, as she knew how,   with seiðr light of spirit,
> ever was she the delight   of evil wives.[47]

Here it is difficult if not impossible to distinguish seiðr from the wiles of female witches.

Such is not to say that Scandinavian men were not involved in either divination or manipulative magic. The male diviner—*spámaðr*—figures frequently in the sagas, and an isolating, privative ritual (*útiseta*, "sitting out") appears favored among male practitioners.[48] In Ari's *Libellus islandorum*, for instance, the lawsayer Þorgeirr is depicted retiring to his tent to lie alone for a day and a night while considering the ramifications of abandoning paganism in favor of Christianity. He neither speaks nor moves during this time but returns at its end in the possession of the wisest counsel for his community. In other accounts, male seers are depicted as immediate clairvoyants: capable of seeing the unseen automatically, without special ritual or preparation. Such is the case with Þorhall the Seer (*spámaðr*) in *Þiðranda þáttr Síðu-*

Hallssonar, in which the character Þorhall senses the coming death of one of the household members but is unable to predict the manner of death or the identity of the victim. Þorhall's abilities are directly opposed in the narrative to impending household rituals (*blót*) associated with the women of the farm. The figure of Kotkell and his sons (above) also reminds us that men could be involved in manipulative magic as well, despite its predominant female associations. Such behavior, however, exposed men to particular contempt and carried the weight of the legal stigma known as *ergi* (extreme shame, abomination). Even when the art of seiðr became consolidated into the magical repertoire of Óðinn, as appears the case in Snorri's *Ynglingasaga*, these strong overtones remain. Writes Snorri:

Óðinn kunni þá íþrótt, svá at mestr máttr fylgði, ok framði sjálfr, er seiðr heitir, en af því mátti hann vita ørlög manna ok óorðna hluti, svá ok at gera mönnum bana eða óhamingju eða vanheilandi, svá ok at taka frá mönnum vit eða afl ok gefa öðrum. En þessi fjölkynngi, er framið er, fylgir svá mikil ergi, at eigi þótti karlmönnum skammlaust við at fara, ok var gyðjunum kennd sú íþrótt.⁴⁹

Óðinn was acquainted with that most powerful art known as seiðr, and he therefore knew a person's fate and of the future, and also of how to cause people death, or bad luck, or illness, and also of how to take power or wit away from some people and give it to others. But in practicing this magic [*fjölkynngi*], such shame and abomination [*ergi*] occurred that it seemed unseemly for men to deal in it and thus the art was taught to priestesses.

The same passage distinguishes this ritual tradition clearly from Óðinn's other famed skills: divinatory shape-shifting, magic control of elements like fire, wind, and water, solitary trance, the use of incantations (*galdrar*) and lone consultations with dead or hanged men. In a culture in which cross-gender behavior was punishable by lawsuit or death, the female associations of seiðr appear decisive in limiting its practice, despite the tradition's acknowledged power and eventual association with Óðinn. Thus, when King Haraldr Finehair and his chosen successor Eiríkr Blood-ax burn Rögnvaldr Réttilbeini and his fellow seiðr men in Hálogaland, their reason seems to be overt disapproval of the prince's religious practices. As Snorri writes: "King Haraldr disliked seiðr men"; Eiríkr himself, however, could marry a woman (Gunnhildr) versed in the same tradition.⁵⁰

Here, then, we see a final stage in the apparent assimilation of the seiðr ritual into Scandinavian paganism. Beginning as a foreign loan, often performed by practitioners from neighboring cultures, the ritual seems to have become associated with Scandinavian women's roles and linked mythologically to Vanir magic, seasonal household rituals, and the goddess Freyja. In the Eddaic poem *Völuspá*, as we have seen, the distinction between this realm of supernatural activities and the god Óðinn remains clear, although the male sky god wields superior might in the end. Finally, in the view reflected by Snorri's account in *Ynglingasaga*, Óðinn is recognized as a prime user of seiðr, a skill he has learned from Freyja, who brought it with her to Ásgarðr after the primordial battle described in *Völuspá*. But although the ritual thus becomes one of the magical tools of the most powerful of sky gods, it remains distinguished from the rest of his skills and still associated with female behavior.

The underhanded, covert workings of seiðr must have represented a further reason for male aversion to it, at least in public. In a society that valued a forthright male manner and a ready embrace of outward conflict, a ritual allowing the secret manipulation of another's will would violate ideals of proper masculinity. In the depiction of manipulative seiðr in *Laxdœla saga*, both Kotkell and his male clients are depicted as reprehensible for their reliance on magic and their reluctance to fight their battles in the open. Since surreptitious seiðr robbed an opponent both of the awareness of his adversary's attack and possibly also the wit to comprehend it, the act denied both combatants the true glory of fair, open conflict. Such trickery is typical of Óðinn, as we have seen (Chapter 4), but it appears more problematic for his male disciples.

Seiðr thus demonstrates a dynamic process of religious exchange operating in the Viking Age in which individual ritual elements—and sometimes even practitioners—crossed cultural and economic lines, becoming reinscribed within the worldview of the recipient community. Seiðr replicated strongly shamanic rituals among Sámi and Balto-Finns, but it also became assimilated into the preexisting repertoire of religious practices and mythology operating among Scandinavian pagans. This assimilation effected its own substantive changes on the tradition, rendering it a new entity, the product of religious syncresis.

This decentralized, circulating flow and exchange of religious ideas, modeled so aptly by the case of seiðr, most challenged the Christian missionaries of the Viking Age. For as messengers of the new faith, Christianizers sought to extend to the North not an *adaptation* of Christianity, but rather its authentic *replication*. While practicing a ritual sung in a language utterly unfamiliar to the bulk of their converts, the priests and bishops of the Viking Age worked to stem the absorption of their religion's most accessible or appealing symbols into preexisting systems of understanding and practice. That challenge will be examined in the following chapter.

SEVEN

The Coming of the Cross

Religious and Artistic Effects

Vexilla regis prodeunt:
fulget Crucis mysterium,
qua vita mortem pertulit,
et morte vitam protulit.

Abroad the royal banners fly,
And bear the gleaming Cross on high,
That Cross whereon Life suffered death,
And gave us life with dying breath.

In the above hymn to the Holy Cross, the sixth-century Gallo-Roman poet and bishop St. Venantius Fortunatus (535–605) distills the varying images of the holiest of sacred implements into a single expression of faith. For the medieval Christian, the Cross was a symbol to carry forth on banners, shields, and pendants: the emblem of a heavenly ruler as well as his Christian representatives on earth. Its presence over the breast or traced in the air could effect wondrous cures and banish evil. At the same time, the Cross was also a holy relic, discovered where it lay abandoned in Jerusalem and treasured ever after as a source of miraculous healing powers. Divided into myriad pieces and distributed across the Christian world, it retained the power and wonder of the materialized Christ it had borne. It was an animate friend, a conscious servant of God and intercessor for all of humanity until the Final Day. With its feast days, litanies, and myriad representations in Christian art, the Cross towered above the other symbols of the faith, a crucial material reminder of human redemption.

This chapter surveys the development of Cross symbolism, devotion, and display in northern Europe, focusing on the uses made of it in both Christian and pagan communities from Ireland across mainland Scandinavia. By examining manifestations of the Cross in Nordic cultures from the early Viking Age through the thirteenth century, we may observe the assimilation of Christian symbolism and belief in the region from three different sources: the British Isles, the eastern realms of Novgorod and Byzantium, and the continental realms of central Europe. In each case, particular ideas and images of the Cross arrived first as the products of trade and contact, only gradually acquiring a deeper significance in the religious outlooks of the Nordic peoples themselves. On the basis of archaeological and textual evidence, it is possible to ascertain how Nordic pre-Christian communities interpreted the Cross during this period and how they found counterparts to it in the pagan concept of divine implements. By the thirteenth century, however, much of the region had embraced the new faith, and orientations toward the Cross reflected the growth of doctrinal orthodoxy among Christian populations. In this last stage of Christianization, we find accounts of Nordic kings who cannily use the Cross and its attendant symbolism in a manner reminiscent of the Christian monarchs of central and southern Europe. These narratives mark the final triumph of a truly Christian outlook, yet they comment as well on the continued prominence of paganism in the region and, perhaps, in the hearts of Nordic leaders.

Before examining the Cross in the North, we must understand its genesis and development as a symbol in Christianity itself. A common implement of public torture among the Romans, the cross emerged as a symbol of Christianity already in the second century.[1] Christians appear to have traced small crosses on foreheads, lips, or breasts, occasionally etching it on objects as a symbol of their faith. It was only with the advent of tolerance toward Christianity during the fourth century, however, that the symbol could become public. And when it did, it took three prime forms: the Cross of the Vision, the Cross of the Relic, and the gestural cross formed in the air, the *Crux usualis*. Each of these distinct aspects of the Cross became important in Nordic Christianity.

Constantine (c. 280–337) figures prominently in the rise of the Cross in official Christianity. He is credited with a vision of the Cross on the eve of the Battle of the Milvian Bridge (*Ponte Molle*), October 28, 312. On that day, Constantine and his army saw a marvelous sight: a luminous X-shaped cross in saltire ("St. Andrew's Cross"), shining in the sky and bearing the inscription "In This Conquer." Later, in the evening, Constantine dreamed of Christ, who appeared to him again with the sign and commanded him to use it as an emblem.[2] Upon inquiring about its significance, Constantine learned that the symbol in his vision—which soon developed into a standardized *chi-rho* digraph crowned by a wreath—represented Christ. With this symbol emblazoned on the shields and helmets of his forces, Constantine won the battle, marching triumphantly into Rome behind his new emblem of adherence. His act made the Cross one with the divine right of the Christian king, a symbolism built on late Roman statecraft and extended by Constantine's Christian successors, particularly Charlemagne (742–814, r. 768–814), who revived the *chi-rho* digraph during his reign. Among all classes of medieval society, Constantine's visionary cross lived on in legends. It was echoed by the visions of later monarchs in the North, from King St. Oswald of the seventh century through King Valdemar II Sejr of the thirteenth.

While the age of Constantine gave Christianity a powerful Cross emblem, it also gave rise to the cult of the Cross as relic. This more material aspect of the Holy Cross had an even greater popular appeal, shaping the religious ideas and experiences of Christians of all classes throughout the medieval era. The tangible Cross, drenched with the miraculous blood of the Savior, scarred by the nails driven through His limbs, hidden or buried after the Crucifixion, discovered, rediscovered, and preserved in the cathedrals of the Holy Land, motivated more than any other relic the pilgrimages and ex-votos of medieval history. Fractured into pieces and distributed across the Near East and Europe, it reached its peak of popularity during the thirteenth century.[3] The Cross's ability to heal the body as well as save the soul rendered it not simply a *symbol* of power but also a *repository* of it on earth.

The earliest account of the discovery of the True Cross (known as the "Invention") credits the Empress Protonica, wife of Emperor Claudius (41–54), with the act after her conversion and pilgrimage to the Holy Land. The Protonica legend was soon overshadowed, however, by the legend of St. Helena (c. 250–c. 330), Constantine's mother, who visited Jerusalem in the early fourth century. St. Helena is said to have discovered three crosses, recognizing the True Cross by its miraculous power to restore a dead man's body to life. By the mid-fourth century, the Cross of the Relic had become commonplace enough for St. Cyril of Jerusalem to mention it in his catechetical lectures, and St. John Chrysostom (c. 347–407) noted in a homily of 387 that both men and women wear fragments of the Cross encased in jewelry about the neck. By the end of the fourth century, St. Jerome (c. 342–420) was criticizing women for the ostentation of such pendants, while the Roman pilgrim Aetheria (Silvia) recounted Good Friday services in Jerusalem that included the exposure and kissing of a portion of the Cross. Precautions must be taken, she notes, lest the faithful bite off pieces of the sacred relic for personal use. In 614, during a Persian invasion of Jerusalem, the Cross was seized and transported away from the Holy City. Its defilement became the subject of various legends and its return on May 3, 630, was celebrated as an occasion of great triumph and joy. This and other days became high feasts in the liturgical year, marking a fervent and widespread devotion to the material implement of the Crucifixion.[4]

Crusades and pilgrimages alike brought Europeans to the Cross in Jerusalem, but reliquaries and translation brought pieces of it back to Europe. The first relics of the True Cross to arrive in Europe reached Italy and Gaul by the beginnings of the fifth century.[5] St. Venantius Fortunatus composed his hymn to the Cross on the arrival of such a relic at Poitiers in the late sixth century. Charlemagne was celebrated as having received a piece of the True Cross from Patriarch George of Jerusalem in 799.[6] Pope Marinus I (882–

84) presented a piece of the True Cross to the British King Alfred in 883 and King Athelstan received a piece enclosed in crystal from King Hugh of Brittany during his reign (871–99).[7] Bede credits the seventh-century St. Felix with owning a piece which he used to stop a terrible city fire, and Ælfric discusses fragments of the Cross and their powers in a tenth-century homily.[8] In Ireland, King Aed Finnlaith of the northern Ui Néill carried a fragment into battle in 867, defeating the Vikings at Drogheda and ending Scandinavian incursions in the region. In 1123, the western Irish King Toirdelbach Ua Conchubhair of Connacht commissioned the ornate processional Cross of Cong to house a fragment of the True Cross as well.[9]

As the cult of the Cross spread across Christendom, early reticence regarding the wearing of cross images faded. The Iconoclast Controversy was laid to rest doctrinally in the Second Council of Nicaea in 787, which upheld the principle of venerating images of "the precious and vivifying Cross," as well as depictions of Christ, the Blessed Virgin, and the saints. This decree was renewed at the Eighth Ecumenical Council at Constantinople in 869.[10] Medieval saints' lives frequently mention crosses as items of clothing, with or without the addition of a sliver of the True Cross. One of St. Ceolfrið's (642–716) brethren is said to have made a golden cross for himself,[11] and Odo of Cluny notes that St. Gerald of Aurillac (c. 855–909) always wore a golden cross on his belt, forsaking all other jewelry or trappings of his estate.[12] Alcuin recounts the story of a deacon who stole a golden cross that St. Willibrord (658–739) had carried on his travels. In the narrative, the deacon grows seriously ill until he confesses his sin and returns the cross to the deceased saint's shrine.[13] The Anglo-Saxon St. Ælfheah (d. 1012) was said to have returned from the dead to punish a man who stole a pectoral cross from his grave.[14] In these accounts, the cross symbol—like the Cross fragment—figures as an implement of power, one used by the holy man to effect miracles, both before and after his death.

While the visionary and material Cross pervaded medieval legendry, the gestural sign of the Cross—the *Crux usualis*—became a constant part of daily Christian life. Nearly every important official act was begun or concluded with the sign of the Cross, which could be made over oneself, another person, or some object. *Jóns saga Byskups* advises Christians to make the sign of the Cross when rising, before going to sleep, and before eating and drinking.[15] In Snorri's *Hákonar saga Góða*, the Christian King Hákon makes the sign of the Cross over the drink which is forced upon him by his pagan supporters. Thus sanctifying the cup, Hákon seems to break its linkage with Óðinn.[16] Indeed, in the right hands, the *Crux usualis* could have all the power and efficacy of the material relic in impeding the wiles of the devil: an early *Life of St. Bridget* tells of how the Irish saint stops a woman from perjuring through making the sign of the Cross over her. The woman's head and tongue immediately begin to swell until she admits her lie and repents.[17] Thus, it is no surprise that Alcuin (c. 735–804) posits that Christ chose crucifixion instead of some other form of death (e.g., stoning or the sword) for the express purpose of giving Christians a wondrous gesture of power and protection.[18]

The Cross Comes to the British Isles and Atlantic Settlements

The Cross came with the faith to northern Europe, first in Roman Britain and then in Ireland, from the era of Constantine onward. After the Anglo-Saxon invasion, England required reconversion, a task accomplished by missionary monks from both Rome and Ireland. Irish and Anglo-Saxon missionaries in turn converted the Scandinavians, both in the Atlantic settlements of the British Isles and, in part, on mainland Scandinavia. A distinctive embrace of the Cross in British Isles Christianity allows us to trace the pathways and effects of this missionization in the Nordic region as a whole. It differed from either the Christianity of the eastern church or that established in the region by the Frankish mission.

The earliest cross figures in Ireland are inscribed Latin crosses, executed on stone slabs and erected on monastic grounds by the time of St. Patrick (c. 389–461) onward. By the eighth century, the first true high crosses had appeared, carved from sandstone and ornamented on shaft and arms with tight interlace patterning reminiscent of metalwork and manuscript art of the day.[19] The characteristic Celtic ringed form had emerged, possibly in stone imitation of metal processional crosses, which would have had a ring to stabilize shaft and arms. These first Irish stone crosses, unique in Europe at the time, limit figural depictions to the base, where pictures of horsemen, deer, and hunts are placed in rectangular panels. During the ninth century, this figural decoration gradually extended up the shaft and across the arms of the cross itself, retaining, however the same aristocratic themes and even an occasional mysterious figure, such as the antler-headed man of the north shaft at Clonmacnoise, strongly reminiscent of the Celtic Cernunnos.[20] An aristocratic reading for the figural decoration is supported not simply by the strong links of patronage between ruling nobles and monasteries (characteristic of monastic economies in much of Europe) but also by the royal character of many early Irish monks themselves, including the pivotal aristocratic monk-saints Enda (d. c. 530), Finnian (d. c. 579), and Columcille ("Columba"; c. 521–597).

With the tenth-century scriptural crosses of sandstone, along with their granite counterparts in southeastern Ireland, events from the Bible and saints' lives replace earlier aristocratic horsemen and deer. The high cross has now become more emphatically Christian, depicting in neat, rectangular panels scenes useful in the teaching of catechumens or reassuring to the ascetic monk. Portrayals of the Flight into Egypt or Daniel in the lions' den obviate in their clarity the nebulousness of the earlier cross depictions and prepare the way for the final late crosses of the eleventh and twelfth centuries, which depict a crucified Christ or a bishop with miter and crozier. The process of "Christianizing" cross ornamentation has thus come to its completion with the attainment of the Crucifix and the triumph of the cleric, suppressing earlier aristocratic or syncretic influences. The same issues, however, would be replayed again in each of the places to which the Irish brought the Cross and the faith.

While the Irish St. Columba and the Briton St. Ninian (d. c. 432) both undertook missionary work in Scotland and Cumbria, the kingdoms of the Angles, Saxons, and Jutes were initially left to Roman missionaries to evangelize. St. Augustine of Canterbury (d. 604), Pope St. Gregory's reluctant emissary to the English, began his mission in Kent, founding a monastery at Canterbury and sees in London and Rochester. For the history of the Cross, however, we look neither to St. Augustine nor to King St. Edwin (c. 585–633), the Northumbrian monarch who brought Christianity north from his Mercian exile. Rather, the decisive figure for the development of the Anglo-Saxon cross is Edwin's successor, King St. Oswald (605–642), who returned from his exile at Iona a Christianized and Celticized monarch.

Oswald demonstrates the continuity of the Constantinian Cross of the Vision in the distinctive social and cultural milieu of northern Europe. In a dream on the eve of his victorious battle for the throne of Northumbria in 634, the king recapitulates Constantine's vision, seeing a great cross and St. Columba, who explains its significance. If he erects a wooden cross on the battlefield, Oswald is assured, he will gain victory over the pagan Welsh king, Cadwallan. He does so and wins the battle, called ever after the Battle of Heavenfield. As king of Northumbria, he invited the Irish St. Aidan (d. 651) from Iona to Lindisfarne to missionize the Northumbrian people. The Venerable St. Bede (c. 672–735) retells the tale in his *Historia ecclesiastica gentis Anglorum* (731) and Ælfric describes it in memorable terms in his late tenth-century homily on the life of Oswald.[21] The visionary Cross, when experienced by a king, comes to the whole of society through the rulership it announces and the monuments that promulgate it. For generations, Bede relates, the wooden cross of Oswald served not only as a reminder of God's endorsement of their ruler, but as a cure for common diseases: chips of the cross, put in one's cup, could cure men as well as cattle (see Chapter 5).[22] Oswald's notoriety in Iceland was great enough that some of the island's most noted families traced lineage to Jórunn hin óborna ("the illegitimate"), reputedly the natural daughter of the sainted king.[23]

The eighth century in particular saw the creation of distinctive Anglo-Saxon religious works that merged the heroic epic of Germanic paganism with the Christian message. The late eighth-century or early ninth-century poet Cynewulf retells the vision of Constantine as well as St. Helena's discovery of the True Cross in his masterful heroic poem *Elene*. Similarly, in his depiction of the Last Judgment in the poem *Christ*, Cynewulf presents the Cross in terms which unite its material essence as the gallows on which Christ died and its spiritual essence as the standard of the ruling God on high. The central presence of the Cross at the Last Judgment had become a standard part of Christian eschatology through the writings of St. John Chrysostom (c. 347–407), and Cynewulf's portrayal echoes accounts of the Last Judgment in Irish works of his era.[24] Nonetheless, it is hard to mistake the heroic overtones of Cynewulf's description, inherent in both the overall image of the shining Cross and the terms used to describe it and God:

> Đonne sīo bȳman stefen
> ond þæt hāte fȳr,
> ond se engla þrym
> ond se hearda dæg
> ryht ārǣred,
> folcdryht wera
> ūsses Dryhtnes rōd
> bēacna beorhtast
> Heofoncyninges
> bisēon mid swāte
> scīre scīneð.[25]
>
> ond se beorhta segn
> ond sēo hēa duguð,
> ond se egsan þrēa
> ond sēo hēa rōd,
> rīces tō bēacne
> biforan bonnað . . .
> ondweard stondeð
> blōde bistēmed
> hlūtran drēore
> þæt ofer sīde gesceaft

> Then the trumpets' strain
> the fiery heat
> the throng of the angels
>
> and the shining standard,
> and the heavenly host,
> and the throes of fear

the Day of terror	and the towering Cross
upraised as a sign	of the Ruler's might
shall summon mankind	before the King . . .
The Rood of our Savior	red with His blood
over-run with bright gore	upreared before men
with radiant light	shall illumine the wide Creation.
No shadows shall lurk	where the light of the Cross
streams on all nations.[26]	

If the Cross appears active in Cynewulf's poems, it is completely personified in the somewhat earlier *Dream of the Rood*, preserved both in the *Vercelli Book* and in an inscription on the red sandstone Ruthwell Cross of the Galloway Peninsula. Here, particularly in the manuscript version, we hear of a narrator's Constantinian or Oswaldian dream-vision, in which the Cross itself, towering in the sky above, recounts the Passion, Harrowing of Hell, and coming Last Judgment. The narrator is thankful for his vision, which consoles him as he awaits his dying day. Crucially, the bulk of the poem is presented in the voice of the Cross itself, an animate and feeling being, who mourns its role in the death of the Savior and looks forward to the coming judgment of mankind. At the end of the poem, the reader is assured that anyone bearing the Cross *in* or *on* the breast (the Anglo-Saxon is inconclusive here) will be saved:

Ne þearf ðǣr þonne ǣnig	anforht wesan
þe him ǣr in brēostum bereð	bēacna sēlest
ac ðurh ðā rōde sceal	rīce gesēcan
of eorðwege	ǣghwylc sāwl
sēo þe mid Wealdende	wunian þenceð.

No one need   be fearful
who already bears in/on his breast   the best of beacons
for through the Cross   each soul
who wishes to dwell   with the Ruler,
leaving the ways of the world,   will attain that kingdom.[27]

Irish and Anglo-Saxon poems and high crosses thus indicate a productive cult of the Cross in the British Isles by the eighth century, merging both the Cross of the Vision and that of the Relic. This cult pervaded monastic and liturgical life and entered into the religious experiences of the laity through homilies, feasts, and prayer at stone monuments. That the custom of praying at high crosses was important in England but distinct from continental religious practice is reflected by Huneberc's eighth-century *Hodoeporicon of Saint Willibald* (700–786), in which the child Willibald, who has taken seriously ill when only a few years old, is laid at the foot of a stone cross in hopes that God will cure him. Writing in Latin for an immediate audience at Heidenheim, the Anglo-Saxon nun Huneberc notes that nobles and wealthy men in England regularly erect a cross on their property for the "convenience of those who wish to pray daily before it."[28]

In areas where Scandinavian settlers came in close contact with Celtic and Anglo-Saxon Christians, the Cross transferred with little modification. Such was the case on the Isle of Man, where Celtic and Scandinavian settlements appear to have merged with particular syncretic productivity.[29] It was also the case in other parts of the British Isles, Iceland, and southwestern Norway.

Inscribed Latin crosses first appeared on Manx slab monuments in the late seventh century, as Man acquired Christianity from Irish sources. Gradually, however, as the Scandinavian settlement on the island developed, Celtic high crosses with runic inscriptions and dedications began to appear. These incorporate interlace patterns in the Borre and Mammen styles of tenth-century western Scandinavia[30] and bear dedication formulas characteristic of continental Scandinavian monuments, apart from the use of the term *kross* for the more usual *steinn* (stone) when referring to the monument itself.[31] Perhaps the best known of these is the tenth-century Gautr's Cross of Kirk Michael, which includes the names of both its patron ("Mael Brigde, son of Aþakan the Smith") and its carver, Gautr (Fig. 1).[32] The bulk of these inscribed monuments were raised in the memory of a relative (male or female) and show a mixing of names indicative of intermarriage or intercultural influence. In this way, they carry on the tradition of memorial stones preexisting throughout Scandinavia while reflecting the Christian and Celtic influences of the Isle of Man in particular.

That Manx Scandinavians assimilated the Cross as a warrior standard and implement of power—akin to the implements of Nordic gods (see below)—is evident in the iconography of the tenth-century slate cross fragment at Kirk Andreas.[33] Here, flanking a depiction of the cross ornamented with interlace, we find two parallel figures: on the right, Óðinn with his spear and raven, treading on the jaw of a wolf (Fenrir); on the left, Jesus (or a saint), armed with cross and book, treading on a serpent, flanked by a fish (cf. *Genesis* 3:15 as a type of Christ). While the book and raven figure as

Figure 1. Gautr's Cross, Kirk Michael, Isle of Man, tenth century. Monument combines Christian Cross with Scandinavian interlace patterning and Norse runic inscription. Photo courtesy Manx National Heritage.

parallel sources of wisdom, the cross and spear are clearly intended as parallel sources of divine power. The Kirk Andreas Cross seems to assume a conversance with both Scandinavian and Christian religious systems and the willingness to compare them outright in terms of symbolism and imagery. It is a work scarcely imaginable but in the richly syncretic Celtic-Scandinavian, pre-Christian–Christian milieu of the Isle of Man. As Man developed into a cultural hearth for the western and northern islands of Scotland, and from there to the Faroes and Iceland, it appears that this embrace of the Cross spread to Scandinavian settlements throughout the region.

The mixture of Christian and pre-Christian symbolism evident on the Kirk Andreas Cross parallels the figural sculpture of the Gosforth Cross in Cumbria.[34] Here, in addition to interlace patterns, we find a variety of scenes drawn from Christian and Scandinavian sacred histories. A crucified Christ on the bottom of the east shaft is attended by both a man with a spear (probably the Longinus of medieval Christian legend) and a woman with a sweeping gown, who may represent Mary or Mary Magdalen but resembles iconographically similar valkyrie or queen figures on the pre-Christian picture stones of Gotland (Fig. 2). The rest of the scenes on the cross appear references to Ragnarök, the pagan version of the Last Judgment, in which the Æsir and their allies do final battle against the unleashed powers of Loki and his ilk. The Gosforth Cross may represent a Scandinavianized Christian eschatology, one merging pre-Christian and Christian figures and reflecting the popularity of the subject in missionary homilies.[35] It was, as we have seen, an event in which the shining Cross of the Vision played a central role, and thus its appearance on a carved high cross makes good thematic sense, even if its imagery may seem strikingly pagan today.

Although the crosses at Kirk Andreas and Gosforth epitomize syncresis between Scandinavian paganism and British Isle Christianity, they are certainly not alone in this respect. Stone sculptures with analogous content abound in northern England, Scotland, and the western and northern islands.[36] Another stone at Gosforth may depict Þórr fishing for the world serpent.[37] Several crosses in Leeds and Sherburn may include depictions of Völundr/Wayland.[38] Stone monuments were probably paralleled by wooden sculptures as well, although these have failed to survive.

Textual as well as archaeological evidence indicates the spread of this Cross tradition from the British Isles north into Iceland and western Norway. *Landnámabók* includes an account of the Orkney migrant Einarr Þorgeirsson, who marked his new territory in Iceland with three divine symbols—an ax (symbolizing Þórr), an eagle (symbolizing Óðinn), and a cross.[39] High

Figure 2. Pagan Picture Stone, Alskog, Tjängvide, Gotland, probably eighth century. Monument shows stylized depictions of elements of Scandinavian paganism, including Óðinn's eight-legged horse, Sleipnir, a valkyrie figure, and a ship. Photo courtesy Antikvarisk-topografiska arkivet, Stockholm.

crosses of stone appear in coastal Norway in the tenth and eleventh centuries,[40] sharing rune type with the crosses of Man.[41] In *Eiríks saga*, Auðr the Deepminded leaves the Hebrides for Caithness, migrating subsequently to the Orkneys and eventually to Iceland. There, the saga writer states: "Hon bjó í Hvammi. Hon hafði bœnahald í Krosshólum; þar lét hon reisa krossa, því at hon var skírð ok vel trúuð"[42] [She made her home at Hvamm and had a chapel at Krosshólar, where she had crosses set up, for she had been baptised and held the Christian faith].[43] References in the twelfth-century Icelandic Homily Book as well as in an early version of *Jóns saga Biskups* indicate the custom of prayer at outdoor crosses. St. Guðmundr is also portrayed as having erected a standing cross as a site for prayer at Hólar. As *Guðmundar saga* records: "People go there as they do to holy places and burn lights before the cross outside just as they would inside a church, even if the weather is bad."[44]

The Cross in Eastern Scandinavia: Influences from the East

The story of the Cross in the eastern Nordic region, like the story of Christianization itself, differs substantively from that of the Atlantic settlements. Archaeological evidence shows that Nordic chieftains and traders along the Baltic coast met with the symbols of Christianity long before understanding or accepting their theological meanings. Christian art had developed for centuries before arriving in the North, and the pervasive, persistent nature of Christian symbolism in southern and eventually also western and eastern Europe made the adoption of Christian motifs inevitable in those communities that carried on trade with the Christian world. Thus, from a purely art-historical perspective, we can note the arrival of the Cross in Sweden and Finland as early as the sixth century.[45] Only gradually, however, does the Cross begin to carry the supernatural weight associated with it in medieval Christianity. The shift is reflected archaeologically through different uses of the cross in burials, uses which subsided as Christianity itself became firmly established.

   The Cross as talisman and motif becomes prominent in Nordic art, graves, and hoards well before the full embrace of Christianity. A survey of cross pendants and icons in gravefinds from the eleventh to the thirteenth centuries in the Lake Beloe and Kargapol area of Russia shows the adoption of the cross as a sacred object, despite the apparent continuation of a pagan belief system, and may illustrate pagan responses to the Cross throughout northern Europe.[46] In this region at the periphery of the Viking world, crosses do not occur randomly; they are found in only a minority of graves, perhaps those of persons or families nominally Christianized. Further, they appear around the necks of those persons viewed as the society's most vulnerable: women, teenaged boys, and especially children. That these burials are pagan, or only marginally Christian, is indicated by burial type, and by irregularities in the burial site, for example, the placing of a cross at the foot of the deceased, an act incongruous with the Christian burial rite of the era.[47] Significantly, crosses disappeared from graves in the Kargapol region in the thirteenth and fourteenth centuries, as Christianity became established as the dominant faith.

Orthodox style and motifs came with cross pendants from Russia and eastern Europe into the entirety of the Baltic region during the ninth and tenth centuries. By the eleventh century, local Nordic and Baltic artisans had begun manufacturing their versions of such objects in Novgorod, Gotland, and the Gulf of Riga area.[48] Where burial with cross pendants appears a function of status, travel, and wealth—as in the still strongly pagan Turku region of Finland in the eleventh century—such objects are associated with male graves and hoards.[49] A single man might be buried with an array of talismans, Christian and pagan alike, a feature paralleled in graves in Eura[50] and Staraja Ladoga[51] and in Sámi graves and hoards throughout Sweden and Norway.[52] Where Christianity appears to have been taking root as a faith through local missionization, on the other hand—as in Birka, Sweden—the cross pendants tend to appear in women's graves (as in the Russian case), strung about the neck with a chain and clearly worn as a source of luck or intercession.[53]

The importation of Mediterranean and Eastern Christian influences into Nordic art and belief can be traced in the remarkable picture stones of Gotland, a leading center of Viking trade in the east. Trade connections brought Gotlanders in contact with the highly developed commemorative sculpture traditions of the Christian Mediterranean as well as of southeastern Europe, and these soon became translated into pagan monuments on the island.[54] Early cryptic symbols, such as spirals and triangles, gave way in time to more recognizable iconography, as on the eighth-century Alskog, Tjängvide stone (Fig. 2). Here Óðinn's eight-legged steed, Sleipnir, shares ground with figures reminiscent of valkyries, gods, warriors, horses, battles, and a ship under sail. While such monuments give the impression of a thriving but mysterious late pagan religiosity on Gotland, more emphatically Christian imagery soon begins to intrude. In the monuments associated with the eleventh century, we find a cross formée, sometimes encircled or taking on floral details, occupying the same upper position once filled by spirals or Óðinnic emblems. Such designs are almost certainly copied from the pendants that they resemble, and they apparently announce the religious identity of the persons honored by the stone. The mysterious ship motif of earlier centuries becomes replaced with an interlace design and runic inscription comparable to those found on Christian stones on mainland Sweden from the same period. The cross symbol functions as an insignia of Christianity, but in so doing it differs from the high crosses of the British Isles. No longer the animate object of fervent devotion, the Cross here appears but a simple emblem of religious membership, paralleled exactly by similar demarcations of pagan allegiance on stones of the same form.

Eastern religious influences, strong in Karelia as well as Gotland, lessened in importance in areas further to the west. Sweden and Denmark reflect a combination of influences from east, south, and west, and Norway in particular shows influences from England. Production of crosses with western motifs and styles and arms of equal length was well established in various parts of more westerly Scandinavia by the eleventh century, and many of these cross types—especially those found in Norway—have close counterparts in England.[55] The lack of high crosses of the type common in the Atlantic settlements anywhere in the eastern Baltic tells us that we are dealing with a different brand of Christianity, one tied to the prestige trade and political centers to the east and south.

The Frankish Mission and the Arrival of State Christianity

We have seen thus far that the Cross—and with it, Christianity—came to the Nordic region both through the Atlantic settlements of the British Isles and through trade and contact with the eastern Christians of Novgorod and Byzantium. The first of these pathways is fondly and frequently remembered in Nordic hagiography: accounts of British missionary-saints like St. Willibrord (c. 658–739) and St. Boniface (c. 680–754) of Friesland, St. Willihad (d. 789) of Saxony, St. Sunniva (tenth century) of Selja, St. Eskil (died c. 1080) of Södermanland, St. David (early eleventh century) of Västmanland, and St. Henrik (d. c. 1156) of Uppsala and Finland—all point to an almost constant flow of devout Christians from the British Isles. The English sojourns of King Hákon the Good (919–61, king of Norway 934–61), the Swedish St. Botvid (d. 1120), and King Óláfr Tryggvason (968–1000, r. 995–1000) are also cited as the causes of conversion for each of these important

Nordic men. In contrast, the second of these pathways—that of the East—receives little credit in the textual accounts of Nordic Christianization, a fact which probably reflects both the Icelandic biases of our written sources and the deteriorating relations of eastern and western Christianity during the thirteenth century. In any case, both the limited distribution of British Isle high crosses in the Nordic region and the strong archaeological showings of eastern cross pendants should caution us to read the textual history with some reservation.

A third important source of Christian influence in mainland Scandinavia, however, came from the south. Although the continental Christianity arriving from Hamburg-Bremen evinced significantly less devotion to the Cross, it helped establish the notion of a Christian monarchy in the region and the idea of mass conversions. The concept of Christianity as a politically motivated public cult took shape particularly in Denmark and spread north and east. Its influence can be traced in yet another manifestation of Cross iconography, the Christian rune stones of Denmark and Sweden. Although derived in a distant form from the high crosses of the British Isles, these mainland Scandinavian monuments possess their own distinctive form and symbolism and their own apparent functions in the social life of Christianizing Scandinavians. They are functions reflective of public cult membership and a religiosity diffusing into the region from the south.

For Charlemagne (742–814) and his successors, Christianization represented a key means of controlling and potentially subjugating pagan populations to the north. It is clear that by the time of King Haraldr Bluetooth Gormson (baptized c. 965, d. 985), royal conversion was necessary to prevent hostile invasion from the south.[56] By the time of Adam of Bremen's *Gesta Hammaburgensis ecclesiae pontificum* (History of the Archbishops of Hamburg-Bremen, c. 1075), Scandinavian clerics and kings alike had come to resent this southern dominance. But in the figure of St. Ansgar (c. 801–865), we see the effort at its start. Although initiated originally by English exile monks such as Willihad (d. 789; founder of the see of Bremen) and Alcuin (c. 735–804; Charlemagne's adviser at Aachen), and linked to a king strongly associated with the Cross of the Relic, the Carolingian missionary effort of St. Ansgar proved far less interested in spreading devotion to the Cross than its British Isle counterparts.

We know of the life of St. Ansgar through Rimbert's ninth-century *Vita Anskarii*, which details the saint's missionary work in Denmark and Sweden and his final death as archbishop of Hamburg-Bremen.[57] Rimbert's text comments on the sanctity of its subject and the evil of his rivals, and thus its details on the history of the Birka mission in particular must be read with reservation.[58] On the other hand, critics concur that the accounts of Ansgar's visions—which are identified in the text as firsthand testimony from Ansgar himself—probably represent the saint's perceptions as recounted later in life. These show little evidence of devotion to the Cross or embrace of its symbolism. When the saint experiences visions, they involve Jesus, Mary, St. Peter, and John the Baptist. A vision of Mary and female saints (including his mother) leads the young Ansgar toward the religious life, and visions of Peter, John the Baptist, purgatory, heaven, and Christ help build up his resolve to persevere at the monastery thereafter. Where the poet of *Dream of the Rood* takes comfort in his memory of the Cross in his final days, the dying Ansgar's mind turns toward his human intercessors.[59] And where the Rood poet listens to the Cross's account of the Passion, Ansgar experiences the Scourging himself. Stretching his own body out behind Christ's, Ansgar bears the blows of the soldiers' whip and replaces imagistically as well as experientially, the animate, feeling Cross.[60] It is not surprising, then, that Asgar's *Vita* makes no mention of cross amulets or sculptures. The holy objects stolen, desecrated, or recovered in this narrative are all books, which hold the same capacity to punish thieves that earlier *vitae* attributed to pectoral crosses.[61]

Perhaps the pagan ownership of crosses, long commonplace among Scandinavians of status, as we have seen, made narratives of crosses falling into pagan hands less intriguing or incensing than stories of pagan acquisition of books. Perhaps, too, the association of the Cross with the British Isles—promoted on the continent by emigrant missionaries and the popularity of the cult of King St. Oswald[62]—made the symbol less appealing to the hagiographers of Hamburg-Bremen. Whatever the case, however, it is clear that Ansgar and his biographer show little of the devotion to the Cross that so inspired the missionary saints of the British Isles.

Crosses, however, did make their way into mainland Scandinavia, and often in striking monuments. Such is the case with the Jelling Stone, King Haraldr Bluetooth's (c. 958–87) monument to Danish conversion (Fig. 3).[63] Haraldr's acceptance of Christianity in 965 was prompted by two factors, neither of them the Cross. On the one hand, Widukind and Snorri tell us, the powerful Emperor Otta to the south threatened to invade Denmark if he refused the faith.[64] On the other hand, the priest Poppo/Poppa proved the power of the new religion by gripping a red-hot iron with his bare hand and showing it unharmed to the king. In the Jelling Stone, Haraldr identifies himself as the monarch who brought Christianity to the Danes. More than that, however, the stone brought to mainland Scandinavia the sculptural

Figure 3. Jelling Stone, Denmark, late tenth century. Commissioned by King Haraldr Bluetooth Gormson, this monument depicts a Christ in crucifixion and credits Haraldr with the conversion of Denmark. Photo courtesy National Museum, Copenhagen.

tradition characteristic of the British Isles. For the next two centuries, Christian as well as pagan Scandinavians imitated the monument, creating hundreds of similar sculptures in Denmark and Sweden.[65] The Jelling Stone can truly be called a turning point in the history of Cross iconography in mainland Scandinavia.[66]

Like St. Ansgar's vision of the Scourging, however, the Jelling Stone removes the Cross itself from the Passion. Here, we find a central, nimbed Christ, arms outstretched in crucifixion, but without any supporting cross at all. Rather, the space surrounding Christ has been filled with coils of serpents, a decorative choice that links the stone imagistically to an eighth-century Irish book cover from Athlone, County Westmeath. In this cast bronze representation of the Crucifixion, Christ's body dominates the scene, with the cross peaking out only a little at the extremities and elaborate spirals and interlace patterns adorning the Savior's clothes and those of his surrounding attendants.[67] But the Jelling Stone takes this stylistic choice to the extreme, as if to say that the Cross—so central to Christian sculpture and religiosity along the shores of the Irish Sea—holds no interest for the Scandinavian artist at all.

In the two centuries which followed, Haraldr's Jelling Stone served as the model for an unprecedented production of rune stones in central Scandinavia, some two thousand in all. Crosses figure frequently in these monuments, but here the cross is simplified and conventionalized in form, appearing most often as a simple Latin or palmette cross (often apparently modeled on a pendant) surrounded by some interlace patterning and a serpent-shaped runic inscription. Like Haraldr's monument, these later stones present the Cross more as an emblem of religious allegiance than as an object for religious meditation. As in Haraldr's Jelling Stone, they commemorate the deeds and lives of local individuals rather than more distant holy intercessors.[68]

The Divine Implement in Pre-Christian Religion

Where Swedish Christians embraced the Cross as an insignia of religious adherence on memorial stones, their pagan counterparts embraced the symbol of Þórr's hammer in much the same way.[69] Such can be seen in the rune stones of Christians and Þórr worshipers in Södermanland. Here, the cross depiction often combines with an image of a bearded man's head, probably Christ's. On the pagan Þórr stones of the region, this head-and-cross arrangement becomes directly paralleled in a head-and-hammer depiction, pointing again to the Christ-Þórr juxtaposition discussed in previous chapters. The hammer symbol appears as well in numerous late pagan amulets and inscriptions and can in many senses be termed an "anti-cross."[70] Scandinavian metalsmiths' dies from the period show that the same craftsmen made either cross or hammer amulets, depending, presumably, on the religious adherence of customers (Fig. 4).

The apparent equation of the Cross and Þórr's hammer demonstrates the late-pagan tendency to match attractive aspects of Christianity with equally attractive pagan counterparts. The close parallels in size, use, and even form of cross and hammer images from this era make this equation evident, and the survival of cross-and-hammer dies reveals the extent to which the two symbols became viewed as parallel religious items. At the same time, however, equating the Cross and Mjöllnir signals a key demotion of the Cross from the category of animate sacred intercessor to that of inanimate divine implement. In most respects, this demotion was entirely expectable given Nordic paganism, and it goes hardly noticed by modern interpreters unfamiliar with the Christian cult of the Cross during the ninth through thirteenth centuries. But it is an important development for what it tells about the interpretation of Christianity within Nordic pagan communities at this time.

Divine implements play a prominent role in Scandinavian mythology, especially as recounted by Snorri in his *Skáldskaparmál*.[71] Here, a single myth accounts for the origins of Þórr's hammer (Mjöllnir), Óðinn's spear (Gungnir), Sif's hair of gold, Óðinn's golden ring (Draupnir), Freyr's ship (Skíðbladnir), and Freyr's golden boar (Gullinborsti). All are created by dwarves at the behest of the mischievous Loki, who thus attempts to escape the wrath of an irritated Óðinn. As is often the case with Snorri's accounts of Scandinavian mythology, this rendering may present too unified and consistent a picture of these implements, glossing over changes or disputes regarding deities' properties and interests over time. Yet it is clear that the implements described relate centrally to each god's sphere of interest or action. Óðinn's roles in warfare as well as in chieftainship are reflected aptly by the unerring spear, Gungnir, and the ring of plenty, Draupnir. Þórr's hammer, Mjöllnir, becomes crucial to the god's activities in fighting the frost giants who threaten the Æsir. As such, the implements are more than simple possessions: they share integrally in each god's sacred functions.

As with the gods, however, so also their implements vary in the regions and versions of Scandinavian mythology left to us today. While Þórr may be primarily associated with his hammer, for instance, he also possesses a belt of strength and powerful iron gauntlets.[72] Saxo describes the god's primary weapon as a club, and the *Landnámabók* includes an account of Einarr

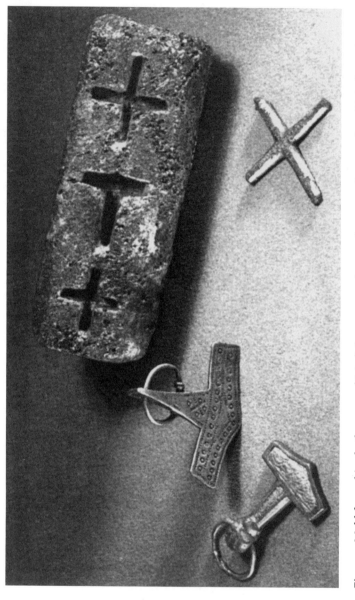

Figure 4. Mold for making both cross and Þórr's-hammer amulets, tenth century. Items such as this indicate the close association of the Christian Cross and Þórr's hammer in late pagan Scandinavia and the production of both types of amulets by the same smiths. Photo courtesy National Museum, Copenhagen.

Þorgeirsson's marking of his new territory with three symbols: a cross, an eagle, and an ax, the last of which is said to represent Þórr.[73] Visual representations of the hammer Mjöllnir itself vary from the earliest iron amulets attached to neckrings[74] to the stylized, sweeping silver hammer amulets of the late tenth and early eleventh centuries, and, finally, to ambiguous, cross-and-hammer objects, such as the Foss Amulet.[75]

Óðinn's relation to divine implements presents a further difficulty. For while Þórr's hammer-club-ax shows certain variation, Óðinn is known by an array of key implements, including his eight-legged horse, Sleipnir, his wolves, Geri and Freki, his ravens, Huginn and Muninn, his valkyries, and his afterlife hall.[76] Thus, while the god is called by skaldic epithets such as Egill's *geirs dróttinn* (Lord of the Spear) and Bragi's *Gungnis váfaðr* (Gungnir's Shaker),[77] Gungnir cannot be seen as Óðinn's sole or even most representative divine implement.

This variation in the form or type of divine implement appears to lessen under the influence of Christianity. In fact, such symbols appear to conventionalize, apparently in imitation of the Christian iconographic tradition. Such is certainly reflected in the portrayal of Óðinn on the Kirk Andreas Cross, discussed above, where Óðinn's depiction with raven and spear is placed in direct juxtaposition to Christ's with cross and book. The system of easily recognized visual symbols developed in western Christian art to identify saints and evangelists spread through manuscript art, stained glass and wall paintings, carvings, and jewelry and became very familiar to artisans of the Viking Age.[78] Similar processes of conventionalization almost certainly underlie the depictions of warriors on horseback and ships under sail on Gotlantic picture stones. And while Þórr's hammer amulets show a good deal of variation in form and style in the early Viking Age, the figures have grown relatively uniform by the late tenth century. The same stylized hammer that develops on silver amulets also comes to dominate Swedish stone monuments of the era.[79] While such relative uniformity can be attributed to craftsmen copying prestige works from trading centers, it may also be viewed as an indication of the development of a notion of standardized iconography, or at least the notion of standardization as a goal and norm.

While divine implements conventionalized in form in late pagan art, the tendency to compare gods through juxtaposition of their tools—apparently an ancient aspect of pagan religion—remained strong. Snorri's account of the creation of Gungnir, Draupnir, and Mjöllnir demonstrates this comparative trait: the gods themselves meet to judge which of their new implements holds the greatest value.[80] The same notion also underlies the battle of Þórr and Hrungnir as depicted in Þódólfr of Hvin's *Haustlöng* and recounted by Snorri in *Skáldskaparmál.* Here, god and giant duel, each hurling his weapon of power at the other. Mjöllnir's victory is also Þórr's:

Sá hann [Hrungnir] þá Þór í ásmóði; fór han ákafliga ok reiddi hamarinn ok kastaði um langa leið at Hrungni. Hrungnir fœrir upp heinina báðum höndum ok kastar í mót; mœtir hon hamrinum á flugi, ok brotnar sundr heinin, fellr annarr hlutr á jörð, ok eru þar af orðin öll heinberg; annarr hlutr brast í höfði Þór, svá at hann fell fram á jörð; en hamarrinn Mjöllnir kom í mitt höfuð Hrungni ok lamði hausinn í smá mola, ok fell han fram yfir Þór, svá at fótr hans lá of háls Þór.[81]

Hrungnir saw Þórr in his godly rage; he strode out furiously and swung the hammer, throwing it from afar at Hrungnir. Hrungnir lifted his hone up with both hands and threw it in return. It hit the hammer in flight and burst into pieces: one part fell to earth and from that has come all flint; the other piece hit Þórr's head, so that he fell down. But the hammer Mjöllnir hit Hrungnir in the middle of the head and smashed his skull into little bits. And he fell over on top of Þórr, so that his feet lay on on Þórr's neck.

These crucial divine implements could also be loaned from one god to another or even from a god to human adherents. This tendency, too, probably reflects Christian influences, particularly when we see humans using surrogates of the divine implement in ritual actions of their own, much as Christians used surrogates of the Holy Cross in their acts of sanctification or prayer. In the Eddaic poem *Helgaqviða Hundingsbana önnor,* Óðinn lends his spear to Dagr so that he can avenge himself on Helgi.[82] Implements can be stolen (as with Þórr's hammer in *Þrymsqviða*) and loaned to other gods (as with Freyr's sword in *För Scirnis*).[83] Þórr's hammer seems to have a function in sanctifying both funeral pyres (as in Snorri's account of Baldr's death) and brides (as in *Þrymsqviða*) and both of these mythic acts appear paralleled in human rituals connected with burial and weddings.[84] Use of a surrogate implement probably underlies Steinþórr's casting of a spear over his enemy's forces in *Eyrbyggja saga* "as in the custom of old,"[85] apparently to designate the men as sacrifices to Óðinn. Finally, Snorri notes at the end of his *Gylfaginning*[86] that Þórr's sons Móði and Magni will recover Mjöllnir where it lies abandoned after the events of Ragnarök, the twilight of the gods. This image strongly resembles King Magnús the Good's recovery and later use of the ax Hel, which had belonged to his father King St. Óláfr.[87] In both cases, the transfer of the sacred weapon to the new generation marks a crucial continuity in power and sacral role within the world.

In some respects, all of these characteristics are shared by the medieval Cross. It too, could be lent and stolen, and its imagery indicated the deity associated with it. It was used ritually to sanctify as well as to protect. Many of these similarities in use may derive from pagan adaptions of Cross-related rituals. In other respects, however, the divine implements of pagan gods are nothing like the Cross. For while the Cross is both independent of Christ and fully conscious, Mjöllnir and Gungnir have no real power to stand on their own. Mjöllnir possesses the ability to withstand Þórr's mightiest blows but exercises no independent harmful effects on the giants who steal it in *Þrymsqviða*. Nor do we see depictions of either hammer or spear as conscious entities, with descriptions of their views during battle or afterward. They are mere vehicles for each god's triumphant power. Thus, it is unlikely that anyone ever wore a Þórr's-hammer amulet as a symbol of devotion to Mjöllnir; devotion to the Cross, on the other hand, pervaded Christian practice of the day.

Cnut the Great and Mixed Religious Symbolism

Attention to the Cross in its various forms can map the pathways of Nordic Christianization and give us a glimpse of pagan interpretations of this complex Christian symbol. With the rise of a Christian monarchy, however, new uses of the Cross developed, drawing on the noble associations that attended both the Cross of the Vision and the Cross of the Relic in European culture. In the statecraft of Cnut, Óláfr, Sigurðr, and Valdemar II, we find both the canny use of Cross symbolism and cogent reminders of the nearness of paganism in the last centuries of the Viking Age.

Given what we have seen regarding Cross devotion in the British Isles, it is natural that King Cnut the Great (c. 995–1035)—grandson of King Haraldr Bluetooth—would turn to the Cross as an attractive imagistic tool in ruling his newly consolidated realm of Denmark-England. Like Constantine, Charlemagne, and Oswald before him, Cnut used religious symbols advantageously. For his English and Anglo-Scandinavian Christian subjects, Cnut proved the model Christian; for his pagan troops and supporters, however, he remained an Óðinnic king.

Cnut, baptized sometime prior to his ascension to the English throne in 1016, used his religious affiliation to advantage in a country weary of pagan Viking invaders. The celebrated miniature portrait of Cnut and Emma in the *Liber vitae* of the New Minster at Westminster (Fig. 5) encapsulates Cnut's knowing usage of the Cross in his political career. The monarch is de-

Figure 5. King Cnut and Queen Emma at Westminster. *Liber vitae*, Westminster New Minster, England, eleventh century. The portrait was commissioned to celebrate Cnut's gift of a golden cross to the monastery and reflects the king's use of Christian symbolism in appealing to his British subjects. Photo by permission of The British Library.

picted beside a gold cross which he donated to the church circa 1031, his right hand outstretched to touch it. His left hand, however, still grasps his sword: he is a king of action and crusade, not a passive recluse. A hovering angel crowns Cnut, completing the visual invocation of the Constantinian formula: a divinely endorsed ruler standing beside his shining emblem of the Cross, at the very foot of an approving Christ in majesty.[88]

When combined with other acts of royal piety—generous endowments of churches and monasteries, and impressive acts of humility—Cnut could scarcely be mistaken for a ruthless pagan king. Often, his public acts of sanctity involved crosses or saints associated with the Cross or martyrdom. On one Easter, for instance, the monk Goscelin writes, Cnut refused his crown, preferring to place it on a crucifix in honor of the King of all and abandoning it there as a gift to the church. He commissioned reliquaries for the remains of St. Vincent at Abingdon and St. Cyriacus at Westminster Abbey and instigated the translation of relics of St. Ælfheah and St. Edmund of East Anglia. Cnut's association with these latter cults almost certainly had political purposes: both saints had been murdered by Viking invaders, and Cnut could find no better way of demonstrating his break with his pagan past.[89]

On the other hand, Cnut's Norse skalds rely on pagan metaphors and imagery in their poems of praise, many of which must have been performed in the hearing of the king's largely pagan forces. Hallvarðr Háreksblesi, for instance, asserts in his *Knútsdrápa*:

> Knútr verr jörð sem ítran
> alls dróttinn sal fjalla.

> Cnut protects the land as the
> Lord of all [does] the splendid
> hall of the mountains [= heaven].[90]

This skaldic image could be as easily interpreted in Óðinnic as Christian terms, with Jörð figuring as the sacred bride of the Scandinavian *hieros gamos* (sacred marriage). Óðinnic imagery was common in skaldic court poetry even after Christianization, and Hallvarðr employs kennings (skaldic metaphors) that link the king to both Freyr and Höðr as well.[91] The fact that many of Cnut's soldiers remained pagan or only nomimally Christian gives added significance to these allusions. Cnut seems to have been willing to let his image cross religious lines, appealing to both his Christian subjects and pagan retainers in terms acceptable to them, uniting all in reverence for the divinely ordained warrior-monarch.

Fram, Fram, Kristsmenn, Krossmen, Konungsmenn!

Despite his Christian predecessors Hákon the Good and Óláfr Tryggvason it is King St. Óláfr (995–1030, r. 1015–30) who becomes known as the true Christianizer of Norway. By the close of Snorri's masterful *Óláfs saga Helga* (written c. 1230–35), we have an image of a steadfastly Christian King St. Óláfr, guided by God and firmly devoted to the Cross. Óláfr has white crosses painted on his soldiers' helmets and shields and marches beneath a banner of white marked with a cross of gold. Further, he instructs his men to invoke the Constantinian threesome—Christ, Cross, and King—in their battle cry, which they do to some confusion in the ensuing Battle of Stiklastaðir, Óláfr's last. The visionary king speaks to his soldiers:

Vér skulum marka lið várt allt, gera herkumbl á hjálmum várum ok skjöldum, draga þar með bleiku á krossinn helga. En ef vér komum í orrostu, þá skulu vér hafa allir eitt orðtak: "Fram, fram, Kristsmenn, krossmenn, konungsmenn!"[92]

We shall mark all our forces, making a battle emblem on our helmets and shields, drawing with white paint the Holy Cross. And when we enter the field, we shall all have one battle cry: "Forward, forward, men of Christ, men of the Cross, men of the King!"

Here, then, it would seem we have the typical invocation of the Cross of the Vision, little altered from either Constantine or Oswald, even if the ruler now sets his forces against supporters of King Cnut, also a Christian monarch. As if to mitigate this lack of congruence, Snorri dwells on Óláfr's insistence that his men be baptized. The king turns away Gauka-Þórir and Afra-Fasti, for instance, until they consent to baptism, and likewise he turns away some five hundred other pagans who offer him help. He promises to punish pagan traitors more harshly than Christian ones, and he forgives the skald Sigvátr his absence since he has gone on pilgrimage to Rome. Finally, he converts Arnljótr to the faith just before the battle is to begin.[93]

Examining the saga as a whole, however, it becomes clear that this attention to the Cross and the role of the Christian leader gains prominence only as the text moves from being a saga based on accounts of King Óláfr's deeds and relations as a Viking leader to a legend designed to make the case for Óláfr's sainthood. For while daily Mass and the feast days of the Church are constant settings in the saga as a whole, and conversion by force a constant theme throughout, the Cross per se plays little role in the narrative until the later chapters of Óláfr's exile to Russia and attempted return to power in Norway. Prior to this point, Snorri describes Óláfr's banner and manner in other terms: although Óláfr's men wear French helmets and shields adorned with the Cross, his standard is white with a dragon.[94] Such seems appropriate for a king described as faithful in principle to Christianity but ruled utterly by his desire for power and his harsh, impulsive nature.

Óláfr is not portrayed as a pagan in Christian clothing by any means, nor is he without his visions. These, however, like those of St. Ansgar, focus on other intercessors or images than the Cross. At the beginning of his career, for instance, Óláfr has a dream-vision of a man "marvelous but also fearsome" who counsels him not to sail to Palestine but to return to Norway where he will rule as king forever.[95] This interlocutor, possibly Christ himself but more likely a previous king of Norway, is paralleled at the close of Óláfr's career by a vision of Óláfr Tryggvason, who appears to assure Óláfr that God supports his quest to recapture Norway from King Cnut. Óláfr's right to regain his throne will be supported by God, since he has received it both by inheritance as well as by divine choice: "God will bear witness that the realm is yours."[96] In contrast to Constantine and Oswald, however, Óláfr sees no Cross with the man.

As Óláfr's fortunes begin to fall at the close of his career, he considers becoming a monk and making a pilgrimage to Jerusalem. While visiting the Russian court, he heals an afflicted boy, a miracle which involves Cross imagery (see Chapter 5).[97] After massaging a boy's swollen boil for some time, the king places pieces of bread in the shape of a cross and feeds these to his patient. The boy's ailment soon disappears.

As Óláfr's sanctity rises in the narrative, so does his association with the Holy Cross, culminating in his strong invocation of the Cross in his final battle. Cross imagery in Snorri's text correlates directly with the intrusion of the European saint's legend as a narrative model and thematic reference point for the later chapters. Where Snorri is writing kingly saga, as in the bulk of his work, he depicts a warrior-king who uses religion as an effective tool for the management and promulgation of allegiance between himself and his subjects. But the Scandinavian St. Óláfr sees himself in direct concourse with his God, even if his cult became associated with a mediating Cross and other more standard images of sainthood through the writings of later hagiographers. It is Óláfr—not the Cross—whom subsequent Norwegian rulers and peasants invoked as their favored intercessor. Armed with his ax, Hel, as his saintly attribute or divine implement, this St. Óláfr becomes the friend to those who call his name, including his son King Magnús the Good, who helps establish the cult in the years immediately following his father's death.[98] Magnús builds Óláfr's shrine and has Sigvátr the Skald compose praise poetry in honor of his father's miracles.[99] And when it

comes time for him to have a vision intimating his own divine right to
conquer and rule, Magnús sees his father, not the Cross.[100]

Sigurðr the Crusader

If King St. Óláfr's legend marks the true arrival of the Cross of the Vision in
mainland Scandinavia, it is King Sigurðr the Crusader (1090–1130; r. 1103–
30) whose legend brings the Cross of the Relic. Preserved at length in Snorri's
Magnússona saga and in brief in Theodric's *Historia de antiquitate regum
Norwegiensium* and the *Ágrip*, this account brings the Crusades and its
intimate association with the Cross into the world of Scandinavian kings.[101]
As an act of devotion or vehicle for political image-making, however, Sigurðr's receipt and translation of a fragment of the True Cross represents one
of the greatest non-events of Scandinavian religious history. Whether out of
pride, lack of piety, or difference in devotion, Sigurðr's failure with respect to
the Church of the Cross tells us much about the ways in which the Cross was
received and ultimately marginalized in conversion-era Scandinavia. Only in
the sequel to the Sigurðr tale—Snorri's account of the destruction of the
Church of the Cross at Konungahella and the rescue of the Relic from the
invading pagan Wends (see below)—do the typical images of Cross devotion
enter into the story.[102] This event, however, postdates Sigurðr's life by five
years (1135) and only underscores the king's indifference.

Sigurðr and his men travel to Palestine in pursuit of glory. After a long
series of battles and visits in England, Spain, and Sicily, Sigurðr and his men
arrive in Jerusalem. There they are greeted by King Baldvini (Baldwin), who
eventually entrusts the king with a fragment of the True Cross:

> Baldvini konungr gerði veizlu fagra Sigurði konungi ok liði miklu með honum. Þá
> gaf Baldvini konungr Sigurði konungi marga helga dóma, ok þá var tekinn spánn af
> krossinum helga at ráði Baldvina konungs ok pátríarka, ok sóru þeir báðir at helgum
> dómi, at þetta tré var af inum helga krossi, er guð sjálfr var píndr á. Síðan var sá
> heilagr dómr gefinn Sigurði konungi, með því at hann sór áðr ok tólf menn aðrir
> með honum, at hann skyldi fremja kristni með öllum mætti sínum ok koma í land
> erkibyskupsstóli, ef hann mætti, ok at krossin skyldi þar vera, sem inn helgi Óláfr
> hvíldi, ok hann skyldi tíund fremja ok sjálfr gera.[103]

> King Baldwin prepared a fine feast for King Sigurðr and many of his men. Then King
> Baldwin gave King Sigurðr many holy relics and a sliver was taken from the Holy
> Cross at the decision of King Baldwin and the patriarch, both of whom swore on that
> holy relic that this wood was from the very Holy Cross on which God had suffered.

Then the holy relic was given to King Sigurðr provided that he, along with twelve of his men, swear that he would work with all his might to further Christianity and bring an archbishop's seat into his land if possible, and that the Cross would be placed where St. Óláfr rests, and that he would advance the cause of tithing and pay tithe himself.

The dream of a Norwegian archbishopric was not realized in Sigurðr's lifetime; rather, it took until 1152 for the English-born papal legate Nicholas Breakspear (later Pope Adrian IV) to establish the archbishopric of Nidaros/Trondheim, freeing the Norwegian church from the control of Lund and giving it authority over Iceland and Greenland.[104] Nor did Sigurðr make good on his promise to deposit the relic near the shrine of St. Óláfr. Rather, he started construction of the wooden Church of the Cross for it at Konungahella (Kungälv) around 1116, fully six years after his return from the Holy Land. Snorri writes reproachfully of the king's decision:

Kross inn helga lét hann vera í Konungahellu ok helt í því eigi eiða sína, er hann sór á Jórsalalandi, en hann framði tíund ok flest allt annat, þat er hann hafði svarit. En þat er hann setti krossinn austr við landsenda, hugði hann þat vera mundu alls lands gæzlu, en þat varð at inu mesta óráði at setja þann helgan dóm svá mjök undir vald heiðinna manna, sem síðan reyndisk.[105]

He kept the Holy Cross at Konungahella and thus broke the oath which he had sworn in Palestine, but he did further the tithes and accomplished most of the other things to which he had sworn. By placing the Cross at the eastern edge of the realm, he thought it would protect the entire land, but it was most unwise to place the holy relic so nearly under the power of pagan men, as it turned out later.

The church was not completed until 1127, seventeen years after Sigurðr's return to Norway and three years before his death. Its eventual destruction and the near loss of the relic are recounted in stirring terms in Snorri's *Magnúss saga Blinda ok Haralds Gilla* (see below).

What kept Sigurðr from keeping his solemn oath of devotion to the Cross and what became of the relic during the many years before the completion of its church? It may be that Sigurðr kept the fragment as a personal talisman, much as other kings before him had done. It may also be that Sigurðr, who by 1116 had become embattled with his brother and co-regent, Eysteinn (1089–1123), wished to set up a separate sphere of sacred power for himself apart from his brother's seat of support at Trondheim. But Sigurðr does not mention receiving the Cross as a great accomplishment in the same way that he boasts of having defeated pagans, swum the Jordan, and tied willow branches along its shores in his altercation with his brother over their relative merits.[106] Thus it is difficult to read his acts as motivated by any fervent devotion, despite the best efforts of Baldwin and the patriarch to inspire one in him. Sigurðr is a soldier, not a saint. The hoped-for devotion to the Cross does little to displace or compete with the already thriving cult of St. Óláfr.

Saving the Cross and Other Crusader Tales

Whatever the realities of the devotional experiences of Scandinavian monarchs and peasants during eleventh and twelfth centuries, the saga texts of the thirteenth century display all the narrative images of Christian devotion and heroism typical of continental literature of their era. In the exciting tale of the pagan Wendish sack of Konungahella in *Magnúss saga Blinda ok Haralds Gilla*, we see a stalwart cleric's defense of the relic of the Cross along with miraculous signs of its power.[107] In accounts of the Danish King Valdemar II Sejr's crusade against the pagan Estonians, Constantine's grand vision becomes recapitulated yet again in the legend of the cross-emblazoned Danish flag. These and other narrative accounts of the Cross reflect the full embrace of Cross symbolism in the region as a product of both religious and cultural adjustment.

Snorri's rendering of the sack of Konungahella follows the lines of typical Crusader tales. The settlement's impending doom is signaled ahead of time by an outbreak of disease and a run of ill fortune, leading many to abandon the city altogether.[108] Then the Wendish King Réttiburr (Ratibor of Pommern, Prussia) arrives with his pagan forces, storming the town and precipitating a fierce battle. Snorri probably knew of the battle through the reminiscences of his foster father, Jón Loftsson (d. 1197), who had been fostered himself at Konungahella and was eleven years old at the time of the siege. In the account, a priest named Andréás plays a notable part in the events of the day, blessing a flaming arrow that kills one of the enemy's otherwise invincible magic soldiers. As the Wends eventually win the victory, however, Andréás manages to save the relic of the Cross from burning and desecration, bearing it in its reliquary into bondage:

Þá fóru þeir Andréás prestr á konungsskipit ok með krossinn helga. Þá kom ótti yfir heiðingja af þeiri bending, er yfir konungsskipit kom hiti svá mikill, at allir þeir þóttusk nær brenna. Konungr bað túlkinn spyrja prest, hví svá varð. Hann sagði, at almáttigr guð, sá er kristnir menn trúðu á, sendi þeim mark reiði sinnar, er þeir dirfðusk þess at hafa með höndum hans píslarmark, þeir er eigi vilja trúa á skapara sinn. "Ok svá mikill kraptr fylgir krossinum, at opt hafa orðit fyrr þvílíkar jartegnir yfir heiðnum mönnum, þá er þeir höfðu hann með höndum, ok sumar enn berari." ... Síðan fór Andréás prestr með krossinn um nóttinna til Sólbjarga, ok var bæði hregg ok rota. Andréás flutti krossinn til góðrar varðveizlu.[109]

Then Andréás the priest and the others went aboard the king's ship with the Holy Cross. The pagans were seized with fear of them because so great a heat came over the king's ship that they thought it near burning. The king commanded the interpreter to ask the priest why this had happened. He said that Almighty God, in whom the Christians believe, had sent them this sign of his anger at those who refused to believe in their maker and yet would dare hold in their hands the sign of his crucifixion. "And so much power is connected with the Cross, that often signs such as this have appeared to pagan men who have handled it—and some signs even clearer." ... Then Andréás the priest journeyed by night to Sólbjargir [a town to the north of Konungahella] amid both wind and rain. Andréás transported the Cross to a place of safety.

Andréás is portrayed as a fearless servant of the Cross, armed with the miraculous assistance of God. In the related account in *Ágrip*, the priest proposes to bring the relic to the shrine of St. Óláfr and the Icelandic Annals record its arrival in Nidaros in 1234 (a century later).[110] It is possible that the ornate Scandinavian reliquary currently housed at the Kammin Cathedral in Pomerania (modern Kamień Pomorski, Poland) represents the original reliquary of Sigurðr's relic of the Cross.[111] Ratibor later converted to Christianity.

While the tale of the pagan sack of Konungahella recapitulates continental accounts of the Persian theft of the Cross in 614, the miraculous vision of the Cross in the Danish crusades against the Estonians recapitulates the Constantinian-Oswaldian sacred vision. In 1219, the Danish King Valdemar II Sejr ("The Victorious," 1170–1241), fighting the pagan Estonians for control of the eastern Baltic coast, was said to have received the red-and-white cross-shaped Danish flag (the *Dannebrog*) as it fluttered down from heaven just before battle. Held aloft during fighting by Valdemar's archbishop Andreas Sunesen, the miraculous emblem of God's favor assured the Danes' triumph over their pagan opponents.[112] Narratives of this type reflect the full assimilation of the Cross as emblem and object of devotion in Nordic Christianity.

Njáls saga reflects this assimilation in its shorthand use of Cross imagery as a device for characterization. Once Christianity has arrived in the narrative (midway through the saga), good characters treat crosses well; evil characters desecrate them. When the villainous Mörðr Valgarðsson returns to Iceland to find the land converted, he attacks his father's crosses to test the new religion. As a result, Mörðr's father soon sickens and dies. When the impetuous but heroic Skarp-Heðinn Njálsson is found dead amid the ashes of his father's estate, he is seen to have burned crosses into his chest, a final act of allegiance to the new faith at the moment of his death.[113]

By the end of the thirteenth century, the Holy Cross had become a normal part of Nordic Christianity, following the same lines and tendencies found in Europe as a whole. A relic of the Cross made its way to Skálholt, Iceland, by 1242,[114] and Hattula Church in Finland became a pilgrimage center for devotees of the Cross during the High Middle Ages.[115] Further fragments arrived in the centuries which followed leading up to the Reformation. Homilies regarding the Cross are found in the Icelandic Homily Book as well as the Old Norwegian Homily Book, and throughout the North, the various feast days of the Cross were honored as holy days of obligation.[116] Never, however, did such devotion to the Cross overshadow pilgrimage and prayer directed toward favored local saints.

The Cross, the most Christian of symbols, became enmeshed in the North in a complex web of interreligious, intercultural exchange so deep-seated and far-ranging that neither pagan nor Christian would have found it easy to disentangle its many strands. An image of torture and sorrow among the early Christians, it became a banner of both heavenly and earthly dominion as well as a material repository of Christ's healing powers. Even tracing its lines in the air could hinder evil. In art, it found expression in iron and silver pendants and in high crosses of wood and stone, the latter particularly in the British Isles and Atlantic Scandinavia.

As the Cross spread across Scandinavia along with the new faith, it became adapted to the social and artistic norms of the region, losing much of its essence as a conscious intercessor and becoming more a simple badge of religious adherence. Its similarity to the divine implements of Scandinavian mythology may have contributed to this decline as it led to a rise in conventionalized Þórr's-hammer amulets and depictions in response. In the long run, when pitted against human intercessors, the Cross failed to inspire Scandinavians as it had the Irish and Anglo-Saxons. While pilgrims flocked to the shrine of an ax-wielding but sainted warrior-king, the Church of the Cross remained unbuilt. And while the Cross graced the banners of Óláfr and Valdemar II, they seem to have taken it as a sign of God's favor rather than as an intercessor in itself. Yet throughout this long history, the Cross served a central role, contributing in its own way to the conversion and redemption of the pagan North. The signs of its fortunes in the Viking-Age North reveal the slow process by which the region ultimately changed its faith.

EIGHT

Achieving Faith

Christian Themes and
Pagan Functions

It is a regrettable fact of saga scholarship that interpreters of Old Icelandic literature have tended to atomize their texts, plundering them for evidence of specific points but less often attempting readings that synthesize or unite. This tendency has been most pronounced in studies examining pre-Christian religion and mythology. Here, the Christian agendas and aesthetics of the saga writers themselves often came to be seen as a problem: a "layer" or "coloring" that had to be removed in the pursuit of the true essence of paganism. More often than not, scholars of Nordic mythology and paganism have skirted the issue of the saga writers' views altogether. The current chapter attempts to reverse this trend by offering overall readings of three sagas: *Óláfs saga Tryggvasonar*, *Víga-Glúms saga*, and *Eiríks saga rauða*. By examining the uses of pagan imagery and detail in these three works, I hope to demonstrate the Christian agendas underlying much of thirteenth-century Icelandic saga literature and the distinctive way in which writers of this era commented on the project of Christianization.

I have selected these three sagas for several reasons. First, they each play an important role in the scholarly reconstruction of Nordic paganism, be it Christianization and public cults (*Óláfs saga*), personal and familial adherence to particular gods (*Víga-Glúms saga*), or ritual (*Eiríks saga*). They are thus often more familiar to scholars for their quasi-ethnographic content and tantalizing details of pre-Christian practice than for their overall plots and themes. Second, despite their pagan content, each of these sagas depicts a different moment and site in the seemingly brief era of Nordic Christianization, from the forced conversion of Óláfr's late tenth-century Norway, to the roughly contemporaneous attenuated paganism of Glúmr's Iceland, to the slightly more willing spread of the new faith in the Greenland colony of the same era, a mission reportedly instigated by King Óláfr Tryggvason himself. All three sagas close with images of a nearly Christianized realm and populace, even if they devote most of their textual attention to portrayals of pagan life. Details of paganism acquire in these works—as in others of the thirteenth century—particular functions within a Christian philosophical and literary tradition. While purporting to focus on the era of conversions, these texts actually help us understand the complex relations of paganism and Christianity in the generations which followed.

Óláfs saga Tryggvasonar: The Duties of a King

En vér viljum heldr rita um þá atburði, er Óláfr konungr kristnaði
Nóreg eða önnur þau lönd, er hann kom kristni á.[1]

But we will rather write about those things that happened when King
Óláfr Christianized Norway or the other lands to which he brought the
Christian faith.

As one of the two longest sagas in Snorri's masterful history of the kings of
Norway, *Heimskringla*, *Óláfs saga Tryggvasonar* offers many insights into
thirteenth-century views of the era of conversions and the role of monarchs
in Christianizing the Nordic region. In many ways prefiguring the career of
King St. Óláfr and rising above the limitations of Norway's first Christian
king, Hákon the Good, Óláfr Tryggvason displays the heroic but ultimately
insufficient attempt of a Christian king to convert his subjects by reason,
force, and divine assistance. While the saga of St. Óláfr presents an abrupt
and imperfect hybridization of the ruthless Viking king and the vita of a
sainted noble monarch (as seen in Chapter 7), *Óláfs saga Tryggvasonar* presents a unified and coherent portrayal of the past conflict between Christian
and pagan ideologies. In it, Snorri uses paganism to construct an image of
ideal Christian conduct, exemplified in King Óláfr's short but glorious reign.

In many respects, Snorri's saga draws on earlier, largely hagiographic
accounts of King Óláfr's life. These included a late twelfth-century Latin *vita*
authorized by Oddr Snorrason and subsequently translated into Icelandic
and a second similar pair of Latin and Icelandic texts by Gunnlaugr Leifsson
of roughly the same period.[2] A comparison of these source works—partly
but imperfectly surviving—and Snorri's great masterpiece helps clarify the
careful uses Snorri makes of details of pagan life. Snorri does not seek to
produce an omnibus version of Óláfr's life built of all details in previous
works; rather, he carefully selects the events and their order which he will
include in his work. He also draws liberally from other texts, including such
works as Gregory's *Dialogues*.[3]

Christianity is not new to Norway at the outset of the saga. King Hákon
the Good has already brought it once from England (as detailed in *Hákonar
saga Góða*), attempting to propagate the faith in Norway during his reign
(934–61).[4] Óláfr's opponents at the start of his life—Queen Gunnhildr and
her sons, King Haraldr Gráfeldr Eiríksson and Guðrøðr Eiríksson—have
also adopted Christianity during a sojourn in England, attempting to com-
pel its acceptance in Norway during their reign by destroying pagan tem-

ples.[5] These foundations are discounted in Snorri's text, however, by aspersions of factionalism, brutality, the meddling of King Haraldr Bluetooth Gormson of Denmark, and widespread popular discontent. Snorri portrays the Norwegian farmers as essentially pagan in all respects, blaming their king for recurrent poor harvests and awaiting a ruler whose divine alliances will ensure the kingdom's health and prosperity. Narratively, the stage is thus set for a valiant King Óláfr, who will reunite Norway in the manner of his pagan ancestor King Haraldr Finehair while simultaneously awakening it to the true faith of Christianity.

In the meantime, however, Snorri erects a suitable foil to Óláfr, the shrewd Jarl Hákon, whose Óðinnic allegiances are stated explicitly in the text. Hákon repairs the temples destroyed by Gunnhildr and Haraldr Grayskin, restoring the fertility of the land.[6] His paganism turns from ignorance to obstinacy, however, when he rejects the Christianity imposed upon him by King Haraldr Bluetooth.[7] After accepting baptism, Haraldr nonetheless strands the priests he is supposed to bring back to Norway, making a sacrifice to Óðinn in repentence for his Christian lapse:

En er hann kom austr fyrir Gautasker, þá lagði hann at landi. Gerði hann þá blót mikit. Þá kómu þar fljúgandi hrafnar tveir ok gullu hátt. Þá þykkisk jarl vita at Óðinn hefir þegit blótit ok þá mun jarl hafa dagráð til at berjask.[8]

And as he came east along the Gaut skerries, he made a landing. He raised a great sacrifice [*blót*] there. Two ravens came flying by and cawed loudly. It seemed to the jarl that Óðinn had accepted his sacrifice well and that he would gain good luck in battle.

In his later conflict with the Jomsvikings, who again attempt to bend the jarl to Christianity, Hákon is said to have sacrificed his son Erlingr in exchange for victory. The battle turns to his favor only after the onset of a mysterious hailstorm, clearly associated with a pagan sky god.[9]

Imagistically, Snorri devotes considerable attention to the final defeat of this last pagan ruler of Norway. The jarl's downfall is precipitated by two evil acts: his use of guile to lure Óláfr back to Norway (presumably to be killed) and his repeated indiscretions with women of high status. Because these faults are Óðinnic, Hákon is ensnared by the very acts that tie him to Óðinnic discipleship. Thus, Snorri can take particular pleasure in the ignoble plight of the jarl at his death, cowering in a hole beneath his mistress's pigsty, hiding from an angry populace and listening to the speech of the new King Óláfr as he stands atop a rock nearby.[10] Hákon's fall reflects not only his own ill luck but also his god's moral inferiority.

Prophetic dreams, typical of Óðinnic narrative, figure prominently in Hákon's final hours.[11] While hiding in a cave with Hákon, the thrall Karkr has a dream in which a dark man tells him that "Ulli" is dead. Hákon interprets the dream to mean that his son Erlendr has been killed. Karkr's second dream—the same man telling him that all the sounds are blocked—is interpreted as a sign that Hákon's own remaining days are few. While sleeping with his master beneath the pigsty, Karkr dreams of receiving a gold necklet at the hands of Óláfr, a portent Hákon interprets as a sign that Karkr will betray him for reward but which in fact betokens Karkr's beheading after he surrenders. Finally, while asleep himself, Hákon has such a terrifying dream that he shrieks aloud in his sleep, causing Karkr to awaken in a start and slit his master's throat. Hákon's death is violent, seemingly accidental, and completely foreshadowed: the hallmarks of an Óðinnic fate but also the justice of a Christian God. With his end, Snorri can truly write that the days of paganism in Norway are numbered: "Þá var sú tíð komin, at fyrirdœmask skyldi blótskaprinn ok blótmennirnir, en í stað kom heilög trúa ok réttir siðir"[12] [The time had come when sacrifices and pagan priests were doomed, and in their place came the holy faith and correct worship].

In terms of actual chronology, Snorri's history up to this point suffers from some of the inevitable inaccuracies of the chroniclers' art.[13] Óláfr is made to deal with famous rulers in an order difficult to reconcile with what is known from other historical sources. Born in 968, in the aftermath of his father's death, Óláfr supposedly found refuge first in the estate of his maternal grandfather Eiríkr Bjóðaskalli and then at the home of Hákon the Old of Sweden, where he is said to have lived for two years, until age three.[14] At that point (i.e., c. 971), he flees with his mother Ástriðr to Garðaríki (Russia) but is intercepted, Snorri tells us, by Estonian Vikings, spending the next six years (971–77) in Estonia.[15] He is recovered by his uncle Sigurðr Eiríksson and brought to the court of King Valdamarr (Vladimir the Great of Russia) at a time when the ruler is still grand duke of Hólmgarðr (Novgorod; 970–80).[16] Óláfr grows to manhood in the court of the king, who becomes czar of Garðaríki (980–1015). He leaves court to raid in the west and marries Queen Geira, the daughter of King Búrizláfr of Wendland (Boleslav I of Poland; r. 992–1025).[17] Given the chronology of the subsequent events, Óláfr's marriage could have occurred at the latest in 989, and probably several years earlier, when Óláfr was between fifteen and eighteen years old. The dates of Boleslav's reign call for a later date, between 992 and when Óláfr comes to the throne of Norway in 995. Anachronistically, Óláfr and his father-in-law are then said to join the forces of Emperor Otta of Saxland (Otto II of Germany, r. 973–83) to force King Haraldr Bluetooth of Denmark (reigned

c. 958–84) to accept Christianity, a conversion which occurred earlier, sometime in the early 960s.[18] Otto's invasion of Denmark, for its part, probably
occurred c. 975.[19] Some five years after leaving Russia (i.e., in the early 990s),
Óláfr arrives in England, where he describes himself as a Russian-born
warrior named Ali, is Christianized, and marries Queen Gyða of England,
sister of King Óláfr Kváran (Óláfr or Anlaf Cuarán of Dublin, d. c. 992).[20]
Convinced by a ruse to return to Norway, Óláfr becomes king there in 995,
and rules until his death in the year 1000. The details of Óláfr's Russian
sojourn and marriage to Queen Geira thus overlap in difficult ways with
Óláfr's English sojourn and marriage to Queen Gyða. Whereas the first set of
events push for a dating in the early 990s, the later call for an earlier dating in
the late 980s.

Part of the reason behind these discrepancies must lie in the strong
desire of Snorri and his sources to align Óláfr with the forces of a triumphant western Christianity, arriving in Scandinavia from the south and west
and finding no counterpart or competition from the Christianity of the
Orthodox East. Thus, Óláfr assists in a battle that Christianizes Denmark,
even though King Haraldr Bluetooth must have accepted the faith at the
latest in 965, three years before Óláfr's birth. Óláfr's own conversion is
forestalled until his arrival in England, where he meets with a prescient
Christian hermit on the Scilly Islands, a detail drawn from Gregory's account of St. Benedict's conversion of Totila the Goth in his *Dialogues*.[21] The
Christian Óláfr, rightful heir to the throne of Norway, then returns to his
native land, putting an end to the reign of the philandering Óðinnic Jarl
Hákon in 995 and bringing Christianity again to the realm.

Erased entirely from this chronolgy is the Christianization of Vladimir
the Great, described in great detail in the eleventh- and twelfth-century
Russian *Primary Chronicle* (*Povest' vremennikh let'*) and dated to 987, that is,
about the time of or somewhat before Óláfr's departure from the court.[22] If,
in fact, Óláfr's friend and support in Vladimir's court, Queen Allógíá, is to
be identified with Vladimir's Queen Anna, then Óláfr would almost certainly have been Christianized in the East. Anna was the Christian sister of
emperors Basil and Constantine of Byzantium and was said to have married
Vladimir only after his conversion in 988. Snorri's choice in this representation is all the clearer when we note that his source, Oddr, not only includes a
description of Vladimir's conversion but also of Óláfr as the agent of his
missionization, returning from Byzantium with the faith and the conviction
that a pagan king faces a terrible fate in hell.[23]

Narratively, however, Snorri sides with the western version of Óláfr's story, which acknowledges the king's Russian past but attributes his Christianization to his British experiences. Such ecclesiastical partisanship is to be expected of a western writer of the thirteenth century, especially given the combined biases of his sources and his own childhood education at Oddi, an estate with strong links to the British Isles. Snorri's foster father Jón Loftsson (d. 1197) was known as the natural grandson of King Magnús Bare-Legs, one of the most Celticized of Norway's kings, and Snorri's foster brother Páll Jónsson had studied at Lincoln before becoming bishop of Skálholt. It is also possible that *Orkneyinga saga* may have been authored at Oddi.[24] More broadly, however, Snorri's privileging of the influences of the western church in Scandinavia allows him to elevate the Atlantic flank of the Viking world as a whole in importance, rendering the British Isles and Iceland as pivotal to the history of the North while Sweden, Finland, and Russia are left as nebulous, exotic loci, lacking in Christian learning and rulership and only tangential to the broader history of the region. Snorri builds a narrative in which a clearly pagan Jarl Hákon will be unseated by a clearly Christian King Óláfr, the latter with the good fortune to have visited the British Isles. Snorri's opening chapters are thus clearly crafted to obviate and extend the pagan-Christian religious oppositions of the era of conversions while erasing the internal oppositions within Christianity itself.

In the middle portion of the saga, Snorri turns his attention to the actual reign of Óláfr. Far from an overall account of Óláfr's political career, however, these chapters focus almost exclusively on the king's missionary activities, both in spreading the faith in Norway and in financing its diffusion to the Atlantic settlements.[25] What seemingly nonreligious political events are included—for example, Óláfr's courtship and altercation with Sigríðr in Stórráða ("the Strongminded") of Sweden—arise in Snorri's telling out of religious differences, a view shared in large part by Snorri's sources, which present Óláfr as a candidate for sainthood.[26] And although Snorri reduces the number of supernatural events in his version of the story from that found in Oddr's version, he focuses with singular attention on the issue of conversion and the labor of Óláfr to Christianize his pagan realm.

Each district and colony of Óláfr's kingdom presents its own challenges to Christianization, and Snorri's Óláfr proves resourceful in turning situations to his advantage. He is aided implicitly by an interested Christian God, who does not appear in physical form or in vision (the stuff of saints' lives), but rather through good luck and miracles in crucial times of need. Óláfr is not depicted beseeching God's help, apart from attending Mass at key moments in the narrative (e.g., upon arrival in Norway, before confronting the pagans, on Michaelmas when converting the Icelanders).[27] Rather, he strides forth in the project of Christianization, confident of God's assistance throughout. God's help produces the miracle of the speeches and the reversal of Eyvindr Kelda's malevolent magic on the eve of Easter.[28] Divine agency is also evident in the miraculous calming of the fjord waters in Óláfr's pursuit of Rauðr inn Rammi ("the Strong"), an event occurring in response to the bishop's prayer and use of liturgical items (incense, candles, a cross, the Gospel, holy water).[29] But God's constancy is to be seen throughout, even when Óláfr is allowed to suffer at the hands of pagan forces and figures. Óláfr's reign prefigures that of King St. Óláfr, whose work on behalf of Christianity and Norway will not succumb to the ravages of time.

Óláfr's Christianity in these chapters is not the advanced, highly mediated medieval religion of Snorri's day but Snori's rendering of the faith of the early Church, where the keys of salvation lie in the willing acceptance of baptism and the provision for priests and churches thereafter. Óláfr's progress takes on the character of the biblical Acts of the Apostles: we see the king progress from district to district, instilling the faith through a combination of interpersonal relations and divine influence. Just as in the Christianizing England of the sixth century, prized by Pope St. Gregory for its frequent miracles (see Chapter 3), Norway of the tenth century becomes the site of numerous miraculous manifestations of a conscious and benevolent God.

Reactions to Óláfr's mission are as varied as the districts of Norway themselves. In Rogaland, men accept the faith after no pagan can deliver a convincing or even audible response to Óláfr's speech.[30] At the Gulathing, conversion occurs easily, after Óláfr promises his sister in marriage to a local noble.[31] In the districts of Sogn, Northfjord, South Fjord, Möre, and Raumsdale, Óláfr must impose the faith through forced baptisms and a destruction of the temple at Lade.[32] No attempt is narrated to convert the *seiðr* practitioners of Tunsberg, however: they are simply invited to a feast and then burned to death.[33] Returning to Þrándheimr (Trondheim)—the same region in which King Hákon had had to yield to pagan demands regarding worship (*Hákonar saga Góða*)—a savvy King Óláfr reveals the essential brutality of his opponents' faith by calling for the human sacrifice of the region's most illustrious nobles, an act which the local pagans prove unwilling to undertake.[34] At the temple in Trondheim, Óláfr demonstrates the impotence of Þórr by destroying his statue and murdering the pagans' chief spokesman.[35] Óláfr's personal charisma and commanding presence lies at the heart of many of these conversions, as is illustrated by the account of Hallfrøðr Vandræðaskáld, who will accept baptism only if Óláfr acts as his sponsor.[36]

Amid this panoply of successful conversions, Óláfr meets with the figure of Óðinn himself.[37] While the Christian God remains serenely silent and aloof in the saga, the demonic Óðinn, garrulous to the end, comes to call personally on the king at Ögvaldsnes. He answers Óláfr's queries regarding kings of old, detailing their modes of worship (Ögvaldr, for instance, worshipped a cow), and entertaining his royal host late into the night. At the bishop's urging, Óláfr at last goes to bed and in the morning has the meat left by the strange one-eyed visitor disposed of. The deceitful Óðinn is thus defeated, as Snorri notes:

Þá segir konungr . . . at þetta myndi engi maðr verit hafa ok þar myndi verit hafa Óðinn, sá er heiðnir menn höfðu lengi á trúat, sagði, at Óðinn skyldi þá engu áleiðis koma at svíkja þá.[38]

Thus the king said . . . that this guest was no man, but rather must have been Óðinn, in whom the pagans had so long believed; and he said that Óðinn should not be given the opportunity to betray them.

With this flourish, Snorri puts an end to the saga's overt Óðinnic presence, one that has succumbed to the superior power of Christianity. It is noteworthy that Snorri includes only this meeting with Óðinn, while his source, Oddr, includes an encounter with Þórr as well. Snorri seems intent on honing the Christian-pagan conflict down to the clear struggle of an invisible but omnipotent God and a visible, limited, demonic Óðinn. The visions of neither Þórr nor St. Martin (who, according to Oddr, is responsible for the miraculous speech impediments of Óláfr's opponents in Rogaland) are allowed to cloud this singular conflict. Óðinn's departure, however, does not mean that he leaves Óláfr alone: in fact, it is largely issues of Óðinnic worship that poison Óláfr's courtship of the Swedish Queen Sigríðr, leading to his eventual downfall at the hands of a combined force of Danish, Swedish, and Norwegian troops, as we shall see below.

In the ethnically mixed and geographically remote district of Hálogaland, Óláfr meets the most vehement resistance to his mission.[39] Rather than relying on the wiles of Óðinn, the folk of this district appear given to the magic of their Sámi and Finnic neighbors. Óláfr's work begins by trying to convert the merchants Sigurðr and Haukr, travelers who have voyaged to England and who manage to elude both the king's entreaties and his chains before fleeing back to the safety of their pagan tracts.[40] From there, the narrative turns to Hárekr of Þjótta, who listens attentively to the king's words in Trondheim but resists conversion until he can return the monarch's hospitality at his own estate in Hálogaland, assisting the king in the conversion of the district.[41] Óláfr refrains from forcing his kinsman Hárekr's conversion in Trondheim, preferring to warn him of the royal ire that he will incur if he continues to resist the faith in the future: "You will find out then whether or not I can punish those who resist Christianity."[42]

In Hálogaland itself, Eyvindr Kinnrifa ("Roughchin") and Rauðr the Strong stand out as two of the staunchest opponents of Christianity in the region and two of the men to whom Óláfr must show the least clemency.[43] Both men are closely associated with Sámi magic: Eyvindr has been engendered by a Sámi incantation (see Chapter 6), while Rauðr is described as having a great following of Sámi who assist him whenever needed. In Rauðr's flight from Óláfr, Sámi magic clearly lies behind the troublesome winds of the fjord, hampering Óláfr's progress until Bishop Sigurðr intervenes through prayer and liturgy. Once captured, both men are exposed to some of the harshest tortures recounted in the saga, punishments for open refusal to convert or outright blasphemy against the Christian God.

Throughout these narratives of easy and difficult conversion, Snorri draws a distinction between pagans who oppose Óláfr out of true religious conviction, however wrongheaded, and those who simply use religious issues as a vehicle for their quest for power. While the former earn the respect of king and author alike, the latter are exposed as worthless political creatures. Thus, Eyvindr Roughchin and Hákon the Jarl emerge as positive figures in the saga while Queen Sigríðr of Sweden and Sveinn Forkbeard emerge as reprehensible, regardless of their religious persuasions.

For Snorri, one of Óláfr's greatest achievements is his missionization of the Atlantic settlements. Snorri devotes considerable attention to details of the Atlantic conversions, establishing Norway, rather than the British Isles, as the center from which Christianity diffuses. This historical representation continues Snorri's tendency to align Christianization with his narrative's most favored polities and characters. While the British Isles win in this respect over Russia and the East in general, they are left behind once Snorri can assert an authentically Norwegian force of Christianity spreading to Iceland, Greenland, and Vinland.

Óláfr's efforts to convert the North Atlantic settlements begin infelicitously with his sending of Þangbrandr the priest, the querulous preacher from Germany or the British Isles, to Iceland.[44] Þangbrandr's poor foundations, however, are soon boosted by Óláfr's own efforts on Michaelmas, in which he succeeds in winning over Kjartan Óláfsson, the finest Icelander then at court.[45] By chapter 84, the Icelandic contingent in Trondheim defends itself against Þangbrandr's ravings, accepting baptism en masse and avoiding the king's ire.[46] In chapter 95, Óláfr sends Gízurr Hvíti ("the White") and Hjalti Skeggjason back to Iceland, where they will soon be successful in propagating the faith nationwide.[47] Meanwhile, Óláfr turns attention to the Greenland-Vinland settlements. In chapter 86, he welcomes Leifr Eiríksson to court, and in chapter 96, he sends him back to Greenland, commissioned to convert the settlement to the faith.[48]

In the closing chapters of *Óláfs saga Tryggvasonar*, Snorri presents a stirring account of Óláfr's final undoing, resisting his source Oddr's assertion that the king survived to become a hermit-pilgrim in the Holy Land and permitting him instead to disappear amid the final throes of a long and heroic battle.[49] Óláfr's fall is precipitated by the evil of other monarchs, largely due to issues associated with Óðinn worship. In the early days of their courtship, Óláfr sends Sigríðr a large golden ring that he has looted from the desecrated temple at Lade. The ring had been commissioned by Hákon the Jarl and was therefore likely a votive offering to Óðinn, perhaps a material allusion to Óðinn's own celebrated ring, Draupnir, which Snorri describes in his *Prose Edda*.[50] Whether it is the fault of a miserly Hákon, dishonest smiths, or a wily Óðinn, however, the ring turns out to be brass inside, a fact which infuriates the queen. Even more perturbing, however, is their actual meeting the following spring when Óláfr insists that his bride convert. Sigríðr's flat refusal provokes Óláfr's immediate rage: he slaps the queen in the face and calls her a pagan bitch (*hundheiðna*), putting an end to the wedding for good.[51] The later ill-willed meddling of the spurned Sigríðr is thus closely linked to Óðinnic issues, in fact the same issues of duplicity, adherence, and treatment of women that (in a different manner) caused the downfall of the Óðinnic Hákon.

In the subsequent chapters, Sigríðr convinces her eventual husband, Sveinn Tjúguskegg ("Forkbeard") of Denmark, to oppose Óláfr, leading to the Battle of Svölð and the defeat and disappearance of Óláfr. She also befriends Eiríkr, son of the Óðinnic Hákon the Jarl. When Sveinn tries to marry his Christian sister, Þyri, to the pagan King Búrizláfr (King Óláfr's former father-in-law), Óláfr gives her shelter, eventually marrying her himself.[52] Óláfr treats his own sister Ingibjörg more nobly, forcing her future husband Rögnvaldr the Jarl of West Gautland to accept baptism before consenting to the marriage. The evils of Óláfr's opponents are further indicated by their sending Sigvaldi the Jarl of the Jomsvikings to delay and eventually lure the king into an ambush, a tactic that parallels again the deception of Jarl Hákon in bringing Óláfr back to Norway.[53] With the battle and odds stacked against him through unfair circumstances, Óláfr commends his soul to God, leading his men with the fervent exhortation: "May

God decide my fate, but I shall never flee!"[54] Óláfr's later leap overboard after the battle turns against him, badly wounded and almost certain to die, must thus be seen as an attempt to save himself or his body from final humiliation rather than any actual attempt at survival.[55] For Snorri, Óláfr dies a king to the last, the willing and worthy opponent of a devious Óðinnic force.

In *Óláfs saga Tryggvasonar*, then, Snorri presents a complex and compelling story of Norway's first great Christian king, one in which images of religious adherence play key thematic roles. Nearly all of Óláfr's narrated actions pertain to the Christianization of his realm and his political undoing stems directly from animosity created by his Christian views and the covert workings of a recalcitrant Óðinnic cult. Christian and pagan act as opposite charges useful in contrasting characters and politics at every turn; where pagan practices and religiosity are described, they serve this broader thematic purpose. Christianity hovers beside the figures most favored in any dyadic conflict within the narrative, a rhetorical strategy which necessitates at times the erasure or downplay of Christian adherence when it proves thematically infelicitous. Such repositioning appears in Snorri's handling of Óláfr's early opponents, the Christian Gunnhildr and King Haraldr, as well as in his treatment of Óláfr's eastern sojourn in Russia. The British Isles source of Christianity, favored at the outset of the saga when Óláfr is converted, gives way to the negative portrayal embodied in Þangbrandr, when Norway has emerged as the prime source of the faith for the Atlantic settlements. Once Trondheim becomes the center for Nordic Christianity, British missionaries can be marginalized or disparaged in Snorri's text. Throughout the saga, Óláfr emerges as Snorri's ideal of the just Christian monarch: one grimly and effectively committed to the conversion of his realm, a figure equal to the task of unseating Óðinn as well as other lesser gods, but defeated in the end by the nefarious workings of demonic pagan forces. His fall in the end is one of martyrdom but not defeat for the Christian faith.

Paganism Imagined: *Víga-Glúms saga*

Hann vaknaði, ok léz Glúmr verr vera við Frey alla tíma síðan.[56]

Glúmr awoke and said that from now on things would be worse between him and Freyr.

The mid-thirteenth-century *Víga-Glúms saga* presents the life and times of the Icelandic chieftain Glúmr Eyjólfsson, an irascible leader and poet who lived in an era roughly simultaneous to that of King Óláfr Tryggvason. His character and dealings as *goði* (priest-chieftain) of the district of Þverá, by the thirteenth century an important Benedictine center, resemble both those of Hrafnkell, the calculating and ruthless *goði* of Freyr in *Hrafnkels saga*, and those of Egill Skalla-Grímsson, the taciturn, belligerent, poetic genius of *Egils saga Skalla-Grímssonar*.[57] As in each of these better-known sagas, the story of Glúmr relies on details of sky-god worship for important parts of its plot motivation, explication, and punctuation. We follow the feuds and intrigues of the descendants of Helgi Magri ("the Lean") as they lapse from Helgi's partial Christianity (muted or suppressed entirely in the text) to an embrace of competing pagan sky gods, chiefly Freyr and Óðinn. Glúmr appears born and destined to live as an adherent of Óðinn, an adherence that appears realized when he meets with the favor of his maternal grand-father in Norway, receiving the marks of the family's power and dignity—a cloak, spear, and sword linked imagistically to Óðinn. An intercult rivalry between Freyr and Óðinn simmers beneath the surface of the text, expressed in the narrative through Glúmr's prophetic dreams and poems (typical of Óðinnic narratives) as well as through key ritual actions at the local temple of Freyr.

At the same time, *Víga-Glúms saga* reflects an author of deep Christian outlook and learning. He produces a text that uses paganism as the thematic basis for a portrayal of a proud and vengeful society, one which can escape its failings only with the final acceptance of Christianity. The textual depic-tion of paganism, at first so seemingly ethnographic and intimate, becomes comprehensible in a Christian light, in fact, through reference to Pope St. Gregory's ideas of pride and its effects on men of leadership. Pagan be-haviors become embodiments of Christian sin.

Pagan imagery is closely tied to characterization in the opening por-tions of *Víga-Glúms saga*.[58] The narrative opens with an account of Helgi the Lean's taciturn son, Ingjaldr, and his own worthy and enterprising son, Eyjólfr. After befriending a Norwegian merchant, Eyjólfr journeys to Nor-way, where he rises above initial mistreatment to become a popular guest at his host's estate. At a moment of local crisis, Eyjólfr defeats an ill-willed berserker named Asgautr. In turn, his grateful hosts help him obtain in marriage Ástríðr, the daughter of the chieftain (*hersir*) Vígfúss of Voss. He returns to Iceland with reputation and marriage connections established.

Throughout this opening portion, no explicit mention of religious adherence is noted, but the author hints at religious factors in a manner presumably clear to a thirteenth-century audience. Ingjaldr is described as having inherited Helgi's *goðorð* (chieftainship, a status with both secular and sacral aspects; see Chapter 3). On arriving in Norway, Eyjólfr declines to visit the court of King Hákon the Good, Norway's first Christian king, noting that he is not suited to follow him. In the pagan Voss, on the other hand, Eyjólfr defeats a berserker and marries into the family of Vígfúss. He meets his future in-laws for the first time at a Yule feast, and the pagan nature of this celebration is later underscored by the description of a Winter's Nights feast in the same vicinity a generation later.

These initial subtle references to paganism give way in the text to explicit mention of pagan worship during the subsequent generation. Another of Helgi's children, Ingunn, has married Hámundr Heljarskinn ("Death-Skin"), whose descendants are clearly associated with a temple to Freyr at Hripkelsstaðir.[59] This clan becomes Glúmr's major rivals in the district and eventually prove his nemesis. In chapter 9, after Glúmr has managed to stave off their encroachments on his father's estate, their leader, Þorkell, makes a sacrifice and appeals to Freyr for revenge:

Ok áðr Þorkell fór á brott frá Þverá, þá gekk han til hofs Freys, ok leiddi þagat uxa gamlan ok mælti svá: "Freyr," sagði hann, "er lengi hefir fulltrúi minn verit, ok margar gjafar at mér þegit ok vel launat—nú gef ek þér uxa þenna til þess at Glúmr fari eigi únauðgari af Þverárlandi, en ek fer nú. Ok láttu sjá nökkurar jartegnir, hvártú þiggr eða eigi." En uxanum brá svá við, at hann kvað við ok féll niðr dauðr; ok þótti Þorkatli vel hafa við látið, ok var nú hughægra, er hánum þótti sem þegit mundi heitið.[60]

Before Þorkell left Þverá farm he went to the sanctuary of Freyr, leading with him an old ox, and spoke as follows: "Freyr," he said, "you have long been my patron (*fulltrúi*), and have received many gifts from me and have rewarded them well: here I give you this ox, in order that Glúmr may leave Þverá no less willingly than I leave it now. Let me have some sign whether or not you accept my gift." At that, the ox was so startled that he bellowed and fell down dead; and that, Þorkell took to mean that the god-head was well inclined, and he felt more at ease then, because he thought his sacrifice had been accepted.[61]

Near the end of the narrative, Glúmr himself has a dream of Freyr that confirms local views of the god's role in his downfall:

En áðr Glúmr riði heiman, dreymdi hann at margir menn væri komnir þar til Þverár at hitta Frey, ok þóttiz hann sjá mart manna á eyrunum við ána, en Freyr sat á stóli. Hann þóttiz spyrja, hverir þar væri komnir. Þeir segja: "Þetta ero frændr þínir framliðnir, ok biðjum vér nú Frey, at þú sér eigi á brott færðr af Þverár-landi, ok tjóar ekki, ok svarar Freyr stutt ok reiðuliga, ok minniz nú á uxa-gjöf Þorkels ens háfa." Hann vaknaði, ok léz Glúmr verr vera við Frey alla tíma síðan.[62]

But before Glúmr left his home he dreamed that many had come to Þverá to meet Freyr, and it seemed to him as though he saw many assembled on the gravel banks by the river where Freyr was sitting on his throne. He dreamed that he asked who had gathered there, and that he was given the answer: "They are your departed kinsmen, and we are praying to Freyr that you be not driven from Þverá farm. But it is of no avail, Freyr answers shortly and wrathfully, and recalls the gift of an ox which Þorkell the Tall made him." Glúmr awoke and said that from now on things would be worse between him and Freyr.[63]

The saga's Óðinnic imagery is equally compelling, although presented more subtly. Upon arrival in Norway, Glúmr finds his maternal grandfather seated on the high seat with cloak and spear in a manner clearly reminiscent of Óðinn: "Þat mark hafði hann til hans, at hann sá mann mikinn ok vekligan í öndvegi í skautfeldi blám, ok lék sér at spjóti gullreknu"[64] (But this was how recognized him: he saw a large and distinguished-looking man in the high-seat. He was clad in a hooded cloak of black fur and amused himself playing with a gold-inlaid spear).[65] Glúmr participates in the estate's winter sacrifice to the *dísir* (female household spirits) and defeats Björn, another berserker who has been oppressing the local community.[66] In return, Vígfúss acknowledges Glúmr as a scion of the clan and promises to pass on to him the family's authority and honor (*ríki* and *virðing*) after his own death. Glúmr later experiences this transfer of power through a dream-vision in which Vígfúss's guardian spirit appears to him in a giant valkyrie guise:

Þat er sagt at Glúmr dreymdi eina nótt. Hann þóttiz vera úti á bæ sínum ok sjá út til fjarðarins. Hann þóttiz sjá konu eina ganga utan eptir héraðinu ok stefndi þangat til Þverár; en hon var svá mikil, at axlirnar tóku út fjöllin tveggja vegna. En hann þóttiz ganga ór garði á mót henni, ok bauð henni til sín. Ok síðan vaknaði hann. Öllum þótti undarligt, en hann segir svá: "Draumr er mikill ok merkiligr, en svá mun ek hann ráða, at Vígfúss móðurfaðer minn mun nú vera andaðr, ok mindi kona sjá hans hamingja vera, er fjöllum hæra gekk. Ok var hann um aðra menn fram um flesta luti at virðingu, ok hans hamingja mun leita sér þangat staðfestu, sem ek em." En um sumarit er skip kómu út, spurðiz andlát Vígfúss. Þá kvað Glúmr vísu:

"Fara sá'k holms und hjalmi
hauks í miklum auka,
jörð, at Eyjafirði,
ísungs! fíradísi,
þá svá't dóms í draumi
dals ótta mer þótti
felliguðr með fjöllum
folkvandar bjöð standa."[67]

It is said that one night Glúmr had a dream: he dreamed that he was standing outside of his farm, looking toward the fjord. And he thought he saw a woman come from the fjord and proceed through the district, heading toward Þverá. She was so huge that her shoulders touched the mountains on both sides. He dreamed that he left his farm and went in to invite her in. Then he awoke. This dream seemed strange to all he told it, but he said this: "This dream is significant and notable; and I would interpret it in this wise: Vígfúss, my maternal grandfather, very likely passed away, these days, and this woman who walked there, taller than the mountains, probably is his guardian spirit [*hamingja*; see Chapter 3]. He was more distinguished than other men, and his guardian spirit is likely seeking to take up her abode with me." And when ships from Norway arrived there the following summer they brought with them the news that Vígfúss had died. Then Glúmr spoke this verse:

> Methinks, that huge and helm-clad,
> hitherward a woman
> proceeded swiftly, heading,
> silver-dís, toward Þverá,
> high as the hills towering,
> head-dress Frigg, in my
> dream I deemed her Óðinn's
> daughter, warrior-choosing [= valkyrie].[68]

Glúmr's poem regarding the vision underscores its Óðinnic imagery. Glúmr becomes a great chieftain, known for his able leadership, ruthless power-mongering, complex poems, and artful speech. Up until he gives away his cloak and spear, apparently symbols of his familial tie to Óðinn, he behaves in a characteristically Óðinnic fashion.

Although Glúmr adopts all the trappings of an Óðinn worshipper—clothing and weapons, a taste for poetry, and a distaste for farmwork—he never explicitly acknowledges allegiance to the god. In fact, the saga writer includes a passage that explicitly depicts Glúmr as reliant on only his own goods and mettle. For conversation one evening, Glúmr asks each of his guests to name their patrons or sources of support (*fulltrúi*): "Nú skulum vér taka oss fulltrúa ok skemtum oss; mun ek kjósa fyrst, ok ero .III. mínir fulltrúar—einn er fésjóðr minn, annarr ex mín, þriði stokkabúr"[69] [Now let us entertain ourselves by choosing patrons. I will choose first. I have three patrons: the first is my bag of money, the second is my axe, the third the storehouse]. While his enemy Þorkell gratefully acknowledges Freyr as his *fulltrúi* (see above), Glúmr makes no such claim concerning Óðinn. Rather, he places his trust firmly in his own possessions and strength. In thirteenth-century Christian symbolism, he is thus revealed not as a worshiper of

Óðinn but as a victim of the sin of pride: the wrongheaded belief that one's success derives from one's own efforts and worth. This same sin of pride that ultimately leads to Glúmr's foolhardy poems regarding his murder of Þorvaldr Krókr ("Hook") and his giving away of the cloak and sword which have assured his success up until then.[70] The outward signs of Óðinn worship thus become an artful narrative embodiment of the deadly sin of pride, an artistic means of expressing a key Christian theme within the context of an imagined pagan past.

For Pope St. Gregory—and the Christian tradition he epitomized for thirteenth-century authors—pride represented one of the most ever-present and pernicious of sins. It lay behind the original Fall and afflicted both the secular and the religious in different guises. In his *Moralia in Job*, Gregory explores the workings of pride in a manner reminiscent of Cassian and characteristic of Church teaching ever after. By imagining themselves responsible for their own successes, the prideful lose sight of God as the first cause of all good, failing to understand his role in their lives.[71] In his *Cura pastoralis*, as well as in the *Moralia*, Gregory details the disastrous effects of pride as it afflicts rulers in particular: the ruler's initial desire to serve God and subjects is turned by the ceaseless praise of sycophantic courtiers until he begins to imagine himself as superior to all and as the author of his own success. From there it is an inevitable decline into tyranny, as the ruler becomes seized by intolerant fits of rage and anger and treats all with disdain and vitriol.[72] Here, in Gregory's profile of the prideful ruler we find the core elements of Glúmr's character.

Glúmr's complete possession by the sin of pride is illustrated especially in his fits of rage, ostensibly an aspect of Óðinnic behavior but presented in the text as one of the key weaknesses which ultimately defeat him as chieftain:

Glúmr veik heim, ok setti at hánum hlátr; ok brá hánum svá við, at hann gerði fölvan í andliti ok hrutu ór augum hánum tár þau, er því voro lík, sem hagl þat er stórt er. Ok þann veg brá hánum opt við síðan, þá er víghugr var á hánum.[73]

Glúmr went home and fell to laughing. He was so agitated that he became pale, and there fell out of his eyes tears as large as hailstones, and that is how he was often stirred in later times when the fighting spirit came upon him.[74]

Here, the imagery of Óðinnic fury is meshed seamlessly with the Christian portrayal of pride. Glúmr appears completely controlled by his temper, unable to resist the temptation to wreak vengeance and violence when crossed. Even after losing all in later life, he remains enslaved by the sin, as he tries to lure his rivals Einarr and Guðmundr to their deaths through a false overture of forgiveness, an act which links him to the Óðinnic villains of *Óláfs saga Tryggvasonar*.[75]

So omnipresent is the image and issue of pride for the author of *Víga-Glúms saga* that he places its castigation even in the mouth of his pre-Christian characters. When the family's rival Sigmundr disparages Glúmr's abilities to defend his patrimony, Ástríðr is made to quote the biblical proverb in response: "Pride (*ofsinn*) often cometh before a fall, Sigmundr, and so does injustice, and this may happen to you, too."[76] Likewise in the same chapter, Sigmundr ridicules Glúmr for his prideful ways since returning from Norway. These details, incongruous within the paganism that the author depicts, reveal the unified Christian outlook and agenda behind the saga.

Pride continues to beset Glúmr throughout his career, although his fury tempers with age. Where the sin leads the youthful Glúmr to violence, it leads the aged chieftain to foolhardy boasting. After having successfully murdered his enemy Þorvaldr Hook and blamed the deed on another, Glúmr cannot resist the temptation to boast about his trickery in a poem. When confronted with a lawsuit at the thing, he promises to swear an oath of innocence at three temple sanctuaries in the area, presumably connected to the three major sky gods, Óðinn, Þórr, and Freyr.[77] At the one oath-taking recounted in the saga, however, Glúmr prevaricates craftily and then gives away both his cloak and spear to the witnesses that have supported his claim.[78] In so doing, he discards the items linked to his continued luck and precipitates his eventual defeat at a subsequent meeting of the Althing.

As the saga closes, however, Glúmr seems to have put his old ways behind him, accepting Christianity and receiving burial in the local church:

Ok vóro þau lok viðskipta þeirra Glúms ok Eyfirðinga. En er kristni kom út hingat, tók Glúmr skírn, ok lifði .III. vetr síðan ok var byskupaðr í banasótt af Kol byskupi, ok andaðiz í hvítaváðum. Þá bjó Már Glúmsson í Fornhaga ok hafði þar látit kirkju gera, ok var Glúmr þar jarðaðr, ok svá Már, þá er hann andaðiz, ok mart annarra manna, því at langa hríð var engi kirkja í Hörgárdal, nema sú ein.[79]

That was the end of the dealings between Glúmr and the Eyfirðing clan. When Christianity came to the country Glúmr had himself baptised, and lived three more years after that. He was confirmed by Bishop Kol in his last illness and died in his white baptismal robe. At that time Már Glúmsson dwelled at Fornhagi and had a church built there. Glúmr was buried there, as was Már when he died, together with many others, because for a long time there was no other church in Horgárdal.[80]

By closing the saga with these strong images of conversion, the author underscores the change of heart that transformed Iceland from a recalcitrant pagan realm, foolishly given to the excesses of pride, to a chastened Christian land, one in which leaders behave according to Christian doctrines of noble rulership. The religious underpinnings of *Víga-Glúms saga* become apparent, and we can appreciate the knowing deployment of pagan imagery and practice in the presentation of an essentially Christian theme. If *Ólafs saga Tryggvasonar* presents a picture of the stirring conversion of a pagan land under a worthy Christian ruler, *Víga-Glúms saga* presents the problematic workings of life under an irascible but capable pagan chieftain. His reign and morals are brought to a close by the arrival of Christianity, an arrival recounted in careful detail in works like *Eiríks saga*.

Christianizing the Spirit: Guðríðr and the Conversion of Greenland

> *Lux orta est iusto*
> *et rectis corde laetitia.*
>
> *Light dawns for the just*
> *and gladness for the upright of heart.*
> —Psalm 96 (97):11

In the context of the North Atlantic, the Greenland colony and its Vinland offshoot represented an intriguing and significant topic. Icelanders could take pride in this past extension of Icelandic settlement, and some of the prominent families of thirteenth-century Icelandic society counted Greenlanders or Vinland colonists among their ancestors. Thus, it is not surprising that a number of sagas from the era record and celebrate the history of the western experiments. *Eiríks saga rauða* and the *Grœnlendiga saga* section of *Ólafs saga Tryggvasonar* as recorded in *Flateyjarbók* are two accounts that survive.[81]

But these accounts are more than documentary histories. In the case of *Eiríks saga rauða* in particular, we find a text with a deeper agenda, incorporating the thematic, theological, and narrative characteristics of medieval Christian literature, demonstrating the superiority of the Christian God over past pagan competitors, and outlining the progression of conversions necessary to transform a pagan society into a truly Christian one. In this broad narrative scheme, three close depictions of pagan rites play pivotal roles. Comparison of *Eiríks saga* with the *Grœnlendiga saga*, generally regarded as its immediate source or parallel, reveals the careful deployment of these scenes by the writer of *Eiríks saga* and the clear role they play in accomplishing a Christian agenda.

Dag Strömbäck offers the earliest analysis of *Eiríks saga* in his discussion of *seiðr*.[82] For Strömbäck, pointing out the strong interest of the saga writer in depicting the life of Guðríðr—the mother-progenitor of several important Icelandic bishops—suffices to account for the text's attention to her role in the detailed description of the *seiðr* ritual. Halldór Hermannsson sees the text as centered on relating the lives and adventures of Þorfinnr Karlsefni along with Guðríðr, but waylaid by the narrative attractiveness and singular legendary importance of Eiríkr the Red, whose history dominates the first chapters of the text.[83] Further analysis of the narrative's structure awaited the 1970s, when Theodore Anderson's study of the family saga genre spurred scholarly interest in the structural underpinnings of these distinctly Icelandic literary works.[84] Bernadine McCreesh, however, points out the inadequacies of Anderson's formalist theory in accounting for the structure of *Eyrbyggja saga* and other sagas that contain depictions of the Christianization of Scandinavia.[85] McCreesh reveals the symmetrical placement of pagan and Christian depictions in these sagas and their placement so as to highlight the pivotal conversion of Iceland. *Eiríks saga*, McCreesh argues, follows this alternative pattern closely. Patricia Conroy finds structural links between *Laxdæla saga* and *Eiríks saga*, perceiving in each a narrative pattern focusing on the life of a woman of note through her various marriages and adventures.[86]

The reading offered here draws on each of these analyses but focuses particularly on the textual agenda that emerges from both the deployment of pagan imagery and the close attention to the life of the character Guðríðr. I argue that *Eiríks saga* presents an extension to the depictions of Christianization presented in works like *Óláfs saga Tryggvasonar* and *Víga-Glúms saga*. Here we see not just the attempt to Christianize in name, nor the evident need of Christian enlightenment in the pagan North, but the careful, progressive nature of Christianization in the era of conversions, the process of coming to the faith that necessitates royal commission, personal espousal, and a gradual consolidation of society under the rules of the Church.

Three Pagan Moments

Three moments stand out as vivid descriptions of pagan rituals in the saga. These moments depict, not the elite religious convictions of king or chieftain, but the vernacular religiosity of ordinary settlers, men and women contending with a harsh struggle for survival in the Greenland and Vinland colonies. They portray the conflict between Christian and pagan practice on the popular level and its changing dynamics in the Viking world.

The first of these moments, the famous account of a *seiðr* séance (see Chapter 6 of the present study), depicts the Christian Guðríðr Þorbjarnardóttir obliged by norms of hospitality and human mercy to assist in a pagan ritual. The event occurs early on in the narrative, soon after the arrival of Guðríðr and her family in the still predominantly pagan Greenland. The second key moment occurs midway through the saga, soon after the initial Christianization of the colony through the missionary efforts of Leifr Eiríksson and his royal backer, King Óláfr Tryggvason of Norway. The same Guðríðr is now obliged to talk with her deceased husband when he returns from the dead to solve the mystery of their farmstead's violent hauntings. The community, Þorsteinn explains, has been lax in its observance of the Christian burial rite and the bodies of the recently deceased must be reinterred in a church. When this situation is rectified, the protracted hauntings cease. Finally, the third moment occurs late in the saga, when the struggling band of Vinland colonists unwittingly partake of whale meat supplied in response to a prayer to Þórr. When the Christians realize the agency through which the meat has come, they quickly dispose of it (which has made them ill in the meantime), pray to God for fish, and receive God's bountiful reward in an abundant catch. The existence of even one of these striking scenes of Christian–non-Christian conflict, of divided loyalties in moments of duress, would make the text of interest to the student of Nordic religions; the occurrence of all three creates a kind of mosaic of pagan practice, a base of memorable scenes upon which to construct the saga's Christian theme. In order to appreciate this thematic framework fully, however, we must examine each scene in greater detail.

The *seiðr* scene in *Eiríks saga* has already been discussed at length in Chapter 6 of the present study. It is important for the purpose of this chapter, however, to point out a few aspects related to the interplay of Christian and pagan. Þorbjörn and his daughter Guðríðr—second- and third-generation Christians from a colony of displaced British Isle–Scandinavians in Iceland—have journeyed to Greenland to make a new life in the colony dominated by their friend and benefactor, the incorrigibly pagan Eiríkr the Red. Þorbjörn appears a staunch Christian, but he does not live apart from his pagan neighbors and associates. In fact, Guðríðr Þorbjarnardóttir has grown up in the fostership of the pagan Ormr of Arnarstapi, whose wife, Halldís, instructs Guðríðr in the performance of the *seiðr* chant before she leaves Iceland. Þorbjörn and his company of migrants run into difficulties on the sea and both Ormr and Halldís perish en route to Greenland. When Þorbjörn and his remaining company arrive in Herjólfsnes, they are storm-tossed and weakened from disease and in grave need of hospitality.

In Herjólfsnes, things have not gone much better. A famine has plagued the region and people are worried about the coming year. Nonetheless, Þorbjörn and his fellow migrants are warmly received by the pagan Þorkell, a local farmer of high esteem in charge of the vicinity's pagan rituals. As the saga writer explains:

því at Þorkell var þar mestr bóndi, þá þótti til hans koma at vita nær létta mundi óárani þessu, sem yfir stóð. Býðr Þorkell spákonunni heim, ok er henni þar vel fagnat sem siðr var til, þá er við þess háttar konum skyldi taka.[87]

Because Þorkell was the leading householder there it was thought to be his responsibility to find out when these hard times which now troubled them would cease, so he invited the *seiðr* woman to his home, and a good reception was prepared for her, as was the custom when a woman of this kind should be received.[88]

It is in this context of hospitality and need that Guðríðr is prevailed upon to aid Þorbjörg in the pagan ritual. She and her family have been treated kindly by their host and her service would assist them in a manner important to their peace of mind. That she does so illustrates her kindness and latitude; on the other hand, her father refuses to remain in the house during the proceedings and must be sent for after the séance has ended. In thanks for her assistance, Þorbjörg prophesies about Guðríðr's eventual return to Iceland and the future greatness of her descendants, three of whom become bishops:

[V]egar þínir liggja út til Íslands, ok man þar koma frá þér bæði mikil ætt ok góð, ok yfir þínum kynkvíslum skína bjartari geislar en ek hafa megin til at geta slíkt vandliga sét.[89]

[Y]our ways lie out to Iceland, where there will spring from you a great and goodly progeny, and over the branches of your family will shine beams brighter than I have power to see precisely as they are.[90]

Here, then, we see *seiðr* as an integral part of a decentralized religious system, a ritual mounted by the populace itself in response to questions of communal significance and financed through the generosity of the vicinity's most prominent resident. All are invited to participate, but not explicitly required: rather, they choose it in response to feelings of communal responsibility and interest and some, such as Guðríðr, feel the weight of the communal will strongly enough to set aside their own differing religious convictions for the duration of the ritual. The Herjólfsnes community has chosen a pagan response to a situation of need just as the later Vinland community will choose Christian prayer when faced with similar famine toward the end of the saga.

The second key moment of Christian-pagan ritual interference in the saga concerns hauntings, and is discussed in Chapter 4 of this study. It again depicts the religious experiences of ordinary people on a farm rather than the more elite practices of leaders or clergy. Guðríðr and her husband, Þorsteinn Eiríksson, are staying in Lysafjörðr for the winter. The estate they share with another Þorsteinn and his wife, Sigríðr, soon falls prey to disease, and an ill-liked foreman, Garðar, is the first to die. Soon, however, more and more of the household take ill and Sigríðr sees a vision of herself and Þorsteinn Eiríksson among all the other dead of the farm, tormented by Garðar. Both Sigríðr and Þorsteinn Eiríksson die, but both revive for a short while: Sigríðr as a ghost to terrify the dying Þorsteinn, Þorsteinn himself as a kind of messenger from God, sent to address his wife. After Guðríðr has consented to the meeting, Þorsteinn predicts her future marriage to an Icelander, counseling her to give their money to the Church and the poor. To the rest of those listening, he explains the source of the hauntings:

[E]n þar mælti hann svá at allir heyrðu, at þeir menn væri sælir, er trúna heldu, ok henni fylgði öll hjálp ok miskunn, ok sagði þó, at margir heldi hana illa; "er þat engi háttr, sem hér hefir verit á Grœnlandi, síðan kristni kom hér, at setja menn niðr í óvígða mold við litla yfirsöngva. Vik ek mik láta flytja til kirkju ok aðra þá menn, sem hér hafa andazk, en Garðar vil ek brenna láta á báli sem skjótast, því at hann veldr öllum aptrgöngum þeim, sem hér hafa verit í vetr."[91]

[B]ut what he did say so that everyone heard was that those men were truly blest who kept their faith well, and that salvation and mercy attended upon them; though many, he added, kept their faith ill. "Nor is that a good custom which has obtained here in Greenland since the coming of Christianity, to lay men down in unconsecrated ground with only a brief service sung over them. I want to be borne to church, and likewise those others who have died here; but I want Garðar to be burnt on a pyre as soon as possible, for he is the cause of all the hauntings that have taken place here this winter."[92]

To stop the hauntings—manifestations of a disordered afterlife for the dead—the community must observe with care the ritual strictures of Christian burial.

This passage presents a Christian-pagan conflict on several fronts. First, the community appears poorly schooled in proper burial rites, exposing their deceased to the likelihood of becoming ghosts and ignoring the logical choice of the newly built church as the resting place for Christian dead. These discrepancies render them, in Þorsteinn's characterization, bad Christians— well-intentioned converts who have strayed too far down the road of syncresis. In a thirteenth-century context when "dying the good death"—that is, with a clear and shriven conscience, recourse to all the proper sacraments, and the surety of sanctified ground for burial—was seen as a gift for the dying, the haphazard and perfunctory ritual acts of the Greenland Christians appear extreme.[93] In addition to these errors, however, the foreman Garðar appears intentionally opposed to God, figuring as a demonic tormenter in his after-death apparition. Þorsteinn's instructions regarding Garðar's body support this view: although Christian (at least nominally), Garðar's body is to be cremated in the old pagan way. We see a direct conflict between those who truly embrace the new faith and the prevaricating false Christian, who in fact serves the devil. Finally, on a subtler but equally important level, the return of Þorsteinn represents a contrast between the ritual relations of Christians and pagans with their dead. While the ghost terrifies pagans, the Christian Guðríðr fears nothing from her Christian husband. He has come back on an errand from God, in the way that saints and others sometimes do, bearing a message proved divine through its eventual efficacy in halting the hauntings. Had his recommendations failed to curtail the mounting visitations of the dead, their origins would have been suspect. But the fact that they correct the situation, as well as the ritual errors of the local community, reveals God's approval of Þorsteinn's appearance and the special grace attached to Guðríðr in receiving the communication. Through Guðríðr's exceptional faith, the entire community is brought closer to ritual orthodoxy, and its supernatural harassment ends.

The third prime moment of popular Christian-pagan conflict in the saga occurs in Vinland, where the company led by Þorfinnr Karlsefni spends winter on an island they name Straumsey. One of the members of the company, Þórhallr Veiðimaðr ("the Hunter"), parallels Garðar in his disagreeable ways and pagan backsliding. Crucially, he is identified as an *illa kristinn*—a bad Christian.[94] When the hunting and fishing fail during the winter, the community prays to God, but to no avail. Þórhallr then steals away from the company and is found three days later:

Hann lá þar ok horfði í lopt upp ok gapði bæði munni ok nösum ok þuldi nökkut. Þeir spurðu, hví hann var þar kominn. Hann kvað þá engu þat varða.[95]

He lay on a peak of a crag, staring up at the sky with his mouth and nostrils both agape, and reciting something. They asked him why he had gone to such a place, but he told them that was no business of theirs.[96]

Soon after, a strange whale washes ashore, and the grateful community sets about slaughtering and boiling it. The same beaching of a whale occurs in *Grœnlendiga saga*, although without any mention of a Þórhallr.[97] While the whale proves a welcome and useful source of food for the settlers in *Grœnlendiga saga*, it immediately sickens the community in *Eiríks saga*. Now Þórhallr boasts of the superior aid of his god, revealing the apparent meaning of the ritual the community had witnessed shortly before:

Þá mælti Þórhallr: "Drjúgari varð inn rauðskeggaði nú en Kristr yðvarr. Hefir ek þetta nú fyrir skáldskap minn, er ek orti um Þór fulltrúann; sjaldan hefir han mér brugðizk."[98]

Then said Þórhallr: "Red Beard proved a better friend now than your Christ. This is what I get for the poem I made about Þórr my patron [*fulltrúi*]. Rarely has he failed me."[99]

The horrified settlers dispose of the meat and turn to God for help and are soon rewarded with successful fishing and foraging for the rest of the winter.[100]

The account further details Þórhallr's topical poems and recounts his disputes with Þorfinnr Karlsefni regarding which direction the community should proceed. When Þórhallr and his band disappear entirely, Þorfinnr attempts to find them. But in the end, Þórhallr is lost for good, apparently shipwrecked and enslaved in Ireland. It is significant that this exemplar of popular religious adherence to a god looks to Þórr rather than Óðinn: the saga's author depicts not the high-flown religious ideals of a pagan aristocrat but the earthy and pragmatic views of the folk.

It is also noteworthy that these three moments of popular religious practice concern the activities of Scandinavians alone, be they Christians, pagans, or members of the intermediate category of "bad Christian." The Irish in the saga figure only as incidental characters: the apparent Christian faith of neither the slaves aboard Þorfinnr's ship nor of the Irish who eventually capture and enslave Þórhallr and his men bears comment in the text. Nor are the Skraelings, the indigenous population of Vinland, depicted as pagans. The saga writer describes their strange manners, warfare, clothing, and hair, but he does not use them as part of his Christian agenda. Neither side witnesses strange religious rituals, although the two Skraeling youths captured by the Scandinavians are eventually baptized. Rather, the Christian-pagan conflict is confined entirely to the central Scandinavian community, a narrative decision that clarifies the conflict and underscores the importance of the inner mission for the souls of converted Christians.

Guðríðr and Female Sainthood

Eiriks saga is generally dated today to the latter half of the thirteenth century, although its two earliest vellum manuscripts derive from the fourteenth and fifteenth centuries, respectively.[101] Apparently composed after *Grænlendiga saga*, and at least in partial revision of it, it reflects a shifting perspective on sanctity and Christian life shaped by the rise of lay saints and mendicant preaching throughout Europe.[102]

In the context of thirteenth-century Christian spirituality, the figure of Guðríðr proves remarkably timely. As André Vauchez has shown, canonized sainthood during this period evolved from an earlier focus on monastics, royalty, and knights toward an embrace of the laity: people engaged in the active life who demonstrated sanctity in their deeds and outlook.[103] Barely a century before, it would have seemed far-fetched that an ordinary man or woman living outside of the contemplative *stabilitas* of the *cenobium* (monastery) would have any great hope of salvation. At least, such people were not exalted through formal canonization or celebrated in costly vitae. The wealthy and landed of Europe retired to monastic life in their later years for just this reason; only in *fuga mundi*—a flight from the world—could one escape the snares and corruption of earthly existence. The old saintly ideal was typified by monastics like St. Benedict (c. 480–c. 547) with his careful and peaceful rule, and Hildegard of Bingen (1098–1179, never officially canonized) with her ethereal songs of praise for the Virgin. They subscribed to a methodical, contemplative rule, aimed at the goal of perpetual prayer, a *vita angelica* on earth.[104] Even the seeming adventurer-saints of this earlier period, like St. Brendan of Ireland (c. 484–c. 577)—whose voyages were recounted in one of the most popular books of the entire Middle Ages—went on his peregrinations in pursuit of quiet meditation.

But with the thirteenth century, the outlook began to shift. The mendicant orders formed at the very outset of the century: St. Francis of Assisi (c. 1181–1226) received permission to found the Franciscans in 1209, and St. Dominic (1170–1221) founded the Order of Preachers (the Dominicans) in 1216. Both saints shifted their early interest in converting Muslims and heretics into missions among the overlooked masses of Christians of the European countryside. Their orders made preaching to the laity a central task, and the exemplary lives and marvelous works of humble saints held obvious attractiveness for audiences. The rapid spread of this remarkable development to northern Europe coincided with the transformation of the story of *Grœnlendiga saga* into *Eiríks saga rauða*.

The mendicant phenomenon itself was a product of an earlier renewal, one associated centrally with the Cistercian monk St. Bernard of Clairvaux (1090–1153). His system of contemplation led the faithful to meditate on the human emotions and feelings of Christ and Mary. Devotion grew out of the faithful's identification with these figures as fellow human beings. This new spirituality combined with the creation of penitentialism and tertiary orders (confraternities) as means of living a contemplative life within the context of worldly existence. Rather than entering a monastery or convent, the faithful could don the robe or habit of the tertiary, live a life of privation and prayer within the family home, and win heaven for themselves and their families. Devotionalism and frequent recourse to the sacraments (especially Penance) gave the laity tools for cleansing themselves of the corruption of the world.[105]

These developments shed important light on Guðríðr of *Eiríks saga*. Already identified in *Grœnlendiga saga* as having undertaken a pilgrimage to the south and then embraced a tertiary lifestyle in her later years, and famed as the progenitress of three important Icelandic bishops, the saga writer seeks to reveal Guðríðr's sanctity along lines well established in the vitae and legends of his day. Her narrative acts display *caritas*—an open charity for others—an essential ingredient for the saintly life. Her experiences include supernatural signs, markers that she is particularly favored by God or set apart for a particular purpose. Above all, she evinces the humility essential for a female saint in particular: acting not to usurp male leadership and control but simply to carry out the will of God, "confounding the mighty" in her humble but authentic holiness.

Guðríðr's *caritas* is demonstrated by her willingness to help the afflicted of the farmstead of Herjólfnes, consenting to sing the incantation that permits the *seiðr* practitioner to complete her ritual. Guðríðr is confronted by a conflict of letter versus spirit of the law: choosing in the end to act out of Christian charity rather than cling to specific strictures of the faith. The rightness of her decision is demonstrated by the seer's perception of Guðríðr's shining destiny. As in other sagas relating the lives of Óláfr Tryggvason, King St. Óláfr, and the Icelandic St. Jón, the pagan prophet(ess) sees but cannot fully comprehend the superior light of Christianity hovering around the hero. This scene of pagan ritual thus places Guðríðr in company with some of the greatest Christian saints or near-saints of the region, conferring a notoriety that cannot have been taken lightly by the saga's thirteenth-century audience.[106]

Børresen points out that female saints and mystics ran the risk of upsetting God's order if their acts of piety or words interfered centrally with the inherent superiority of men in temporal and spiritual matters. While the male saint could take the active role of the critical Voice in the Desert, the female saint's actions grow out of modest humility, following the submissive model of the Virgin Mary.[107] As the abbot Alphonsos, confessor to St. Birgitta (1303–1373) would later write in his introduction to one of the outspoken Birgitta's books of revelations:

Quod Deus omnipotens tam in Veteri quam in Nouo Testamento ad ostendendum omnipotenciam suam sepe infirma mundi elegit sibi tam in femineo sexu quam in masculis, vt confundat sapientes.[108]

Both in the Old as well as in the New Testaments, God the Almighty has often selected for the revelation of his omnipotence a lowly one of the world, be that person of the female or male sex, that He may confound the wise.

God could choose to confound the wise and learned through conferring revelation onto lowly women, holy fools, impoverished hermits, or humble tradesmen, all figures who became promoted for their sanctity in the thirteenth century.

This saintly subservience is evident in Guðríðr's second great supernatural experience: her conference with her deceased husband, Þorsteinn. When Þorsteinn revives and asks to speak with his wife, the saga writer carefully underscores Guðríðr's resigned submission to God's will. While the Guðríðr of *Grœnlendiga saga* makes no answer to Þorsteinn's call,[109] the Guðríðr of *Eiríks saga* consents fearlessly to speak with him, noting: "Vera kann at þetta sé ætlat til nökkura þeira hluta, er síðan sé í minni hafðir, þessi inn undarligi hlutr, en ek vænti, at guð gæzla mun yfir mér standa"[110] [It may be . . . that this marvel is intended as one of those things which are to be stored in our hearts hereafter; yet I trust that God's keeping will stand over me].[111] Her lines echo those stated of Mary in the Gospel of Luke regarding the early wonders connected with Jesus' birth and childhood (Luke 2:19, 51), in which the Virgin submits to the marvels of the moment but stores them up for later reflection. By characterizing the moment in this way, Guðríðr identifies it as a wonder of divine origin, an assumption which is proved true by the respite it brings the community. From the standpoint of contemporary female sanctity, it is important that the saga emphasize the lack of hubris or self-interest in these wonders: Guðríðr's will, like Mary's, must be wholly turned toward God's service.

The saga writer underscores Guðríðr's overall subservience to authority through careful textual changes. Her marriage to Þorfinnr is brokered by her father-in-law, Eiríkr, even though, as the text notes, her status as a widow would permit her to exercise greater independence.[112] In *Grænlendiga saga*, she is a prime instigator of Þorfinnr's expedition to Vinland and figures prominently in decision making while there.[113] In *Eiríks saga*, in contrast, she is a mere follower, her presence in the party becoming known only through the mention of her being left behind at Straumsfjörðr while her husband attempts to find Þórhallr.[114] In her later repatriation to Iceland, Guðríðr's role in Þorfinnr's household is changed as well: while *Grænlendiga saga* portrays her as an active farmwife, eventually displaced by her daughter-in-law, *Eiríks saga* presents her as a dutiful daughter-in-law herself, winning over Þorfinnr's skeptical mother through her remarkable nature.[115] The details of the sagas can be reconciled; they are not differences of real substance but of emphasis, and they appear calculated in the case of *Eiríks saga* to present Guðríðr in an idealized, saintly light.

In this sense, Guðríðr is a wholly different kind of saint than the King St. Óláfr discussed in the last chapter. Óláfr's sanctity is largely confirmed by sacred signs after his death—a plethora of miracles, the growth of a cult around his shrine, the development of Trondheim as a pilgrimage center— all proofs of strong and efficacious devotion to him as a saint. In *Eiríks saga*, in contrast, the saga writer makes no such claims for Guðríðr; her sanctity lies entirely in her behavior and experiences while living. This difference reflects in part the shift in conceptualization inherent in the lay saint, someone similar to the rank-and-file Christian but greater in her more complete fulfillment of God's will. Such is not to suggest that *Eiríks saga* was written in any sense as an official vita for the purpose of campaigning for Guðríðr's recognition as a saint. Rather, it appears that the model of the lay saint's life, common in thirteenth-century Europe and familiar to Scandinavians at this time, influenced the writer's views and portrayal of his saintly character. The imagery of sainthood employed would have met with favor among the writer's ecclesiastical audience and would have resonated with his lay audience as well. Official canonization proceedings occurred only very seldom and only for a small fraction of the persons recognized and celebrated as saints in various parts of medieval Europe. Guðríðr's life, as depicted in *Eiríks saga* at least, would simply serve as a worthy model to emulate.

While the events of Guðríðr's life draw the text toward the narrative model of the saint's *vita*, *Eiríks saga* also displays many of the characteristics of a saga centered on a district, such as *Vatnsdœla saga*, *Laxdœla saga*, or *Eyrbyggja saga*.[116] In this respect, the narrative's popular supernatural moments again advance a Christian agenda: illustrating the gradual process by which a truly Christian society was achieved. This agenda again reflects the inner mission of thirteenth-century European Christianity: its abrupt embrace of the laity as a worthy object of interest and shift from earlier emphases on nobility or foreign infidels. *Eiríks saga* demonstrates the importance of a Christianization that extends beyond the acts of a saintly few toward a thorough restructuring of social institutions and achievement of overall religious orthodoxy. In this greater task, Guðríðr's role declines, becoming overshadowed by a succession of central male leaders who eventually prevail against the Greenland colony's pagan tendencies. The role of the saint as model and guide is thus placed in the broader context of the overall toil for a Christian society.

Again, the three prime moments of supernatural experience act as the ideological backbone of this textual program. In the *seiðr* scene, male authority acts in the interest of maintaining pagan rites, forcing the Christian Guðríðr to contribute to the success of the séance. Guðríðr's father, also Christian, holds no sway over his host's wishes. In absenting himself from the proceedings, Þorbjörn protests, but he remains unable to prevent its occurrence.[117] In the hauntings and Þorsteinn's revival, on the other hand, the colony's faith moves closer to Christian orthodoxy. While the farm's host in *Grœnlendiga saga* is portrayed as a pagan with Christian leanings, farmer Þorsteinn of *Eiríks saga* heads a wholly Christianized farmstead, where only a lack of clerics and laxity regarding burial rites separate the people from true Christian order. In returning from the dead, Guðríðr's Þorsteinn makes God's approval of his return clear, couching it in terms of the Christian afterlife. He has come to accomplish a task for God, leading the community toward proper Christian practice and urging the rejection of those who keep the faith badly, typified later by Þórhallr.[118] While a mosaic of differing faiths or syncresis of pagan and Christian practices may suffice as an environment for a truly saintly figure such as Guðríðr, normal folk require the institutional support and scrutiny afforded only by a diligently Christian community. It falls to the men of the saga to help erect the structures of this new orthodoxy.

Finally, in Þorfinnr's encounters with Þórhallr, Christian and pagan vie directly for preeminence. Þórhallr is a truly "bad Christian" (*illa kristinn*), one who relies equally or more on the patronage of Þórr. His procurement of tainted whale meat for the colonists is rejected immediately once its supernatural origin is made known, and Þorfinnr leads his people toward proper reliance on Christ alone to survive the winter. Þorfinnr rejects his opponent's religious acts but he does not banish the man himself: rather, like the biblical Good Shepherd, he searches for Þórhallr and his men diligently before resigning them to their mysterious loss. Þorfinnr emerges as an ideal Christian leader, devoted to the maintenance of proper Christian rites and attentive to the needs of even his backsliding opponents in faith, one imagistically and ideologically linked to King Óláfr Tryggvason, as discussed above, and contrasting markedly with conniving pagan chieftains like Víga-Glúmr.

This progression of Christianizing events replaces the wonders of a more extraneous kind in *Grœnlendiga saga*. In this earlier work, Þorvaldr Eiríksson's company is warned of an impending Skraeling attack through a loud voice that awakens them from their sleep.[119] Guðríðr, too, experiences a supernatural vision of less centrally Christian nature in this text: a woman much like her in appearance who appears beside her during the Skraelings' visit to the settlement.[120] The writer of *Eiríks saga* is no mere compiler of supernatural detail: his scenes are carefully deployed as part of a broader ideological program. The experiences and convictions of these early Christians, who will return to Iceland at the saga's end, serve as a conceptual background to the celebrated legal conversion of Iceland. They provide a justification for the importance of complete conversion while illustrating the mettle and merit of those Christians who met the challenge. We are to see in them the prototypes for a community of believers well equipped to withstand the temptations of heterodoxy and diligent in the task of Christianizing the land.

Like *Óláfs saga* and *Víga-Glúms saga*, *Eiríks saga* evinces not simply a Christian coloring of pagan history but a unified Christian agenda. Non-Christian ritual is depicted in detail but not out of mere antiquarian curiosity. It serves a specific purpose as the backdrop and motivation for the narrative's exploration of Christian sanctity, institutional change, and the importance of enforcing complete adherence to the faith. Nor can the saga writer be accuseed of pagan sympathies, although he deals with his pagan characters in a fairly kind manner. They are types for the expression of the challenge of the inner mission: to convert the populace not simply in name but also in spirit and practice. The recent history of the Viking colonies gave the Icelandic author unusually rich materials for the expression and exploration of this timely European concern.

Epilogue

The sagas present two worlds to the modern reader, worlds that lie at opposite ends of the five-century period examined in this book. On the one hand, they present the pagan ninth century, an era of Viking exploits and the first conversions to the new faith. On the other hand, they reflect the consolidating world of the thirteenth century, when an expanded monarchy and a well-established Church provided a new context from which to view, sometimes nostalgically, the rugged past of the North. During this era, religion—like society—changed remarkably. At the same time, some aspects of worldview and even religious practice remained unchanged.

Too often, however, scholarship on Nordic paganism has sought to examine the earlier of these eras exclusively. Scholars yearned to know of the pagan religions that preceded Christianity in the North: their gods, myths, rituals, and worldview. So generous are the saga writers in supplying details on these past traditions that it became easy to bracket or dismiss entirely the Christian "coloring" of their accounts. In a nearly archaeological fashion, scholars hoped to peel off the Christian layer of beliefs to gaze without obstruction at prior modes of religious experience. They ignored the intricacies of the Christianity they sought to bracket, its own changing and pluralistic nature. And thus, they took materials prime for the study of religious dynamics and sought instead to reconstruct an image of precontact religious stasis.

But archaeological as well as textual evidence tell us a different story: one of extensive and long-term intercultural contacts and of religious traditions that altered over the course of time. For centuries prior to the Christian conversions, and for generations thereafter, individuals, communities, and kingdoms developed their own specific versions of religion, selecting deities, rituals, and worldview in a manner that supported and explained the realities of their own particular experiences. New ideas diffused into these constructions with new economic and cultural influences while old ideas lingered on as a product of the inherent conservativism of human religiosity. Thus, Nordic religion at any given point in space or time could be seen as both an artifact of its past and a reflection of its present. It represented the ideological, aesthetic, and ethical basis of a community of belief.

The preceding chapters have suggested, I hope, some of the dynamics at work in Nordic religions during the Viking Age. By resisting notions of centralized, monolithic ethnic religions, it becomes possible to discern an array of different religious communities, pagan and Christian alike, operating on local levels and with great variation over time. Certain concepts or issues united many of these communities, regardless of conscious religious claims. These included attitudes toward death and health, some views of gods, and understandings of rituals. Even in the most universalizing of these traditions—that of official Christianity—individual and local variation occurred, and in the era of conversions both pagan religions and Christianity changed through the influence of neighboring faiths.

I have not attempted an exhaustive overview of this complex religious situation, nor has this exploration been framed as a "final word." A complete examination would need to take into account complex social contracts and traditions like pilgrimage, fosterage, jurisprudence, seasonal festivals, marriage, and war. Many studies have examined each of these topics, but much work remains to be done in interrelating the various strands of knowledge regarding Nordic worldviews in the Viking Age. I hope that this book will stimulate further explorations of the religions of the region and their textual portrayals in the Christian sagas of the thirteenth century. If it spurs others to examine this set of issues or appreciate the workings of Nordic communities during the long and tumultuous Viking Age, it will have succeeded in its purpose.

Glossary

áhkká Sámi term for any of various female household spirits residing in particular places within the home and responsible for reproduction and the proper functioning of the household. These include Máttaráhkká, Sáráhkká, Juksáhkká, and Uksáhkká.

Balto-Finns Any of the various populations of Karelia and the Gulf of Finland region speaking languages of the Finnic branch of the Finno-Ugric language family. Modern Balto-Finnic languages include Finnish, Karelian, Estonian, Votic, Vepsian, and Livonian.

benedictiones Latin term for the former possessions of a saint, venerated in shrines (see *relics, translatio*).

berserkr A class of Scandinavian warriors known for their battle frenzy. The term associates the tradition with the wearing of bear skins, perhaps as an initiation.

blót Old Norse term for sacrifice. The term usually denotes some sort of animal offering and was performed at temples or in homes.

dísir Old Norse term for female household spirits, recipients of winter sacrifices in the home.

Eddaic poems A set of poems first written down in the late twelfth or thirteenth century but probably deriving from earlier poetic traditions. They provide important evidence regarding pagan myths and beliefs and their interaction with Christianity.

Finno-Ugric language family A group of related languages spoken by various peoples across North Eurasia, including Sámi and Balto-Finns.

fóstr Old Norse term for fosterage, the temporary adoption of another's child, usually to effect alliances between families or clans.

fulltrúi Old Norse term for a patron, a deity with whom an individual enjoyed an especially warm or confident relation.

fylgja   Old Norse term for an individual's guardian spirit, often visible near death (also *hamingja*).

galdr   Old Norse term for a magic formula used in healing as well as in maintaining luck.

Germanic language family   A group of closely related Indo-European languages spoken by peoples in continental Europe, the British Isles, and Scandinavia. Old Norse, the language of Viking-Age Scandinavians, belongs to this language group, as does Old English, the precursor to modern English.

goði   Pagan Scandinavian priest-chieftain, whose duties included both religious and secular functions.

hamingja   Old Norse term for an individual's guardian spirit, often visible near death (also *fylgja*).

hieros gamos   Anthropological term (derived from Greek) for the "sacred marriage": a mystical union between a male sky god and female earth goddess. Common concept in Nordic agrarian religions, reflected in rituals.

hof   Old Norse term for a temple site, usually a building but often with surrounding inviolable land.

Indo-European language family   A widespread group of languages spoken by most peoples in Europe, including the Scandinavians. Its spread is associated archaeologically with the development and spread of sedentary agricultural communities in Europe.

loitsu   Finnish term for magic formulas used in healing as well as in maintaining luck.

noaide, noaidevuohttá   Sámi term for shaman and shamanism, a key aspect of Sámi pagan religion.

nornor   Old Norse term for female spirits associated with fate. Snorri refers to them as Urðr, Verðandi and Skuld—i.e., Past/Fate, Present, and Future/Destined.

relics   (Latin *reliquiae*) Earthly remains of a saint, venerated in shrines (see *benedictiones, translatio*).

rune   A system of writing widespread among pagan Germanic peoples and associated with magic and healing.

sájva   Sámi term for guardian spirits. In Sámi shamanism, the shaman relied on three such beings: *sájva-lâddie* (a bird spirit), *sájva-guölie* (a fish spirit), and *sájva-sârvá* (a reindeer bull spirit).

Sámi   Any of various populations of Scandinavia who spoke a language belonging to the Sámic branch of the Finno-Ugric language family.

Sámi communities lived as hunter-gatherers, with some degree of rein-deer husbandry. They came into close trading contact with Balto-Finns and Scandinavians.

Scandinavians Any of various populations in Scandinavia who spoke a form of Old Norse. Scandinavian populations spread from mainland Scandinavia to the British Isles and the Atlantic and were the dominant forces in the entire region during the Viking Age.

seidi Sámi term for idol or altar, often of stone, located in the wilderness and protected by various taboos. It was a site of sacrifices among Sámi pagans.

seiðr A pagan ritual practiced in Scandinavian communities for the pur-pose of divination or control of other people's wills. Seiðr practitioners were predominantly women.

shaman, shamanism Anthropological term for a widespread variety of re-ligious specialists and practices involving ecstatic trance and concepts of spirit travel.

siida Sámi term for a system of land use which featured collective land ownership and seasonal migration within the tract.

thing Old Norse term for a regional assembly in which laws were recited and disputes settled. Icelandic society developed a system of regional things as well as an annual island-wide assembly known as the Althing.

tietäjä Finnish term for a religious specialist skilled in healing and the manipulation of luck, associated with the widespread religious tradi-tion known as shamanism.

translatio Latin term for the ceremonial transferral of the relics or former possessions of a saint (see *relics, benedictiones*).

väki Finnish term for the inherent power of objects or entities, useful in gaining magical control over them. Väki is related to widespread con-ceptualizations of power known in anthropology as *mana*.

valkyrjor Old Norse term for a group of female spirits associated with the god Óðinn and responsible for conduct and death in battle.

Winter's Nights festival Household rituals taking place during winter and mentioned frequently in the sagas. Participants were apparently limited to family or household members and selected guests. The rituals, in-volving *blót*, were presided over by women, although men witnessed or participated in them.

Notes

Introduction

1. *Eyrbyggja saga*, ch. 4; Sveinsson and Þórðarson, 1935, 7–8.
2. Snorri Sturluson, *Heimskringla: Óláfs saga Tryggvasonar*, ch. 76; Aðalbjarnarson 1941 I, 323.
3. Snorri Sturluson, *Heimskringla: Óláfs saga Helga*, ch. 133; Aðalbjarnarson 1945 II, 229–231.

Chapter 1. The Cultures and History of the Viking North

1. For bibliographic overviews of this research tradition, see Lindow 1988 and *Bibliographia studiorum Uralicorum* 1990.
2. For discussion of this tendency, see Næss 1985, Olsen 1986, Voss 1987, Arnold 1990, Zachrisson 1991b.
3. See Zachrisson 1988, 1991b, 1992 for a critique of this entrenched view.
4. Durant 1950, 659.
5. Bäckman 1983, 1991; Rydving 1987, 1995.
6. Archaeological: Kajanoja 1984, Lehtosalo-Hilander 1984, Huurre 1979, 1984, Meinander 1984, Nuñez and Taavitsainen 1993, Salo 1984; palynological: Tolonen 1984, Lempiäinen and Häkkinen 1995, 1996; linguistic: Itkonen 1984, Korhonen 1984, Koivulehto 1984, Suhonen 1984; genetic: Nevanlinna 1984, Piazza et al. 1995.
7. Siiriäinen 1991.
8. Carpelan 1984.
9. Siiriäinen 1991, Julku 1995, Itkonen 1984, Korhonen 1984, Koivulehto 1984, Sammallahti 1984.
10. Wiik 1993.
11. Taavitsainen 1987.
12. Carpelan 1984.
13. Bitner-Wróblewski 1991, Wyszomirska-Werbart 1991, Lehtosalo-Hilander 1984, Grundström 1994, Talvio 1994.
14. Valonen 1980, 1984; Hajdú 1975.
15. Sherman 1997, Kovalev 1997.

16. Zenkovsky 1974, 64–67.
17. Khazanov 1984, Krupnik 1993, 1996; Wheelersburg and Kvist 1996.
18. Carpelan 1984, Taavitsainen 1987.
19. Valonen 1980, 1984.
20. Outakoski 1991.
21. Jutikkala and Pirinen 1984, Valonen 1980.
22. Siiriäinen 1991.
23. Vahtola 1995.
24. Linguistic: Sammallahti 1984, Valonen 1984; archaeological: Carpelan 1984, Eronen and Zetterberg 1996, Julku 1995, Zetterberg, Eronen and Briffa 1994; genetic: Eriksson 1984.
25. Sammallahti 1984.
26. Davidson 1976, Nuñez and Taavitsainen 1993, Wyszomirska-Werbart, 1991.
27. Roesdal 1987, 97–103; Ramskou 1962.
28. Blindheim and Tollnes 1972.
29. Benveniste 1973; Dumézil 1973, 1977; Polomé 1982; Puhvel 1970, 1987.
30. Karras 1998, 73–85.
31. Jochens 1995, 1996, Lövkrona 1992, Sawyer and Sawyer 1993.
32. Durrenberger 1992.
33. Byock 1982, 1988; Lindow 1994a.
34. Hunter 1997, Batey, Jesch, and Morris 1993.
35. Einarsson 1994.
36. Hunter 1997.
37. *Orkneyinga saga*, ch. 105, as discussed in Simpson 1967, 73.
38. O Còrrain 1972.
39. Hunter 1997.
40. Hunter 1997.
41. Bruce-Mitford 1979, Martin 1991.
42. De Paor 1967, Chadwick 1983.
43. Ó Cuív 1967.
44. Jóhannesson 1974, Madsen 1990, Arge 1993, Debes 1993, Hansen 1993, Sayers 1994.
45. Sayers 1994.
46. Cormack 1994, 91–92.
47. De Paor 1967.
48. Snorri Sturluson *Heimskringla: Magnússona saga*, ch. 27; Aðalbjarnarson 1951, III, 267.
49. Pelteret 1991.
50. Chadwick 1983, de Paor 1967, Durrenberger 1992, Samson 1991.
51. *Hávamál*, str. 41; Kunz 1962, 23.
52. Sammallahti 1984.
53. Sammallahti 1984, Valonen 1980, 1984.
54. Zachrisson 1988, 1991b, 1992.
55. For discussion of *Siida*, see Nickul 1977, Ruong 1982, Bergman 1990.
56. Storå 1971, Bäckman 1983, Ränk 1981, Fjellström 1987, Kjellström 1987, Rydving 1987 and 1995, Pentikäinen 1995.

57. "Ac hyra ār is mǣst on þǣm gafole þe ðā Finnas him gyldað" Whitelock 1967, 19.

58. Ruong 1982, 46; Vahtola 1995.

59. "Þā Finnas, him þūhte, ond þā Beormas sprǣcon nēah ān geþēode" (To him, the Finnas and the Beormas spoke nearly the same language) Whitelock 1967, 18.

60. *Egils saga*, ch. 14; Nordal 1933, 35–37.

61. *Egils saga*, ch. 7, 8; Nordal 1933, 16–22.

62. *Egils saga*, ch. 10; Nordal 1933, 27.

63. Ruong 1982, Nickul 1977, Carpelan 1984.

64. Ruong 1982, 47.

65. *Egils saga*, ch. 17; Nordal 1933, 43.

66. *Egils saga*, ch. 10; Nordal 1933, 27–28.

67. Whitelock 1967, 19–20.

68. Lehtosalo-Hilander 1984, Dreijer 1989, Salo 1991, Thunmark-Nylén 1995.

69. Talvio 1994.

70. Siiriäinen 1991.

71. Snorri Sturluson *Heimskringla: Ólafs saga helga* ch. 80; Aðalbjarnarson 1945, II, 114–117.

72. McGovern 1985.

Chapter 2. Religions in the Viking Age

1. Luckert 1984.

2. Geertz 1965, 1973.

3. Luckert 1984, 4.

4. See especially Asad 1983, Hofstee 1985.

5. Grimm 1965, Benveniste 1973; Dumézil 1973, 1977; Polomé 1982; Puhvel 1970, 1987; Holmberg-Harva 1926; Krohn 1932; Ajkhenvald et al. 1989.

6. Pentikäinen 1978, 36–45; Hastrup 1981, Schjødt 1990.

7. Finnestad 1990.

8. Brown 1981, 1–22; Gurevich 1988, Vauchez 1993.

9. Strömbäck 1975; Sawyer and Sawyer 1987, 1993; Hultgård 1990, 1992.

10. Strömbäck 1975, Gíslason 1990.

11. Von Schubert 1962, Levison 1946, Schnürer 1956, Meyvaert 1977, Brooke 1994.

12. Gurevich 1988, 39–40.

13. Rumble 1994.

14. *Historia Norwegiae*; Storm 1880, 152.

15. Christiansen 1980, 126–131.

16. Von Schubert 1962, Schnürer 1956, Lieu and Montserrat 1996.

17. *Hungrvaka*, ch. 13, Kahle 1905, 92; see also Gíslason 1990, 232.

18. Daly 1961.

19. Turville-Petre 1953, 112.

20. Schnürer 1956, 391.

21. Turville-Petre 1953, 113.

22. Turville-Petre 1953, 117–118.

23. Compare the views of Nordal 1952 and Sveinsson 1953 with Turville-Petre 1953, 1972; Lönnroth 1964, 1965a, 1965b, 1969, 1976, 1991; Strömbäck 1975; Clover 1985; Hill 1995.

24. Von See 1988, 69–83; see also Faulkes 1983.

25. Turville-Petre 1953, 117–118.

26. *Liber de miraculis sanctae dei genitricis Mariae*; Crane 1925, no. xx.

27. Turville-Petre 1953, 114.

28. Vauchez 1993, 141–152.

29. Turville-Petre 1953, 124.

30. Schnürer 1956, 438–444.

31. Ramskou 1962, Wikander 1978.

32. Schubert 1921, Vauchez 1993, 45–50.

33. Martin 1991, 67.

34. Von Schubert 1962, Levison 1946, Schnürer 1956, Kors and Peters 1972, Peters 1978, Vauchez 1993.

35. Schnürer 1956, 406–407.

36. Kors and Peters 1972, 44–47.

37. *Liber de gloria martyrum*, ch. 79 as discussed in Schnürer 1956, 199.

38. Smith and Urban, 1977.

39. Christensen 1980, 126–131.

40. Snorri Sturluson *Heimskringla: Óláfs saga Tryggvasonar*, ch. 31; Aðalbjarnarson 1941, I, 266; *Dialogues*, Book II, ch. 14, as discussed in Strömbäck 1975, 103, and Turville-Petre 1953, 136.

41. Schnürer 1956, 395.

42. As quoted in Schnürer 1956, 393.

43. Schnürer 1956, 393.

44. Lönnroth 1969, Faulkes 1983.

45. *Óláfs saga Tryggvasonar*, ch. 76; Aðalbjarnarson 1941, I, 322–323.

46. Smith and Urban 1977.

47. See Gíslason 1990 for discussion.

48. Ajkhenvald et al. 1989.

49. Lindow 1995.

50. Simpson 1967, 22–23.

51. Zachrisson 1987b, 1988; Meinander 1985; Lehtosalo-Hilander 1990, Purhonen 1990; Wyszomirska-Werbart 1991.

52. Gordon 1984, 188–191.

53. Turville-Petre 1964, 106–125.

54. Sørensen 1986.

55. Snorri Sturluson, *Heimskringla: Óláfs saga Helga*, ch. 133; Aðalbjarnarson 1945, II, 227–234.

56. Tacitus *Germania* ch. 39, 40; Lund 1988, 100–101.

57. Bäckman 1983, 30.

58. As discussed in Turville-Petre 1964, 237.

59. Turville-Petre 1972, 4–5.

60. Turville-Petre 1964, 244–247.

61. Snorri Sturluson, *Heimskringla: Hákonar saga Góða*, ch. 15–18; Aðalbjarnarson 1941, I, 169–173.

62. Gíslason 1990, 246.

63. See Simpson 1967, 18.

64. *Eyrbyggja saga* ch. 9; Sveinsson and Þórðarson 1935, 14–16.

65. *Hrafnkels saga* ch. 5–6; Cawley 1935, 22–26.

66. Rimbert *Vita Anskarii*, ch. 17; Odelman 1986, 33.

67. Snorri Sturluson, *Heimskringla: Haraldssona saga*, ch. 25; Aðalbjarnarson 1951, III, 334–337.

68. Snorri Sturluson, *Heimskringla: Óláfs saga Tryggvasonar*, ch. 27; Aðalbjarnarson 1941, I, 259–262.

Chapter 3. Gods, Guides, and Guardians

1. Luckert 1984, 6.

2. Zuesse 1987.

3. See, for instance, Eliade 1958a, Hultkrantz 1966, Dumézil 1977, Régis Boyer 1981, Polomé 1982, Honko et al. 1993.

4. Purhonen 1996; see also Lehtosalo-Hilander 1987, Pentikäinen 1978, Ajkenvald et al. 1989, Honko et al. 1993.

5. Lehtosalo-Hilander 1987, Ajkenvald et al. 1989.

6. Jónas Gíslason 1990, 246.

7. Gräslund 1967.

8. "Frœnda sinna, þeira er heygðir höfðu verit" Snorri Sturluson, *Heimskringla: Hákonar saga Góða*, ch. 14; Aðalbjarnarson 1941, I, 168.

9. Nordland 1969; Bäckman 1975, 1983; Pettersson 1987.

10. Gimbutas 1956, Mikkelsen 1986, Görman 1987, Salo 1987, Siiriäinen 1991, Honko et al. 1993, DuBois 1997.

11. Mikkelsen 1986; see also Durkheim 1915.

12. Gimbutas 1956, Siiriäinen 1991.

13. Ajkenvald et al. 1989, Siiriäinen 1991.

14. Siiriäinen 1991.

15. Honko et al. 1993, 63–81.

16. Kuusi et al. 1977, 522–523.

17. Norlander-Unsgaard 1985, Kuusi et al. 1977, Sarmela 1983, 1995; Honko et al. 1993.

18. Honko et al. 1993, 117–139.

19. Koivulehto 1984; see also De Vries 1970, section 235.

20. *Njáls saga* ch. 55; Ásmundarson 1894, 162.

21. Miller 1988.

22. *Edda: Guðrúnarqviða in Þriðia*; Kuhn 1962, 232–233; Snorri Sturluson, *Heimskringla: Magnússona saga*, ch. 27; Ed. Aðalbjarnarson 1951, III, 267–268.

23. Ränk 1981, Pettersson 1983.

24. See, for example, Dumézil 1948, Rooth 1961, Schjødt 1981; Aðalsteinsson 1990.

25. For Scandinavian terms, see Turville-Petre 1964, de Vries 1970; for *Hiisi*, see Koski 1987.

26. Tacitus *Germania*, ch. 39; Lund 1988, 100.

27. Bäckman 1977, Vorren 1987, Rydving 1995, 20; Pentikäinen 1995, 149–156.

28. *Kristnisaga* ch. 2; Kahle 1905, 6–10.

29. Ström 1986.

30. *Germania* ch. 12; Lund 1988, 80.

31. Ström 1954; Roesdahl 1987, 153; Turville-Petre 1964, 221–224.

32. Snorri Sturluson, *Heimskringla: Óláfs saga helga*, ch. 91; ed. Aðalbjarnarson 1945 II, 134–146.

33. *Njáls saga* ch. 96; Ásmundarson 1894, 228–229.

34. Ramskou 1962, 29–30.

35. Ränk 1955; on Scandinavian counterparts, see Ström 1954.

36. Honko et al. 1993.

37. Bäckman 1984.

38. Bäckman 1984, 38.

39. Rydving 1995, 129–133, 153.

40. *Edda: Helgaqviða Hjörvarðzsonar* str. 34–35; Kuhn 1962, 148.

41. Víga-Glúms saga ch. 9; Þorláksson 1880, 26–30.

42. Ström 1954.

43. *Edda: Helgaqviða Hundingsbana in fyrri, Helgaqviða Hundingsbana önnor, Sigrdrífomál*; Kuhn 1962, 130–139, 150–161, 189–197.

44. *Völsungasaga*. Olsen 1906–8.

45. See, for example, Eliade 1951, Mercier 1977, Bäckman and Hultkrantz 1977, Siikala 1987, Glosecki 1989, Honko et al. 1993.

46. Eliade 1951, 1958; Mercier 1977, Siikala 1987a, Conquergood et al. 1989.

47. Bäckman 1975.

48. Siikala 1992, 50, 101, 187–195.

49. Valonen 1983, Görman 1987, Troelsen 1987.

50. Gimbutas 1956, Lempiäinen and Häkkinen 1995.

51. Turville-Petre 1964, 249, 256.

52. *Edda: Völuspá*, str. 22, 24; Kuhn 1962, 5–6.

53. *För Scírnis*; Kuhn 1962, 69–77.

54. Snorri Sturluson *Prose Edda: Gylfaginning*, ch. 37; Faulkes 1983, 31.

55. Snorri Sturluson *Heimskringla: Ynglingasaga*, ch. 4. Aðalbjarnarson 1941, I, 12–13.

56. *Edda: Locasenna*. Kuhn 1962, 96–110.

57. *Kristnisaga*, ch. 10; Kahle 1905, 30.

58. Jaffee 1997.

59. Turville-Petre 1964, 174, Mitchell 1983.

60. *Gylfaginning* ch. 23; Faulkes 1983, 23–24.

61. Tacitus, *Germania*, ch. 40.2; Lund 1988, 100.

62. Krohn 1932; Kuusi 1963; Koivusalo 1993, 1995; DuBois 1997.

63. Snorri Sturluson, *Prose Edda: Skáldskaparmál*, ch. 5; Jónsson 1935, 108–110; *Edda: Völuspá*. Kuhn 1962, 1–16.

64. Dumézil, 1973, Salo 1990.

65. Bäckman 1991, Krohn 1932, Lindow 1994b, Rydving 1995, Salo 1987, Sayers 1990, Turville-Petre 1964.

66. Hastrup 1981, Siikala 1992, 136–140.

67. For Balts, Slavs, see Biezais 1976, Eisen 1995, Greimas 1992, Moszyński 1992, Puhvel 1987, Sayers 1990; for Finno-Ugric peoples, see Holmberg-Harva 1926, Honko et al. 1993, Pentikiäinen 1995.

68. Ross 1981.

69. Rydving 1995, 22; Pentikäinen 1995, 232–237.

70. L Dies Jovis = ON Þórsdagr, OE Þunresdæg = Thursday; Turville-Petre 1963, 101.

71. L Dies Mercurii = ON Óðinsdagr, OE Wodnesdæg = Wednesday; Turville-Petre 1963, 73.

72. Misane 1997.

73. Cf. Turville-Petre 1964, 62ff.

74. *Gylfaginning*, ch. 20; Faulkes 1983, 22.

75. Tr. Young 1954, 50.

76. *Edda: Hárbarðzlióð*. Kuhn 1962, 78–87.

77. Snorri Sturluson, *Prose Edda: Skáldskaparmál*, ch. 5; Jónsson 1935, 108–110.

78. See *Gylfaginning*, ch. 15, 38; Faulkes 1982 17, 32.

79. Ælfric, *De falsis diis*, in Homilies; Pope 1967–68, II, XXI, 667–724; *Hauksbók*, Jónsson and Jónnson 1892–96.

80. Ælfric, *De falsis diis*; Pope 1968, 669.

81. See especially Dumézil 1973.

82. Ström 1987.

83. *Egils saga Skalla-Grímssonar* ch. 56; Nordal, 1933, 148–163; see discussion Turville-Petre 1963, 69.

84. Turville Petre 1964, 86, and 1972, 1–19.

85. *Víga-Glums saga* ch. 6; Þorláksson, 1880, 15–19.

86. *Landnámabók: Sturlubók*, ch. 399, *Hauksbók*, ch. 356; both in Benediktsson 1968, II, 396.

87. *Eyrbyggja saga*, ch. 49; Sveinsson and Þórðason 1935.

88. Dumézil 1973, Davidson 1990, 31.

89. Hultgård 1992.

90. *Landnámabók: Sturlubók*, ch. 218, *Hauksbók*, ch. 184; Benediktsson 1968, II, 249–253.

91. *Eiríks saga rauða*, ch. 8; Hermannsson 1944, 23.

92. *Njáls saga* ch. 102; Ásmundarson 1894, 247–248.

93. Adam of Bremen *Gesta Hammaburgensis*, B. Schmeidler 1917, as discussed in Turville-Petre 1964, 244–247.

94. Snorri Sturluson, *Heimskringla: Óláfs saga Tryggvasonar*, ch. 69; Aðalbjarnarson 1941, I, 317–318.

95. Snorri Sturluson, *Heimskringla: Hákonar saga góða*, ch. 16; Aðalbjarnarson 1941, I, 171.

96. *Óláfs saga Tryggvasonar*, ch. 64; Aðalbjarnarson 1941, I, 312–314.

97. Baasten 1986, Evans 1986, McCready 1989.

98. Matthew 25:31–46.

99. Baasten 1986, 93–95.
100. Brown 1981, McCready 1989, Noble and Head 1995.
101. Rimbert, *Vita Anskarii*, Odelman 1986.
102. Cormack 1994; see also Jokipii 1989.
103. Sawyer 1987, 71–72.
104. McCready 1989.
105. McCready 1989, 22.
106. Brown 1981.
107. *Sturlunga saga: Prestssaga Guðmundar góða*, ch. 4; Bjarnarson 1908, I, 171.
108. "Uia haiþuiar þan þiakn" Gordon 1984, 187.
109. "þur uiki þasi runaR," ("Þórr hallow these runes") Gordon 1984, 187.
110. Gordon 1984, 188–191.
111. *Eyrbyggja saga*, chs. 3–4; Sveinsson and Þórðason 1935, 6–10.
112. *Hrafnkels saga*, ch. 2; Cawley 1932, 4.
113. Turville-Petre 1964, 260.
114. Hastrup 1981.
115. Þuríðr gyja Sölmundardóttir and Þuríðr hofgyja Véþormsdóttir: *Land-námabók: Sturlubók*, ch. 180, *Hauksbók*, ch. 276; Benediktsson 1968, II, 223, 321; Turville-Petre 1964, 261.
116. *Hof; Kristnisaga* ch. II, subchapter 11; Kahle 1905, 9.
117. *Njáls saga*, ch. 102; Ásmundarson 1894, 245–248.
118. Turville-Petre 1964, 261.
119. Sawyer 1992.
120. *Óláfs saga Tryggvasonar*, ch. 55; Aðalbjarnarson 1941, I, 305.
121. *Óláfs saga Tryggvasonar*, ch. 62; Aðalbjarnarson 1941, I, 311.
122. Sawyer and Sawyer 1986, 9, 60.

Chapter 4. Visitors from Beyond

1. Ibn Fadhlan, ed. Wikander 1968; trans. Simpson 1967, 199.
2. Bäckman 1983.
3. Carpelan 1984, Zachrisson 1987b, 1988, 1991a, 1991b, 1992.
4. Lehtosalo-Hilander 1987, 1990.
5. Snorri Sturluson, *Heimskringla: Óláfs saga helga*, ch. 133; Aðalbjarnarson 1945, II, 227–234; see Introduction for quotation of passage.
6. Lehtosalo-Hilander 1990.
7. Snorri Sturluson, *Heimskringla: Ynglingasaga*, ch. 8; Aðalbjarnarson 1941, I 20–22.
8. Thunmark-Nylén 1995.
9. Ramskou 1962, 49.
10. Batey 1993, Kaland 1993.
11. Simpson 1967; Roesdahl 1987; Christensen, Ingstad, and Myhre 1992; Batey 1993; Kaland 1993; Scott 1996.
12. Bruce-Mitford 1979.
13. Simpson 1967, 192.
14. Kaland 1993.

15. Blindheim and Tollnes 1972, 49.
16. Pentikäinen 1978, Lehtosalo-Hilander 1987, Ajkenvald et al. 1989, Honko et al. 1993.
17. Bäckman 1983, 38.
18. Pentikäinen 1978.
19. Honko et al. 1993, 566.
20. Bäckman 1975, 1983.
21. Bäckman 1983.
22. Bäckman 1975.
23. Nordland 1969; see also discussion in Bäckman 1975 and 1983, and Pettersson 1987.
24. *Eyrbyggja saga*, ch. 11; ed. Sveinsson and Þórðarson 1935, 19.
25. Translation from Pálsson and Edwards 1989, 38.
26. *Landnámabók*, as quoted and translated in Sayers 1994, 141.
27. Ellis 1943, 90.
28. *Edda: Helgaqviða Hundingsbana önnor*, Kuhn 1962, 150–161.
29. Clover 1986.
30. Gordon 1984, 144.
31. Trans. Terry 1990, 249.
32. *Edda: Helgaqviða Hundingsbana önnor*, str. 45; Kuhn 1962, 160.
33. Terry 1991, 132.
34. *Edda: Helgaqviða Hundingsbana önnor*, str. 46; Kuhn 1962, 160.
35. Ajkenvald et al. 1989; Hultkrantz 1977b, 17.
36. Virtanen 1988; DuBois 1997.
37. Pettersson 1957, 1983, 1987.
38. Ajkenvald et al. 1989; Salo 1987; for issue of borrowing, see Fritzner 1877, Olrik 1905, Krohn 1906, Rosén 1919, von Unwerth 1911; see Pettersson 1987 for discussion of this early view.
39. Pettersson 1987.
40. Manker 1950, Ahlbäck and Bergman 1991, Zachrisson 1991b, Pentikäinen 1995.
41. For stylistic analysis, see Zachrisson 1991b; for relation to shield-poems, see Kabell 1980.
42. Siikala 1992, 125–127.
43. Siikala 1992, 128–129.
44. *Suomen Kansan Vanhat Runot*, I, part 1: variants 349–381; For discussion, see Haavio 1952, 83–105, and Kuusi, Bosley and Branch 1977, 191–194.
45. Snorri Sturluson *Prose Edda: Gylfaginning* ch. 34; Faulkes 1983, 27.
46. Trans. Young 1954, 56.
47. *Edda: Helreið Brynhildar*, Kuhn 1962, 219–222.
48. *Gylfaginning*, ch. 49; Faulkes 1983, 45–48.
49. *Gylfaginning*, ch. 24; Faulkes 1983, 24–25.
50. *Gylfaginning*, ch. 35; Faulkes 1983, 29.
51. *Gylfaginning*, ch. 38–41; Faulkes 1983, 32–34.
52. Snorri Sturluson, *Heimskringla: Ynglingasaga*, ch. 8; Aðalbjarnarson 1941, I, 20.
53. Ellis 1943; For discussion of Njörðr, see Elcqvist 1952.

54. *Gylfaginning*, ch. 52; Faulkes 1983, 53–54.
55. *Gylfaginning*, ch. 52; Faulkes 1983, 53.
56. Richard Boyer 1981.
57. Gregory, *Dialogues*, Book IV, ch. 31.3; Vogüé 1980, 104.
58. *Dialogues*, IV, ch. 32.4; Vogüé 1980, 108.
59. Rimbert *Vita Anskarii*, ch. 3; Odelman 1984, 12.
60. For Marian examples, see *Liber de miraculis sanctae genitricis Mariae*; Crane 1925.
61. Strömbäck 1975, 93.
62. Sveinsson 1943, see discussion in Strömbäck 1975, 95–97; for Icelandic version of the *Dialogues*, see Benediktsson 1963.
63. *Gylfaginning*, ch. 51–53; Faulkes 1983, 49–54; see discussion Hultgård 1990, 353.
64. Vauchez 1993, 86.
65. Storå 1971, 106.
66. *Óláfs saga Helga*, ch. 187; Aðalbjarnarson 1945, II, 339.
67. "Nunna ok einsetukona," *Grœnlendiga saga*, ch. 9; Hermannsson 1944, 61.
68. Batey 1993, 161.
69. See Vauchez 1993, 87.
70. *Grœnlendiga saga*, ch. 5; Hermansson 1944, 53–54.
71. Roesdal 1987, 164.
72. *Egils saga*, ch. 86; Nordal 1933, 142.
73. Pentikäinen 1968.
74. Brown 1981, Noble and Head 1995.
75. Storå 1971, 260, Virtanen 1988, 216.
76. *Eyrbyggja saga*, ch. 33; Sveinsson and Þórðarson 1935, 92.
77. Trans. Pálsson and Edwards 1989, 93.
78. Aðalsteinsson 1987.
79. Kjellström 1976.
80. Koski 1987.
81. Koski 1987, 415.
82. *Laxdœla saga*, ch. 7, 17, 18, 24; Sveinsson 1934, 11–15, 39–43, 66–69.
83. *Landnámabók: Sturlubók*, ch. 110; Benediktsson 1968 I, 147; *Laxdœla saga*, ch. 7; Sveinsson 1934, 11–15; see discussion Conroy and Langen 1988, 124.
84. *Laxdœla saga*, ch. 24; Sveinsson 1934, 66–69.
85. *Grœnlendiga saga*, ch. 6; Hermannsson 1944, 54–56.
86. *Eiríks saga*, ch. 4; Hermannsson 1944, 16.
87. Trans. Jones 1935, 142.
88. *Eiríks saga*, ch. 6; Hermannsson 1944, 17.
89. Trans. Jones 1935, 144.
90. *Eyrbyggja saga*, ch. 11; Sveinsson and Þórðarson 1935, 18–19.
91. *Eyrbyggja saga*, ch. 33–34, 43, 63; Sveinsson and Þórðarson 1935, 90–95, 115–119, 169–176.
92. *Eyrbyggja saga*, ch. 63; Sveinsson and Þórðarson 1935, 169–170.
93. Trans. Pálsson and Edwards 1989, 156.
94. *Eyrbyggja saga*, ch. 63; Sveinsson and Þórðarson 1935, 174–175.
95. *Eyrbyggja saga*, ch. 50–55; Sveinsson and Þórðarson 1935, 137–152.

96. Davidson 1981, Ottósson 1983.
97. *Eyrbyggja saga*, ch. 49; Sveinsson and Þórðarson 1935, 136.
98. *Eyrbyggja saga*, ch. 51; Sveinsson and Þórðarson 1935, 143–144.
99. Trans. Pálsson and Edwards 1989, 134.
100. *Eyrbyggja saga*, ch. 54; Sveinsson and Þórðarson 1935, 148.
101. "En þá var enn lítt af numin forneskjan, þó at menn væri skírðir ok kristnir at kalla," Sveinsson and Þórðarson 1935, 148; trans. Pálsson and Edwards 1989, 138.
102. *Eyrbyggja saga*, ch. 55; Sveinsson and Þórðarson 1935, 150–152.
103. Pálsson and Edwards 1989, 141.
104. McCreesh 1978–79.

Chapter 5. Concepts of Health and Healing

1. Apuleius, *Herbarium* 1961, Old English translation, ed. Cockayne 1961, vol. I.
2. Apuleius XCI; Cockayne 1961, 199–200.
3. Apuleius I, XCV, CXLII, CLX, CXXIX; Cockayne 1961, 71, 209, 265, 289, 241.
4. Apuleius LVI, LXIII; Cockayne 1961, 159, 167.
5. Apuleius LXXV, CLXVIII; Cockayne 1961, 179, 299.
6. Apuleius LXXVII, XC; Cockayne 1961, 181, 195.
7. Apuleius CXIV; Cockayne 1961, 227.
8. Apuleius LX, LXXXIX, LXXXII; Cockayne 1961, 163, 193, 187.
9. Apuleius CIV; Cockayne 1961, 219.
10. Apuleius XCIV, LXII; Cockayne 1961, 207, 165.
11. Apuleius CXV; Cockayne 1961, 229.
12. Apuleius V, LXXX, CXVII, CXLV, CXVI; Cockayne 1961, 95, 183, 231, 269, 229.
13. Sextus Placitus *Medicina de quadrupedibus*. Old English translation, ed. Cockayne 1961, vol. I.
14. Placitus; Cockayne 1961, 345, 355.
15. Placitus; Cockayne 1961, 355, 365.
16. Placitus; Cockayne 1961, 361, 365.
17. Placitus; Cockayne 1961, 369.
18. Placitus; Cockayne 1961, 347, 370.
19. Placitus; Cockayne 1961, 369, 366.
20. *Bald's Leechbook*, Cockayne 1961, vol. II. See also Wright 1955.
21. Brøndegaard 1979, vol. 2, 279–283, 192–194.
22. Brøndegaard 1979, 117–124.
23. Brøndegaard 1979, 288–292.
24. Danish *skrœppe, syre*; Brøndegaard 1979, 124–131.
25. *Edda: Hávamál* str. 137; Kuhn 1962, 39–40.
26. See Evans 1986, 131–134, for commentary on possible glosses of these remedies.
27. Naakka-Korhonen 1983.
28. Snorri Sturluson, *Heimskringla: Magnúss saga ins Góða*, ch. 28; Aðalbjarnarson 1951, III, 45.
29. Tillhagen 1977, 11.

30. Karras 1988, 69–95.
31. As cited in Tillhagen 1977, 12.
32. Tillhagen 1977, 12.
33. Snorri Sturluson, *Heimskringla: Óláfs saga Helga*, ch. 234; Aðalbjarnarson 1945, II, 392–393.
34. *Bald*, XXXV; Cockayne 1961, II, 84–87.
35. *Njáls saga* ch. 57, 63; Ásmundarson 1894, 135, 149.
36. Turunen 1981, "Löyly," 197.
37. Zenkovsky 1974, 47.
38. Vahros 1966, 40.
39. Tacitus, *Germania*, ch. 22; Lund 1988, 88.
40. *Sverris saga*, ch. 50 (67, 68); Kjær 1985, 87; *Arons saga*, ch. 16; Bjarnarson 1908, IV, p. 207.
41. *Eyrbyggja saga*, ch. 28; Sveinsson and Þórðarson 1935, 74.
42. *Sturlunga saga: Saga Þórðar Sighvatssonar Kakala*, ch. 11, *Svínfellinga saga*, ch. 6; Bjarnarson 1908, III, ch. 174, 39; III, 153.
43. *Sturlunga saga: Sturlusaga* ch. 9; Bjarnarson 1908, I, 94. Snorri's bath is mentioned in *Sturlunga saga: Íslendingasaga* ch. 69; Bjarnarson 1908, II, 150.
44. *Sturlunga saga: Íslendingasaga* ch. 86; Bjarnarson 1908, II, 187–188.
45. Bonser 1963, 55.
46. Bonser 1963, 155 ff.; Honko 1962.
47. Bonser 1963, 56.
48. Kealey 1981, 4.
49. Bonser 1963, 58.
50. Bonser 1963, 59–63.
51. Bonser 1963, 59–63, 91.
52. Kealey 1981, 2.
53. Kealey 1981, 18–19.
54. Kealey 1981, 15.
55. *Eiríks saga rauða*, ch. 6; Hermannsson 1944, 15–17.
56. *Eyrbyggja saga*, ch. 52; Sveinsson and Þórðarson 1935, 145–146.
57. *Eyrbyggja saga*, ch. 51; Sveinsson and Þórðarson 1935, 139–145.
58. Davidson 1981, 158.
59. Cameron 1993, 130–158.
60. Hultkrantz 1977b.
61. *Historia Norwegiae*; Storm 1880, 69–124.
62. Siikala 1987b, 1992.
63. Siikala 1987b, 191–192.
64. Siikala 1992, Tillhagen 1977.
65. Ajkenvald et al. 1989.
66. Sköld 1996.
67. Demant-Hall, in Turi and Turi *Lappish Texts*, 1918–19, fn 46, 271.
68. Turi and Turi, *Lappish Texts*, 1918–19, 121, 129.
69. Virtanen 1988, 241.
70. *The Anglo-Saxon Charms*; Grendon 1909, 129–131.
71. "Trēow-wurðunga and stān wurðunga and þone dēofles cræft, þǣr man þā cild þurh þā eorðan tī hð," as quoted in *The Anglo-Saxon Charms*; Grendon 1909, 130.

72. Tillhagen 1977, 291–292; Sarmela 1995, 46–47.
73. Holthoer 1981, 161.
74. Virtanen 1988, 267.
75. *The Anglo-Saxon Charms*; Grendon 1909, 110.
76. Wipf 1975, 47–48.
77. *The Anglo-Saxon Charms*; Grendon 1909, 111.
78. *Edda: Sigrdrífomál*, str. 6, 7, 11; Kuhn 1962, 191–192.
79. Trans. Terry 1990, 162–163.
80. *Edda: Sigrdrífomál* str. 15–18; Kuhn 1962, 193.
81. Trans. Terry 1990, 164.
82. *Egils saga* ch. 72; Nordal 1933, 227–230.
83. Cameron 1993, 139.
84. *Bald*, I:9; Cockayne 1961 vol. II, 54; Cameron 1993, 137.
85. Singer 1955, xxxviii–xxxix, in Cameron 1961, vol. I; see further discussion in Olsan 1992.
86. "Tellam te artemesia ne lassus súm in via" (I will take you artemesia lest I be weary on the way); *Bald*, I: LXXXVI; Cockayne 1961, vol. II, 154–155.
87. *Bald*, I: LXXXV; Cockayne 1961, vol. II, 154–155.
88. *Edda: Oddrúnarqviða*, Kuhn 1962, 234–239.
89. *Grogaldr*, Detter and Heinzel 1903, 185a–186a.
90. *Edda: Sigrdrífomál, Hávamál*; Kuhn 1962, 189–197, 17–44.
91. *Edda: Hávamál*, str. 147, *Grogaldr*, str. 12, *Sigrdrífomál*, str. 9, 11; Kuhn 1962, 42, 191–192; Detter and Heinzel 1903, 186.
92. *Hávamál*, str. 146; Kuhn 1962, 41.
93. *Grogaldr*, str. 6, 7, 10, 13; *Hávamál* str. 148, 149, 150, 156, 158; *Sigrdrífomál* str. 6; Detter and Heinzel 1903, 185a; Kuhn 1962, 42–43, 191.
94. E.g., love—*Hávamál*, str. 161, 162, 164; protection against ill will or ill speech—*Grogaldr*, str. 9, *Sigrdrífomál*, str. 12, 13, *Hávamál*, str. 151, 153; Kuhn 1962, 44, 192; Detter and Heinzel 1903, 185a.
95. *Sigrdrífomál*, str. 7–8; Kuhn 1962, 191.
96. *Grogaldr*, str. 14, *Hávamál* str. 155, 157, 159, 160; Detter and Heinzel 1903, 186a; Kuhn 1962, 43–44.
97. *Grogaldr*, str. 8, 11, *Hávamál* str. 154, *Sigrdrífomál*, str. 10; Detter and Heinzel 1903, 185–186a; Kuhn 1962, 43, 191.
98. *Hávamál*, str. 152; Kuhn 1962, 42.
99. See Weisser-Aall 1968, Jacobsen 1986.
100. *Gylfaginning*, ch. 35; Faulkes 1983, 29–30.
101. *Oddrúnagrátr*, str. 9; Kuhn 1962, 235; *Sigrdrífomál*, str. 9; Kuhn 1962, 191.
102. DuBois 1997.
103. *Oddrúnagrátr* str. 7; Kuhn 1962, 235.
104. *Oddrúnagrátr* str. 9; Kuhn 1962, 235.
105. *Oddrúnagrátr* str. 10; Kuhn 1962, 235; Sprenger 1992, 110–112.
106. See, for example, *Suomen Kansan Vanhat Runot* 6, no. 2, 4638.
107. Weiser-Aall 1968, DuBois 1997; Turi and Turi *Lappish Texts* 1918–19, 129–130.
108. Simpson 1975, Migliore 1983, Sebald 1984.
109. Kors and Peters 1972.

110. Peters 1978, 4–5.
111. Olaus Magnus 1555, book 3, ch. 17.
112. Trans. Foote 1996, 175.
113. *The Anglo-Saxon Charms*; Grendon 1909, Grattan and Singer 1952, Honko 1959, Bonser 1963, Cameron 1993.
114. *The Anglo-Saxon Charms*; Grendon 1909, 164.
115. *Eyrbyggja saga*, ch. 15–20; Sveinsson and Þórðarson 1935, 26–54.
116. Pálsson 1991.
117. Simpson 1975.
118. Singer 1955, xxxii in Cockayne 1961.
119. *Bald*, I:VIIII; Cockayne 1961, vol. II, 54.
120. "þes cræft mæʒ wiþ ælcre feondes costunʒe," Cockayne 1961, vol. II, 54.
121. *Prose Life of St. Cuthbert*, ch. 9; quoted in Bonser 1963, 55.
122. Elder *Gula þingslög*, sections 28–29; ed. Eithun, Rindal, and Ulset 1994, 50–52.
123. Bonser 1963, 171.
124. Snorri Sturluson, *Heimskringla: Óláfs saga Tryggvasonar*, ch. 76; Aðalbjarnarson 1941, I, 322–323.
125. Bonser 1963, 175.
126. Kealey 1981, 23.
127. Snorri Sturluson, *Heimskringla: Óláfs saga Helga*, ch. 189; Aðalbjarnarson 1945, II, 341–342.
128. *Óláfs saga Helga*, chs. 230, 237; Aðalbjarnarson 1945, II, 387, 396–397.
129. Koppenberg 1980, 140.
130. Koppenberg 1980, 141.
131. *Óláfs saga Helga*, ch. 240; Aðalbjarnarson 1945, II, 401.
132. Luckert 1984.

Chapter 6. The Intercultural Dimensions of the Seiðr Ritual

1. For a detailed examination of seiðr in Old Norse texts, see Strömbäck 1935. The current chapter also draws on DuBois 1996.
2. Zuesse 1987. For an overview of past scholarly definitions, see Platvoet 1995, 25–52. Sørensen 1993 would widen the arc of bodily actions included in Zuesse's definition to include meditation and silent prayer.
3. *Eiríks saga rauða*, ch. 4; Hermannsson, 1944, 9–10.
4. Jones 1980, 135.
5. *Eiríks saga rauða*, ch. 4; Hermannsson 1944, 10.
6. Jones 1980, 134.
7. *Eiríks saga rauða*, ch. 4; Hermannsson 1944, 11–12.
8. Jones 1980, 136–137.
9. *Vatnsdøla saga*, ch. 10–12; Sveinsson 1939, 27–36.
10. Strömbäck 1935, 87, 96.
11. Strömbäck 1935, 79ff.
12. She is said to gasp and work her jaws "*slær þá í sundr kiöptunum ok geispar*

miök"; Saxo's term for the practitioner's chant is "morbi simulacione"—"as if dead." Strömbäck 1935, 79.

13. "Svá er sagt, at Gunnhildr lét seið efla ok lét þat seiða, at Egill Skalla-Grímsson skyldi aldri ró bíða á Íslandi, fyrr en hon sæi hann." (It is said that Gunnhildr practiced seiðr and that she worked a seiðr spell that Egill Skalla-Grímsson should never find peace of mind in Iceland until she had seen him), *Egils Saga*, ch. 59; ed. Nordal 1933, 176; *Egils Saga*, trans. Fell 1975.

14. "Drífa keypti at Hulð seiðkonu, at hon skyldi síða Vanlanda til Finnlands eða deyða hann at öðrum kosti. En er seiðr var framiðr, var Vanlandi at Uppsölum. Þá gerði hann fúsan at fara til Finnlands, en vinir hans ok ráðamenn bönnuðu honum ok sögðu, at vera myndi fjölkynngi Finna í fýsi hans." (Drífa hired a seiðr woman named Hulð to work a seiðr spell to bring Vanlandi back to Finnland or otherwise to kill him. When the seiðr took effect, Vanlandi was in Uppsala. He then had a strong desire to go to Finnland, but his friends and advisors forbade it, saying that there must be some Finn magic in his desire.) Snorri Sturluson, *Heimskringla: Ynglingasaga*, ch. 13; Aðalbjarnarson 1941, I, 29.

15. *Laxdœla saga*, ch. 35; Sveinsson 1934, 95–100; see discussion, Strömbäck 1935, 64 ff.

16. *Laxdœla saga*, ch. 37; Sveinsson 1934, 105–106.

17. "At nema kunnostu at Finnum tveim, er hér eru fróðastir á mörkinni," Snorri Sturluson, *Heimskringla: Haralds saga ins Hárfagra*, ch. 33; Aðalbjarnarson 1941, I, 135.

18. *Landnámabók: Hauksbók*, ch. 116; *Sturlubók*, ch. 145; Benediktsson 1968, I, 186.

19. *Haralds saga ins Hárfagra*, ch. 25, ch. 34; Aðalbjarnarson 1941, I, 125–127, 138–139.

20. Snorri Sturluson, *Heimskringla: Óláfs saga Tryggvasonar*, ch. 62–63; Aðalbjarnarson 1941, I, 311–312.

21. Strömbäck 1935.

22. *Borgarthings Kristenrett* I, 16; II, 25; III, 22, as quoted in Strömbäck 1935, 203–205; See also Zachrisson 1991, 192.

23. *Historia Norwegiae*, ed. Storm 1880, 69–124; for discussion of dating, see Anderson 1985, 201.

24. See Strömbäck; also Bäckman 1975 and Bäckman and Hultkrantz 1977.

25. Manker 1938/1950; for more recent approaches to the subject see Ahlbäck and Bergman 1991.

26. *Historia Norwegiae* Storm 1880, 86.

27. See, for instance Kjellström 1991.

28. Siikala 1987a, 45.

29. Siikala 1992, 73.

30. Siikala 1992, 238.

31. Kabell 1980.

32. Haavio 1952, 106–139; Pentikäinen 1995, 188.

33. Ajkenvald 1989.

34. Siikala 1987b, 195; 1992, 239–246.

35. Siikala 1992, 242.

36. Siikala 1992, 239.
37. Siikala 1987b, 193–194; 1992, 207.
38. Haavio 65–82, 140–173.
39. Siikala 1992, 236.
40. Siikala 1987b.
41. Hultkrantz 1977b.
42. Bäckman and Hultkrantz 1977, 59; Norlander-Unsgaard 1985; Apo 1995, 11–49; DuBois 1997.
43. Lundmark 1987; Siikala 1987b.
44. Tacitus *Germania* ch. 8; Lund 1988, 76.
45. "Hon kenndi fyrst með Ásum seið, sem Vönum var títt" (She was first among the Æsir to know of seiðr, which was common among the Vanir), Snorri Sturluson, *Heimskringla: Ynglingasaga*, ch. 3; Aðalbjarnarson 1951, 113.
46. Pálsson 1991.
47. *Edda: Völuspá* str. 22; Kuhn 1962, 6–7.
48. De Vries 1970, section 236.
49. *Ynglingasaga*, ch. 7; Aðalbjarnarson 1941, I, 19.
50. "Haraldi konungi þóttu illir seiðmenn"; Snorri Sturluson, *Heimskringla: Haralds saga ins Hárfagra*, ch. 34; Aðalbjarnarson 1941, I, 138.

Chapter 7. The Coming of the Cross

1. Frolow 1961, 155–157.
2. Eadie 1971, 13–14.
3. Frolow 1961, 111.
4. Frolow 1961, 155, 160–161, 188–190.
5. Miller 1967.
6. Frolow 1961, 198–210.
7. Stevens 1904, 16.
8. Stevens 1904, 15.
9. De Paor and de Paor 1960, 116, 133, 170.
10. Eighth Ecumenical Council at Constantinople, canon iii, as quoted in Miller 1967.
11. Ó Cárrigáin 1994, 14.
12. Odo of Cluny, *Life of St. Gerald of Aurillac*, book II, ch. 3; Sitwell 1995, 328.
13. Alcuin, *Life of St. Willibrord*, ch. 30; Talbot 1995, 209.
14. Rumble 1994, 297.
15. Cormack 1994, 106.
16. Snorri Sturluson, *Heimskringla: Hákonar saga Góða*, ch. 16.
17. *Life of St. Bridget*, O'Brien 1938, 132–133.
18. Stevens 1904, 33.
19. De Paor and de Paor 1960, 124–126.
20. Henry 1940, 42.
21. *Historia Ecclesiastica Gentis Anglorum*, Book III, ch. 2; Cf. Ælfric, *Lives*, ed. Needam 1966, 28–29.

22. Bonser 1963, 182–183.
23. *Njáls saga*, ch. 113; Ásmundarson 1894, 265.
24. McNamara 1975, 128–140.
25. Cook 41, ll. 1061–1066, 1084–1088a.
26. Translation from Kennedy 1960, 152–153.
27. *Dream of the Rood* ll.117–121; Whitelock 1967, 158.
28. Talbot 1995, 146.
29. Kinvig 1975; Page 1983; Margeson 1983; Wilson 1974, 1983.
30. Margeson 1983.
31. Page 1983.
32. "Xmail: brikti: sunr: aþakans: smiþ" "kautX," Page 1983, 136.
33. Kirk Andreas, no. 128; Margeson 1983, 96.
34. Bailey 1980, 127.
35. Hultgård 1990.
36. Liestøl 1983, Bailey 1993.
37. Sørensen 1986.
38. Bailey 1980, 103–116.
39. *Landnámabók: Sturlubók*, ch. 257; Benediktsson 1968, II, 285; Turville-Petre 1964, 84.
40. Sawyer and Sawyer 1993, 103.
41. Johnsen 1968, Birkeli 1982, Page 1983.
42. *Eiríks saga* ch. 1; Hermannsson 1944, 3–4.
43. *Eiríks saga* ch. 1; Jones 1961, 127.
44. "Sækja menn þangat sem til heilagra staða, ok brenna ljósi firir þeim krossi, úti sem inni í kirkju, þótt hregg sé úti," as quoted in Cormack 1994, 106–7.
45. Jokipii 1989, Luoto 1989.
46. Makarov 1989.
47. Makarov 1989, 56–57.
48. Horn Fuglesang 1981, Purkanen 1990, Wyszomirska-Werbart 1991.
49. Luoto 1989.
50. Lehtosalo-Hilander 1990.
51. Meinander 1985.
52. Zachrisson 1986a, 1988.
53. Arbman 1943, Dreijer 1989.
54. Lindqvist 1941, Davidson 1976, 300–317.
55. Purhonen 1990, 38.
56. Cf. Widukind's *Rerum gestarum Saxonicarum*, III.65; Snorri Sturluson, *Óláfs saga Tryggvasonar*, ch. 24–27; Sawyer 1987, 69; Roesdahl 1987, 74.
57. Rimbert, *Vita Anskarii*, tr. and ed. Odelman 1986.
58. Ekenberg 1986, Wood 1987.
59. Rimbert, *Vita Anskarii*, ch. 2–5, 41; Odelman 1986, 17–22, 72–73.
60. Rimbert, *Vita Anskarii*, ch. 29; Odelman 1986, 56–58.
61. Rimbert, *Vita Anskarii*, ch. 10, 16, 17, 18, 29; Odelman 1986, 27, 32–35, 56–58.
62. Clemoes 1983.
63. Bailey 1980, 76, 139; Henry 1983, 66; Sawyer 1987, 70.

64. Widukind, *Rerum gestarum Saxonicarum* III.65; Snorri Sturluson, *Heims-kringla: Óláfs saga Tryggvasonar*, ch. 24–27; Aðalbjarnarson 1941, I, 254–262.

65. Bailey 1980, Hultgård 1992, Sawyer 1992, Sawyer and Sawyer 1993, 14–16.

66. Bailey 1980, 76.

67. De Paor and de Paor 1960, pl. 28.

68. Sawyer 1992.

69. Hultgård 1992.

70. Lindow 1994b.

71. Snorri Sturluson, *Prose Edda: Skáldskaparmál*, ch. 44; Jónsson 1935, 158–161.

72. Snorri Sturluson, *Prose Edda: Gylfaginning*, ch. 21; Faulkes 1983, 22–23

73. See Saxo Grammaticus, *Historia Danica* III, 73; Turville-Petre 1964, 81, 84.

74. *Landnámabók:* Sturlubók, ch. 257; Benediktsson 1968, II, 285; Lindow 1994b, 489.

75. Turville-Petre 1964, 83.

76. Snorri Sturluson, *Gylfaginning*, ch. 38; Faulkes 1983, 32–33.

77. Turville-Petre 1964, 43.

78. Brown 1996.

79. Hultgård 1992.

80. *Skáldskaparmál*, ch. 44; Jónsson 1935, 161.

81. *Skáldskaparmál*, ch. 25; Jónsson 1935, 133–134.

82. *Edda: Helgaqviða Hundingsbana önnor*, Kuhn 1962, 157.

83. *Edda: Þrymsqviða*; Kuhn 1962, 111–115.

84. See *Gylfaginning*, ch. 49; Faulkes 1983, 46; *Þrymsqviða*, Kuhn 1962, 111–115.

85. "At fornum sið," *Eyrbyggja saga*, ch. 44; Sveinsson and Þórðarson 1935, 122.

86. Snorri Sturluson, *Prose Edda: Gylfaginning*, ch. 52. Faulkes 1983, 53.

87. Snorri Sturluson, *Heimskringla: Magnúss saga ins Góða*, ch. 28; Aðalbjarnarson 1951, III, 43–45.

88. Lawson 1993, 137.

89. Lawson 1993, 134, 135–140.

90. Frank 1994, 116.

91. Frank 1994, 117.

92. Snorri Sturluson, *Heimskringla: Óláfs saga Helga*, ch. 204; Aðalbjarnarson 1945, II, 355.

93. *Óláfs saga Helga*, ch. 201, 204, 205, 206, 215; Aðalbjarnarson 1945, II, 349–351, 353–360, 369–370.

94. *Óláfs saga Helga*, ch. 49; Aðalbjarnarson 1945, II, 60–62.

95. "Maðr ok þekkilgir ok þó ógurligr," *Óláfs saga Helga*, ch. 18; Ed. Bjarni Aðalbjarnarson 1945, II, 25.

96. "Guð mun þér bera vitni, at þat er þín eiga," *Óláfs saga Helga*, ch. 187; Aðalbjarnarson 1945, II, 340.

97. *Óláfs saga Helga*, ch. 189; Aðalbjarnarson 1945, II, 341–342.

98. Cf. Snorri Sturluson, *Heimskringla: Magnúss saga ins Goða*, ch. 28; Aðalbjarnarson 1951, III, 43–45.

99. *Magnúss saga ins Goða*, ch. 10; Aðalbjarnarson 1945, II, 20–21.

100. *Magnúss saga ins Goða*, ch. 27; Aðalbjarnarson 1945, II, 43.

101. Snorri Sturluson, *Heimskringla: Magnússona saga*; Aðalbjarnarson 1951; Theodric, *Historia de Antiquitate Regum Norwagiensium*, chapter 33, ed. Storm 1880, 65–66; parallel passages from the *Ágrip* (86–87) printed as footnotes. Storm 65–66.

102. Snorri Sturluson, *Heimskringla: Magnúss saga Blinda ok Haralds Gilla*, ch. 11; Aðalbjarnarson 1951, III, 291–295.

103. *Magnússona saga*, ch. 11; Aðalbjarnarson 1951, III, 250.

104. Snorri Sturluson, *Heimskringla: Haraldssona saga*, ch. 23; Aðalbjarnarson 1951, III, 332–333; Jokipii 1989, 89.

105. *Magnússona saga*, ch. 19; Aðalbjarnarson 1951, III, 257–28.

106. *Magnússona saga*, ch. 21; Aðalbjarnarson 1951, III, 330.

107. Snorri Sturluson, *Heimskringla: Magnúss saga Blinda ok Haralds Gilla*, ch. 11; Aðalbjarnarson 1951, III, 291–295.

108. *Magnúss saga Blinda ok Haralds Gilla*, chs. 9–10; Aðalbjarnarson 1951, III, 288–291.

109. *Magnúss saga Blinda ok Haralds Gilla*, ch. 11; Aðalbjarnarson 1951, III, 295.

110. Cormack 1994, 107.

111. Aðalbjarnarson 1951, III, 295 n. 2.

112. Derry 1979, 52.

113. *Njáls saga*, chs. 107, 132; Ásmundarson 1894, 256, 323.

114. Cormack 1994, 103.

115. Vuorela 1979, 393.

116. Cormack 1994, 103.

Chapter 8. Achieving Faith

1. Snorri Sturluson, *Heimskringla: Óláfs saga Tryggvasonar*, ch. 80; Aðalbjarnarson 1941, I, 328.

2. Turville-Petre 1953, 190–196.

3. Gregory, *Dialogues*, Vogüé and Antin 1980.

4. Snorri Sturluson, *Heimskringla: Hákonar saga Góða*; Aðalbjarnarson 1941 I, 150–197.

5. Snorri Sturluson, *Heimskringla: Haralds saga Gráfeldar*, ch. 2–5; Aðalbjarnarson 1941 I, 203–207.

6. *Óláfs saga Tryggvasonar*, ch. 16; Aðalbjarnarson 1941, I, 241–243.

7. *Óláfs saga Tryggvasonar*, ch. 27; Aðalbjarnarson 1941, I, 259–262.

8. *Óláfs saga Tryggvasonar*, ch. 27; Aðalbjarnarson 1941, I, 260.

9. *Óláfs saga Tryggvasonar*, ch. 42; Aðalbjarnarson 1941, I, 285–286.

10. *Óláfs saga Tryggvasonar*, ch. 49; Aðalbjarnarson 1941, I, 296–298.

11. *Óláfs saga Tryggvasonar*, ch. 48–49; Aðalbjarnarson 1941, I, 293–298.

12. *Óláfs saga Tryggvasonar*, ch. 50; Aðalbjarnarson 1941, I, 299.

13. Bagge 1991, 52–57.

14. *Óláfs saga Tryggvasonar*, ch. 4–6; Aðalbjarnarson 1941, I, 228–230.

15. *Óláfs saga Tryggvasonar*, ch. 6; Aðalbjarnarson 1941, I, 230.

16. *Óláfs saga Tryggvasonar*, ch. 7; Aðalbjarnarson 1941, I, 230–231.

17. *Óláfs saga Tryggvasonar*, ch. 22; Aðalbjarnarson 1941, I, 252–253.

18. *Óláfs saga Tryggvasonar*, ch. 26–27; Aðalbjarnarson 1941, I, 255–262; for earlier date, see Widukind's *Rerum gestarum Saxonicarum*, III, 65, Roesdahl 1987, 162.

19. *Víga-Glúms saga*; Hollander 1972, 19.

20. *Óláfs saga Tryggvasonar*, ch. 32; Aðalbjarnarson 1941, I, 267–269.

21. Gregory, *Dialogues*, book II, ch. 14; see Strömbäck 1975, 103.

22. Zenkovsky 1974, 65–71.

23. Oddr Snorrason, *Saga Óláfs Tryggvasonar*, ch. 13; Jónsson 1932, 25.

24. Turville-Petre 1953, 220–222; Pálsson and Edwards 1989, 5.

25. *Óláfs saga Tryggvasonar*, ch. 53–59, 65–84, 95–96; Aðalbjarnarson 1941, I, 302–309, 314–333, 347–348; as discussed in Bagge 1991, 46.

26. *Óláfs saga Tryggvasonar*, ch. 61; Aðalbjarnarson 1941, I, 310.

27. *Óláfs saga Tryggvasonar*, ch. 46, ch. 67, ch. 82; Aðalbjarnarson 1941, I, 291, 315–316, 329–330.

28. *Óláfs saga Tryggvasonar*, ch. 55, ch . 63; Aðalbjarnarson 1941, I, 305–306, 311–312.

29. *Óláfs saga Tryggvasonar*, ch. 79–80; Aðalbjarnarson 1941, I, 325–328.

30. *Óláfs saga Tryggvasonar*, ch. 55; Aðalbjarnarson 1941, I, 305–306.

31. *Óláfs saga Tryggvasonar*, ch. 56–57; Aðalbjarnarson 1941, I, 306–307.

32. *Óláfs saga Tryggvasonar*, ch. 59; Aðalbjarnarson 1941, I, 308–309.

33. *Óláfs saga Tryggvasonar*, ch. 62; Aðalbjarnarson 1941, I, 311.

34. *Hákonar saga Góða*, ch. 15–18; Aðalbjarnarson 1941, I, 169–170; *Óláfs saga Tryggvasonar*, ch. 65–67; Aðalbjarnarson 1941, I, 314–316.

35. *Óláfs saga Tryggvasonar*, ch. 68–71; Aðalbjarnarson 1941, I, 315–319.

36. *Óláfs saga Tryggvasonar*, ch. 83; Aðalbjarnarson 1941, I, 330–332.

37. *Óláfs saga Tryggvasonar*, ch. 64; Aðalbjarnarson 1941, I, 312–314.

38. *Óláfs saga Tryggvasonar*, ch. 64; Aðalbjarnarson 1941, I, 314.

39. *Óláfs saga Tryggvasonar*, ch. 74–80; Aðalbjarnarson 1941, I, 320–328.

40. *Óláfs saga Tryggvasonar*, ch. 74; Aðalbjarnarson 1941, I, 320.

41. *Óláfs saga Tryggvasonar*, ch. 75, 77; Aðalbjarnarson 1941, I, 321–324.

42. "Skuluð þér þá vita, hvárt ek kann refsa þeim, er neitam kristninni" *Óláfs saga Tryggvasonar*, ch. 75; Aðalbjarnarson 1941, I, 322.

43. *Óláfs saga Tryggvasonar*, ch. 76, 78–80; Aðalbjarnarson 1941, I, 322–328.

44. *Óláfs saga Tryggvasonar*, ch. 73; Aðalbjarnarson 1941, I, 319–320.

45. *Óláfs saga Tryggvasonar*, ch. 82; Aðalbjarnarson 1941, I, 329–330.

46. *Óláfs saga Tryggvasonar*, ch. 84; Aðalbjarnarson 1941, I, 332–333.

47. *Óláfs saga Tryggvasonar*, ch. 95; Aðalbjarnarson 1941, I, 347.

48. *Óláfs saga Tryggvasonar*, ch. 86, 96; Aðalbjarnarson 1941, I, 334, 347–348.

49. *Óláfs saga Tryggvasonar*, ch. 89–103; Aðalbjarnarson 1941, I, 337–357.

50. See, for example, Snorri Sturluson, *Heimskringla: Gylfaginning*, ch. 49; Faulkes 1983, 45–48.

51. *Óláfs saga Tryggvasonar*, ch. 61; Aðalbjarnarson 1941, I, 310.

52. *Óláfs saga Tryggvasonar*, ch. 92; Aðalbjarnarson 1941, I, 341–343.

53. *Óláfs saga Tryggvasonar*, ch. 99–100; Aðalbjarnarson 1941, I, 350–353.

54. "Ráði guð fyrír lífi mínu, en aldri mun ek á flótta leggja." *Óláfs saga Tryggvasonar*, ch. 102; Aðalbjarnarson 1941, I, 355.

55. *Óláfs saga Tryggvasonar*, ch. 111; Aðalbjarnarson 1941, I, 365–366.
56. *Víga-Glúms saga*, ch. 26; Þorláksson 1880, 78.
57. *Hrafnkels saga*, ed. Cawley 1932; *Egils saga Skalla-Grímssonar*, ed. Nordal 1933.
58. *Víga-Glúms saga*, chs. 1–4; Þorláksson 1880, 1–13.
59. *Víga-Glúms saga*, ch. 5; Þorláksson 1880, 13–15.
60. *Víga-Glúms saga*, ch. 9; Þorláksson 1880, 29–30.
61. Tr. Hollander 1972, 49.
62. *Víga-Glúms saga*, ch. 26; Þorláksson 1880, 78.
63. Tr. Hollander 1972, 109.
64. *Víga-Glúms saga*, ch. 6; Þorláksson 1880, 16.
65. Tr. Hollander 1972, 34.
66. *Víga-Glúms saga*, ch. 6; Þorláksson 1880, 15–19.
67. *Víga-Glúms saga*, ch. 9; Þorláksson 1880, 26–27.
68. Tr. Hollander 1972, 46–47.
69. *Víga-Glúms saga*, ch. 14; Þorláksson 1880, 40.
70. *Víga-Glúms saga*, ch. 25; Þorláksson 1880, 75–77.
71. Gregory, *Moralia in Job*, books 24, 26, and 34, as discussed in Baasten 1986, 24–26.
72. Gregory, *Cura pastoralis*, part III, ch. 20, *Moralia*, book 34, as discussed in Baasten 1986, 34–35.
73. *Víga-Glúms saga*, ch. 7; Þorláksson 1880, 23.
74. Tr. Hollander 1972, 42.
75. *Víga-Glúms saga*, ch. 28; Þorláksson 1880, 86–87.
76. "Illa sezt opt ofsinn, Sigmundr, ok rangendi—kann ok vera at þat hendi þik." *Víga-Glúms saga*, ch. 7; Þorláksson 1880, 22.
77. *Víga-Glúms saga*, ch. 24; Þorláksson 1880, 72–75.
78. *Víga-Glúms saga*, ch. 25; Þorláksson 1880, 75–77.
79. *Víga-Glúms saga*, ch. 28; Þorláksson 1880, 86–87.
80. Tr. Hollander 1972, 118.
81. *Eiríks saga rauða, Grœnlendiga saga*; Hermannsson 1944.
82. Strömbäck 1935, 49–60.
83. Hermannsson 1944, vii.
84. Anderson 1967.
85. McCreesh 1978–79.
86. Conroy 1980.
87. *Eiríks saga*, ch. 4; Hermannsson 1944, 9–10.
88. Tr. Jones 1961, 134.
89. *Eiríks saga*, ch. 4; Hermannsson 1944, 11–12.
90. Tr. Jones 1961, 136.
91. *Eiríks saga*, ch. 6; Hermannsson 1944, 17.
92. Tr. Jones 1961, 143.
93. Vauchez 1993, 86.
94. *Eiríks saga*, ch. 8; Hermannsson 1944, 21–22.
95. *Eiríks saga*, ch. 8; Hermannsson 1944, 22–23.
96. Tr. Jones 1961, 148.

97. *Grœnlendiga saga*, ch. 7; Hermannsson 1944, 56.

98. *Eiríks saga*, ch. 9; Hermannsson 1944, 23.

99. Tr. Jones 1961, 149.

100. *Eiríks saga*, ch. 9; Hermannsson 1944, 23.

101. AM 544, 4° and 557, 4°; Hermannsson 1944, viii.

102. McCreesh 1978–79.

103. Vauchez 1993, 95–106.

104. Vauchez 1993, 97.

105. Vauchez 1993, 99.

106. Strömbäck 1933, 57.

107. Børresen 1991, 42.

108. Børresen 1991, 36.

109. *Grœnlendiga saga*, ch. 6; Hermannsson 1944, 55.

110. *Eiríks saga*, ch. 6; Hermannsson 1944, 15–16.

111. Tr. Jones 1961, 143.

112. *Eiríks saga*, ch. 7; Hermannsson 1944, 19.

113. *Grœnlendiga saga*, ch. 7; Hermannsson 1944, 56–58.

114. *Eiríks saga*, ch. 12; Hermannsson 1944, 28–29.

115. *Grœnlendiga saga*, ch. 9; Hermannsson 1944, 60–61; *Eiríks saga*, ch. 14; Hermannsson 1944, 30–31.

116. *Vatnsdøla saga*, Sveinsson 1939; *Laxdœla saga*, Sveinsson 1934; *Eyrbyggja saga*, Sveinsson and Þórðarson 1935.

117. *Eiríks saga*, ch. 4; Hermannsson 1944, 12.

118. *Eiríks saga*, ch. 6; Hermannsson 1944, 16.

119. *Grœnlendiga saga*, ch. 5; Hermannsson 1944, 52–54.

120. *Grœnlendiga saga*, ch. 7; Hermannsson 1944, 57.

Bibliography

Primary Sources

Wherever possible, the names and titles of translations are included for the convenience of student and researcher.

Adam of Bremen (Adamus Bremensis). *Gesta Hammaburgensis ecclesiae pontificum.* Ed. Bernhard Schmeidler. Hanover: Hahn, 1917.

Ælfric. *Ælfric's Catholic Homilies.* Ed. Malcolm Godden. Early English Text Society SS 5. London: Oxford University Press, 1979.

———. *Homilies of Ælfric: A Supplementary Collection.* 2 vols. Ed. John C. Pope. London: Early English Text Society, 1967–68.

———. *Lives of Three English Saints.* Ed. G. I. Needham. London: Methuen, 1966.

———. *St. Oswald, King and Martyr.* Ed. G. I. Needham. In *Ælfric, Lives of Three English Saints.* London: Methuen, 1966.

Alcuin. *Life of St. Willibrord.* Tr. C. H. Talbot. In *Soldiers of Christ: Saints and Saints' Lives from Late Antiquity and the Early Middle Ages.* Ed. Thomas F. X. Noble and Thomas Head. University Park: Pennsylvania State University Press. Pp. 189–212.

The Anglo-Saxon Charms. Ed. Felix Grendon. *Journal of American Folklore* 21, no. 84 (1908): 105–237.

Apuleius. *Herbarium.* Old English translation. In *Leechdoms, Wortcunning, and Starcraft of Early England*, vol. 1. Ed. Thomas Oswald Cockayne. Intro. Charles Singer. London: Holland Press, 1961.

Ardo. *Life of Saint Benedict.* Tr. Allen Cabaniss. In *Soldiers of Christ: Saints and Saints' Lives from Late Antiquity and the Early Middle Ages.* Ed. Thomas F. X. Noble and Thomas Head. University Park: Pennsylvania State University Press, 1995. Pp. 213–254.

Ari Thorgilsson. *Íslendingabók.* Ed. Jakob Benediktsson. *Íslenzk fornrít* 1. Reykjavik: Hið Íslenzka Fornritafélag, 1968.

Arons saga. Vol. 4. Ed. Björn Bjarnarson. Reykjavík: Sigurður Kristnjánsson, 1908.

Bald's Leechbook. (British Museum: Royal 12, D. XVII). Ed. C. E. Wright. London: Allen & Unwin, 1955. Also 2 in *Leechdoms, Wortcunning, and Starcraft of Early England*, vol. 2. Ed. Thomas Oswald Cockayne. Intro. Charles Singer. London: Holland Press, 1961. All references in the present study use the Cockayne text.

Bede. *Historiae ecclesiasticae gentis Anglorum.* Ed. Alfred Holder. Freiburg I.B.: Mohr, 1882. Tr. and ed. Bertram Colgrave and R. A. B. Mynors. *Bede's Ecclesiastical History of the English People.* Oxford: Clarendon Press, 1969.

The Book of Beasts. Tr. and ed. T. H. White. New York: Dover, 1984.

Cynewulf. *The Christ of Cynewulf.* Ed. Albert S. Cook. Boston: Ginn, 1900. Tr. Charles W. Kennedy. In *An Anthology of Old English Poetry.* New York: Oxford University Press, 1960. Pp. 131–154.

Dream of the Rood. In *Sweet's Anglo-Saxon Reader in Prose and Verse.* Ed. Dorothy Whitelock. Oxford: Clarendon Press, 1967. Pp. 153–159.

Edda. Die Lieder des Codex Regius nebst verwandten Denkmälern. Ed. Hans Kuhn. Heidelberg: Carl Winter, 1962. Tr. Patricia Terry. *Poems of the Elder Edda.* Philadelphia: University of Pennsylvania Press, 1990.

Egils saga Skalla-Grímssonar. Ed. Sigurður Nordal. *Íslensk fornrít* 2. Reykjavík: Hið Íslenzka Fornritafélag, 1933. Tr. Christine Fell. *Egil's Saga.* London: J. M. Dent & Sons; Toronto: University of Toronto Press, 1975.

Eiríks saga rauða. Ed. Einar Ól. Sveinsson og Matthías Þórðarson. *Íslenzk fornrít* 4. Reykjavík: Hið Íslenzka Fornritafélag, 1935. Tr. Gwyn Jones. *Eirik the Red and Other Icelandic Sagas.* Oxford: Oxford University Press, 1961.

Eiríks saga rauða. In *The Vinland Sagas.* Ed. Halldór Hermannsson. Ithaca: Cornell University Press, 1944.

Den eldre Gulatingslova. Ed. Bjørn Eithun, Magnus Rindal, and Tor Ulset. Oslo: Riksarkivet, 1994.

Eyrbyggja saga. Ed. Einar Ólafur Sveinsson and Matthías Þórðarson. *Íslenzk fornrít* 4. Reykjavík: Hið Íslenzka Fornritafélag, 1935. Tr. Hermann Pálsson and Paul Edwards. *Eyrbyggja saga.* London: Penguin, 1989.

Friðþjófs saga ins frœkna. Ed. L. Larsson. Halle, 1901.

Gísla saga Súrssonar. Ed. Agneta Loth. Editiones Arnamagnæanæ, Series A, vol. 5. Copenhagen: Munksgaard, 1960. Tr. Ralph B. Allen. *The Saga of Gisli Son of Sour.* New York: Harcourt, Brace, 1936.

Gregory the Great, Pope. *Dialogues.* Ed. Adalbert de Vogüé. Tr. Paul Antin. Paris: Éditions du Cerf, 1980.

———. *The Life of St. Gregory and His Dialogues: Fragments of an Icelandic Manuscript from the Thirteenth Century.* Ed. Hreinn Benediktsson. Editiones Arnamagnæanæ, Series B, vol. 4. Copenhagen: Munksgaard, 1963.

Grœnlendiga saga. In *The Vinland Sagas.* Ed. Halldór Hermannsson. Ithaca: Cornell University Press, 1944.

Grogaldr. In *Sæmundar Edda, mit einem Anhang,* Ed. F. Detter and R. Heinzel. Leipzig: Verlag von Georg Wigand, 1903. Pp. 185–186.

Gulaþingslög (elder). In *Den eldre Gulatingslova.* Ed. Bjørn Eithun, Magnus Rindal, and Tor Ulset. Oslo: Riksarkivet, 1994.

Hávamál. Ed. David A. H. Evans. London: Viking Society for Northern Research, 1986.

Historia Norwegiae. In *Monumenta historica Norvegiae: Latinske kildeskrifter til Norges historie i middelalderen.* Ed. Gustav Storm. Kristiania: A. W. Brøgger, 1880. Pp. 69–124.

The History of the Cross-Tree down to Christ's Passion. In *Icelandic Legend Versions.*

Ed. M. Overgaard. Editiones Arnamagnæanæ, Series B, vol. 26. Copenhagen: Munksgaard, 1968.

History of the Holy Rood-Tree: A Twelfth Century Version of the Cross-Legend. Ed. Arthur S. Napier. Early English Text Society 103. London: Early English Text Society. 1894. Repr., Millwood, N.Y.: Kraus Reprint, 1973.

Hrafnkels saga. Ed. Frank Stanton Cawley. Cambridge: Harvard University Press, 1932. Tr. Hermann Pálsson. *Hrafnkel's Saga and Other Icelandic Stories.* London: Penguin, 1971.

Hrolfs saga kraka. Ed. D. Slay. Editiones Arnamagnæanæ, Series B, vol. 1. Copenhagen: Munksgaard, 1960.

Huneberc of Heidenheim. *Hodoeporicon of Saint Willibald.* Tr. C. H. Talbot. In *Soldiers of Christ: Saints and Saints' Lives from Late Antiquity and the Early Middle Ages.* Ed. Thomas F. X. Noble and Thomas Head. University Park: Pennsylvania State University Press, 1995. Pp. 141–164.

Hungrvaka. Ed. B. Kahle. In *Kristnisaga, Þáttr Þorvalds ens Víðförla, Þáttr Ísleifs Biskups Gizurarsonar, Hungrvaka,* 87–126. Altnordische Saga-Bibliothek 11. Halle: Verlag von Max Niemeyer, 1905.

Ibn Fadhlan. Travel account. Ed. Stig Wikander. *Araber, Vikingar, Väringar.* Lund: Svenska Humanistiska Förbundet, 1978.

Kristnisaga. Ed. B. Kahle. In *Kristnisaga, Þáttr Þorvalds ens Víðförla, Þáttr Ísleifs Biskups Gizurarsonar, Hungrvaka.* Altnordische Saga-Bibliothek 11. Halle: Verlag von Max Niemeyer, 1905. Pp. 1–58.

Landnámabók. (*Sturlubók* and *Hauksbók*). Ed. Jakob Benediktsson. *Íslenzk fornrít* 1. Reykjavík: Hið Íslenzka Fornritafélag, 1968.

Laxdœla saga. Ed. Einar Ól. Sveinsson. *Íslenzk fornrít* 5. Reykjavík: Hið Íslenzka Fornritafélag, 1934. Tr. Magnus Magnusson and Hermann Pálsson. *Laxdœla Saga.* New York: Penguin, 1969.

Liber de miraculis sanctae dei genitricis Mariae. Ed. T. F. Crane. Ithaca, N.Y.: Cornell University Press, 1925.

Life of Saint Bridget: The Old Irish Life of St. Brigid. Ed. and tr. M. A. O'Brien. *Irish Historical Studies* 1, no. 2 (1938): 121–134.

Njáls saga. Ed. Valdemarr Ásmundarson. Reykjavík: Sigurður Kristjánsson, 1894. Tr. Magnus Magnusson and Hermann Pálsson. *Njal's Saga.* London: Penguin, 1960.

Oddr Snorrason. *Saga Óláfs Tryggvasonar.* Ed. Finnr Jónsson. Copenhagan: Glydendal, 1932.

Odo of Cluny. *The Life of Saint Gerald of Aurillac.* Tr. Gerard Sitwell. In *Soldiers of Christ: Saints and Saints' Lives from Late Antiquity and the Early Middle Ages.* Ed. Thomas F. X. Noble and Thomas Head. University Park: Pennsylvania State University Press, 1995. Pp. 293–362.

Ohtere. Accounts of voyages, appended to Anglo-Saxon translation of Orosius's *Historia adversum paganos.* In *Sweet's Anglo-Saxon Reader in Prose and Verse.* Ed. Dorothy Whitelock. Oxford: Clarendon Press, 1967. Pp. 17–22.

Olaus Magnus. *Historia de gentibus septentrionalibus.* 1555. Repr., Westmead: Gregg International Publishers Limited, 1971. Tr. Peter Fisher and Humphrey Higgens. *Description of the Northern Peoples.* Ed. Peter Foote. London: Hakluyt Society, 1996.

Örvar-Odds saga. Ed. R. C. Boer. Altnordische Saga-Bibliothek Hft. 2, Halle a.S.M. Niemeyer, 1892. Tr. Paul Edwards and Hermann Pálsson. *Arrow-Odd: A Medieval Novel.* New York: New York University Press, 1970.

Osbern. *Translatio Sancti Ælfegi Cantuariensis archiepiscopi et martyris.* Tr. and ed. Alexander R. Rumble and Rosemary Morris. In *The Reign of Cnut: King of England, Denmark and Norway.* Ed. Alexander R. Rumble. London: Leicester University Press, 1994. Pp. 284–316.

Rimbert. *Vita anskarii.* Ed. G. Waitz. *Scriptores rerum Germanicarum in usum scholarum ex monumentis Germaniae historicis recensi.* Hanover, 1884. Tr. and ed. Eva Odelman. *Boken om Ansgar. Rimbert: Ansgars liv.* Stockholm: Proprius Förlag, 1986.

Saxo Grammaticus. *Historia Danica.* Ed. Petrus Erasmus Muller and Joannes Mattias Velschow. Havniae, 1839–58.

Sextus Placitus. *Medicina de quadrupedibus,* vol. 1. Old English translation. Ed. Thomas Oswald Cockayne. Intro. Charles Singer. London: Holland Press, 1961.

Snorri Sturluson. *Prose Edda.* (= *Snorra Edda*) Prologue and *Gylfaginning.* Ed. Anthony Faulkes. Oxford: Clarendon Press, 1982. *Skáldskaparmál.* Ed. Guðni Jónsson. *Edda Snorra Sturlusonar með Skáldatali.* Reykjavík: Sigurður Kristjánsson, 1935. *Háttatal.* Ed. Anthony Faulkes. Oxford: Clarendon Press, 1991. Tr. Jean I. Young. *The Prose Edda: Tales from Norse Mythology.* Berkeley: University of California Press, 1954.

———. *Heimskringla.* Ed. Bjarni Aðalbjarnarson. Reykjavík: Hið Íslenzka Fornritafélag, 1941–45. Sagas: *Ynglingasaga* (I. 9–83), *Haralds saga ins Hárfagra* (I. 94–149), *Hákonar saga Góða* (I. 150–97), *Haralds saga Gráfeldar* (I. 198–224), *Óláfs saga Tryggvasonar* (I. 225–372), *Óláfs saga Helga* (II. 3–451), *Magnúss saga ins Góða* (III. 3–67), *Magnússona saga* (III. 238–77), *Magnúss saga Blinda ok Haralds Gilla* (III. 278–302), *Haraldssona Saga* (III. 303–346). Tr. Erling Monsen and A. H. Smith. *Heimskringla; or, The Lives of the Norse Kings.* New York: Dover, 1990.

Sturlunga saga. 4 vols. Ed. Björn Bjarnarson. Reykjavík: Sigurður Kristjánsson, 1908. Tr. Julia H. McGrew. 2 vols. New York: Twayne Publishers and the American-Scandinavian Foundation, 1970.

Suomen Kansan Vanhat Runot. 33 vols. Helsinki: Suomalaisen Kirjallisuuden Seura, 1908–.

Svenska trollformler. Ed. Bengt af Klintberg. Stockholm: Wahlström & Widstrand, 1965.

Sverrisaga. Ed. A. Kjær. In *Det Arnamagnæanske Haandskrift 81 a Fol.* (*Skálholtsbók yngsta*). Oslo: Den Norske Historiske Kildeskriftkommission, 1985. Tr. J. Sephton. *The Saga of King Sverri of Norway.* London: David Nutt, 1899. Repr., Felinfach: Llanerch, 1994.

Tacitus. *Germania.* Ed. Allan A. Lund. Heidelberg: Carl Winter, Universitätsverlag, 1988.

Theodric. *Historia de Antiquitate Regum Norwagiensium.* In *Monumenta historica Norvegiae: Latinske kildeskrifter il Norges historia i middelalderen.* Ed. Gustav Storm. Kristiania: A. V. Brøgger, 1880. Pp. 60–68.

Turi, Johan, and Per Turi. *Lappish Texts.* Ed. K. B. Wiklund and Emilie Demant-Hall. Copenhagen: A. F. Host & Son, 1918–19.

Vatnsdøla saga. Ed. Einar Ól. Sveinsson. *Íslenzk fornrit* 8. Reykjavík: Hið Íslenzka Fornritafélag, 1939. Tr. Gwyn Jones. *The Vatnsdalers' Saga*. Princeton, N.J.: Princeton University Press, for the American-Scandinavian Foundation, 1944.

Víga-Glúms saga. In *Íslenzkar fornsögur*. Ed. Guðmundur Þorláksson. Kaupmannahöfn: Hið Íslenzka Bókmentafélag, 1880. Tr. Lee M. Hollander. *Víga-Glúm's Saga and the Story of Ögmund Dytt*. New York: Twayne, 1972.

Völsunga saga. Ed. Magnus Olsen. Samfund til Udgivelse af Gammel Nordisk Litteratur, 36. Copenhagen: S. L. Møller, 1906–8. Tr. Jesse L. Byock. *The Saga of the Volsungs*. Berkeley: University of California Press, 1990.

Widukind of Corvey. *Rerum gestarum Saxonicarum libri tres*. Ed. H.-E. Lohmann and P. Hirsch. Hanover: Hahn, 1935.

Secondary Sources

Ahlbäck, Tore (ed.) 1987. *Saami Religion: Based on papers read at the Symposium on Saami Religion held at Åbo, Finland, on the 16th–18th of August 1984*. Scripta Instituti Donneriani Aboensis XII. Stockholm: Almqvist & Wiksell International.

———, ed. 1990. *Old Norse and Finnish Religions and Cultic Place-Names. Based on papers read at the Symposium on Encounters between Religions in Old Nordic Times and on Cultic Place-Names, held at Åbo, Finland, on the 19th–21st of August 1987*. Åbo: Donner Institute for Research in Religious and Cultural History.

Ahlbäck, Tore, and Jan Bergman, eds. 1991. *The Saami Shaman Drum. Based on papers read at the Symposium on the Saami Shaman Drum held at Åbo, Finland, on the 19th–20th of August 1988*. Åbo: Donner Institute for Research in Religious and Cultural History.

Ajkhenvald, A., E. Helimski, and V. Petrukhin. 1989. "On Earliest Finno-Ugric Mythologic Beliefs: Comparative and Historical Considerations for Reconstruction." In *Uralic Mythology and Folklore* (Ethnologica Uralica 1). Ed. M. Hoppál and J. Pentikäinen. Budapest and Helsinki: Suomalaisen Kirjallisuuden Seura. Pp. 155–160.

Anderson, Clinton. 1967. *Anglo-Saxon Saints and Heroes*. New York: Fordham University Press.

Anderson, Theodore M. 1967. *The Icelandic Family Saga: An Analytic Reading*. Cambridge: Harvard University Press.

———. 1985. Kings' Sagas (*Konungasögur*). In *Old Norse-Icelandic Literature: A Critical Guide*. Ed. Carol J. Clover and John Lindlow. Ithaca, N.Y.: Cornell University Press. Pp. 197–238.

Apo, Satu. 1995. *Naisen väki*. Helsinki: Suomalaisen Kirjallisuuden Seura.

Arbman, Holger. 1943. *Birka I. Die Gräber. Text*. Uppsala: Almqvist & Wiksell.

Arge, Símun V. 1993. "On the Landnam of the Faroe Islands." In *The Viking Age in Caithness, Orkney, and the North Atlantic*. Ed. Colleen E. Batey, Judith Jesch, and Christopher D. Morris. Edinburgh: Edinburgh University Press. Pp. 465–472.

Arnold, Bettina. 1990. "The Past as Propaganda: Totalitarian Archaeology in Nazi Germany." *Antiquity* 64: 464–78.

Asad, T. 1983. "Anthropological Conceptions of Religion: Reflections on Geertz." *Man*, n.s., 18: 237–259.

Aðalsteinsson, 1987. "Wrestling with a Ghost in Icelandic Popular Belief." *Arv* 43: 7–20.

———. 1990. "Gods and Giants in Old Norse Mythology." *Temenos* 26: 7–22.

Baasten, Matthew. 1986. *Pride According to Gregory the Great: A Study of the Moralia.* Studies in the Bible and Early Christianity, vol. 7. Lewiston, Ontario: Edwin Mellen Press.

Bäckman, Louise. 1975. *Sájva: Föreställningar om hjälp- och skyddsväsen i heliga fjäll bland samerna.* Stockholm Studies in Comparative Religion 13. Stockholm: Norstedts.

———. 1983. "Förfäderskult? En studie i samernas förhållande till sina avlidna." In *Lasta: SáDS áigecála 1*, 11–48. Ed. Elina Helander. Umeå: Sámiid Dutkiid Searvi.

———. 1984. "The Akkas: A Study of Four Goddesses in the Religion of the Saamis (Lapps)." In *Current Progress in the Methodology of the Science of Religions.* Ed. Witold Tyloch. Warsaw: Polish Scientific Publishers. Pp. 31–39.

———. 1991. "Vearalden Olmai—Världens Man—Frey eller Kristus?" In *Studier I religionshistoria tillägnade Åke Hultkranta.* Ed. L. Bäckman, U. Drobin, P.-A. Berglie. Löberöd: Bokförlaget Plus Ultra. Pp. 71–96.

Bäckman, Louise, and Åke Hultkrantz. 1977. *Studies in Lapp Shamanism.* Stockholm Studies in Comparative Religion 16. Stockholm: Almqvist & Wiksell.

Bagge, Sverre. 1991. *Society and Politics in Snorri Sturluson's Heimskringla.* Berkeley: University of California Press.

Bailey, Richard N. 1980. *Viking Age Sculpture in Northern England.* London: Collins.

Batey, Colleen E. 1993. "The Viking and Late Norse Graves of Caithness and Sutherland." In *The Viking Age in Caithness, Orkney, and the North Atlantic.* Ed. Colleen E. Batey, Judith Jesch, and Christopher D. Morris. Edinburgh: Edinburgh University Press. Pp. 148–164.

Batey, Colleen E., Judith Jesch, and Christopher D. Morris. 1993. *The Viking Age in Caithness, Orkney, and the North Atlantic.* Edinburgh: Edinburgh University Press.

Benveniste, Emile. 1973. *Indo-European Language and Society.* Tr. Elizabeth Palmer. Coral Gables: University of Miami Press.

Bergman, Ingela. 1990. "Rumsliga strukturer in samiska kulturlandskap." *Förvännen* 85: 273–282.

Bibliographia studiorum Uralicorum. 1990. Vol. 2. *Perinnetieteet, Ethnology, and Folkloristics.* Helsinki: Suomalaisen Kirjallisuuden Seura.

Biezais, Haralds. 1976. *Lichtgott der alten Letten.* Scripta Instituti Donneriani Aboensis 8. Stockholm: Almqvist & Wiksell.

Birkeli, Fridtjov. 1982. *Hva vet vi om kristningen av Norge? Utforskningen av norsk kristendoms- og kirkehistorie fra 900- til 1200-tallet.* Oslo: Universitetsforlaget.

Bitner-Wróblewsky, Anna. 1991. "Between Scania and Samland: From Studies of Stylistic Links in the Baltic Basin during the Early Migration Period." *Förvännen* 86, no. 4, 225–241.

Blindheim, Charlotte, and Roar L. Tollnes. 1972. *Kaupang: Vikingenes handelsplass.* Oslo: Ernst G. Mortensens Forlag.

Bonser, Wilfrid. 1963. "The Medical Background of Anglo-Saxon England: A Study in History, Psychology, and Folklore." London: Wellcome Historical Medical Library.

Børresen, Kari. 1991. "Birgitta's Godlanguage: Exemplary Intention, Inapplicable Content." Pp. 21–71. In *Birgitta, hendes værk og hendes klostre i Norden*. Ed. Tore Nyberg. Odense: Odense Universitetsforlag.

Boyer, Régis. 1981. *La religion des anciens Scandinaves*. Paris: Payot.

Boyer, Richard. 1981. "The Role of the Ghost Story in Mediaeval Christianity." In *The Folklore of Ghosts*. Ed. Hilda R. Ellis Davidson and W. M. S. Russell. Cambridge: Folklore Society. Pp. 177–192.

Brøndegaard, V. J., ed. 1979. *Folk og flora: Dansk etnobotanik*. Tønder: Rosenkilde og Bagger.

Brooke, Daphne. 1994. *Wild Men and Holy Places: St. Ninian, Whithorn, and the Medieval Realm of Galloway*. Edinburgh: Canongate.

Brown, Michelle P. 1996. *The Book of Cerne: Prayer, Patronage, and Power in Ninth-Century England*. Toronto: The British Library and the University of Toronto Press.

Brown, Peter. 1981. *The Cult of the Saints: Its Rise and Function in Latin Christianity*. Chicago: University of Chicago Press.

Bruce-Mitford, Rupert. 1979. *The Sutton Hoo Ship Burial: A Handbook*. London: Trustees of the British Museum.

Bruhn, Ole, 1993. "Earl Rognvald and the Rise of Saga Literature." In *The Viking Age in Caithness, Orkney, and the North Atlantic*. Ed. Colleen E. Batey, Judith Jesch, and Christopher D. Morris. Edinburgh: Edinburgh University Press. Pp. 240–247.

Byock, Jesse L. 1982. *Feud in the Icelandic Saga*. Berkeley: University of California Press.

———. 1988. *Medieval Iceland: Society, Sagas, and Power*. Berkeley: University of California Press.

Cameron, M. L. 1993. *Anglo-Saxon Medicine*. Cambridge: Cambridge University Press.

Carpelan, Christian. 1984. "Katsaus saamelaisten esihistoriaan." In *Suomen väestön esihistorialliset juuret*, 97–108. Bidrag till Kännedom av Finlands Nature och Folk h. 131. Helsinki: Finska Vetenskaps-Societeten. Pp. 97–108.

Carver, Martin. 1998. *Sutton Hoo: Burial Ground of Kings?* Philadelphia: University of Pennsylvania Press.

Chadwick, Nora K. 1983. "The Vikings and the Western World." In *The Impact of the Scandinavian Invasions on the Celtic-Speaking Peoples c. 800–1100 A.D.*, 13–42. Ed. Brian Ó Cuív. Baile Átha Cliath: Institiúid Ard-Léinn Bhaile Átha Cliath.

Chirat, H. 1967. *The New Catholic Encyclopedia*. S.v. "Cross, finding the." New York: McGraw-Hill.

Christensen, Arne Emil, Anne Stine Ingstad, and Bjørn Myhre. 1992. *Oseberg-Dronningens grav: Vår arkeologiske nasjonalskatt i nytt lys*. Oslo: Schibsted.

Christiansen, Eric. 1980. *The Northern Crusades: The Baltic and the Catholic Frontier, 1100–1525*. Minneapolis: University of Minnesota Press.

Clemoes, Peter. 1983. *The Cult of St. Oswald on the Continent.* Jarrow Lecture, 1983. Jarrow on Tyne: Rev. H. Saxby.

Clover, Carol J. 1985. "Icelandic Family Sagas (*Íslendigasögur*)." In *Old Norse-Icelandic Literature: A Critical Guide.* Ed. Carol J. Clover and John Lindow. Ithaca, N.Y.: Cornell University Press. Pp. 239–315.

———. 1986. "Maiden Warriors and Other Sons." *Journal of English and Germanic Philology* 85, no. 1: 35–49.

Clover, Carol J., and John Lindow, eds. 1985. *Old Norse-Icelandic Literature: A Critical Guide.* Ithaca, N.Y.: Cornell University Press.

Comparetti, Domenico. 1898. *The Traditional Poetry of the Finns.* London: Longmans, Green.

Conquergood, Dwight, Paja Thao, and Xa Thao. 1989. *I Am a Shaman: A Hmong Life Story with Ethnographic Commentary.* Southeast Asian Refugee Studies Occasion Papers. Minneapolis: Center for Urban and Regional Affairs.

Conroy, Patricia. 1980. "*Laxdœla Saga* and *Eiríks Saga Rauða*: Narrative Structure." *Arkiv för Nordisk filologi* 95: 34–50.

Conroy, Patricia, and T. C. S. Langen. 1988. *Laxdœla saga: Theme and Structure. Arkiv för Nordisk Filologi* 103, no. 1: 118–41.

Cormack, Margaret. 1994. *The Saints in Iceland: Their Veneration from the Conversion to 1400.* Bruxelles: Société des Bollandistes.

Cramp, Rosemary. 1965. *Early Northumbrian Sculpture.* Jarrow Lecture, 1965. Jarrow on Tyne: Rev. H. Saxby.

Czaplicka, M. A. 1914. *Aboriginal Siberia: A Study in Social Anthropology.* Oxford: Clarendon Press.

Daly, Lowrie J. 1961. *The Medieval University, 1200–1400.* New York: Sheed and Ward.

Davidson, Hilda R. Ellis. 1976. *The Viking Road to Byzantium.* London: George Allen & Unwin.

———. 1981. "The Restless Dead: An Icelandic Ghost Story." In *The Folklore of Ghosts.* Ed. Hilda R. Ellis Davidson and W. M. S. Russell. Cambridge: Folklore Society. Pp. 155–176.

———. 1988. *Myths and Symbols in Pagan Europe: Early Scandinavian and Celtic Religions.* Syracuse: Syracuse University Press.

———. 1990. "Religious Practices of the Northern Peoples in Scandinavian Tradition." *Temenos* 26: 23–34.

Debes, Hans Jacob. 1993. "Problems Concerning the Earliest Settlement in the Faroe Islands." In *The Viking Age in Caithness, Orkney, and the North Atlantic.* Ed. Colleen E. Batey, Judith Jesch, and Christopher D. Morris. Edinburgh: Edinburgh University Press. Pp. 465–472.

De Paor, Liam. 1967. "The Age of the Viking Wars (9th and 10th Centuries)." In *The Course of Irish History.* Ed. T. W. Moody and F. X. Martin. Cork: Mercier Press. Pp. 91–106.

De Paor, Máire, and Liam de Paor. 1960. *Early Christian Ireland.* London: Thames and Hudson.

Derry, T. K. 1979. *A History of Scandinavia: Norway, Sweden, Denmark, Finland, and Iceland.* Minneapolis: University of Minnesota Press.

Donner, K. 1915. *Bland samojeder i Sibirien, åren 1911–13, 1914.* Helsinki: Suomen Tiedeakatemia.

Dreijer, Matts. 1989. Ansgars och Unnis Birka-rike. *Forntid og nutid* 36, no. 2: 85–99.

DuBois, Thomas. 1992. "Integrating Finno-Ugric Mythology into a Scandinavian Mythology Course." *Studies in Finnish Language and Culture: Proceedings of the Fourth Conference on Finnish Studies in North America.* Helsinki: Council for Instruction of Finnish for Foreigners (UKAN), 1992:41–49.

———. 1996. "Seiðr, Sagas, and Saami: Religious Exchange in the Viking Age." In *Northern Peoples, Southern States: Maintaining Ethnicities in the Circumpolar World.* Ed. Robert P. Wheelersburg. Umeå: CERUM. Pp. 43–66.

———. 1997. "Continuities through Change: The Ritual Life of Finnish Women before and after Christianity." *Journal of Finnish Studies* 1, no. 1: 5–24.

Dumézil, Georges. 1948. *Loki.* Vol. 1 of Les dieux et les hommes. Paris: G.-P. Maisonneuve.

———. 1973. *Gods of the Northmen.* Ed. Einar Haugen. Berkeley: University of California Press.

———. 1977. *Les dieux souverains des Indo-Européens.* Paris: NRF-Gallimard.

Durant, Will. 1950. *The Age of Faith: A History of Medieval Civilization—Christian, Islamic and Judaic—from Constantine to Dante: A.D. 325–1300.* New York: Simon and Schuster.

Durkheim, Émile. 1915. *The Elementary Forms of Religious Life.* Tr. Joseph Ward Swain. New York: Allen and Unwin.

Durrenberger, E. Paul. 1992. *The Dynamics of Medieval Iceland: Political Economy and Literature.* Iowa City: University of Iowa Press.

Eadie, John W., ed. 1971. *The Conversion of Constantine.* New York: Holt, Rinehart, and Winston.

Einarsson, Bjarni F. 1994. *The Settlement of Iceland: A Critical Approach. Granastaðr and the Ecological Heritage.* Göteborg: Gothenburg University.

Eisen, Matthias Johann. 1919 [1995]. *Eesti mütoloogia.* 2d ed. Tallinn: Mats.

Ekenberg, Anders. 1986. " 'Ansgars liv' som helgonbiografi." In *Boken om Ansgar. Rimbert: Ansgars liv.* Tr. and ed. Eva Odelman. Stockholm: Proprius Förlag. Pp. 133–146.

Elgqvist, Eric. 1952. *Studier rörande Njordkultens spridning bland de nordiska folken.* Lund: Olins Antikvariat.

Eliade, Mircea. 1951. *Le chamanisme et les techniques archaïques de l'extase.* Paris: Payot.

———. 1958a. *Rites and Symbols of Initiation.* Tr. Willard R. Trask. New York: Harper & Row.

———. 1958b [1996]. "The Prestige of the Cosmogonic Myth." *Diogenes* 23 (Autumn): 1–13. Repr., In *Theories of Myth.* Ed. Robert A. Segal. New York: Garland. Pp. 129–141.

Eriksson, Aldur W. 1984. "Saamelaisten perinnölliset erikoispirteet." *Suomen väestön esihistorialliset juuret.* Tvärminnen symposiumi 17–19 Jan. 1980. In *Bidrag till Kännedom av Finlands Natur och Folk* h. 131. Helsinki: Finska Vetenskaps-Societeten. Pp. 109–136.

Eronen, Matti, and Pentti Zetterberg. 1996. "Ailigasjärven liekopuiden arvoitus." *Hiidenkivi* 3 (1996): 10–12.

Evans, G. R. 1986. *The Thought of Gregory the Great.* Cambridge: Cambridge University Press.

Faulkes, Anthony. 1983. "Pagan Sympathy: Attitudes to Pagandom in the Prologue to *Snorra Edda.*" In *Edda: A Collection of Essays.* Ed. Robert J. Glendinning and Haraldur Bessason. Winnipeg: University of Manitoba Press.

Fell, Christine, Peter Foote, James Graham-Campbell, and Robert Thomson, eds. 1983. *The Viking Age in the Isle of Man.* London: Viking Society for Northern Research.

Fellows-Jensen, Gillian. 1983. "Scandinavian Settlement in the Isle of Man and Northwest England: The Place-Name Evidence." In *The Viking Age in the Isle of Man.* Ed. Christine Fell, Peter Foote, James Graham-Campbell, and Robert Thomson. London: Viking Society for Northern Research. Pp. 37–52.

Finnestad, Ragnhild Bjerre. 1990. "The Study of Christianization of the Nordic Countries: Some Reflections." In *Old Norse and Finnish Religions and Cultic Place-Names.* Ed. Tore Ahlbäck. Scripta Instituti Donneriani Aboensis 13. Stockholm: Almqvist & Wiksell. Pp. 256–272.

Fjellström, Phebe. 1987. "Cultural- and Tradition-Ecological Perspectives in Saami Religion." In *Saami Religion: Based on papers read at the Symposium on Saami Religion, held at Åbo, Finland, on the 16th–18th of August 1984.* Ed. Tore Ahlbäck. Scripta Instituti Donneriani Aboensis 12. Åbo: Donner Institute for Research in Religious and Cultural History. Pp. 34–45.

Fletcher, Eric. 1981. *Benedict Biscop.* Jarrow Lecture, 1981. Jarrow on Tyne: Rev. H. Saxby.

Forsblom, Valter W. 1927. *Finlands svenska folkdiktning VII: Folktro och trolldom 5, Magiska folkmedicin.* Helsingfors: Svenska litteratursällskapet i Finland.

Frank, Roberta. 1994. "King Cnut in the Verse of His Skalds." In *The Reign of Cnut: King of England, Denmark and Norway.* Ed. Alexander R. Rumble. London: Leicester University Press. Pp. 106–124.

Fritzner, Johan. 1877. *Lappernes Hedenskab og Troldomskunst sammenholdt med andre Folks, isaer Nordmaendenes, Tro og Overtro.* Historisk Tidsskrift utg. af d. Norske Historiske Foreningen 4.

Frolow, A. 1961. *La relique de la vraie croix: Recherches sur le développment d'un culte.* Paris: Institut Français d'Études Byzantines.

Fuglesang, Signe Horn. 1981. "Crucifixion Iconography in Viking Scandinavia." In *Proceedings of the Eighth Viking Congress, Århus, 24–31 August 1977.* Odense: Odense University Press.

Geertz, Clifford. 1965 [1979]. "Religion as a Cultural System." In *Anthropological Approaches to the Study of Religion.* Ed. Michael Banton. London: Tavistock Publications. Repr., in *Reader in Comparative Religion: An Anthropological Approach.* Ed. William A. Lessa and Evon Z. Vogt. New York: Harper & Row. Pp. 78–92.

———. 1973. *The Interpretation of Cultures.* New York: Basic Books.

Gimbutas, Marija. 1956. *The Prehistory of Eastern Europe, Part I: Mesolithic, Neolithic, and Copper Age Cultures in Russia and the Baltic Area.* American School of Prehistoric Research Bulletin, no. 20. Cambridge, Mass.: Peabody Museum.

Gíslason, Jónas. 1990. "Acceptance of Christianity in Iceland in the Year 1000 (999)." In *Old Norse and Finnish Religions and Cultic Place-Names. Based on papers read at the Symposium on Encounters between Religions in Old Nordic Times and on Cultic Place-Names, held at Åbo, Finland, on the 19th–21st of August 1987.* Ed. Tore Ahlbäck. Åbo: Donner Institute for Research in Religious and Cultural History. Pp. 223–255.

Goodall, Blake. 1979. *The Homilies of St. John Chrysostom on the Letters of St. Paul to Titus and Philemon: Prolegomena to an Edition.* University of California Publications in Classical Studies, vol. 20. Berkeley: University of California Press.

Gordon, E. V. 1984. *An Introduction to Old Norse.* 2d ed. Rev. by A. R. Taylor. Oxford: Clarendon Press.

Görman, Marianne. 1987. "Nordic and Celtic: Religion in Southern Scandinavia during the Late Bronze Age and Early Iron Age. In *Old Norse and Finnish Religions and Cultic Place-Names.* Ed. Tore Ahlbäck. Scripta Instituti Donneriani Aboensis 13. Stockholm: Almqvist & Wiksell. Pp. 329–343.

Graham-Campbell, James A. 1993. "The Northern Hoards of Viking-Age Scotland." In *The Viking Age in Caithness, Orkney, and the North Atlantic,* 173–86. Ed. Colleen E. Batey, Judith Jesch, and Christopher D. Morris. Edinburgh: Edinburgh University Press.

Grant, Michael. 1993. *The Emperor Constantine.* London: Weidenfeld & Nicolson.

Gräslund, Anne-Sofie. 1967. "Ett forhistoriskt brödfynd från Östergötland." *Förvännen* 62: 257–260.

Grattan, J. H. G., and C. Singer. 1952. *Anglo-Saxon Magic and Medicine Illustrated Specially from the Semi-Pagan Text "Lacnunga."* Oxford: Oxford University Press.

Greimas, Algirdas J. 1992. *Of Gods and Men: Studies in Lithuanian Mythology.* Tr. Milda Newman. Bloomington: Indiana University Press.

Grimm, Jakob. 1965. *Deutsche Mythologie.* Darmstadt: Wissenschaftiche Buchgesellschaft.

Grundström, Elina. 1994. "Hopeatie." *Hiidenkivi* 3: 10–15.

Gurevich, Aron. 1988. *Medieval Popular Culture: Problems of Belief and Perception.* Cambridge: Cambridge University Press.

Haavio, Martti. 1952. *Väinämöinen: Eternal Sage.* FF Communications no. 144. Helsinki: Suomalainen Tiedeakatemia.

Hagu, Paul. 1987. "Setukaisten sadonjumala Peko." In *Viron veräjät: Näkökulmia folkloreen.* Ed. Leea Virtanen. Tr. Eva Lille. Helsinki: Suomalaisen Kirjallisuuden Seura. Pp. 145–160.

Hajdú, Peter. 1975. *Finno-Ugrian Languages and Peoples.* Tr. G. F. Cushing. London: Andre Deutsch.

Hansen, Steffan Stummann. 1993. "Viking-Age Faroe Islands and Their Southern Links in the Light of Recent Finds at Toftanes, Leirvik." In *The Viking Age in Caithness, Orkney, and the North Atlantic.* Ed. Colleen E. Batey, Judith Jesch, and Christopher D. Morris. Edinburgh: Edinburgh University Press. Pp. 473–486.

Harjula, Janne. 1996. "Kiukaisissa hiihdettiin jo rautakaudella." *Hiidenkivi* 2: 24–25.

Hartman, Sven. S. 1969. *Syncretism. Based on papers read at the Symposium on Cultural Contact, Meeting of Religions, Syncretism, held at Åbo on the 8th–10th of September, 1966.* Stockholm: Almqvist & Wiksell.

Harvo, Uno. *See* Holmberg-Harva.

Hastrup, Kirsten. 1981. "Cosmology and Society in Medieval Iceland: A Social Anthropological Perspective on World-View." *Ethnologia Scandinavica*: 63–78.

Hatt, Jean-Jacques. 1971. "Celtic Symbols." In *The Conversion of Constantine*. Ed. John W. Eadie. New York: Holt, Rinehart, and Winston. Pp. 34–38.

Helm, Karl. 1955. "Mythologie auf alten und neuen Wegen." *Beiträge zur Geschichte der deutschen Sprache und Literatur 77*: 347–65.

Henry, Françoise. 1940. *Irish Art in the Early Christian Period*. London: Methuen.

———. 1983. "The Effects of the Viking Invasions on Irish Art." In *The Impact of the Scandinavian Invasions on the Celtic-speaking Peoples c. 800–1100 A.D.* Ed. Brian Ó Cuív. Dublin: Dublin Institute for Advanced Studies. Pp. 61–72.

Hill, Thomas D. 1995. "Guðlaugr Snorrason: The Red-Faced Saint and the Refusal of Violence. *Scandinavian Studies* 67, no. 2: 145–152.

Hinnebusch, W. A. 1967. *The New Catholic Encyclopedia*. S.v. "Rosary." New York: McGraw-Hill.

Hofstee, W. 1985. "The Interpretation of Religion: Some Remarks on the Work of Clifford Geertz." *Neue Zeitschift für Systematische Theologie und Religionsphilosophie 27*: 145–58.

Holmberg-Harva, Uno. 1926. *Die Religion der Tscheremissen*. FF Communications no. 61. Helsinki: Suomalainen Tiedeakatemia.

———. 1945. "Lemminkäisen matka Päivölän pitoihin." *Virittäjä* 49: 219–225.

———. 1964. *Finno-Ugric, Siberian Mythology*. Vol. 4 of *The Mythology of All Races*. New York: Cooper Square.

Holthoer, R. 1981. *Birch-Bark Documents from Novgorod Relating to Finland and Scandinavia. Acta Universitatis Uppsaliensis 19*. Uppsala: University of Uppsala.

Honko, Lauri. 1959. *Krankheitsprojektile: Untersuchung über eine urtümliche Krankheitserklärung*. FF Communications no. 178. Helsinki: Suomalainen Tiedeakatemia.

———. 1962. *Geisterglaube in Ingermanland*. FF Communications no. 185. Helsinki: Suomalainen Tiedeakatemia.

———. 1963. *Itkuvirsirunous*. In *Suomen kirjallisuus I: Kirjoittamaton kirjallisuus*. Helsinki: Suomalaisen Kirjallisuuden Seura and Otava. Pp. 81–128.

———. 1974. "Balto-Finnic Lament Poetry." *Studia Fennica 17*. Helsinki: Suomalaisen Kirjallisuuden Seura.

Honko, Lauri, Senni Timonen, and Michael Branch, eds. 1993. *The Great Bear: A Thematic Anthology of Oral Poetry in the Finno-Ugrian Languages*. Helsinki: Suomalaisen Kirjallisuuden Seura.

Hultgård, Anders. 1990. "Old Scandinavian and Christian Eschatology." In *Old Norse and Finnish Religions and Cultic Place-Names. Based on papers read at the Symposium on Encounters between Religions in Old Nordic Times and on Cultic Place-Names, held at Åbo, Finland, on the 19th–21st of August 1987*, 344–57. Ed. Tore Ahlbäck. Åbo: The Donner Institute for Research in Religious and Cultural History.

———. 1992. "Religiös förändring, kontinuitet och ackulturation/synkretism i vikingatidens och medieltidens skandinaviska religion." In *Kontinuitet i kult och tro från vikingatid till medeltid*, 49–104. Ed. Bertil Nilsson. Uppsala: Lunne Böcker.

Hultkrantz, Åke. 1966. "An Ecological Approach to Religion." *Ethnos 31*: 131–50.

———. 1977a. "Ecological and Phenomenological Aspects of Shamanism." In *Studies in Lapp Shamanism*, 9–35. Ed. Louise Bäckman and Åke Hultkrantz. Stockholm: Almqvist & Wiksell.

———. 1977b. "Means and Ends in Saami Shamanism." In *Studies in Lapp Shamanism*, 40–61. Ed. Louise Bäckman and Åke Hultkrantz. Stockholm: Almqvist & Wiksell.

———. 1987. "On Beliefs in Non-Shamanic Guardian Spirits among the Saamis." *Saami Religion. Based on papers read at the Symposium on Saami Religion held at Åbo, Finland, on the 16th–18th of August 1984*, 110–23. Ed. Tore Ahlbäck. Scripta Instituti Donneriani Aboensis 12. Stockholm: Almqvist & Wiksell.

Hunter, John R. 1997. "The Early Norse Period." In *Scotland: Environment and Archaeology, 8000 B.C.–A.D. 1000*, 241–54. Ed. Kevin J. Edwards and Ian B. Ralston. Chichester: John Wiley.

Hunter, John R., Julie M. Bond, and Andrea M. Smith. 1993. "Some Aspects of Early Viking Settlement in Orkney." In *The Viking Age in Caithness, Orkney, and the North Atlantic*. Ed. Colleen E. Batey, Judith Jesch, and Christopher D. Morris. Edinburgh: Edinburgh University Press. Pp. 272–284.

Huurre, M. 1979. *9000 vuotta Suomen esihistoriaa*. Keuru: WSOY.

———. 1984. "Itä-Suomen rautakautinen asutus arkeologian valossa." *Suomen väestön esihistorialliset juuret*. Tvärminnen symposiumi 17–19 Jan. 1980. In *Bidrag till Kännedom av Finlands Natur och Folk* h. 131. Helsinki: Finska Vetenskaps-Societeten. Pp. 303–318.

Itkonen, Terho. 1984. "Suomessa puhutun suomen kantasuomalaiset juuret." *Suomen väestön esihistorialliset juuret*. Tvärminnen symposiumi 17–19 Jan. 1980. In *Bidrag till Kännedom av Finlands Natur och Folk* h. 131, 347–64. Helsinki: Finska Vetenskaps-Societeten. Pp. 347–364.

Jacobsen, Grethe. 1986. *Kvindeskikkelser og kvindeliv i Danmarks middelalder*. Copenhagen: Tønder.

Jaffee, Martin. 1997. "Spoken, Written, and Incarnate: Ontologies of Textuality in Classical Rabbinic Judaism." Paper delivered at the conference Voice, Text, and Hypertext at the Millennium, 29 Oct.–1 Nov. 1997, Seattle, Wash. University of Washington.

Jochens, Jenny. 1995. *Women in Old Norse Society*. Ithaca, N.Y.: Cornell University Press.

———. 1996. *Old Norse Images of Women*. Philadelphia: University of Pennsylvania Press.

Johansson, Maija, 1984. *Suomalaiset muinaispuvut ja korut*. Asiantuntijat Leena Söyrinki-Harmo and Leena Tomanterä. Helsinki: Kalevala Koru Oy and Valtion audiovisuaalinen keskus.

Johnsen, Ingrid Sannes. 1968. *Stuttruner i vikingetidens innskrifter*. Oslo: Universitetsforlaget.

Jokipii, Mauno. 1989. "Ruotsin ja Länsi-Suomen lähetyspyhimysten muistoja." *Suomen museo* 96: 61–131.

Jørgensen, Ellen. 1909. *Helgendyrkelse i Danmark: Studier over kirkekultur og kirkeligt liv fra det 11te aarhundredes midte til reformationen*. København: H. Hagerups Forlag.

Julku, Kyösti. 1995. "Miten Lappi asutettiin?" *Hiidenkivi* 4: 14–17.

Jutikkala, Eino, and Kauko Pirinen. 1984. *A History of Finland*. 4th rev. ed. Tr. Paul Sjöblom. Espoo: Weilin & Göös.

Kabell, Aage. 1980. *Skalden und Schamanen*. FF Communications no. 227. Helsinki: Suomalainen Tiedeakatemia.

Kajanoja, Pauli. 1984. "Mitä kampakeraamisen kultuurialueen kraniologiset löydökset kertovat suomalaisten sukujuurista?" *Suomen väestön esihistorialliset juuret*. Tvärminnen symposiumi 17–19 Jan. 1980. In *Bidrag till Kännedom av Finlands Natur och Folk* h. 131. Helsinki: Finska Vetenskaps-Societeten. Pp. 49–54.

Kalan, Sigrid H. H. 1993. "The Settlement of Westness, Rousay." In *The Viking Age in Caithness, Orkney, and the North Atlantic*. Ed. Colleen E. Batey, Judith Jesch, and Christopher D. Morris. Edinburgh: Edinburgh University Press. Pp. 308–317.

Karras, Ruth Mazo. 1988. *Slavery and Society in Medieval Scandinavia*. New Haven, Conn.: Yale University Press.

Kealey, Edward J. 1981. *Medieval Medicus: A Social History of Anglo-Norman Medicine*. Baltimore: Johns Hopkins University Press.

Kee, Alistair. 1982. *Constantine versus Christ*. London: SCM Press.

Kennedy, Charles W. 1960. *An Anthology of Old English Poetry*. New York: Oxford University Press.

Khazanov, A. M. 1984. *Nomads and the Outside World*. Cambridge: Cambridge University Press.

Kinvig, R. H. 1975. *The Isle of Man: A Social, Cultural, and Political History*. Rutland, Vt.: Charles E. Tuttle.

Kjellman, Hilding. *La deuxième collection anglo-normande des miracles de la Sainte Vierge*. Paris: Edouard Champion, 1922.

Kjellström, Rolf. 1976. "Är traditionerna om Stalo historiskt grundade?" In *Nordisk folkltro: Studier tillägnade Carl-Herman Tillhagen*. Ed. Bengt af Klintberg, Reimund Kvideland, and Magne Velure. Lund: Nordiska Museet. Pp. 155–178.

———. 1987. "On the Continuity of Old Saami Religion." In *Saami Religion: Based on papers read at the Symposium on Saami Religion, held at Åbo, Finland, on the 16th–18th of August 1984*. Ed. Tore Ahlbäck. Scripta Instituti Donneriani Aboensis 12. Åbo: Donner Institute for Research in Religious and Cultural History. Pp. 24–33.

Kluckholm, Clyde. 1942 [1979]. "Myths and Rituals: A General Theory." *Harvard Theological Review* 35 (January): 45–79. Repr., in *Reader in Comparative Religion: An Anthropological Approach*. Ed. William A. Lessa and Evon Z. Vogt. New York: Harper & Row. Pp. 66–78.

Koivulehto, Jorma. 1984. "Itämerensuomalais-germaaniset kosketukset." In *Suomen väestön esihistorialliset juuret*. Tvärminnen symposiumi 17–19 Jan. 1980. In *Bidrag till Kännedom av Finlands Natur och Folk* h. 131. Helsinki: Finska Vetenskaps-Societeten. Pp. 191–206.

Koivusalo, Esko. 1993. "Ukon vakoista vakaille Ukoille." *Kieliposti* 1: 13–18.

———. 1995. "Milloin Ukko ylijumala pärskyi? Mikael Agricolan Ukko-säkeiden arvoitus." *Hiidenkivi* 3: 26–27.

Koppenberg. Peter. 1980. *Hagiographische Studien zu den Biskupa Sögur: Unter besonderer Berücksichtigung der Jóns saga helga*. Bochum: Scandica Verlag.

Korhonen, Mikko. 1984. "Suomalaisten suomalais-ugrilainen tausta historiallisvertailevan kielitieteen valossa." *Suomen väestön esihistorialliset juuret.* Tvärminnen symposiumi 17–19 Jan. 1980. In *Bidrag till Kännedom av Finlands Natur och Folk* h. 131. Helsinki: Finska Vetenskaps-Societeten. Pp. 55–72.

Kors, Alan C., and Edward Peters, eds. 1972. *Witchcraft in Europe 1100–1700: A Documentary History.* Philadelphia: University of Pennsylvania Press.

Koski, Mauno. 1987. "A Finnic Holy Word and Its Subsequent History." In *Old Norse and Finnish Religions and Cultic Place-Names. Based on papers read at the Symposium on Encounters between Religions in Old Nordic Times and on Cultic Place-Names, held at Åbo, Finland, on the 19th–21st of August 1987.* Ed. Tore Ahlbäck. Åbo: Donner Institute for Research in Religious and Cultural History. Pp. 404–440.

Kovalev, Roman. 1997. "The Transfer of Finno-Ugrian Strategies into Rus' Culture." Paper delivered at the 1997 Annual Convention of the American Association for the Advancement of Slavic Studies, Seattle, 20–23 Nov. 1997.

Krohn, Kaarle. 1906. "Lappische Beiträge zur germanischen Mythologie." *Finnishugrische Forschungen* 6: 155–80.

———. 1932. *Zur Finnischen Mythologie.* Vol. 1. FF Communications no. 104. Helsinki: Suomalainen Tiedeakatemia.

Krupnik, Igor. 1993. *Arctic Adaptations: Native Whalers and Reindeer Herders of Northern Eurasia.* Hanover, N.H.: University of New England Press.

———. 1996. "Northern People, Southern Records." The Yamal Nenets in Russian Population Counts, 1695–1989." In *Northern Peoples, Southern States: Maintaining Ethnicities in the Circumpolar World.* Ed. Robert P. Wheelersburg. Umeå: CERUM. Pp. 67–92.

Kuusi, Matti. 1963. *Suomen kirjallisuus I:Kirjoittamaton kirjallisuus.* Helsinki: Suomalaisen Kirjallisuuden Seura.

Kuusi, Matti, Keith Bosley, and Michael Branch, eds. 1977. *Finnish Folk Poetry: Epic.* Helsinki: Suomalaisen Kirjallisuuden Seura.

Kvideland, Reimund, and Henning K. Sehmsdorf, eds. 1988. *Scandinavian Folk Belief and Legend.* Minneapolis: University of Minnesota Press.

Lappalainen, P. 1967. *Puumalan historia I.* Kuopio: WSOY.

Laulajainen, Leena. 1995. *Marilaiset, laulun ja uhritulien kansa.* Helsinki: Otava.

Lawson, M. K. 1993. *Cnut: The Danes in England in the Early Eleventh Century.* London: Longman.

Lehtosalo-Hilander, Pirkko-Liisa. 1984. "Suomen nuoremman rautakauden esineistö kansallisuusolojen heijastajana." *Suomen väestön esihistorialliset juuret.* Tvärminnen symposiumi 17–19 Jan. 1980. In *Bidrag till Kännedom av Finlands Natur och Folk* h. 131. Helsinki: Finska Vetenskaps-Societeten. Pp. 283–302.

———. 1987. "The Conversion of the Finns in Western Finland." In *The Christianization of Scandinavia: Report of a Symposium held at Kungälv, Sweden, 4–9 August 1985.* Ed. Birgit Sawyer, Peter Sawyer, and Ian Wood. Alingsås, Sweden: Viktoria Bokförlag. Pp. 31–35.

Leksikon des Mittelalters 1995. Munich: Lexma Verlag.

———. 1990. Le Viking finnois. *Finskt museum* 97: 55–72.

Lempiäinen, Terttu, and Kaisa Häkkinen. 1995. "Koska maanviljely tuli Suomeen?" *Hiidenkivi* 6: 11–14.

Lenhammar, Harry. 1982. *Genom tusen år: Huvudlinjer i Nordens Kyrkohistoria.* Uppsala: Uppsala universitet.

Lévi-Strauss, Claude. 1955a. "The Structural Study of Myth." *Journal of American Folklore* 67: 428–44. Repr., in *Reader in Comparative Religion: An Anthropological Approach.* Ed. William A. Lessa and Evon Z. Vogt. New York: Harper & Row. Pp. 185–197.

———. 1955b. *Tristes tropiques.* Paris: Plon.

———. 1964. *Mythologiques II: Du miel au cendre.* Paris: Plon.

———. 1968. *Mythologiques III: L'Origine de manières de table.* Paris: Plon.

———. 1971. *Mythologiques IV: L'Homme nu.* Paris: Plon.

Levison, Wilhelm. 1946. *England and the Continent in the Eighth Century.* Oxford: Clarendon Press.

Lid, Nils. 1951. "The Mythical Realm of the Far North." In *Laos: Études comparëes de folklore our d'ethnologie régionale.* Ed. Sigurd Erixon. Stockholm: Almqvist & Wiksell.

Liestøl, Aslak. 1983. "An Iona Rune Stone and the World of Man and the Isles." In *The Viking Age in the Isle of Man.* Ed. Christine Fell, Peter Foote, James Graham-Campbell, and Robert Thomson. London: Viking Society for Northern Research. Pp. 85–94.

Lieu, Samuel N. C., and Dominic Montserrat. 1996. *From Constantine to Julian: Pagan and Byzantine Views: A Source History.* London: Routledge.

Lindow, John. 1988. *Scandinavian Mythology: An Annotated Bibliography.* New York: Garland.

———. 1994a. "Bloodfeud and Scandinavian Mythology." *Alvíssmál* 4: 51–68.

———. 1994b. "Thor's *hamarr.*" *Journal of English and Germanic Philology* 93, no. 4 (Oct.): 485–503.

———. 1995. "Supernatural Others and Ethnic Others: A Millenium of World View." *Scandinavian Studies* 67, no. 1: 8–31.

———. 1997. "*Íslendingabók* and Myth." *Scandinavian Studies* 69, no. 4: 454–64.

Lindqvist, Sune. 1941. *Gotlands Bildsteine.* 2 vols. Stockholm: Walhström & Widstrand.

Ljungberg, Helge. 1938. *Den nordiska religionen och kristendomen: Studier över det nordiska religionsskiftet under Vikingatiden.* Stockholm: Hugo Gebers Förlag.

Lönnroth, Lars. 1964. "Tesen om de två kulturerna: Kristiska studier i den islänska sagaskrivningens sociala förutsättninger." *Scripta Islandica* 15: 1–97.

———. 1965a. "Det litterära porträttet i latinsk historiografi och islänsk sagaskrivning—en komparativ studie." *Acta Philologica Scandinavica* 27: 68–117.

———. 1965b. *European Sources of Icelandic Saga-Writing: An Essay Based on Previous Studies.* Stockholm: Boktryckeri AB Thule.

———. 1969. "The Noble Pagan: A Theme in the Sagas." *Scandinavian Studies* 41: 1–29.

———. 1976. *Njáls Saga: A Critical Introduction.* Berkeley: University of California Press.

———. 1991. "Sponsors, Writers, and Raiders of Early Norse Literature." In *Social Approaches to Viking Studies.* Ed. Ross Samson. Glasgow: Cruithne Press. Pp. 3–10.

Lövkrona, Inger, ed. 1992. *Kvinnospår i medeltiden*. Lund: Lund University Press.

Luckert, Karl W. 1984. "Coyote in Navajo and Hopi Tales." In *Navajo Coyote Tales: The Curly Tó Aheedlíinii Version*. Tr. Berard Haile. Lincoln: University of Nebraska Press. Pp. 3–19.

Lundmark, Bo. 1985. "'They Consider Sun to Be a Mother to All Living Creatures': The Sun-Cult of the Saamis." *Arv* 41: 179–188.

———. 1987. "Rijkuo-Maja and Silbo-Gåmmoe—Towards the Question of Female Shamanism in the Saami Area." In *Saami Religion: Based on papers read at the Symposium on Saami Religion held at Åbo, Finland, on the 16th–18th of August 1984*. Ed. Tore Ahlbäck. Scripta Instituti Donneriani Aboensis 12. Stockholm: Almqvist & Wiksell. Pp. 158–169.

Luoto, Jukka. 1989. "Suomen varhaiskristillisyydestä." *Suomen museo* 96: 133–52.

Madsen, Heini. 1990. *Færøerne i 1000 år*. Vadum: Skúvanes.

Makarov, N. A. 1989. "On the Christianization of the Rural Areas of Russia in the 11th–13th Centuries: Burials with Crosses and Small Icons in Beloserie Cemeteries." *Suomen Museo* 96: 49–59.

Malinowski, Bronislaw. 1926 [1954]. "Myth in Primitive Psychology." Repr., in *Magic, Science, and Religion, and Other Essays by Bronislaw Malinowski*. Ed. Robert Redfield. Garden City, N.J.: Doubleday. Pp. 93–148.

Manker, Ernst. 1950. *Die lappische Zaubertrommel*. 2 vols. Stockholm: Hugo Gebers Förlag.

Margeson, Sue. 1983. "On the Iconography of the Manx Crosses." In *The Viking Age in the Isle of Man*. Ed. Christine Fell, Peter Foote, James Graham-Campbell, and Robert Thomson. London: Viking Society for Northern Research. Pp. 95–106.

Martin, John Stanley. 1991. "The Transference of Attitudes to Islam from France to Scandinavia in the *Elie de Saint Gille* and *Elis Saga ok Rósamundu*." In *The Audience of the Sagas. Eighth International Saga Conference, held at Gothenburg University, August 11–17, 1991*. Gothenburg: Gothenburg University. 2: 67–79.

McCready, William D. 1989. *Signs of Sanctity: Miracles in the Thought of Gregory the Great*. Studies and Texts 91. Toronto: Pontifical Institute of Mediaeval Studies.

McCreesh, Bernadine. 1978–79. "Structural Patterns in the *Eyrbyggja Saga* and Other Sagas of the Conversion." *Mediaeval Scandinavica* 11: 271–280.

McGovern, Thomas H. 1991. "Climate, Correlation, and Causation in Norse Greenland." *Arctic Anthropology*, 28, no. 2: 77–100.

McKinnell, John. 1994. *Both One and Many: Essays on Change and Variety in Late Norse Paganism*. Rome: Il Calamo.

McNamara, Martin. 1975. *The Apocrypha in the Irish Church*. Dublin: Dublin Institute for Advanced Studies.

Meinander, C. F. 1983. "Om introduktionen av sädesodling i Finland." *Suomen Museo* 90: 5–20.

———. 1984. "Kivikautemme väestöhistoria." *Suomen väestön esihistorialliset juuret*. Tvärminnen symposiumi 17–19 Jan. 1980. In *Bidrag till Kännedom av Finlands Natur och Folk* h. 131. Helsinki: Finska Vetenskaps-Societeten. Pp. 21–48.

———. 1985. "Odin i Staraja Ladoga." *Finskt museum* 92: 65–69.

Mercier, Mario. 1977. *Chamanisme et chamans: Le vécu dans l'expérience magique*. Paris: Pierre Belfond.

Meyvaert, Paul. 1977. "Diversity within Unity: A Gregorian Theme." In *Benedict, Gregory, and Others.* London: Variorum Reprints. Pp. 141–162.

Migliore, Sam. 1983. "The Doctor, the Lawyer, and the Melancholy Witch: European Witchcraft in the 16th and 17th Centuries." *Anthropologica* 25, no. 2: 163–192.

Mikkelsen, Egil. 1986. "Religion and Ecology: Motifs and Location of Hunters' Rock Carvings in Eastern Norway." In *Words and Objects: Toward a Dialogue between Archaeology and History of Religion.* Ed. Gro Steinsland. Oslo: Norwegian University Press. Pp. 127–141.

Miller, J. H. 1967. *The New Catholic Encyclopedia.* S.v. "Cross." New York: McGraw-Hill.

Miller, William Ian. 1988. "Ordeal in Iceland." *Scandinavian Studies* 60: 189–218.

Misane, Agita. 1997. "The Notion of Exchange and Reciprocity during the Viking Age and Its Religious Connotations." Unpublished paper, presented at the University of Washington, 30 May 1997.

Moreau, Jacques. 1971. "Syncretic Propaganda." In *The Conversion of Constantine.* Ed. John W. Eadie. New York: Holt, Rinehart, and Winston. Pp. 46–51.

Morris, Christopher. 1993. "The Birsay Bay Project: A Résumé." In *The Viking Age in Caithness, Orkney, and the North Atlantic.* Ed. Colleen E. Batey, Judith Jesch, and Christopher D. Morris. Edinburgh: Edinburgh University Press. Pp. 285–307.

Moszyński, Leszek. 1992. *Die vorchristliche Religion der Slaven im Lichte der slavischen Sprachwissenschaft.* Cologne: Böhlau Verlag.

Moyne, Ernest J. 1981. *Raising the Wind: The Legend of Lapland and Finland Wizards in Literature.* Newark: Prentice-Hall.

Naakka-Korhonen, Mervi. 1983. "Lääkekasvien keruusta ja viljelystä maassamme." In *Kansa parantaa.* Ed. Pekka Laaksonen and Ulla Piela. Helsinki: Suomalaisen Kirjallisuuden Seura. Pp. 114–129.

Naert, Pierre. 1957. "Askraka." *Arkiv för Nordisk Filologi* 67: 176–181.

Næss, Jenny Rita, ed. 1985. *Arkeologi og etnisitet.* Stavanger: Arkeologisk museum i Stavanger.

Nenola-Kallio, Aili. 1982. *Studies in Ingrian Laments.* FF Communications no. 234. Helsinki: Suomailainen Tiedeakatemia.

Nenonen, Marko. 1992. *Noituus, taikuus ja noitavainot Ala-Satakunnan, Pohjois-Pohjanmaan ja Viipurin Karjalan maaseudulta vuosina, 1620–1700.* Helsinki: Suomen Historiallinen Seura.

Neuland, Lena. 1977. *Jumis: Die Fruchtbarkeitsgottheit der alten Letten.* Stockholm Studies in Comparative Religion 15. Stockholm: Almqvist & Wiksell.

Nevanlinna, H. R. 1984. "Suomalaisten juuret geneettisen merkkiominaisuustutkimuksen valossa." *Suomen väestön esihistorialliset juuret.* Tvärminnen symposiumi 17–19 Jan. 1980. In *Bidrag till Kännedom av Finlands Natur och Folk* h. 131. Helsinki: Finska Vetenskaps-Societeten. Pp. 157–174.

New Catholic Encyclopedia. 1967. Prepared by an editorial staff at the Catholic University of America. New York: McGraw-Hill.

Nickul, Karl. 1977. *The Lappish Nation: Citizens of Four Countries.* Bloomington: Indiana University Press.

Nioradze, G. 1925. *Der Schamanismus dei den sibirischen Völkern.* Stuttgart: Strecker und Schroder.

Noble, Thomas F. X., and Thomas Head, eds. 1995. *Soldiers of Christ: Saints and Saints' Lives from Late Antiquity and the Early Middle Ages.* University Park: Pennsylvania State University Press.

Nordal, Sigurður. 1952. "Time and Vellum." *Annual Bulletin of the Modern Humanities Research Association* 24: 5–18.

Nordin, Fredrik. 1891 [1993]. *En gotländsk bondgård för 1.500 år sedan.* Stockholm: Historiska Förlaget.

Nordland, Odd. 1969. "Valhall and Helgafell. Syncretistic Traits of the Old Norse Religion." In *Syncretism. Based on papers read at the Symposium on Cultural Contact, Meeting of Religions, Syncretism held at Åbo on the 8th–10th of September, 1966.* Ed. Sven S. Hartman. Stockholm: Almqvist & Wiksell. Pp. 66–99.

Norlander-Unsgaard, Siv. 1985. "On Gesture and Posture, Movements, and Motion in the Saami Bear Ceremonialism." *Arv* 41: 189–99.

———. 1987. "On Time-Reckoning in Old Saami Culture." In *Saami Religion: Based on papers read at the Symposium on Saami Religion, held at Åbo, Finland, on the 16th–18th of August 1984.* Ed. Tore Ahlbäck. Stockholm: Almqvist & Wiksell. Pp. 81–93.

Nuñez, Milton, and Jussi Pekka Taavitsainen. 1993. *Keitä ja mistä: Suomalaisten tarina I.* Jyväskylä (Finland): WSOY.

Ó Carrigáin, Éamonn. 1994. *The City of Rome and the World of Bede.* Jarrow Lecture 1994.

O Còrrain, D. 1972. *Ireland before the Normans.* Dublin: Gill and Macmillan.

Ó Cuív, Brian. 1967. "Ireland in the Eleventh and Twelfth Centuries." In *The Course of Irish History.* Ed. T. W. Moody and F. X. Martin. Cork: Mercier Press. Pp. 107–122.

Odelman, Eva, ed. 1986. *Boken om Ansgar. Rimbert: Ansgars liv.* Stockholm: Proprius Förlag.

Ohrt, F. 1938. "Om Merseburgformlerne som galder: En efterladt afhandling." *Danske studier* 35: 125–36.

Olrik, Axel. 1905. "Nordisk og lappisk Gudsdyrkelse." *Danske studier* 2: 39–57.

Olsan, Lea. 1992. "Latin Charms of Medieval England: Verbal Healing in a Christian Oral Tradition." *Oral Tradition* 7, no. 1: 116–142.

Olsen, Bjørar. 1986. "Norwegian Archaeology and the People without (Pre-)History: Or How to Create a Myth of a Uniform Past." *Archaeological Review from Cambridge* 5: 25–42.

Orrman, Eljas. 1981. "The Progress of Settlement in Finland during the Late Middle Ages." *Scandinavian Economic History Review* 29, no. 2: 129–143.

Ottósson, Kjartan G. 1983. *Fróðárundur í Eyrbyggju. Studia Islandica* 42. Reykjavík: Bókaútgáfa Menningarsjóðs.

Outakoski, Nilla. 1991. *Lars Levi Laestadiuksen saarnojen maahiskuva.* Scripta Historica 17. Oulu: Oulun Historiaseura.

Page, R. I. 1983. "The Manx Rune-Stones." In *The Viking Age in the Isle of Man.* Ed. Christine Fell, Peter Foote, James Graham-Campbell, and Robert Thomson. London: Viking Society for Northern Research. Pp. 133–146.

Pálsson, Gísli. 1991. "The Name of the Witch: Sagas, Sorcery and Social Context." In *Social Approaches to Viking Studies,* 157–68. Ed. Ross Samson. Glasgow: Cruithne Press.

Pálsson, Hermann, and Paul Edwards. 1989. *Vikings in Russia: Yngvar's Saga and Eymund's Saga.* Edinburgh: Edinburgh University Press.

Pelteret, David. 1991. "Slavery in the Danelaw." In *Social Approaches to Viking Studies.* Ed. Ross Samson. Glasgow: Cruithne Press. Pp. 179–190.

Pentikäinen, Juha. 1978. *Oral Repertoire and World View: An Anthropological Study of Marina Takalo's Life History.* FF Communications no. 219. Helsinki: Suomalainen Tiedeakatemia.

———. 1995. *Saamelaiset: Pohjoisen kansan mytologia.* Helsinki: Suomalaisen Kirjallisuuden Seura.

Peters, Edward. 1978. *The Magician, the Witch, and the Law.* Philadelphia: University of Pennsylvania Press.

Pettersson, Olof. 1957. *Jabmek and Jabmeaimo.* Lunds universitets årskrift N.F. Vol. 1, no. 52, issue 6. Lund: Lunds universitet.

———. 1983. "The God Ruto: Some Phenomenological Reflections." *Arv* 39: 157–68.

———. 1987. "Old Nordic and Christian Elements in Saami Ideas about the Realm of the Dead." In *Saami Religion: Based on papers read at the Symposium on Saami Religion, held at Åbo, Finland, on the 16th–18th of August 1984.* Ed. Tore Ahlbäck. Stockholm: Almqvist & Wiksell. Pp. 69–83.

Piazza, Alberto, Sabina Rendine, Eric Minch, Paolo Menozzi, Joanna Mountain, and Luigi L. Cavalli-Sforza. 1995. "Genetics and the Origin of European Languages." *Proceedings of the National Academy of Science (U.S.A.)* 92 (June): 5836–40.

Piganiol, André. 1971. "Neither Mystic nor Imposter." In *The Conversion of Constantine.* Ed. John W. Eadie. New York: Holt, Rinehart, and Winston. Pp. 39–45.

Plavoet, Jan. 1995. "Ritual in Plural and Pluralist Societies: Instruments for Analysis." In *Pluralism and Identity: Studies in Ritual Behaviour.* Ed. Jan Platvoet and Karel van der Toorn. Leiden: E. J. Brill. Pp. 25–52.

Polomé, Edgar C. 1982. *Language, Society, and Paleoculture.* Ed. Anwar S. Dil. Stanford, Calif.: Stanford University Press.

Puhvel, Jaan, ed. 1970. *Myth and Law among the Indo-Europeans: Studies in Indo-European Comparative Mythology.* Berkeley: University of California Press.

———. 1987. *Comparative Mythology.* Baltimore: Johns Hopkins University Press.

Purhonen, Paula. 1990. "Cross Pendants from Iron-Age Finland." In *Fenno-Ugri et Slavi 1988. Papers presented by the participants in the Finnish-Soviet archeological symposium "Studies in the material culture of the peoples of eastern and northern Europe."* Helsinki: National Board of Antiquities. Pp. 33–57.

———, ed. 1996. *Vainionmäki—A Merovingian Period Cemetery in Laitila, Finland.* Helsinki: National Board of Antiquities.

Ramskou, Thorkild. 1962. *Hedeby: Vikingetidens internationale handelsby.* Copenhagen: Munksgaard.

Ränk, Gustav. 1948. "Die Hausgottheiten der Frauen und das Geschlechtstabu bei den nordeurasische Völkern." *Ethnos* 13: 153–70.

———. 1981. *Der mystische Ruto in der samischen Mythologie: Eine religionsethnologische Untersuchung.* Acta Universitatis Stockholmiensis. Stockholm Studies in Comparative Religion 21. Stockholm: Almqvist & Wiksell.

———. 1983. "The North-Eurasian Background of the Ruto Cult." *Arv* 39: 169–78.

Ringgren, Helmer. 1969. "The Problems of Syncretism." In *Syncretism: Based on papers read at the Symposium on Cultural Contact, Meeting of Religions, Syncretism Held at Åbo on the 8th–10th of September, 1966*. Ed. Sven S. Hartman. Stockholm: Almqvist & Wiksell. Pp. 7–14.

Robinson, Vaughan, and Danny McCarroll, eds. 1990. *The Isle of Man: Celebrating a Sense of Place*. Liverpool: Liverpool University Press.

Roesdahl, Else. 1987. *The Vikings*. Tr. Susan M. Margeson. London: Penguin.

Rooth, Anna Birgitta. 1961. *Loki in Scandinavian Mythology*. Lund: C. W. K. Gleerup.

Rosén, Helge. 1919. "Om lapparnas dödsrikesföreställningar." *Fataburen* 10, no. 2: 16–27.

Ross, Margaret Clunies. 1981. "An Interpretation of the Myth of Þórr's Encounter with Geirrøðr and His Daughters." In *Speculum Norroenum: Norse Studies in Memory of Gabriel Turville-Petre*. Ed. Ursula Dronke, Guðrún Helgadóttir, Gerd Wolfgang Weber, Hans Bekker-Nielsen. Odense: Odense University Press. Pp. 370–391.

Rumble, Alexander R., ed. 1994. *The Reign of Cnut: King of England, Denmark, and Norway*. London: Leicester University Press.

Ruong, Israel. 1982. *Samerna i historia och nutiden*. Stockholm: Bonnier Fakta.

Rydving, Håkan. 1987. "Scandinavian-Saami Religious Connections in the History of Research." In *Old Norse and Finnish Religions and Cultic Place-Names*. Ed. Tore Ahlbäck. Scripta Instituti Donneriani Aboensis 13. Stockholm: Almqvist & Wiksell. Pp. 358–373.

———. 1995. *The End of Drum-time: Religious Change among the Lule Saami, 1670–1740s*. Acta Universitatis Upsaliensis. *Historia Religionum* 12. Uppsala: Almqvist & Wiksell.

Saami Religion: Based on papers read at the Symposium on Saami Religion, Held at Åbo, Finland, on the 16th–18th of August 1984. 1987. Ed. Tore Ahlbäck. Scripta Instituti Donneriani Aboensis 12. Åbo: Donner Institute for Research in Religious and Cultural History.

Sallamaa, Kari. 1983. "Nouse lempi liehumaan." In *Kansa parantaa*. Ed. Pekka Laaksonen and Ulla Piela. *Kalevalaseuran vuosikirja* 63. Helsinki: Suomalaisen Kirjallisuuden Seura. Pp. 253–261.

Salo, Unto. 1984. "Esihistoriallisen asutuksen jatkuvuudesta Suomen rannikolla." *Suomen väestön esihistorialliset juuret*. Tvärminnen symposiumi 17–19 Jan. 1980. In *Bidrag till Kännedom av Finlands Natur och Folk* h. 131. Helsinki: Finska Vetenskaps-Societeten. Pp. 175–190.

———. 1987. "Agricola's Ukko in the Light of Archaeology: A Chronological and Interpretative Study of Ancient Finnish Religion." In *Old Norse and Finnish Religions and Cultic Place-Names. Based on papers read at the Symposium on Encounters Between Religions in Old Nordic Times and on Cultic Place-Names, held at Åbo, Finland, on the 19th–21st of August 1987*. Ed. Tore Ahlbäck. Åbo: Donner Institute for Research in Religious and Cultural History. Pp. 92–190.

———. 1991. "Kontakterna mellan Finland och Sverige under järnåldern 500 f.Kr.–1150 e.Kr." *Budkavlen* 70: 5–17.

Sammallahti, Pekka. 1984. "Saamelaisten esihistoriallinen tausta kielitieteen valossa." *Suomen väestön esihistorialliset juuret*. Tvärminnen symposiumi 17–19 Jan.

1980. In *Bidrag till Kännedom av Finlands Natur och Folk* h. 131. Helsinki: Finska Vetenskaps-Societeten. Pp. 137–156.

———. 1993. "Suomalaisten ja saamelaisten juuret." *Kieliposti* 1: 10–12.

Samson, Ross, ed. 1991. *Social Approaches to Viking Studies.* Glasgow: Cruithne Press.

Sarmela, Matti. 1983. "The Finnish Bear-Hunting Drama." *Mémoires de la Société Finno-Ougrienne* 183: 283–300.

———. 1995. *Suomen perinneatlas.* Helsinki: Suomalaisen Kirjallisuuden Seura.

Sawyer, Birgit. 1992. "Kvinnor som brobyggare—om de vikingatida runstenarna som historiska källor." In *Kvinnospår i medeltiden.* Ed. Inger Lövkrona. Lund: Lund University Press.

Sawyer, Birgit, and Peter Sawyer. 1993. *Medieval Scandinavia from Conversion to Reformation, circa 800–1500.* Minneapolis: University of Minnesota Press.

Sawyer, Birgit, Peter Sawyer, and Ian Wood. 1987. *The Christianization of Scandinavia. Report of a symposium held at Kungälv, Sweden, 4–9 August 1985.* Alingsås, Sweden: Viktoria Bokförlag.

Sawyer, Peter. 1987. "The Process of Christianization in the Tenth and Eleventh Centuries." In *The Christianization of Scandinavia. Report of a symposium held at Kungälv, Sweden, 4–9 August 1985.* Ed. Birgit Sawyer, Peter Sawyer, and Ian Wood. Alingsås, Sweden: Viktoria Bokförlag. Pp. 68–87.

Sayers, William. 1990. "Weather Gods, Syncretism, and the Eastern Baltic." *Temenos* 26: 105–114.

———. 1994. "Management of the Celtic Fact in *Landnámabók.*" *Scandinavian Studies* 66, no. 2: 129–153.

Schjødt, Jens Peter. 1981. "Om Loki endnu engang." *Arkiv för nordisk filologi* 96: 49–86.

———. 1990. "Horizontale und vertikale Achsen in her vorchristlichen skandinavischen Kosmologie." In *Old Norse and Finnish Religions and Cultic Place-Names. Based on Papers Read at the Symposium on Encounters between Religions in Old Nordic Times and on Cultic Place-Names, held at Åbo, Finland, on the 19th–21st of August 1987.* Ed. Tore Ahlbäck. Åbo: Donner Institute for Research in Religious and Cultural History. Pp. 35–57.

Schnürer, Gustav. 1956. *Church and Culture in the Middle Ages.* Tr. George J. Undreiner. Paterson, N.J.: St. Anthony Guild Press.

von Schubert, Hans. 1962. *Geschichte der christlichen Kirche im Frühmittelalter: Ein Handbuch.* Hildesheim: Georg Olms Verlagsbuchhandlung.

Scott, Barbara G. 1996. "Archaeology and National Identity: The Norwegian Example." *Scandinavian Studies* 68, no. 3: 321–342.

Sebald, Hans. 1984. "Shaman, Healer, Witch: Comparing Shamanism with Franconian Folk Magic. *Ethnologia Europaea* 14: 125–142.

Sherman, Heidi M. 1997. "Was Ladoga the First Town in Northern European Russia?" Paper delivered at the 1997 National Convention of the American Association for the Advancement of Slavic Studies, Seattle, 20–23 Nov. 1997.

Siikala, Anna-Leena. 1987a. *The Rite Technique of the Siberian Shaman.* FF Communications no. 220. Helsinki: Suomalainen Tiedeakatemia.

———. 1987b. "Singing of Incantations in Nordic Tradition." In *Old Norse and Finnish Religions and Cultic Place-Names.* Ed. Tore Ahlbäck. Scripta Instituti Donneriani Aboensis 13. Stockholm: Almqvist & Wiksell. Pp. 191–205.

———. 1992. *Suomalainen šamanismi: Mielikuvien historiaa.* Helsinki: Suomalaisen Kirjallisuuden Seura.

Siiriäinen, Ari. 1991. "Finland, a Part of Europe: The Long Term Perspective." Paper delivered at the 1991 Finnish Studies Symposium "Finland Before Christianity," organized by the Programme in Finnish Studies at the University of Toronto and the Canadian Friends of Finland, 17 Nov. 1991.

Simpson, Jacqueline. 1967. *Everyday Life in the Viking Age.* New York: Dorset Press.

———. 1975. "Legends of Icelandic Magicians." London: D. S. Brewer and Rowman and Littlefield for The Folklore Society.

Sköld, Peter. 1996. "Saami and Smallpox in Eighteenth-Century Sweden: Cultural Prevention of Epidemic Disease." In *Northern Peoples, Southern States: Maintaining Ethnicities in the Circumpolar World.* Umeå: CERUM. Pp. 93–111.

Small, Alan, Charles Thomas, and David M. Wilson. 1973. *St. Ninian's Isle and its Treasure.* 2 vols. London: Oxford University Press.

Smith, Jerry C., and William L. Urban, eds. and tr. 1977. *The Livonian Rhymed Chronicle.* Bloomington: Indiana University Press.

Smith, John Holland. 1971. *Constantine the Great.* London: Hamish Hamilton.

Sørensen, Birgitte Refslund. 1993. "Changing Reasons for Ritual Performance: A Discussion of a Sinhalese Harvest Ritual." *Folk* 35: 65–89.

Sørensen, Preben Meulengracht. 1986. "Thor's Fishing Expedition." In *Words and Objects: Towards a Dialogue between Archaeology and History of Religion.* Ed. Gro Steinsland. Oslo: Norwegian University Press. Pp. 298–315.

Sprenger, Ulrike. 1992. *Die Altnordische Heroische Elegie.* Berlin: Walter de Gruyter.

Steinsland, Gro., ed. 1986. *Words and Objects: Toward a Dialogue Between Archaeology and History of Religion.* Oslo: Norwegian University Press.

Stevens, William O. 1904 [repr. 1977]. *The Cross in the Life and Literature of the Anglo-Saxons.* Yale Studies in English 22. Reissued with a new introduction by Thomas D. Hill. Hamden: Archon Books.

Storå, Nils. 1971. *Burial Customs of the Skolt Lapps.* FF Communications no. 210. Helsinki: Suomalainen Tiedeakatemia.

Ström, Åke V. 1987. "Personal Piety in Nordic Paganism." In *Old Norse and Finnish Religions and Cultic Place-Names. Based on papers read at the Symposium on Encounters between Religions in Old Nordic Times and on Cultic Place-Names, held at Åbo, Finland, on the 19th–21st of August 1987.* Ed. Tore Ahlbäck. Åbo: Donner Institute for Research in Religious and Cultural History. Pp. 374–380.

Ström, Folke. 1954. *Diser, nornor, valkyrjor: Fruktbarhetskult och sakralt kungadöme in Norden.* Stockholm: Almqvist & Wiksell.

———. 1974. "Nið, Ergi, and Old Norse Moral Attitudes." The Dorothea Coke Memorial Lecture, delivered 10 May 1973 at University College, London. London: Viking Society for Northern Research.

———. 1986. "Bog Corpses and *Germania.*" Ch. 12 in *Words and Objects: Towards a Dialogue between Archaeology and History of Religion.* Ed. Gro Steinsland. Oslo: Norwegian University Press. Pp. 223–239.

Strömbäck, Dag. 1935. *Sejd: Textstudier i nordisk religionshistoria.* Stockholm: Hugo Gebers Förlag.

———. 1975. *The Conversion of Iceland: A Survey.* Tr. Peter Foote. London: Viking Society for Northern Research.

Suhonen, Seppo. 1984. "Lainasanat balttilais-itämerensuomalaisten kontaktien kuvastajina." *Suomen väestön esihistorialliset juuret.* Tvärminnen symposiumi 17–19 Jan. 1980. In *Bidrag till Kännedom av Finlands Natur och Folk* h. 131. Helsinki: Finska Vetenskaps-Societeten. Pp. 207–226.

Suomen väestön esihistorialliset juuret. Tvärminnen symposiumi 17–19 Jan. 1980. 1984. *Bidrag till Kännedom av Finlands Natur och Folk h. 131.* Helsinki: Finska Vetenskaps-Societeten.

Sveinsson, Einar Ól. 1943. "Á Njálsbuð." In *Ízlenzk fornrít* 12, lxxi–lxxii. Reykjavik: Hið Íslenzka Fornritafélag.

———. 1953. *The Age of the Sturlungs.* Ithaca: Cornell University Press.

Taavitsainen, J.-P. 1987. "Wide-range Hunting and Swidden Cultivation As Prerequisites of Iron Age Colonization in Finland. *Suomen Antropologi* 12, no. 4: 213–234.

Talvio, Tuukka. 1994. "Pohjolan aarrekätköihin päätyi arabialaisia hopearahoja." *Hiidenkivi* 3: 16–20.

Thunmark-Nylén, Lena. 1995. *Die Wikingerzeit Gotlands.* Vol. 1, *Abbildungen der Grabfunde.* Stockholm: Kungl. Vitterhets Historie och Antikvitets Akademien.

Tillhagen, Carl-Herman. 1977. *Folklig läkekonst.* Falköping: LTS Förlag.

Tolonen, Kimmo. "Paleoekologin puheenvuoro." *Suomen väestön esihistorialliset juuret.* Tvärminnen symposiumi 17–19 Jan. 1980. In *Bidrag till Kännedom av Finlands Natur och Folk* h. 131. Helsinki: Finska Vetenskaps-Societeten. Pp. 319–326.

Troelsen, Bjarne. 1987. *Nordisk bondereligion: Tolkning og dokumentation.* Århus: Forlaget Systime.

Turner, Victor. 1969. *The Ritual Process: Structure and Anti-Structure.* Chicago: Aldine Publishing.

Turunen, Aimo. 1981. *Kalevalan sanat ja niiden taustat.* Joensuu (Finland): Karjalaisen Kulttuurin Edistämisäätiö.

Turville-Petre, Gabriel. 1953. *Origins of Icelandic Literature.* Oxford: Clarendon Press.

———. 1964. *Myth and Religion of the North: The Religion of Ancient Scandinavia.* New York: Holt, Rinehart, and Winston.

———. 1972. *Nine Norse Studies.* London: Viking Society for Northern Research.

von Unwerth, Wolf. 1911. *Untersuchungen über Totenkult und Oðinnverehrung bei Nordgermanen und Lappen, mit Excursen zur altnordischen Literaturgeschichte.* Germanistische Abhandlungen 37. Breslau: M & M Marcus.

———. 1914. "Óðinn und Rota." *Beitrage zur Geschichte der deutschen Sprache und Literatur* 39: 213–221.

Vahros, Igor. 1966. *Zur Geschichte und Folklore der Grossrussichen Sauna.* FF Communications no. 197. Helsinki: Suomalainen Tiedeakatemia.

Vahtola, Jouko. 1995. "Keitä olivat kveenit, kainulaiset ja pirkkalaiset?" *Hiidenkivi* 1: 22–27.

Valonen, Niilo. 1980. "Varhaisia lappalais-suomalaisia kosketuksia." *Ethnologia Fennica* 10: 21–124.

———. 1983. "Ancient Folk Poetry in Eastern Karelian Petroglyphs." *Ethnologia Fennica* 12: 9–48.

———. 1984. "Vanhoja lappalais-suomalaisia kosketuksia." In *Suomen väestön esihistorialliset juuret* (Bidrag till Kännedom av Finlands Natur och Folk h. 131). Helsinki: Finska Vetenskaps-Societeten. Pp. 73–96.

Vauchez, André. 1993. *The Laity in the Middle Ages: Religious Beliefs and Devotional Practices.* Ed. Daniel E. Bornstein. Tr. Margery J. Schneider. Notre Dame: University of Notre Dame Press. Orig. *Les laïcs de Moyen Age: Pratiques et expériences religieuses.* Paris: Éditions du Cerf, 1987.

Virtanen, Leea. 1988. *Suomalainen kansanperinne.* Helsinki: Suomalaisen Kirjallisuuden Seura.

Vorren, Ørnulv. 1986. "Om kyst-samiske torvgamer i Finnmark." *Norveg* 29: 23–40.

———. 1987. "Sacrificial Sites, Types, and Functions." In *Saami Religion: Based on papers read at the Symposium on Saami Religion, held at Åbo, Finland, on the 16th–18th of August 1984.* Ed. Tore Ahlbäck. Scripta Instituti Donneriani Aboensis 12. Stockholm: Almqvist & Wiksell. Pp. 94–109.

Voss, Jerome A. 1987. "Antiquity Imagined: Cultural Values in Archaeological Folklore." *Folklore* 98, no. 1: 80–90.

Vries, Jan de. 1970. *Altgermanische Religionsgeschichte.* Berlin: de Gruyter.

Vuorela, Toivo. 1979. *Kansanperinteen sanakirja.* Porvoo: WSOY.

Weiser-Aall, Lily. 1968. *Svangerskab og fødsel i nyere norsk tradition: En kildekritisk studie.* Oslo: Norwegian University Press.

———. 1969. "Syncretism in Nordic Folklore Medicine: Critical Periods during Pregnancy." In *Syncretism. Based on papers read at the Symposium on Cultural Contact, Meeting of Religions, Syncretism held at Åbo on the 8th–10th of September, 1966.* Ed. Sven S. Hartman. Stockholm: Almqvist & Wiksell. Pp. 100–109.

Wheelersburg, Robert P., ed. 1996. *Northern Peoples, Southern States: Maintaining Ethnicities in the Circumpolar World.* Ed. Robert P. Wheelersburg. Umeå: CERUM.

Wheelersburg, Robert, and Roger Kvist. 1996. "Saami and the Swedish State: Theories on the Origins of Reindeer Pastoralism." In *Northern Peoples, Southern States: Maintaining Ethnicities in the Circumpolar World*, 141–68. Ed. Robert P. Wheelersburg. Umeå: CERUM.

Whitelock, Dorothy, ed. 1967. *Sweet's Anglo-Saxon Reader in Prose and Verse.* Oxford: Clarendon Press.

Wiik, Kalevi. 1993. "Suomen syntyvaiheita." *Kieliposti* 1: 4–9.

Wikander, Stig. 1978. *Araber, Vikingar, Väringar.* Lund: Svenska Humanitiska Förbundet.

Wilson, David M. 1974. *The Viking Age in the Isle of Man: The Archaeological Evidence.* C. C. Rafn Lecture 3. Odense: Odense University Press.

———. 1983. "The Art of the Manx Crosses of the Viking Age." In *The Viking Age in the Isle of Man.* Ed. Christine Fell, Peter Foote, James Graham-Campbell, and Robert Thomson. London: Viking Society for Northern Research. Pp. 175–187.

Wipf, K. A. 1975. "Die Zaubersprüche im Althochdeutschen." *Numen* 22, no. 1: 42–69.

Wood, Ian. 1987. "Christians and Pagans in Ninth-Century Scandinavia." In *The Christianization of Scandinavia. Report of a symposium held at Kungälv, Sweden, 4–9 August 1985.* Ed. Birgit and Peter Sawyer and Ian Wood. Alingsås, Sweden: Viktoria Bokförlag. Pp. 36–67.

Wrenn, C. L. 1967. *A Study of Old English Literature*. New York: W. W. Norton.

Wyszomirska-Werbart, Bozena. 1991. "Baltic and Scandinavian Connections in Southern Area of the Baltic Sea during the Late Iron Age." In *Regions and Reflections in Honor of Märta Strömberg*. Ed. Kristina Jennbert et al. Lund: Almqvist & Wiksell. Pp. 231–247.

Zachrisson, Inger. 1987a. "Arkeologi och etnicitet: Samisk kultur mellersta Sverige ca 1–1500 e Kr." In *Samer och germaner i det förhistoriska Norrland*. Ed. Per H. Ramqvist. *Bebyggelsehistorisk tidskrift* 14: 24–41.

———. 1987b. "Sjiele Sacrifices, Odin Treasures, and Saami Graves?" In *Saami Religion: Based on Papers Read at the Symposium on Saami Religion, held at Åbo, Finland, on the 16th–18th of August 1984*. Ed. Tore Ahlbäck. Stockholm: Almqvist & Wiksell. Pp. 61–68.

———. 1988. "The So-Called Scandinavian Cultural Boundary in Northern Sweden in Viking Times—Ethnic or Socio-Economic?" *Acta Borealia* 1, no. 2: 70–97.

———. 1991a. "The Saami Shaman Drums: Some Reflexions from an Archaeological Perspective." In *The Saami Shaman Drum. Based on Papers Read at the Symposium on the Saami Shaman Drum held at Åbo, Finland, on the 19th–20th of August 1988*. Ed. Tore Ahlbäck and Jan Bergman: Åbo: Donner Institute for Research in Religious and Cultural History. Pp. 80–95.

———. 1991b. "The South Saami Culture: In Archaeological Finds and West Nordic Written Sources from A.D. 800–1300." In *Social Approaches to Viking Studies*. Ed. Ross Samson. Glasgow: University of Glasgow Press. Pp. 191–199.

———. 1992. "Saami Prehistory in the South Saami Area." In *Readings in Saami History, Culture, and Language III*. Ed. Roger Kvist. Umeå: Institute for Sámi Studies. Pp. 9–23.

Zenkovsky, Serge A. 1974. *Medieval Russia's Epics, Chronicles, and Tales*. New York: E. P. Dutton.

Zetterberg, Pentti, Matti Eronen, and J. Briffa. 1994. "Evidence on Climatic Variability and Prehistoric Human Activities between 165 B.C. and 1400 B.C. derived from Subfossil Scots Pines Found in a Lake in Utsjoki, Northernmost Finland." *Bulletin of the Geological Society of Finland* 66: 107–124.

Zuesse, E. M. 1987. *The Encyclopedia of Religion*. Ed. Mircea Eliade. S.v. "Ritual," vol. 12: 405–422. New York: Macmillan.

Index

Note on alphabetization: No distinction is made between accented and unaccented vowels; č is alphabetized as *ch* and ð and þ are alphabetized as *th*.